FOUNDATIONS OF MARKETING THEORY

Toward a General Theory of Marketing

Shelby D. Hunt

M.E. Sharpe
Armonk, New York
London, England

Copyright © 2002 by M. E. Sharpe, Inc.

All rights reserved. No part of this book may be reproduced in any form
without written permission from the publisher, M. E. Sharpe, Inc.,
80 Business Park Drive, Armonk, New York 10504.

Library of Congress Cataloging-in-Publication Data

Hunt, Shelby D.
Foundations of marketing theory : toward a general theory of marketing / Shelby D. Hunt
p. cm.
Includes bibliographical references and index.
ISBN 0-7656-0929-0 (cloth: alk. paper) — ISBN 0-7656-0930-4 (pbk.: alk. paper)
1. Marketing. I. Title.

HF5415.H873 2002
658.8'001—dc21 2002066976

Printed in the United States of America

The paper used in this publication meets the minimum requirements of
American National Standard for Information Sciences
Permanence of Paper for Printed Library Materials,
ANSI Z 39.48-1984.

MV (c) 10 9 8 7 6 5 4 3 2 1
MV (p) 10 9 8 7 6 5

This book,
as was "the little green book,"
is dedicated to my wife,
Suzanne.

CONTENTS

PREFACE

Cynical observers claim that science in the traditional sense is already corrupted, spoiled, and lost. However, realism is a philosophy which encourages us to fight for science, for its methods and ethics. If anything, this is a good social reason for keeping up the high spirit of critical realism about science.

—Ilkka Niiniluoto

The first version of this work was entitled *Marketing Theory: Conceptual Foundations of Research in Marketing* (Hunt 1976a). Often referred to as the "little green book," its purpose was to explore philosophical issues in marketing and provide a "tool kit," based on the philosophy of science, for developing and analyzing marketing theory. The slender, 150-page monograph was not to be *on* the philosophy of science, or *about* it, but rather it was to apply the philosophy of science to issues in marketing theory. The second edition, often referred to as the "big red book," was entitled *Marketing Theory: The Philosophy of Marketing Science* (1983b). Although much larger than the little green book, it continued to use the philosophy of science to explore and explicate the nature of concepts such as "explanation," "laws," and "theories" in marketing theory and research. As such, it was definitely evolutionary in nature.

The third version was entitled *Modern Marketing Theory: Critical Issues in the Philosophy of Marketing Science* (Hunt 1991a). The "blue book" differed markedly from its predecessors. Part I of the "blue book" continued the applications orientation of its forerunners, which focused on the traditional topics in the philosophy of marketing science. However, Part II addressed the "philosophy debates" in marketing using a historical methodology. Stated briefly, many marketing scholars in the philosophy debates questioned whether there can possibly be genuine progress in the development of knowledge in any science, argued for relativism as a philosophical foundation for marketing, and argued against epistemic values such as *truth* and *objectivity* in marketing theory and research.

By the late 1980s, it had become clear that the philosophy debates were becoming increasingly unproductive: discussions of ideas were shifting toward *ad hominem* discourse, epistemology was morphing into "epistobabble" (Coyne 1982), honest mischaracterizations were becoming "nastiness and purposeful distortions" (Hirschmann 1989, p. 209), and a concern for civility was being replaced with "ridicule" (Pechmann 1990, p. 7). Furthermore, by then, the nihilistic implications of relativism were becoming clear. Believing that a major factor contributing to the muddled status of the philosophy debates was a lack of understanding of the various "isms" in the philosophy of science, for example, logical positivism and logical empiricism, Part II of Hunt (1991a) included four new chapters in a section entitled "Philosophy of Science: Historical Perspectives and Current Status." Its aim was to use a historical approach to raise the level of debate to a more informed level.

The structure of this fourth edition of *Marketing Theory* results from discussions I have had with instructors who have used the blue book. It is apparent that there are at least three different kinds of marketing theory courses. Some instructors want a book that focuses exclusively on the traditional marketing theory topics, as did the green and red books. Others are much more interested in the philosophy debates and wish to focus exclusively on them, as did Part II of the blue book. And still others want text material that covers both the traditional topics and the philosophy debates. Accordingly, this book addresses the interests of the first group. A companion volume, *Controversy in Marketing Theory: For Reason, Realism, Truth, and Objectivity* (Hunt 2003), addresses the interests of the second group. Instructors in the third group have the option of using the two books together.

All those who have attempted to find publishers for works that have small markets know the difficulty of the task. Therefore, I should like to thank M.E. Sharpe for agreeing to publish this work, and, in particular, Harry M. Briggs, Executive Editor, for encouraging me once again to revise *Marketing Theory*.

Many colleagues have encouraged me to write this (final?) edition of *Marketing Theory* and provided suggestions as to specific topics to be included, excluded, or revised. I gratefully acknowledge the encouragement, comments, and suggestions of Dennis Arnett (Texas Tech University), Danny Bellenger (Georgia State University), Adam Finn (University of Alberta), David Gardner (University of Illinois), Michael Hyman (New Mexico State University), Robert Lusch (Texas Christian University), Carl McDaniel (University of Texas, Arlington), Robert Morgan (University of Alabama), William Pride (Texas A&M University), Arturo Vasquez-Parraga (University of Texas,

PanAmerican), Scott Vitell (University of Mississippi), and Arch Woodside (Tulane University).

Over the years, my doctoral students, as well as students in theory courses at other universities, have provided numerous helpful suggestions. I thank them all. Finally, but very importantly, thanks go to Raylynn Dorny, Bessie Jones, and Jill Stephens for their extensive assistance in manuscript preparation.

S.D.H.

FOUNDATIONS OF MARKETING THEORY

1 INTRODUCTION

Question: Prove to me I should study logic!

Answer: How would you know that it was a good proof?

—Epictetus

Marketing research books usually contain sections on issues such as experimental research designs, data collection procedures, the availability and desirability of secondary data, sampling methods, data analysis, and the writing of research reports. Because this monograph discusses none of these topics, how can it claim to be about "marketing research"? Most books on *advanced* research topics in marketing discuss items such as factor analysis, multiple discriminant analysis, cluster analysis, multiple regression, dummy variable regression, canonical correlation, and structural equation modeling. Because there are few equations in this monograph, why have graduate students referred to this work as *advanced* issues in marketing research? Finally, students often describe most contemporary works on marketing theory as "impractical," with no relevance to the real world. How can this monograph concern marketing theory and further assert that the study of theory is the most *practical* intellectual pursuit of anyone interested seriously in marketing research? Is this entire monograph an inherent contradiction in terms? Let's examine these contradictions and determine whether they are real or only apparent.

1.1 THREE CONTRADICTIONS?

Few students of marketing would deny that much marketing research attempts to explain, predict, and understand marketing phenomena. Thus, much research is directed at explaining why some products have failed and attempting to predict which new products will succeed; explaining why certain retail institutions have declined and predicting which retail institutions will emerge; explaining why some promotional programs have succeeded and predicting the characteristics of successful future programs; and explaining why consumers have allocated their expenditures according to certain patterns and predicting how consumers will purchase in the future. Thus, explanation, prediction, and understanding are fundamental to marketing research.

Care should be taken to distinguish between *marketing* research and *market* research. Marketing research (or, alternatively, scholarly research in marketing) always seeks to expand the total knowledge base of marketing. In general, market research attempts to solve a particular company's marketing problem. To evaluate a particular department store's image would be a market research problem. To explore whether department stores have images *at all* is a marketing (scholarly) research problem. To attempt to determine the best location for a particular warehouse is a market research problem. To attempt to develop a model for locating warehouses in *general* is a marketing research problem. The following question can serve as a litmus test for differentiating *market* research from *marketing* research: "After conducting this research project, what will we then know about marketing in *general* that we do not know now?" In short, "What will be the contribution of this research to knowledge about marketing?" Unfortunately, many dissertation research proposals and even some completed dissertations fail this test. Although the line differentiating marketing research from market research may sometimes be fine, the distinction is useful and conceptually important.

Myers, Massy, and Greyser (1980) have drawn similar distinctions among basic research, problem solving research, and what they refer to as "problem-oriented" research. They suggest that problem-oriented research lies between basic research and problem solving research and "may be fundamental or highly applied, but its driving force is the desire to make a contribution to the solution of an important practical problem" (1980, p. 157). Does problem-oriented research "lie between" basic research and problem-solving research? If "basic" research is considered to be roughly synonymous with "marketing" research and "problem solving" research is considered to be roughly synonymous with "market" research, then problem-oriented research is *not* "between" the two. Problem-oriented research is a subclass of *marketing* research because it is research directed at general *classes* of marketing problems and because it is generalizable *across* different firms. Problem-oriented research is, simply, a kind of basic research in marketing that is normative-driven rather than positive-driven (see section 1.3.1). It seeks answers to normative questions such as "How *should* retail establishments price their merchandise?" rather than answers to positive questions such as "How *do* retail establishments price their merchandise?" Both questions are appropriate for "basic" or "marketing" research.

The first apparent contradiction dissolves if we note that this monograph is substantially concerned with exploring the basic methodological issues attendant on the explanation, prediction, and understanding of marketing phenomena. These basic methodological issues are customarily given only cursory treatment, at best, in most marketing research texts. Such texts focus primarily (and probably justifiably, given their target markets) on the conventional topics previously mentioned (data collection, sampling, etc.). Fortunately, for the present endeavor, many of the basic methodological issues in research and scientific inquiry have been extensively developed in the philosophy of science and are applicable to marketing research. *The major purpose of this monograph will be to draw upon the vast storehouse of analytical methods in the philosophy of science in order to systematically explore the basic methodological issues underlying marketing research.* The philosophical orientation of this monograph, sometimes referred to as "contemporary empiricism" or "modern empiricism," may be described as a combination of critical pluralism and scientific realism.[1] Critical pluralism is the view that, because both dogmatism and relativism are antithetical to science, we should both (1) adopt a tolerant, open posture toward new theories and methods and (2) subject all such theories and methods to critical scrutiny—nothing is, or can be, exempt (Hunt 1991b). Claims of "incommensurability" represent neither a state of nature to be accommodated nor a problem to be addressed—they are a convenient catchall for squelching debate or avoiding critical scrutiny.

Scientific realism, following Hunt (1990), is the view that:

- the world exists independently of its being perceived (classical realism);
- the job of science is to develop genuine knowledge about the world, even though such knowledge will never be known with certainty (fallibilistic realism);
- all knowledge claims must be critically evaluated and tested to determine the extent to which they do, or do not, truly represent, correspond, or accord with the world (critical realism); and
- the long-term success of any scientific theory provides reason to believe that something like the entities and structure postulated by that theory actually exists (inductive realism).

Note that a philosophy encompassing critical pluralism and scientific realism is open, without being anarchistic; it is critical, without being nihilistic; it is tolerant, without being relativistic; it is fallible, without being subjectivistic; it is absolutist, without being ABSOLUTIST.

As used here, to be "absolutist" is to maintain that there exist trustworthy criteria for evaluating the merit of competing knowledge-claims. To be "ABSOLUTIST" is to maintain that one knows with certainty that one's criteria will guarantee the production of true knowledge-claims. Thus, "ABSOLUT-ISM" equates with Siegel's (1987) "vulgar absolutism."

The second apparent contradiction is (a) that "advanced" topics in marketing research universally seem to be quantitatively sophisticated and (b) that quantitative techniques are conspicuous by their absence in this monograph, yet (c) students who have used this work generally consider it advanced. The contradiction is illusory. Quantitative techniques represent a tool kit for conducting research. Many mathematical and statistical models are difficult to understand, and, hence, *advanced.* Similarly, the philosophy of science is a tool kit that students may perceive as being relatively advanced. Students may find the tool kit to be of moderate difficulty for two reasons. First, few students have been formally exposed to the philosophy of science, and the first exposure to new material is always the most difficult. The reader must not only comprehend the *substance* of the tool kit but also must learn the *vocabulary.* Every effort has been made to "dejargonize" the presentation. Nevertheless, just as students must understand terms such as *differentiation* and *integration* to learn the role of calculus in marketing research, so must they understand terms such as *retrodiction* and *deductive-nomological explanation* to appreciate the usefulness of the philosophy of science tool kit in marketing research.

Some marketing commentators have charged that the history of marketing (not unlike the history of other social sciences) can be interpreted as a history of marketing fads. Every few years a new tool kit appears that promises to be the key to marketing problems. Thus, marketing has been blessed with motivation research, operations research, Markov processes, systems analysis, the behavioral sciences, mathematical models, multidimensional scaling, psychographics, conjoint analysis, structural equation models, and multi-attribute models. Although each tool kit has value in conducting research in marketing, advocates of the various tool kits often tend to oversell and over-promise. Therefore, a caveat concerning the philosophy of science seems appropriate. Just as marketing research problems are not solved by restating our ignorance in mathematical symbols, so, too, the present philosophy-of-science tool kit provides no panaceas, no magic formulas.

The second reason some students may find this presentation moderately difficult is that we shall attempt to analyze rigorously a topic (often referred to as "the scientific method") about which students have some notoriously nonrigorous (though often firmly held) notions. Unfortunately, rigor and difficulty often travel in tandem. If the analysis is both complete and clear (rigorous), this will maximize the opportunity for others to point out errors. When analyses are incomplete and ambiguous, the temptation is often strong for authors to dismiss their errors as misinterpretations. Because ambiguity should never be confused with profundity, I plead guilty to the charge of attempted rigor.

The last apparent contradiction is (a) students believe that theory is impractical, yet (b) this book concerns theory while (c) claiming to be devoted to a practical intellectual pursuit. The fallacy lies in the false dichotomy of theoretical-practical. Almost all marketing practitioners, most marketing academicians, and, sadly, too many marketing researchers perceive theoretical and practical as being at the opposite ends of a continuum. This perception leads to the conclusion that as any analysis becomes more theoretical, it must become less practical. To puncture this misperception, one need only note that a theory is a systematically related set of statements, including some lawlike generalizations, that is empirically testable. The purpose of theory is to increase scientific understanding through a systematized structure capable of both explaining and predicting phenomena. Thus, any structure that purports to be theoretical must be capable of explaining and predicting phenomena. Any structure that has neither explanatory nor predictive power is not a theory. Because the explanation and prediction of marketing phenomena are eminently practical concerns, the study and generation of marketing theory are practical pursuits of the first order.

The *theoretical-practical* issue is not the only false dichotomy in marketing. Consider the *behavioral-quantitative* classification. Incredibly, some marketing educators still inquire of prospective faculty whether they are quantitative *or* behavioral. This false dichotomy automatically presumes that no one can be both behaviorally oriented and at the same time be well-grounded in quantitative methodology. The presumption is, of course, unfounded. The *rigor-relevance* dichotomy has also been shown to be false on the grounds that it wrongly assumes that research cannot be both rigorous *and* relevant (Kassarjian 1989; Hunt 1989a).

1.2 OBJECTIVES OF MONOGRAPH

The primary objective here will be to explore systematically some of the basic methodological issues underlying marketing research. As discussed earlier, the analytical methods to be developed and employed will be drawn from the tool kit of critical pluralism and scientific realism, with insights from logical empiricism, critical rationalism (falsificationism), and pragmatism where appropriate. Numerous other tool kits exist in the philosophy of science: classical empiricism, phenomenalism, rationalism, instrumentalism, logical positivism, conventionalism, relativism, constructivism, and, recently, "Weltanschauungen-ism." The differentiating characteristics of these various "isms" need not detain us, because this work, unlike its companion volume (Hunt 2003), is not *on* the philosophy of science, but, rather, attempts to *use* the philosophy of science. This is not a philosophy of science book disguised in the trappings of marketing research. Much of the philosophy of science is not even mentioned, let alone developed, in this work. Philosophy of science issues and methods are introduced and discussed only when they are deemed useful for explicating some particular methodological issue in marketing research.

One way to clarify the purpose of this work is to give some examples of the basic methodological issues that will be explored. Although certainly not exhaustive, the following list should prove reasonably representative of these issues:

1. How does one scientifically explain marketing phenomena?
2. Is it possible to be able to explain marketing phenomena without being able to predict them?
3. Is functionalism a different method of explaining phenomena?
4. How does explanation differ from causation?
5. Can one understand marketing phenomena without being able to explain or predict them?
6. What is the role of laws and lawlike generalizations in marketing research?
7. How do empirical generalizations differ from laws?
8. Are the axioms in a theory "assumed to be true"?
9. How do universal laws differ from statistical laws?
10. What is theory, and what is its role in marketing research?
11. How can formalization help in analyzing marketing theory?
12. Why must theories contain lawlike generalizations?
13. Why must theories be empirically testable?
14. How can marketing phenomena best be classified?

Before analyzing these questions, some preliminary matters require attention. These preliminary issues can be best examined in the context of the "Is marketing a science?" controversy. The controversy was sparked by an early *Journal of Marketing* article written by Converse (1945) and entitled "The Development of a Science of Marketing." Prominent writers who then entered the debate included Bartels (1951), Hutchinson (1952), Baumol (1957), Buzzell (1963), Taylor (1965), and Halbert (1965). After raging throughout most of the 1950s and 1960s, the controversy has since waned. The waning may be more apparent than real because many of the substantive issues underlying the marketing science controversy overlap with the 1970s "broadening the concept of marketing" debate. Fundamental to both controversies are some radically different perspectives on the essential characteristics of both *marketing* and *science.* An exploration of the basic nature of both these notions will provide a frame of reference for the rest of this monograph.

1.3 THE NATURE OF MARKETING

What is marketing? What kinds of phenomena are appropriately termed marketing phenomena? How do marketing activities differ from nonmarketing activities? What is a marketing system? How can the marketing process be distinguished from other social processes? Which institutions should one refer to as marketing institutions? *In short, what is the proper conceptual domain of the construct labeled "marketing?"*

Prior to the definition of marketing formulated in 1985, the American Marketing Association (AMA) defined marketing as "the performance of business activities that direct[s] the flow of goods and services from producer to consumer or user." This position came under attack from various quarters as being too restrictive. Specifically, an official position paper by the Marketing Staff of the Ohio State University (1965, p. 43) suggested that marketing be considered "the process in a society by which the demand structure for economic goods and services is anticipated or enlarged and satisfied through the conception, promotion, exchange, and physical distribution of goods and services." Note the conspicuous absence of the notion that marketing consists of a set of business activities (as in the AMA definition). Rather, marketing is viewed as a societal *process.*

Next to plunge into the semantic battle were Philip Kotler and Sidney Levy. Although they did not specifically propose a new definition of marketing, Kotler and Levy (1969a) suggested that the concept of marketing be broadened to include nonbusiness organizations. They observed that nonbusiness organizations, including churches, police departments, and public schools, have products and customers and use the normal tools of the marketing mix. Therefore, Kotler and Levy concluded that these organizations perform marketing activities, or at least marketing-like activities. Thus, "the choice facing those who manage nonbusiness organizations is not whether to market or not to market, for no organization can avoid marketing. The choice is whether to do it well or poorly, and on this necessity the case for organizational marketing is basically founded" (1969a, p. 15). In the same issue of the *Journal of Marketing*, William Lazer discussed the changing boundaries of marketing. He pleaded that "what is required is a broader perception and definition of marketing than has hitherto been the case—one that recognizes marketing's societal dimensions and perceives of marketing as more than just a technology of the firm" (1969, p. 9). Thus, Kotler and Levy desired to broaden the notion of marketing by including not-for-profit organizations, and Lazer called for a definition of marketing that recognized marketing's expanding societal dimensions.

David Luck (1969, p. 54) took sharp issue with Kotler and Levy by insisting that marketing be limited to those business processes and activities that ultimately result in a *market* transaction. Luck noted that even thus bounded, marketing would still be a field of enormous scope and that marketing specialists could still render their services to nonmarketing causes. Kotler and Levy (1969b, p. 57) then accused Luck of a new form of myopia and suggested that "the crux of marketing lies in a *general idea of exchange* rather than the narrower thesis of market transactions." They further contended that defining marketing "too narrowly" would prevent students of marketing from applying their expertise to some of the most rapidly growing sectors of the society.

Other marketing commentators began to espouse the dual theses that (1) marketing be broadened to include nonbusiness organizations and that (2) marketing's societal dimensions deserve scrutiny. Thus, Ferber (1970) prophesied that marketing would diversify into the social and public policy fields. And Robert Lavidge sounded a similar call to arms by admonishing marketers to cease evaluating new products solely on the basis of whether they *could* be sold. Rather, he suggested that they evaluate new products from a societal perspective, that is, *should* the products be sold?

> The areas in which marketing people can, and must, be of service to society have broadened. In addition, marketing's functions have been broadened. Marketing no longer can be defined adequately in terms of the activities involved in buying, selling, and transporting goods and services. (Lavidge 1970, p. 27)

The movement to expand the concept of marketing probably became irreversible when the *Journal of Marketing* devoted an entire issue in 1971 to marketing's changing social/environmental role. At that time, Kotler and Zaltman coined the term *social marketing*, which they defined as "the design, implementation, and control of programs calculated to influence the acceptability of social ideas and involving considerations of product planning, pricing, communication, distribution, and marketing research" (1971, p. 5). In the same issue, marketing technology was applied to fund raising for the March of Dimes (Mindak and Bybee 1971), health services (Zaltman and Vertinsky 1971), population problems (Farley and Leavitt 1971), and the recycling of solid waste (Zikmund and Stanton 1971). Further, Dawson chastised marketers for ignoring many fundamental issues pertaining to the social relevance of marketing activities:

> Surely, in these troubled times, an appraisal of marketing's actual and potential role in relation to such [societal] problems is at least of equal importance to the technical aspects of the field. Yet, the emphasis upon practical problem-solving within the discipline far outweighs the attention paid to social ramifications of marketing activity. (Dawson 1971, p. 71)

Kotler then expanded his earlier position concerning broadening the concept of marketing and articulated a "generic" concept of marketing. He proposed that the essence of marketing is the *transaction*, defined as the exchange of values between two parties. Kotler's generic concept of marketing states, "Marketing is specifically concerned with how transactions are created, stimulated, facilitated, and valued" (1972b, p. 49). By the mid-1970s empirical evidence indicated that, at least among marketing educators, the broadened concept of marketing represented a *fait accompli.* A study by Nickels (1974) showed that 95 percent of marketing educators believed that the scope of marketing should be broadened to include nonbusiness organizations. Similarly, 93 percent agreed that marketing goes beyond just economic goods and services, and 83 percent favored including in the domain of marketing many activities whose ultimate result is not a market transaction. Also by the mid-1970s, the American Marketing Association was calling for a reevaluation and modification of its formal definition of marketing. Today it is noncontroversial that marketing has an important role to play in nonbusiness organizations.

Three questions are central to understanding the definition (broadening the concept) of marketing controversy. First, what kinds of phenomena and issues *do* the various marketing writers perceive to be included in the scope of marketing? Second, what kinds of phenomena and issues *should* be included in the scope of marketing? Third, how can marketing be defined both to encompass systematically all of the phenomena and issues that should be included, and, at the same time, to exclude systematically all other phenomena and issues? That is, a good definition of marketing must be both properly inclusive and exclusive. All three questions cry out for rigorous analysis. However, because a complete explication of Questions 2 and 3 depends in part on a satisfactory exposition of Question 1, the present analysis will begin by examining the various kinds of phenomena and issues that marketing writers often seem to put within the confines of marketing. In short, what is the scope of marketing?

1.3.1 The Scope of Marketing

The scope of marketing is unquestionably broad. Often included are diverse subject areas such as consumer behavior, pricing, purchasing, sales management, product management, marketing communications, comparative marketing, social marketing, the efficiency/productivity of marketing systems, marketing ethics, the role of marketing in economic development, packaging, channels of distribution, marketing research, societal issues in marketing, retailing, wholesaling, the social responsibility of marketing, international marketing, commodity marketing, and physical distribution. Though lengthy, this list of topics does not exhaust the possibilities. Not all writers would include all of the topics under the general rubric of marketing. However, the point deserving emphasis here is that different commentators on marketing would *disagree* as to which topics should be excluded. The disagreement stems from fundamentally different perspectives and can be best analyzed by attempting to develop some common ground for classifying the diverse topics and issues in marketing.

During a presentation at the 1972 fall conference of the American Marketing Association, Philip Kotler made some observations concerning how to classify marketing phenomena using the concepts *micro*, *macro*, *normative*, and *positive.*[2] These observations spurred the development of the classificatory schema detailed in Table 1.1. The schema proposes that all marketing phenomena, topics, and issues can be categorized using the three categorical dichotomies of (1) profit sector/nonprofit sector, (2) micro/macro, and (3) positive/normative. The three categorical dichotomies yield $2 \times 2 \times 2 = 8$ classes or cells in the schema. Thus, the first cell includes all marketing topics that are micro-positive and in the profit sector. Similarly, the second cell includes all marketing activities that are micro-normative and in the profit sector, and so on throughout the table. This model of the scope of marketing was first proposed in an article entitled "The Nature and Scope of Marketing" (Hunt 1976b). The model has come to be known as the Three Dichotomies Model.

Some definitions are required to interpret properly the schema presented in Table 1.1. *Profit sector* includes the study of organizations or other entities whose stated objectives include the realization of profit. Also included are studies that adopt the *perspective* of profit-oriented organizations. Conversely, *nonprofit sector* includes the study and perspective of all organizations and entities whose stated objectives do not include the realization of profit. *Positive* marketing adopts the perspective of attempting to describe, explain, predict, and understand the marketing activities and phenomena that actually exist. This perspective examines what *is.* In contrast, *normative* marketing adopts the perspective of attempting to prescribe what marketing organizations and individuals ought to do or what kinds of marketing systems a society ought to have. That is, this perspective examines what *ought to be* and what organizations and individuals *ought to do.* The grounds for the "ought" may be ethical/moral or instrumental/rational (see section 8.2).

Of the three dichotomies proposed to organize the total scope of marketing, the micro-macro dichotomy is probably the most ambiguous. Drawing upon the distinction between microeconomics and macroeconomics, the original paper distinguished between micromarketing and macromarketing on the basis of aggregation: *micro* referred to the marketing activities of individual units (firms and consumers or households), while *macro* referred to a higher level of aggregation, either marketing systems or groups of consumers. However, as was pointed out, topics such as "Does marketing have special social responsibilities?" would not fit the macro label on the basis of a level of aggregation criterion. Given that most marketers desire to classify topics similar to the "social responsibilities" issue as *macro*, how should the specification of *macro* be modified?

Some marketers suggested an "internalities versus externalities" classification. That is, micromarketing focuses on the internal marketing interests of firms, whereas macromarketing focuses on the interests of society with regard to marketing activities. Specified in this way, macromarketing would include topics such as "social responsibilities," efficiency, productivity, and whether "the poor pay more." And this is all to the good. However, the specification would not encompass topics such as the legal aspects of marketing, comparative marketing, and relationships in channels of distribution. None of these topics necessarily focuses on the "interests of society," yet many marketers would like to include them under the *macro* rubric because the topics are very different from *micro* topics such as "How do (or should) firms determine their advertising budgets?" Therefore, an "interests of society" criterion is not sufficient.

Thus, it would appear that macromarketing is a multidimensional construct. Therefore, I argue, a complete specification of macromarketing would (should) include the following criteria: Macromarketing refers to the study of (1) marketing systems, (2) the impact of marketing systems on society, and (3) the impact of society of marketing systems. Criterion (1) is a level of aggregation criterion that allows the inclusion of topics such as comparative marketing, the institutional structure of marketing, and relationships in channels of distribution. Criterion (2) is a generalized "interests of society" criterion that brings in topics such as "social responsibilities" and the role of marketing in economic development. Criterion (3) recognizes that society impacts on marketing and would include topics such as the legal aspects of marketing and the consequences for marketing of different political and social value systems. This multidimensional perspective has been adopted by the *Journal of Macromarketing* (Fisk 1982, p. 3).

An examination of Table 1.1 reveals that most of the early (circa 1920) approaches to the study of marketing reside in cell 3, profit sector/macro/positive. The institutional, commodity, and functional approaches analyzed existing (positive) business activities (profit sector) from a marketing systems (macro) perspective. However, not all of the early marketing studies were profit/macro/positive. L.D.H. Weld's (1920) classic, *The Marketing of Farm Products*, not only examined existing distribution systems for farm commodities but also attempted to evaluate normative issues such as "Are there too many middlemen in food marketing?"[3] Thus, Weld's signally important work was both profit/macro/positive and profit/macro/normative. Similarly, the Twentieth Century Fund study, *Does Distribution Cost Too Much?* (Stewart 1939), took an essentially profit/macro/normative perspective. Other important works that combined the profit/macro/positive and the profit/macro/normative perspectives include those of Harold Barger (1955), Reavis Cox (1965), and Neil Borden (1942).

Table 1.1

The Three Dichotomies Model of Marketing

Positive	Normative
Profit sector	
Micro	
1. Problems, issues, theories, and research concerning: a. Individual consumer buyer behavior b. How firms determine prices c. How firms determine products d. How firms determine promotion e. How firms determine channels of distribution f. Case studies of marketing practices	2. Problems, issues, normative models, and research concerning how firms *should:* a. Determine the marketing mix b. Make pricing decisions c. Make product decisions d. Make promotion decisions e. Make packaging decisions f. Make purchasing decisions g. Make international marketing decisions h. Organize their marketing departments i. Control their marketing efforts j. Plan their marketing strategy k. Apply systems theory to marketing problems l. Manage retail establishments m. Manage wholesale establishments n. Implement the marketing concept
Macro	
3. Problems, issues, theories, and research concerning: a. Aggregate consumption patterns b. The institutional approach to marketing c. The commodity approach to marketing d. Legal aspects of marketing e. Comparative marketing f. The efficiency of marketing systems g. Whether the poor pay more h. Whether marketing spurs or retards economic development i. Power and conflict relationships in channels of distribution j. Whether marketing functions are universal k. Whether the marketing concept is consistent with consumers' interests	4. Problems, issues, normative models, and research concerning: a. How marketing can be made more efficient b. Whether distribution costs too much c. Whether advertising is socially desirable d. Whether consumer sovereignty is desirable e. Whether stimulating demand is desirable f. Whether the poor should pay more g. What kinds of laws regulating marketing are optimal h. Whether vertical market systems are socially desirable i. Whether marketing should have special social responsibilities

Table 1.1 *(continued)*

Positive	Normative
Nonprofit sector	
Micro	
5. Problems, issues, theories, and research concerning: a. Consumers' purchasing of public goods b. How nonprofit organizations determine prices c. How nonprofit organizations determine products d. How nonprofit organizations determine promotion e. How nonprofit organizations determine channels of distribution f. Case studies of public goods marketing	6. Problems, issues, normative models, and research concerning how nonprofit organizations *should:* a. Determine the marketing mix (social marketing) b. Make pricing decisions c. Make product decisions d. Make promotion decisions e. Make packaging decisions f. Make purchasing decisions g. Make international marketing decisions (e.g., CARE) h. Organize their marketing efforts i. Control their marketing efforts j. Plan their marketing strategy k. Apply systems theory to marketing problems
Macro	
7. Problems, issues, theories, and research concerning: a. The institutional framework for public goods b. Whether television advertising influences elections c. Whether public service advertising influences behavior (e.g., Smokey the Bear) d. Whether existing distribution systems for public goods are efficient e. How public goods are recycled	8. Problems, issues, normative models, and research concerning: a. Whether society should allow politicians to be "sold" like toothpaste b. Whether the demand for public goods should be stimulated c. Whether "low informational content" political advertising is socially desirable (e.g., ten-second "spot" commercials) d. Whether the U.S. Army should be allowed to advertise for recruits

Source: Hunt (1991). Reprinted by permission of the author.

Although the profit/micro/normative (cell 2) orientation to marketing can be traced at least back to the 1920s and notable works such as Reed (1930) and White and Hayward (1924), the movement reached full bloom in the early 1960s with proponents of the managerial approach to marketing such as McCarthy (1960). The managerial approach adopts the perspective of the marketing manager, often (but not necessarily) the marketing manager in a large manufacturing corporation. Therefore, the emphasis is micro and in the profit sector. The basic question underlying the managerial approach is: "What is the optimal marketing mix?" Consequently, the approach is unquestionably normative.

During the mid-1960s, writers such as Lazer and Kelley (1962), Adler (1967), and Fisk (1967) began advocating a *systems approach* to marketing. Sometimes the systems approach used a profit/micro/normative perspective and applied to marketing certain sophisticated optimizing models (such as linear and dynamic programming) developed by the operations researchers. Other writers used the systems approach in a profit/macro/positive fashion to analyze the complex interactions among marketing institutions. Finally, some used the systems approach to include the profit/macro/normative:

> The method used in this book is called the general systems approach. In this approach the goals, organization, inputs, and outputs of marketing are examined to determine how efficient and how effective marketing is. Constraints, including competition and government, are also studied because they affect both the level of efficiency and the kinds of effects obtained. (Fisk 1967, p. 3)

During the late 1960s, the *environmental approach* to marketing was promulgated by writers such as Holloway and Hancock (1964, 1968) and Scott and Marks (1968). This approach emphasized an analysis of the environmental constraints on marketing activities. These constraints included consumer behavior, culture, competition, the legal framework, technology, and the institutional framework. Consequently, this approach may be classified as profit/macro/positive.

Two trends surfaced in the 1970s. The first was the trend toward *social marketing* as proposed by Kotler (1972b), Kotler and Levy (1969a), and Kotler and Zaltman (1971) and as promulgated by others.[4] Social marketing, with its emphasis on the marketing problems of nonprofit organizations, is nonprofit/micro/normative. The second can be termed the *societal issues* trend. It concerns topics as diverse as consumerism, ethics, marketing and ecology, the desirability of political advertising, social responsibility, and whether the demand for public goods should be stimulated.[5] All of these works share the common element of *evaluation.* They attempt to evaluate the desirability or propriety of certain marketing activities or systems, and, therefore, should be viewed as either profit/macro/normative or nonprofit/macro/normative.

In 1985, two decades after the Ohio State University position paper, the debate within the American Marketing Association culminated in a new "official" definition: "Marketing is the process of planning and executing the conception, pricing, promotion, and distribution of ideas, goods, and services to create exchanges that satisfy individual and organizational objectives" (Bennett 1988, p. 115). The new definition does not completely satisfy all those who participated in the debate. For example, I believe that the words "in organizations and society" should be inserted after "the process." Nonetheless, most agree that it is a substantial improvement over its predecessor. We should note in particular the emphasis on *exchange* and the "broadening" of marketing to include "ideas." Thus, suitably interpreted, the definition accommodates all eight cells of the Three Dichotomies Model.

In conclusion, it is possible to classify all the approaches to the study of marketing and all the topics usually considered within the scope of marketing by using the three categorical dichotomies of profit sector/nonprofit sector, positive/normative, and micro/macro. This does not imply that reasonable people cannot disagree as to which topics should fall within the scope of marketing. Nor does it even imply that reasonable people cannot disagree as to which cell in Table 1.1 is most appropriate for each topic. (For example, the study of the efficiency of marketing systems may have both positive and normative aspects.) Rather, Table 1.1 provides a useful analytical framework, as shall be demonstrated in the next section.

1.3.2 Is Marketing a Science?

The previous discussion on the scope of marketing now enables us to clarify some of the issues with respect to the definition (broadening the concept) of marketing controversy and the "Is marketing a science?" debate. Most marketing practitioners and some marketing academicians perceive the entire scope of marketing to be profit/micro/normative (cell 2 of Table 1.1). That is, practitioners often perceive the entire domain of marketing to be the analysis and improvement of the decision-making processes of marketers. This perspective is exemplified by the definition of marketing suggested by Canton (1973). Most marketing academicians—but assuredly not all—would chafe at delimiting the proper subject matter of marketing to simply the profit/micro/normative dimensions. Most would, at the very least, include all the phenomena, topics, and issues in the top half of Table 1.1 (i.e., cells 1 through 4). As a result of the "broadening the concept of marketing" debate, including in the definition of marketing *all* eight cells in Table 1.1 has probably become the majority position in marketing academe.

Now, returning to the "Is marketing a science?" controversy, the preceding analysis suggests that a primary factor explaining the nature of the controversy is the widely disparate notions of marketing held by the participants. The common element shared by those who hold that marketing is not (and cannot be) a science is the belief that the entire conceptual domain of marketing is cell 2—profit/micro/normative. Hutchinson clearly exemplifies this position:

> There is a real reason, however, why the field of marketing has been slow to develop a unique body of theory. It is a simple one: marketing is not a science. It is rather an art or a practice, and as such much more closely resembles engineering, medicine, and architecture than it does physics, chemistry, or biology. The medical profession sets us an excellent example, if we would but follow it; its members are called "practitioners" and not scientists. It is the work of physicians, as it is of any practitioner, to apply the findings of many sciences to the solution of problems. . . . It is the drollest travesty to relate the scientist's search for knowledge to the market research man's seeking after customers. (Hutchinson 1952, p. 287)

Note first that Hutchinson confuses problem-solving or *market* research (seeking after customers) with problem-oriented, basic or *marketing* research (expanding the knowledge base of marketing). And no one would deny that the "seeking after customers" is not science. Second, if, as Hutchinson implies, the entire conceptual domain of marketing is profit/micro/normative, then marketing is not and (more important) probably *cannot* be a science. However, if the conceptual domain of marketing is expanded to include both micro/positive and macro/positive phenomena, then marketing *could* be a science. That is, if phenomena such as consumer behavior and systems of distribution are included in the conceptual domain of marketing, there is no reason why the study of these phenomena could not be deserving of the designation "science."

Other disciplines, including economics, psychology, sociology, and philosophy, have experienced similar discipline-definitional controversies. It is not at all uncommon for an economist to review a colleague's work and proclaim, "This isn't *really* economics." Several decades ago, a definitional debate raged in philosophy. Some philosophers preferred a narrow approach, confining the philosophy of science to the method of investigating ordinary language systems. Other philosophers, including Karl R. Popper (1959, p. 19), rebelled at such an emasculation of philosophy of science. Popper noted that all definitions of disciplines are largely arbitrary in content. That is, they primarily represent an agreement to focus attention on some problems, issues, and phenomena, to the exclusion of others. Popper believed that to so define philosophy of science would almost, *by definition*, preclude philosophy from making substantive contributions to the total body of scientific knowledge.

A major problem with narrowly circumscribing the appropriate subject matter of a discipline is that it can seriously trammel research and other scientific inquiry. Kaplan (1964, p. 70) refers to the problem as "premature closure." When some marketers confine their conceptualization of the total scope of marketing to its micro-normative dimensions, they *prematurely close* their thinking and the thinking of others over which they have influence. This may be a particularly pernicious process for marketing because, it may be argued, studies that attempt to describe, classify, explain, and predict the micro-positive and macro-positive aspects of marketing may do more for the micro-normative dimension of marketing in the long run than will studies that are specifically restricted to micro-normative marketing. As Kaplan has observed, "Tolerance of ambiguity is as important for creativity in science as it is anywhere else" (1964, p. 71).

Is marketing a science? Differing perceptions of the scope of marketing have been shown to be a primary factor in the controversy over this question. The second factor contributing to the controversy has been differing perceptions concerning the basic nature of science, a subject that will now occupy our attention.

1.4 THE NATURE OF SCIENCE

The question of whether marketing is a science cannot be adequately answered without a clear understanding of the basic nature of science. So what is a science? Some writers claim that there is nothing that distinguishes science from any form of inquiry: "[S]cience is whatever society chooses to call science" (Anderson 1983, p. 26). This perspective is not discussed and evaluated here, but in this work's companion volume (Hunt 2003) and in Hunt (1984, 1989a). Nonrelativistic writers maintain that there are distinguishing features of science and often, in marketing, cite the perspective proposed by Buzzell. A science is:

- a classified and systematized body of knowledge,
- organized around one or more central theories and a number of general principles,
- usually expressed in quantitative terms,
- knowledge which permits the prediction and, under some circumstances, the control of future events. (Buzzell 1963, p. 37)

Buzzell then proceeded to note that marketing lacked the requisite theory and principles to be termed a science.

Although the Buzzell perspective on science has much to recommend it, the requirement "organized around one or more central theories" seems overly restrictive. This requirement confuses the successful culmination of scientific efforts with *science itself.* Was the study of chemistry not a science before discoveries such as the periodic table of elements? The major purpose of science is to develop laws and theories to explain, predict, understand, and control phenomena. Withholding the label "science" until a discipline has "central theories" would not seem reasonable.

The previous comments notwithstanding, requiring a science to be organized around one or more central theories is not completely without merit. There are strong honorific overtones in labeling a discipline a science. The label often signifies that the discipline has "arrived" in the eyes of other scientists. In large part, the label "science" is conferred upon a discipline only when the discipline has matured enough that it contains several "central theories." Thus, physics achieved the status of a science before psychology, and psychology achieved it before sociology. However, the total conceptual content of the term "science" is decidedly not just honorific. Marketing does not, and should not, have to wait to be knighted by others to be a science. How, then, do sciences differ from other disciplines, if not by virtue of having central theories?

Consider the discipline of chemistry—unquestionably a science. Chemistry can be defined as "the science of substances—their structure, their properties, and the reactions that change them into other substances" (Pauling 1956, p. 15). Using chemistry as an illustration, three observations will enable us to clarify the distinguishing characteristics of sciences. First, a distinct science must have a distinct subject matter, a set of phenomena that serves as a focal point for investigation. The subject matter of chemistry is *substances*, and chemistry attempts to understand, explain, predict, and control phenomena related to substances. Other disciplines, such as physics, are also interested in substances. However, chemistry can meaningfully lay claim to being a separate science because physics does not *focus on* the reactions of substances.

What is the basic subject matter of marketing? Most marketers now perceive the ultimate subject matter of marketing to be the *transaction.* Harking back to the chemistry analogue, marketing might then be viewed as the science of transactions—their structure, their properties, and their reactions with other phenomena. Given this perspective, the subject matter of marketing would certainly overlap with that of other disciplines, notably economics, psychology, and sociology. The analysis of transactions is considered in each of these disciplines. Yet, only in marketing is the transaction the *focal point.* For example, transactions remain a tangential issue in economics, where the primary focus is on the allocation of scarce resources (Leftwich 1966, p. 2). *Therefore, the first distinguishing characteristic is that any science must have a distinct subject matter.* To the extent that the transaction is the basic subject matter of marketing, marketing would seem to fulfill this requirement.

A distinct subject matter alone is not sufficient to distinguish sciences from other disciplines because all disciplines have a subject matter (some less distinct than others). The previously cited perspective of chemistry provides a second insight into the basic nature of science. Note the phrase "their structure, their properties, and [their] reactions." Every science seeks to describe and classify the structure and properties of its basic subject matter. Likewise, the term *reactions* suggests that the basic subject matter of chemistry is presumed to be systematically interrelated. Thus, the second distinguishing characteristic: *Every science presupposes the existence of underlying uniformities or regularities among the phenomena that comprise its subject matter. The discovery of these underlying uniformities yields empirical regularities, lawlike generalizations, laws, principles, and theories.*

The basic question for marketing is not whether there now exist several central theories that serve to unify, explain, and predict marketing phenomena. Rather, the following should be asked: "Are there underlying uniformities and regularities among the phenomena that constitute the subject matter of marketing?" This question can be answered affirmatively on two grounds—one *a priori* and one empirical. Marketing is a discipline investigating human behavior. Insofar as numerous uniformities and regularities have been observed in other behavioral sciences, there is no *a priori* reason for believing that the subject matter of marketing is devoid of uniformities and regularities. The second ground for believing that the uniformities exist is empirical. In the past four decades, the quantity of scholarly research conducted on marketing phenomena probably exceeds the total of *all* prior research in marketing. Efforts in the consumer behavior dimension of marketing have been particularly prolific. Who can deny that *some* progress has been made or that *some* uniformities have been identified? In short, who can deny that there exist uniformities and regularities in the subject matter of marketing? I, for one, cannot.

The task of delineating the basic nature of science is not yet complete. Up to this point, we have utilized chemistry to illustrate that all sciences involve (1) a distinct subject matter, (2) the description and classification of the subject matter, and (3) the presumption that underlying the subject matter are uniformities and regularities that science seeks to discover. The chemistry example provides a final observation. Note that "chemistry is the *science* of. . . ." This suggests that sciences can be differentiated from other disciplines (and pseudosciences) by the method of analysis. At the risk of being somewhat tautologous, sciences employ a set of procedures that are commonly referred to as the scientific method. The historical significance of the development and acceptance of the method of science cannot be overstated. The scientific method has been called "the most significant intellectual contribution of western civilization" (Morris 1955, p. 63). Is the method of science applicable to marketing?

One way of interpreting this monograph is to view it as an articulation of the application of the scientific method to marketing. Therefore, comments here on the scientific method should be viewed as strictly introductory in nature. One immediate observation is that there is no reason whatsoever to presume that the scientific method of analysis is any less appropriate to marketing than it is to other disciplines. Similarly, scholarly researchers in marketing, though often holding rather distorted notions concerning topics such as the role of laws and theories in research, seem to be at least as technically proficient as researchers in other areas.

The second observation concerning the scientific method involves the "unity of scientific method controversy." Three questions frame this issue: Is there a single scientific method? Do different sciences require different methods? Are several scientific methods appropriate for the same science? Zaltman et al. (1973, p. 93) state that *the* scientific method is a myth. Conversely, Bergmann (1957, p. 164) states that "there is one and only one scientific method." Similarly, whole volumes have been written on the unity of the scientific method (Neurath et al. 1955; Jeffrey 1966; Kaiser 1993; Snyder 1978). The unity of scientific method controversy has far-reaching implications for marketing. In fact, a basic understanding of the foundations of this controversy is an absolute precondition to comprehending fully the rest of this monograph. Consequently, the next section will be devoted to an exposition of this issue. The analysis will draw heavily from the works of Gustov Bergmann, Carl Hempel, Harvey Kyburg, Richard Rudner, and Wesley Salmon.[6]

1.5 THE UNITY OF SCIENTIFIC METHOD

The claim is sometimes made that marketing and other social sciences require a scientific method that differs somewhat from the method of the physical sciences. Do the various sciences require different scientific methods? Are there several equally appropriate methods for any particular science? Those who respond affirmatively to these questions support the Multi-Scientific-Method (MSM) thesis. Those who respond negatively support the Single-Scientific-Method (SSM) thesis. Such is the substance of the unity of science issue. Analyzing it requires an appreciation for (1) the differences between the *methodology* of a discipline and the *techniques* of a discipline and (2) the importance of carefully distinguishing between issues in the context of discovery versus issues in the context of justification. (The context of justification is sometimes referred to as the context of validation.)

The techniques of a discipline are the specific tools and apparatus, both conceptual and physical, that researchers in a discipline have found useful in the conduct of inquiry. Marketing uses devices such as consumer panels, questionnaires, pupilometers, Likert scales, multiple regression, multidimensional scaling, surveys, random sampling, and multiple classification analysis. Some of these tools are conceptual, and some are physical. The tools used encompass the *techniques* of marketing research. Chemistry employs test tubes, thermocouples, spectrometers, and cyclotrons. Some techniques, such as strictly experimental research designs, are much more common in the physical sciences than in marketing or most of the social sciences. Unfortunately, many advocates of the MSM thesis point to these differences in techniques to support their position. However, the scientific method is not restricted to certain kinds of hardware (test tubes, cyclotrons, pupilometers), to techniques of gathering data (experiments, surveys), to techniques of measuring phenomena (thermometers, Likert scales), or, most certainly, to techniques of analyzing data (regression, multiple classification analysis, canonical correlation). Astronomy is unquestionably a science, and yet its techniques are in some respects closer to those of marketing than to those of physics (note the conspicuous lack of laboratory experimentation in astronomy). To the extent that advocates of the MSM thesis rely on these differences in techniques for evidential support, their position becomes either (a) trivial or (b) untenable: trivial, because different sciences obviously use different techniques in research; untenable, because the *techniques* of a science should not be confused with the *methodology* of a science. What, then, is the methodology of science?

Philosophers of science agree that *the methodology of science is its logic of justification.* That is, the scientific method consists of the rules and procedures on which a science bases its acceptance or rejection of its body of knowledge, including hypotheses, laws, and theories.[7] To the extent that advocates of the MSM thesis are not simply referring to different techniques, they are really claiming that different sciences have (or should have?) different bases on which to assess the truth content of their disciplines. This, indeed, is a radical claim and one that has been thoroughly discredited (Rudner 1966, p. 4). As Hempel has observed:

> The thesis of the methodological unity of science states, first of all, that, notwithstanding many differences in their techniques of investigation, all branches of empirical science test and support their statements in basically the same manner, namely by deriving from them implications that can be checked intersubjectively and by performing for those implications the appropriate experimental or observational tests. This, the unity of method thesis holds, is true also of psychology and the social and historical disciplines. In response to the claim that the scholar in these fields, in contrast to the natural scientists, often must rely on empathy to establish his assertions, logical-empiricist writers stressed that imaginative identification with a given person often may prove a useful heuristic aid to the investigator who seeks to guess at a hypothesis about that person's beliefs, hopes, fears, and goals. But whether or not a hypothesis thus arrived at is factually sound must be determined by reference to objective evidence: the investigator's empathic experience is logically irrelevant to it. (Hempel 1969, p. 91)

As Siegel (1985) argues, the methodological criteria of science that collectively constitute the scientific method (SM) can best be expressed as a "commitment to evidence," as exemplified by "a concern for explanatory adequacy, however that adequacy is conceived; and insistence on testing, however testing is thought to be best done; and a commitment to inductive support, however inductive inference is thought to be best made" (p. 528). Thus, "science's commitment to evidence, by way of SM, is what justifies its claim to respect—science is to be taken seriously precisely because of its commitment to evidence" (p. 530). However, the preceding conclusions by Siegel about scientific method do not imply that he claims that science is the *only* domain in which the epistemic worthiness of beliefs, hypotheses, or claims may be putatively established on the basis of evidence. Rather, "SM extends far beyond the realm of science proper. But this is only to say that SM can be utilized widely. It is still properly labeled *scientific* method" (p. 530).

Therefore, the unity of science stems from the common acceptance by the sciences of a methodology for the justification (confirmation, validation, corroboration) of knowledge. One of the primary objectives of this monograph will be to explore systematically this logic of justification as applied to marketing. That is, we shall explore the basic nature of the scientific understanding, explaining, and predicting of marketing phenomena. In the process, the unique roles of hypotheses, laws, lawlike generalizations, empirical generalizations, and theories will be developed.

This section began by delineating two rival theses: the Multi-Scientific-Method thesis and the Single-Scientific-Method thesis. Supporters of the MSM thesis have been shown often to confuse the techniques of a science with its methodology. A second shortcoming of the MSM thesis is even more important: *advocates of the MSM thesis often confuse the context of discovery with the context of justification.*

1.5.1 Discovery Versus Justification

How does one go about discovering scientific hypotheses, laws, and theories? What kinds of tools and procedures will assist the researcher in uncovering them? Are some procedures better than others? Are some procedures correct and others incorrect? Is there a single procedure that is guaranteed to produce results? Should a theory or law be evaluated on the basis of how that theory or law was generated? What was the genesis of Reilly's Law? How did John Howard and Jagdish Sheth create their theory of buyer behavior? All these issues and questions should be considered in the *context of discovery.* If there existed a set of systematic rules and procedures that were optimal for the discovery of hypotheses, laws, and theories, this set of rules and procedures would constitute a *logic of discovery.*

How does one scientifically *explain* marketing phenomena? Can one explain marketing phenomena without being able to *predict* them? What are the roles of laws and theories in explaining and predicting phenomena? Must theories be empirically testable? Are the axioms of a theory assumed to be true? Must theories contain lawlike generalizations? These issues and questions belong in the *context of justification.* As previously noted, the set of rules and procedures that delineate the criteria for accepting or rejecting knowledge (hypotheses, laws, and theories) in science constitutes its *logic of justification.*

Salmon has observed that treating issues that appropriately belong in the context of discovery as if they belong in the context of justification often leads one to commit the "genetic fallacy." He offers the following statement as an extreme illustration of the genetic fallacy: "The Nazis condemned the theory of relativity because Einstein, its originator, was a Jew" (1963, p. 12). Obviously, in this extreme example, the fact that Einstein was a Jew should have been ignored in assessing the validity of the theory of relativity. Unfortunately, in the literature of science, dividing issues into discovery and justification is frequently much more difficult, and, thus, a trap is laid for the unsuspecting researcher.

Bergmann (1957, p. 51) has noted that many philosophers of science, including Hegel and John Dewey, have confused the discovery of scientific knowledge with its justification. The confusion of discovery with justification seems widespread in all the sciences, and marketing is no exception. This writer (1971) has previously observed that Robert Bartels's (1968) "The General Theory of Marketing" should perhaps be evaluated in the context of discovery, rather than justification. Similarly, Bartels (1970) has offered a metatheory of marketing comprising seven axioms. To what extent are these seven axioms proposed as rules for *discovering* marketing theory, and to what extent are they to be used to *evaluate* marketing theory? Likewise, William Lazer (1962) believes that there are two approaches for developing models and theories in marketing—*abstraction* and *realization.* Abstraction begins with "perceptions of marketing situations," whereas realization begins with "theoretical and abstract statements about marketing." Which aspects of these approaches belong in the context of discovery, and which in the context of justification? Similarly, in discussing the scientific method, Zaltman, Pinson, and Angelmar (1973, p. 12) propose a model of the research process composed of the following nine states:

1. Assessment of relevant existing knowledge
2. Concept formation and specification of hypotheses
3. Acquisition of meaningful data
4. Organizing and analyzing data in relevant ways

5. Evaluation of and learning from results
6. Dissemination of research information
7. Providing explanations
8. Making predictions
9. Engaging in necessary control activities

The reader should attempt to determine which of these stages should be evaluated in the context of discovery, and which in the context of justification. It is hoped that the chart in Figure 1.1 will be of some assistance.

Figure 1.1 attempts to provide guidance as to which issues are in the context of discovery and which are in the context of justification. The top half of the chart shows four procedures for generating (discovering) empirical generalizations, laws, and theories. These procedures are simply illustrative and by no means exhaust the possibilities. The bottom half details a variety of issues in justification, and, again, the issues by no means exhaust the subject. Because the entire remainder of this monograph will be devoted to exploring the issues in the bottom half of Figure 1.1, our attention here will be directed to the top half, that is, the alternative routes to the discovery of scientific knowledge.

One route in Figure 1.1 shows that dreams sometimes play an important role in scientific discovery. Hempel relates the story of how the chemist Kekulé discovered the structure of the benzene molecule:

> He had long been trying unsuccessfully to devise a structural formula for the benzene molecule when, one evening in 1865, he found a solution to his problem while he was dozing in front of his fireplace. Gazing into the flames, he seemed to see atoms dancing in snakelike arrays. Suddenly, one of the snakes formed a ring by seizing hold of its own tail and then whirled mockingly before him. Kekulé awoke in a flash: he had hit upon the now famous and familiar idea of representing the molecular structure of benzene by a hexagonal ring. (Hempel 1966, p. 16)

Similarly, it is claimed that the goddess of Namakkal visited the great Indian mathematician Ramanujan (1887–1920) and revealed mathematical formulas to him (Salmon 1963, p. 10). Thus, sometimes a dream can prompt a scientific discovery.

A second path to discovery, the eureka route, can be illustrated by Archimedes' (287–212 B.C.) principle. Supposedly, Archimedes noticed that his bathwater rose in height when he immersed himself. Shouting "Eureka!" he proclaimed that any body immersed in a fluid would be "buoyed up" with a force equal to the weight of the displaced fluid. Likewise, schoolchildren are told the story of how Newton discovered the universal law of gravitation when an apple dropped on his head. The point of these examples (fables?) concerning the dream and eureka routes is that serendipity plays a prominent

Figure 1.1 **Discovery Versus Justification**

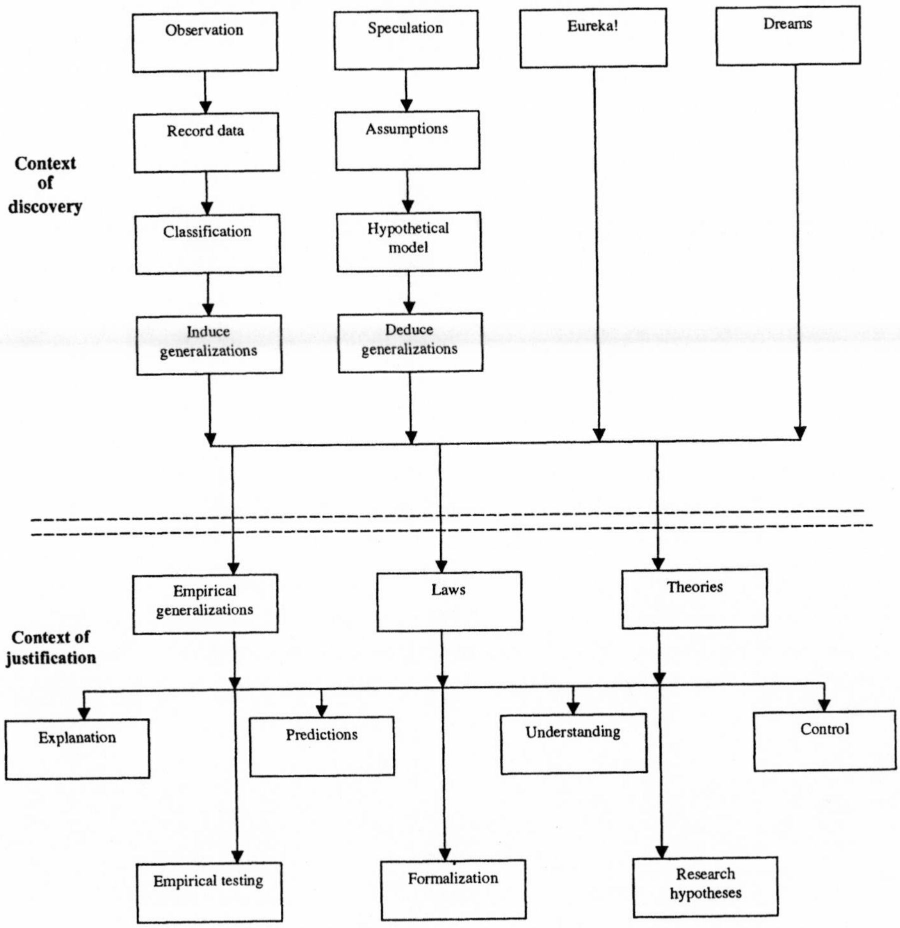

Source: Hunt (1991). Reprinted by permission of the author.

role in scientific discovery. *Many, if not most, major scientific discoveries are flashes of perceptual insight and are not the result of following some rigorously prescribed procedure.*

Consider, now, the first route in Figure 1.1, which starts with *observation*, and the second route, which starts with *speculation*. The first route is a variant of the generalized *inductivist* route, and the second is a form of the generalized *deductivist* route. The deductivist route plays a prominent role in much economic theory, while marketing theoreticians seem to advocate an inductivist route. Thus, McGarry (1936), in the very first volume of the *Journal of Marketing*, maintained that the "scientific method" in marketing involves the four steps of (1) selecting facts, (2) registering these facts, (3) rearranging the facts so as to bring order out of chaos, and (4) finding a formula or conclusion. Similarly, three decades later, Schwartz (1963, p. 135) argues that "there appears to be no way of avoiding the laborious empirical method in discovering marketing theory." Conversely, Fisk (1971, p.10) notes that "the first step in applying the scientific method is to think of an hypothesis." Is the *inductivist* route the preferred procedure for marketing, as many marketing theorists suggest? To answer this question, we must examine more carefully the basic nature of this route.

Let us suppose that a marketing theorist desires to explore phenomena relating to consumer purchase behavior. In particular, let us suppose that the theorist has decided to focus on the phenomenon of brand loyalty as the "dependent" variable. The inductivist route suggests that the first steps for the theorist would be observation and the recording of data. What would the theorist observe? "Everything," the strict inductivist might reply. Yet, we might then point out that observing and recording everything would be impossible because the number of potential phenomena that could be observed and recorded at any point in time is virtually infinite (phase of the moon, height of the tides, temperatures, etc.). The inductivist would probably then become somewhat defensive, chastise us for taking his statement "too literally," and respond, "Of course, you should not observe and record all phenomena! Just observe and record all data *relevant* to the problem of brand loyalty." Readers should attempt to place themselves in the role of the bewildered research assistant who has just been instructed to observe and record all data *relevant* to the problem of brand loyalty and ignore all phenomena *irrelevant* to brand loyalty. By what criterion is the research assistant to separate relevant phenomena from the irrelevant variety? The strict inductivist will finally admit that the charge to the research assistant must be first to think of some *a priori* hypotheses concerning which phenomena might be systematically related to brand loyalty and then to make observations and record data *relevant* to those hypotheses. That is, data are never *a priori* relevant or irrelevant to a *problem* such as brand loyalty. Rather, data can only be *a priori* relevant or irrelevant to hypotheses (however crude or tentative) concerning certain phenomena and brand loyalty.

After observation and the recording of data comes the classification stage in the inductivist route. By now the reader should recognize that the appropriate question is, "On what basis should the data be classified?" Again, because the number of ways a set of data can be classified is virtually unlimited, the data must be classified on some basis that is likely to be useful for exploring *a priori* hypotheses. In conclusion, the strict inductivist approach to theory building is untenable, because speculation and the creation of *a priori* hypotheses are absolutely essential parts of any *systematic procedure* of theory discovery and creation. Actual research does not proceed according to the stages suggested by the strict inductivists, and the inductivist route certainly cannot be defended as the *preferred* procedure.

Given the previous analysis of the strict inductivist route for generating theory, why do so many marketing theorists tout its virtues? Perhaps many marketing theorists have reacted (overreacted?) to certain perceived deficiencies in conventional economic theory. Economic theory is perceived to be deductive in nature. Economic theory is also often perceived to be unrealistic and divorced from the real world. As Alderson (1965, p. 18) has noted, "economists have shown a notable preference for elegance over relevance." Nevertheless, it is erroneous to believe that the deficiencies of economic theory are to be found in the context of discovery. That is, to the extent that economic theory is deficient, the cause lies not in the economists' deductive procedures for generating theory. Rather, the truth of economic theory must be analyzed and evaluated in the context of justification. To what extent has economic theory been tested and found accurately to depict the real world? These and other questions that are appropriate to the context of justification will be discussed in Chapter 6.

This section began by proposing that advocates of the Multi-Scientific-Method thesis often confuse issues and procedures in the context of discovery with issues and procedures in the context of justification. Proponents of MSM point out the wide variety of "methods" for the discovery of laws and theories in science. We must grant their premise, but not their conclusion. Granted, there exists no single set of procedures that is guaranteed to lead to the discovery of laws and theories. Also, there exists no single set of procedures that can be defended as optimal. *Therefore, there is no single logic of discovery.* Nevertheless, the conclusion that many scientific methods exist does not necessarily follow, because the scientific method concerns the context of justification, not discovery, and *there does exist a single logic of justification that is common to all science.* The reader should clearly recognize the difference between *discovery* and *justification* because we shall be referring to it on numerous occasions throughout this monograph.

1.6 CONCLUSIONS ON MARKETING SCIENCE

The purpose of this introductory chapter has been to detail the objectives of this monograph and to discuss some preliminary issues. The primary objective has been stated to be the utilization of the tool kit of the philosophy of science for systematically exploring some of the basic methodological issues underlying marketing research. The preliminary issues explored have been in the context of the "Is marketing a science?" controversy. In attempting to explore this controversy, we have found it necessary to delve into the basic nature of both marketing and science and to distinguish between methodology and techniques and between discovery and justification. The analysis suggests several conclusions.

The scope of the area called marketing has been shown to be exceptionally broad. Marketing has micro/macro dimensions, profit sector/nonprofit sector dimensions, and positive/normative dimensions. Reasonable people can disagree as to which combination of these dimensions (refer to the eight cells in Table 1.1) represents the *appropriate* total scope of marketing. If marketing were restricted to the profit/micro/normative dimension (as many practitioners would do), then marketing would not be a science and could not become one. Sciences involve the explanation, prediction, and understanding of phenomena, and, therefore, any discipline that is purely evaluative (normative) is not a science. At least for marketing academe, restricting the scope of marketing to its profit/micro/normative dimension is unrealistic, unnecessary, and, without question, undesirable.

Once the appropriate scope of marketing has been expanded to include at least some *positive* dimensions (cells 1, 3, 5, and 7 in Table 1.1), then the explanation, prediction, and understanding of these phenomena could be a science. The question then becomes whether the study of the positive dimensions of marketing has the requisite characteristics of a science. Aside from the strictly honorific overtones of *nonmarketers* accepting marketing as a science, the substantive characteristics differentiating sciences from other disciplines have been shown to be (1) a distinct subject matter, (2) the description and classification of the subject matter, (3) the presumption of underlying uniformities and regularities in the subject matter, and (4) the adoption of the method of science for studying the subject matter. The *positive* dimensions of marketing have been shown to have a subject matter properly distinct from that of other sciences. The marketing literature is replete with description and classification. There have been discoveries (however tentative) of uniformities and regularities in marketing phenomena. Finally, although Kenneth Longman (1971, p. 10) deplores "the rather remarkable lack of scientific method employed by scientists of marketing," I suggest that marketing researchers are at least as committed to the method of science as are researchers in other disciplines. Therefore, we can conclude that the study of the *positive* dimensions of marketing can be appropriately referred to as *marketing science.*

1.7 THE THREE DICHOTOMIES MODEL: AN EVALUATION

Since its first publication in 1976, the "Three Dichotomies Model of Marketing" has evoked substantial interest and significant controversy. For an early review and analysis of the controversy, see Arndt (1981a). Many marketing academicians have expressed views such as "I basically agree with the model except for the following characteristic. . . ." This section will address the major "except fors" that have been proposed. Although the positive/normative dichotomy has sparked the most spirited comments, it is fair to say that all aspects of the model have been questioned. And this is as it should be, because models in general are not (a positive observation) and should not be (a normative observation) inscribed in stone for all time.

Although numerous colleagues have volunteered their observations on the Three Dichotomies Model, the "except fors" discussed here have come primarily from (1) the participants at the first Macromarketing Conference held at the University of Colorado in 1976 (Slater 1977), (2) letters to the editor of the *Journal of Marketing* by Donald P. Robin (1977, 1978) and Michael Etgar (1977), and (3) an article by Michael R. Hyman, Robert Skipper, and Richard Tansey (1991). These writers have charged that the positive/normative dichotomy is (1) false, (2) dangerous, (3) unnecessary, (4) meaningless, and (5) useless. It is further claimed that (6) all of marketing thought is normative. Each charge will be discussed, in turn. First, however, it will be useful to provide a brief review of the positive/normative dichotomy in the philosophy of science.

1.7.1 The Positive/Normative Dichotomy in Philosophy of Science

David Hume (1711–1776) is generally given credit for being the first philosopher to point out that statements concerning the verb "is" are different in kind from statements containing the verb "ought." In particular, Hume observed that no set of statements containing only descriptive terms and no copula except "is" can logically yield a conclusion containing an "ought." The positive/normative dichotomy is the version of Hume's "is/ought" dichotomy discussed in John Neville Keynes's (1891) classic work, *The Scope and Method of Political Economy.* There he defined a positive science as "a body of systematized knowledge concerning what is" and a normative science as "a body of systematized knowledge discussing criteria of what ought to be" (pp. 34–35). Keynes pointed out that "confusion between them is common and has been the source of many mischievous errors" (p. 46). The *Dictionary of Philosophy* clarifies the view in philosophy about the is/ought dichotomy:

> **Is/Ought Dichotomy.** Also, *fact/value dichotomy*. Statements containing the verb *is* are related to descriptive or factual claims and are of a different order from those containing the verb *ought* (*should*), which are related to judgments, evaluations, or commands. It is impossible (logically, formally, conceptually) to derive an "ought" (or "should") statement from an "is" (factual) statement, a normative statement from a statement of facts; it is impossible to have a valid deductive argument in which the premises state descriptions and the conclusion states prescriptions or imperatives. (Angeles 1981, p. 138)

The "is/ought fallacy" is one of the most widely accepted ideas in philosophy and is related to the "naturalistic fallacy" in the area of ethics, which is: "The fallacy of deriving (deducing) ethical statements from nonethical statements" (Angeles 1981, p. 186). Indeed, the is/ought fallacy and the naturalistic fallacy are two of only four fallacies that are given special attention under the heading of "Philosophical Fallacies" in *The Encyclopedia of Philosophy* (Edwards 1972, vol. 3, p. 178).

So, the is/ought (i.e., positive/normative) dichotomy forms the foundation for one of the most important classes of fallacies in all of philosophy. It is a dichotomy that has proved its usefulness in many disciplines for several centuries. Yet, critics contend that when the dichotomy is applied to the *marketing* discipline, it is, among other things, so ambiguous as to render it useless. On *prima facie* grounds such a conclusion is implausible. Specific analyses of specific criticisms provide other grounds.

1.7.2 Is the Positive/Normative Dichotomy False?

Some writers have suggested that *the positive/normative dichotomy is a false dichotomy because we cannot escape from our own value systems.* This premise is probably true: we probably cannot escape from our value systems. Nevertheless, the premise does not imply that the positive/normative dichotomy is false; to accede to this conclusion would be to capitulate to despair and to commit the "philosophers' fallacy of high redefinition" (Hunt 1990).

There is an analogous problem in other disciplines. Consider journalism. It stresses *objectivity* in reporting: journalists attempt to keep their personal value systems out of their *news* writing. All knowledgeable people recognize the impossibility of keeping the news columns completely free of editorializing. Nevertheless, the goal of separating news from opinion remains one of the ethical pillars of journalism. It does so because the credibility of journalists would be irreparably damaged if they abandoned the *goal* of objectivity simply because they found its complete *achievement* to be unattainable. Furthermore, holding the goal of objectivity in high regard is itself a *value*—and, for many, a highly important value. (Alas, for some "journalists" it is quite unimportant.)

So it is in marketing. Granted, marketing research cannot be value-free. But this does not imply that we should not *attempt* to separate the positive issue of whether marketers perceive themselves as having "social responsibilities" from the normative issue of whether marketers *should* have social responsibilities. Nor does it imply that we should not attempt clearly to separate the issue of whether the poor do in fact "pay more" from the issue of whether it is *wrong* for them to pay more. Nor, finally, does it imply that we should not attempt to separate how managers do in fact make marketing decisions from how they *should* make those decisions. The importance of the positive/normative dichotomy as a goal for clear thinking and analysis is in no way impaired because that goal is, in principle, not completely attainable.

1.7.3 Is the Positive/Normative Dichotomy Dangerous?

A few colleagues have proposed that *the positive/normative dichotomy is dangerous because it may lead people to downgrade the importance of micro/normative marketing.* However, the model does not imply that micro/normative marketing is unimportant or unworthy of attention. On the contrary, the study of how marketing decisions *should* be made is extremely important. To believe otherwise is to grossly misinterpret the model. Unquestionably, some people, now that they have a taxonomic schema showing the various dimensions of marketing, may choose to deemphasize micro/normative marketing. Further, this deemphasis *may* have unfortunate consequences. Nevertheless, many marketers *still* consider the entire scope of marketing to be its micro-normative dimension, and this *has had* demonstrably unfortunate consequences.

The positive/normative dichotomy puts micro/normative marketing "in its place." It does not imply that its "place" is unimportant. The potential advantages of awakening people to the fact that there are dimensions to marketing *beyond* the micro/normative dimension greatly outweigh any possible dangers of downgrading the importance of micro/normative marketing.

1.7.4 Is the Positive/Normative Dichotomy Unnecessary?

Robin charges that *the positive/normative dichotomy is "unnecessary" for considering the "Is marketing a science?" controversy because "using scientific explanation in marketing simply requires that the normative statements be used as antecedent conditions"* (Robin 1977, p. 136). To illustrate his point of using normative statements in scientific explanations, he offers the following "explanation" as an example:

Antecedent conditions

C_1 = Long-run profit maximization is the primary objective of the organization.
C_2 = One or more competitors of approximately equal economic strength exist in the market.
C_3 = The organization has the opportunity of offering several different variations of a new product, at varying prices, with different promotional possibilities, and through a variety of channels.
C_4 = The products of the firm are such that buyers can adequately determine their value (functional and/or psychological).

Generally accepted propositions

L_1 = Strong competitors can and will produce products desired by buyers if a large enough number desire them.
L_2 = Buyers purchase goods in a manner that they perceive to be in their best interest at the time of the purchase.

Thus:

Given C_1, C_2, C_3, C_4, L_1, and L_2, the firm must organize the controllable variables available to it (i.e., the marketing mix) so as to develop and maintain a satisfied group of buyers. (Robin 1977, pp. 137–38)

Robin concludes, "It should be noted that the antecedent condition C_1 represents an assumed organizational objective that is, as previously explained, a *normative judgment*" (Robin 1977, p. 138).

Is the positive/normative dichotomy unnecessary? Do normative statements play a role in scientific explanation? To evaluate these questions, we must refer to the meaning of *positive statements* versus *normative statements.* Recall that the positive/normative dichotomy provides categories based on whether the focus of the analysis is primarily descriptive or prescriptive. Positive marketing adopts the perspective of attempting to describe, explain, predict, and understand the marketing activities, processes, and phenomena that actually exist. This perspective examines *what is.* In contrast, normative marketing adopts the perspective of attempting to prescribe what marketing organizations and individuals ought to do or what kinds of marketing systems a society ought to have. That is, this perspective examines what *ought to be* and what organizations and individuals *ought to do.* Thus, one signal (but not the *only* one) of a normative statement is the existence of an *ought* or *should* or some similar term.

Returning to Robin's "explanation," are there any normative statements? In particular, is C_1 normative, as Robin indicates? Clearly, it is a *positive* statement, not a normative one. C_1 states that "long-run profit maximization is the primary objective of the organization." If C_1 were normative, it would state, "Long-run profit maximization *ought to be* the primary objective of the organization." As a matter of fact, there are *no* normative statements in Robin's "explanation." Note that C_2 states that "competitors of approximately equal economic strength *exist,*" not that they "ought to exist." Further, C_3 and C_4 state that "the organization *has*" and that "products of the firm are"—both are positive statements.

There are no normative statements in Robin's "explanation" precisely because (as Robin himself points out) in scientific explanation "the explanandum [the statement to be explained] must be logically derivable from the explanans [the statements doing the explaining]." And any statement with an "ought" *cannot* be an antecedent condition in a logically valid scientific explanation. Thus, far from showing that the positive/normative dichotomy is *unnecessary*, Robin's "explanation" gives powerful justification for considering the dichotomy to be *necessary.* Robin's later analysis agreed:

> In my simple model, C_1 (antecedent condition No. 1) was given: "Long-run profit maximization is the primary objective of the organization." Professor Hunt states, "Clearly it (C_1) is a *positive* statement not a normative one." He further states that there are *no* normative statements in Robin's 'explanation.'" *I completely agree on both accounts.* (Robin 1978, p. 6; italics added)

1.7.5 Is the Positive/Normative Dichotomy Meaningless?

Robin also suggests that *the positive/normative dichotomy is "meaningless" because the information derived from a positive "study is of little interest unless it is given prescriptive overtones. . . . That is, the positive issues are barren except where they have prescriptive implications"* (1977, p. 136). We can begin our analysis of this comment by asking: To *whom* are positive studies "of little interest" unless there are prescriptive implications? Is it to the marketing manager? Are all positive studies "barren" unless they provide immediate guidance as to how the marketing manager can make better decisions? This seems to be the "meaningfulness" criterion that Robin is proposing.

No one would dispute that many of the positive studies in marketing have managerial implications. There is no doubt that the explanations and predictions from positive studies frequently serve as useful guides for developing normative decision rules and normative models. However, the view that all positive studies are "meaningless" unless they assist the marketing manager is exactly the kind of narrow perception of the scope of marketing that has for so long caused so much mischief in our discipline. The discipline of marketing does not exist solely and exclusively to serve the needs of the marketing manager, just as the discipline of psychology does not exist solely to serve the needs of the clinical psychologist. Research in marketing has many aims. Fortunately, the American Marketing Association (AMA) now specifically acknowledges that there are numerous "constituencies" for marketing research. The AMA Task Force on the Development of Marketing Thought identified five such groups: academicians (including students), managers, public policy members, special interest groups, and consumers (Monroe et al. 1988).

The prime directive for scholarly research is the same for marketing as for all sciences: *to seek knowledge.* The knowledge must be intersubjectively certifiable and capable of describing, explaining, and predicting phenomena. At some times, the knowledge may assist marketing managers in making decisions. At other times, the knowledge may guide legislators in drafting laws to regulate marketing activities. At still other times, the knowledge may assist the general public in understanding the functions that marketing activities perform for society. Finally, the knowledge may simply assist marketing scholars in *knowing*, a not inconsequential objective.

1.7.6 Is the Positive/Normative Dichotomy Useless?

In a restatement of his position, Robin (1978, p. 6) agrees that "normative statements are not part of scientific explanatory models." Nevertheless, he still concludes that "*any attempt to classify marketing phenomena on the basis of a positive/normative dichotomy will lead either to confusion or a useless set of relationships.*" His conclusion is based in part on the observation that the positive and normative "parts of our world are so inseparably intermingled." Robin in this case seems to be echoing Etgar's observation that "Hunt's classification fails to pass a major test by which categorical schemes should [readers please note: this is a normative statement] be judged: namely, self-exclusivity—the principle that under a specific classificatory scheme, such as normative/positive, a given phenomenon should be classified as falling into one category only" (Etgar 1977, p. 146).

Is lack of self-exclusivity a fatal flaw? I think not. First of all, it is unnecessary to concede the *positive* issue of whether the positive/normative (P/N) dichotomy is completely lacking in self-exclusivity. Many studies in marketing are either overwhelmingly positive (such as descriptive analyses of the channels of distribution for farm products) or overwhelmingly normative (such as models for the optimal allocation of media expenditures). Thus, it is clear that the classification in the model of many, if not most, marketing studies and phenomena is not in doubt; and this is all that is required for a taxonomic schema to be viable (Van Fraassen 1980, p. 16).

Second it is unnecessary to concede the *normative* issue of whether lack of self-exclusivity would render the P/N dichotomy "useless." Though the exclusivity of classificational schemata is indeed desirable (see section 8.1.3), it is false that a lack of self-exclusivity is, by itself, a fatal flaw. Indeed, many useful classificational schemata lack self-exclusivity. For example, most universities evaluate their faculties on the dimensions of teaching, research, and service. Please note that these dimensions are closely related; some would even believe them to be "inseparably intermingled." Research activities often carry over into teaching and service activities. Likewise, teaching activities impact on research and service. Is this a "fatal flaw" of the teaching/research/service trichotomy, making it "useless?" Because normative economics is not independent of positive economics, should all economic thought be lumped into one side? Certainly, economists think not (Friedman 1953). So it is with the positive/normative dichotomy in marketing. The positive dimensions impact on the normative dimensions. The normative dimensions impact on the positive dimensions. The results are synergistic and thus useful to the discipline of marketing.

1.7.7 Is All of Marketing Thought Normative?

Hyman, Skipper, and Tansey (hereafter "HST") (1991) evaluate the positive/normative dichotomy as flawed because the meanings of "ought" and "should," (my rule of thumb for separating normative from positive) depend on their context. They then offer the following as their own rule of thumb for "normative": "*All normative sentences and only normative sentences offer a reason for action*" (p. 420; italics in original). Using their criterion, they conclude: "[A]lmost all marketing phenomena are normative phenomena, almost all marketing issues are normative issues, almost all marketing theories are normative theories, and almost all marketing answers are normative answers" (p. 420). They base their conclusion on their analyses of the concepts "ownership," "obligation," "rights," "values," and "needs." These terms, as well as "exchange," "price," "purchasing," "advertising," "promotion," "product," "power," and "conflict" (among many others), "are so blatantly normative that little argument is needed" (p. 420). Therefore, "marketing language is so saturated with value-laden terms and marketing theories are so thoroughly imbued with normative claims that no translation into positive language is conceivable" (p. 420). The implications for HST of finding the positive half of the positive/normative dichotomy to be an empty set in marketing are: "[M]ost of our empirical studies in marketing have been conducted on empirically untestable positions" and "the only way to make marketing positive is to start anew" (p. 421).

It is worth noting that HST are far too modest in claiming only that *marketing* is overwhelming normative. Consider the discipline of economics. It unquestionably focuses extensively (obsessively?) on price and its role in exchange relationships and clearing markets. But, if price and exchange are irretrievably normative, as concluded by HST, then, no doubt, economics is overwhelming normative and no part of it is a positive science. Likewise, political science relies heavily on the concepts of power and conflict. Yet, these too, according to HST, are normative. Thus, no positive research is possible in contemporary political science. How about social psychology, sociology, or anthropology? Clearly, according to simple extensions of the logic of HST, all these areas are overwhelmingly normative and no positive, empirical research is conducted in any of these areas. In short, according to HST's logic, all the social sciences are overwhelmingly normative and they all, like marketing, should "start anew." Have HST found the Achilles' heel of the social sciences? Must we all "start anew?" Is the sky truly falling on the social sciences?

Although some may warmly applaud and others eagerly embrace the skeptical conclusions of HST (most for reasons other than HST's logic), I do not. Therefore, I will endeavor, following the analysis in Hunt (1991c), to show that their analysis is problematic and neither marketing nor other social sciences need discard all the research that has been conducted in the past few decades—we need not "start anew."

To examine HST's conclusion that all of marketing thought is normative, it will be helpful to work from an example. Consider the case of a marketing researcher running a marketing panel who reviews the purchase diary of Mary Smith, one of the consumers in the panel. After reviewing Mary's purchase diary for a particular day, the researcher notes: "Mary Smith now owns one box of ten Hostess Twinkies after exchanging $5.00 with her local Safeway Supermarket." Is this statement by the marketing researcher positive or normative? Most marketing researchers and other social scientists would, no doubt, put this statement on the positive side of the positive/normative dichotomy. After all, the statement does not observe that the price of Twinkies was lower at United Supermarket and *prescribe* that Mary *should* have purchased her Twinkies there. It does not *judge* that it was *wrong* for Mary to buy the Twinkies at Safeway based on some criterion, such as a claim that Safeway treats its employees unfairly. It does not claim that Mary *ought* to have purchased the Twinkies at a supermarket evincing proper environmental concern. Nor does it *evaluate* Mary and find her to be a *bad* mother for allowing her children to eat such nutritionally empty products as Hostess Twinkies. The statement makes none of these normative claims. Rather, the statement claims that Mary in fact made a particular purchase at a particular store at a particular price and now owns a particular product. That is, the intent of the statement is to make the positive assertion that the evidence supports the fact that Mary made the purchase. However, HST would claim otherwise. On the basis that "ownership," "price," and "exchange," are "blatantly normative," all statements containing such terms are normative, and, therefore, for HST are "forbidden" in positive marketing research. We need to explore how HST could reach such an idiosyncratic view.

What are the criteria for HST's conclusion that ownership, exchange, and price are irretrievably normative? They use their rule of thumb that "all normative sentences and only normative sentences offer a reason for action" in their evaluation of "ownership":

> *Ownership* is a normative term. Ownership can exist only within a normative framework—a web of promises and obligations. Only persons can own property, because only persons have property rights within a value system established by a set of laws. . . . Our proposed rule classifies sentences about ownership as normative, because mere ownership is a reason for acting a certain way (*not stealing*, for instance). (HST 1991, p. 420; italics added)

Thus, HST would contend that "Mary owns a box of Twinkies" is normative because "mere ownership is a reason for acting a certain way." To evaluate their reasoning we should first note that "Mary owns a box of Twinkies" is not, by itself, "a reason for acting a certain way." That is, the ownership of Twinkies does not provide a reason for not stealing—for thieves steal (Twinkies and other items) all the time. Rather, "Mary owns a box of Twinkies" must be conjoined with the values of the observer (it is right or wrong to steal) for the statement to be a reason for acting in a certain way (i.e., stealing or not stealing). In contrast, the normative statement "it is wrong to steal" offers, by *itself*, a reason for acting in a certain way.

The reason why "Mary owns a box of Twinkies" is not by itself a reason for acting is that it is (as previously discussed) a positive statement, not a normative one. The fact that societies set criteria for "ownership" does not imply that all individuals agree with the criteria, or that they agree to be bound by the criteria, or even that they are *aware* of such criteria. However, if an individual does evaluate the criteria of ownership as *right*, such an individual has a reason for acting.

The situation will be even clearer if we examine a statement that HST, themselves, classify as positive: "By tonight it ought to be snowing in Chicago" (p. 418). By conjoining this statement with "I hate to fly when it snows," we have "a reason for acting." Thus, by HST's criterion, the *positive* "snowing statement" suddenly is transformed into a *normative* assertion. Indeed, it is difficult to imagine *any* positive assertion that could not become "a reason for acting" (on HST's logic) by someone, somewhere, somehow.

The point of the preceding analysis is not to emphasize that HST's criterion for normativity is even more ambiguous than my original, "ought/should" rule-of-thumb (though it surely is). Rather, the point is to reemphasize HST's "context" insight. Recalling HST's (correct) conclusion that "ought" and "should" can occur in either positive or normative statements depending on context, we note that "own," "exchange," and "price" may likewise appear in either positive or normative assertions. Such terms are not "forbidden" to marketing science because they do not *automatically* make a statement normative. Thus, HST's idiosyncratic conclusion that almost all marketing thought is normative stems in part from the inconsistent application of their own "context" insight. I say "in part" because their highly suspect ontology also contributes to the confusion.

What is the ontology implied by HST's analysis—what, for them, *exists*? HST contend that ownership exists only within a "normative framework," a "web," a "value system," a "set of laws" (p. 420). HST are certainly correct that ownership, exchange, and price exist only within a societal context. Furthermore, the denotation of the terms "ownership," "exchange," and "price" is certainly different from "rock," "Twinkies," and "Mary." But why does this bother HST?

HST do not specifically state their ontology, but they gave clues to it in the draft of their paper that they (graciously) provided me and which was accepted for presentation. On page 9 of that draft they state: "Ownership cannot be a positive term because it cannot be measured by any imaginable tool of science." On the next page they further amplify their ontology by claiming that some concepts are normative because they "cannot be physically detected."

We now are in a position to better understand the second reason why HST reach their idiosyncratic conclusion that all marketing thought is normative. For HST, Hostess Twinkies exist because "Hostess Twinkies" denotes a physical entity that is observable and can be readily measured by simple counting. Likewise, Mary Smith exists because "Mary Smith" denotes a physical entity. But, the assertion "Mary Smith owns a box of Twinkies after exchanging $5.00 with Safeway Supermarket" is normative because "ownership," "exchange," and "price" are not tangible, physical entities, but exist only within a societal system ("only persons own property"). It is easy now to see how HST can review the vocabulary of marketing (and, by implication, all the social sciences) and can find almost nothing on the positive half of the positive/normative dichotomy. They have discovered that the social sciences use many concepts that are intangible and unobservable, that is, distinctively *social*—and such concepts violate their physicalist ontology.

As the philosophy of science learned (or should have learned) with the demise of logical positivism, a physicalist ontology, especially for the *social sciences*, results in an impoverished vocabulary that is simply not capable of serving the needs of science or society. As argued here and in Hunt (1990), the ontology of scientific realism, with its claim that the long-term success of a scientific theory gives us reason to believe that something like the entities and structure of that theory actually exists, seems to suit better the needs of social science (and much natural science). Entities need not be tangible or observable to exist.

Hyman, Skipper, and Tansey (1991) quite rightly remind us that nothing in science is beyond critical examination. Lakatos (1978) was fundamentally misguided when he claimed that scientific progress required research programs to have a "hard core" that was beyond questioning, beyond critique. Nothing in marketing, nothing in the social sciences, nothing in the physical sciences is, or ought to be, immune from critical discussion. If the Three Dichotomies Model is a "truss in the conceptual structure of marketing" (HST 1991, p. 417), this is all the more reason to subject it periodically to critical examination.

Several conclusions are warranted. First, HST are on firm grounds in pointing out that whether a sentence is positive or normative can often be determined only by carefully examining its context. Any rule of thumb, including both theirs and the one that I offered in my original article, can lead one astray. Moreover, they correctly conclude that purportedly positive statements may have a "hidden" normative component. This normative component may be by accident or design. Those who are skilled in rhetoric have long known that their normative views are often more persuasive when disguised as declarative, positive assertions.

Second, HST have not presented credible evidence that the positive/normative dichotomy is so ambiguous as to be useless. Normative statements can be unambiguously separated from positive statements by examining whether the statements, taken in context, make judgments, evaluations, commands, prescriptions, or imperatives. The positive/normative (is/ought) dichotomy has served well the objective of clear thinking for hundreds of years. It, likewise, serves marketing well.

Third, HST's idiosyncratic conclusion that marketing and other social sciences are overwhelmingly normative and should "start anew" (1) stems from the inconsistent application of their own insight that the meanings of words and sentences must be determined within their context, and (2) is grounded on an impoverished physicalist ontology. Such a physicalist ontology should be rejected on the grounds that it yields a vocabulary that would impede, if not thwart entirely, progress in social science.

Finally, the claim that the social sciences are entirely misguided, if not downright pernicious, has become commonplace over the past few decades. However, such cynical and nihilistic views usually come from advocates of deconstructionism, postmodernism, relativism, constructivism, and subjectivism. The positive/normative debate shows that one need not be mesmerized by any of these "isms" into reaching an extremely skeptical conclusion regarding social science. Although all philosophical roads do not lead to skepticism and nihilism, many clearly do—some by intent and others, as in this case, purely by accident.

1.8 THE THREE DICHOTOMIES MODEL AS A GENERAL TAXONOMICAL FRAMEWORK FOR MARKETING

All disciplines have taxonomical frameworks. These frameworks represent a loose consensus among the participants in a discipline concerning the discipline's fundamental nature. These frameworks—which may be explicit or implicit—customarily include the discipline's phenomena to be investigated and general approaches to such investigations. Among other things, the taxonomical framework of a discipline plays a central role in guiding the research efforts of scholars.

The Three Dichotomies Model of marketing would seem to be a general framework that could help resolve some of the critical problems in marketing (Hunt 1978). The framework is (1) properly inclusive, (2) analytically useful,

(3) pedagogically sound, and (4) conceptually robust. The model is *inclusive* and healing rather than *exclusive* and divisive. It succeeds in including within the scope of marketing a wide range of perceptions. Those who view marketing with a traditional *managerial* perspective have a "home" in the profit sector/micro/normative cell. Those who prefer a "broadened" perspective have the nonprofit half of the model. Those who wish to have more attention paid to the societal impact of marketing have the macro-positive and macro-normative cells. Finally, those who desire to focus their attention on the science of marketing have the micro-positive and macro-positive cells. As can be noted, the Three Dichotomies Model brings the various perspectives of marketing *together* rather than attempting to *exclude* people by using pejorative statements such as "What you are interested in is not *really* marketing." The model recognizes that marketers are a diverse group with different perspectives, different "homes," and different contributions to make.

The Three Dichotomies Model is *analytically useful.* It has been used to analyze the various approaches to the study of marketing: the functional, commodity, institutional, managerial, systems, and environmental approaches. The model has also been used to explore the "broadening of the concept of marketing" debate. Finally, it has been instrumental in addressing the "Is marketing a science?" controversy.

The Three Dichotomies Model is *pedagogically sound:* it is useful as a teaching device. Students can readily understand the model. They are familiar with the micro/macro dichotomy from economics, and the profit sector/nonprofit sector dichotomy is straightforward. Only the positive/normative dichotomy is outside the average business student's vocabulary and requires substantial elaboration. It is distressing that many beginning business students, both at the bachelor's and master's levels, perceive marketing to be exclusively advertising and personal selling. Salutary effects on students' views of marketing can be generated by demonstrating the broad scope of marketing with the aid of the model.

Finally, the Three Dichotomies Model is *conceptually robust.* The preceding sections have been devoted to analyzing and evaluating various comments and observations concerning specific aspects of the model. The framework has absorbed the blows with surprisingly little damage. Although the ultimate test of both its conceptual robustness and its desirability as a general taxonomical framework for marketing is *time*, the performance of the model over almost three decades warrants optimism.

1.9 PLAN OF MONOGRAPH

The plan or organization of a monograph is second in importance only to its content. The organization of this monograph posed a dilemma. In order truly to comprehend the nature of laws and theories in marketing, one must first understand and appreciate their usefulness in explaining and predicting marketing phenomena. However, in order to understand the problem of scientific explanation, one must first comprehend the nature of laws and theories. The dilemma parallels the micro/macro teaching problem in economics. Should microeconomics be taught before macroeconomics, or vice versa? This book discusses explanation before laws and theories on the ground that it is sometimes desirable to demonstrate the usefulness of concepts, such as laws and theories, before delving into their basic nature. However, the chapters on laws and theories are relatively self-contained, and readers may, at their discretion, start with the latter chapters first.

Chapter 2 explores several issues concerning the marketing discipline. First, it considers marketing as (1) a university discipline, (2) an applied discipline, (3) a professional discipline, and (4) a set of responsibilities. Next, it explores the nature of marketing research, before concluding by providing an answer for the question: Why is there an aversion to qualitative methods in marketing? Chapter 3 explores the morphology of scientific explanation. That is, how does one go about *explaining* marketing phenomena? Various explanatory models are developed, including the deductive-nomological, deductive-statistical, inductive-statistical, pattern, and functionalist models. Chapter 4 discusses some issues in explanation, such as the relationships among explanation, prediction, retrodiction, and causation. Several marketing explanations, involving areas such as the product life cycle, consumer behavior, price discrimination, and the wheel of retailing, are then analyzed. Chapter 5 investigates the nature of laws in marketing and evaluates the four criteria for lawlike generalizations—generalized conditionals, empirical content, nomic necessity, and systematic integration.

Chapter 6 delineates the characteristics of the various kinds of laws: equilibrium laws, laws of atemporal coexistence, laws of succession, process laws, axioms, fundamental laws, derivative laws, bridge laws, statistical laws, and universal laws. Chapter 7 begins by noting some misconceptions concerning the nature of theory. A perspective on theory is presented, and the three major criteria for theories are detailed. These criteria reveal that theories must (1) contain systematically related sets of statements, (2) contain some lawlike generalizations, and (3) be empirically testable. Chapter 8 examines the role of classification in theory development, contrasts positive theory with normative theory, explores whether deterministic theory in marketing is possible, and examines how "general theories" differ from other theories. Chapter 9 provides a brief overview of the general theory of competition developed by Robert M. Morgan and me and develops three arguments supporting the view that resource-advantage theory is *toward* a general theory of marketing.

QUESTIONS FOR ANALYSIS AND DISCUSSION

1. Do the social sciences and marketing require a different methodology from the physical sciences? If yes, how would it differ? If no, why do so many social science researchers claim that their methodology must be different?
2. Lazer (1962) suggests that there are two approaches to model building in marketing—abstraction and realization (see illustration). Are these approaches two different *methodologies*? Do they belong in the context of discovery or in the context of justification? Which is more *deductive*? Which is more *inductive*? Evaluate the usefulness of models. Which is superior for marketing? Why?

Model building by abstraction:

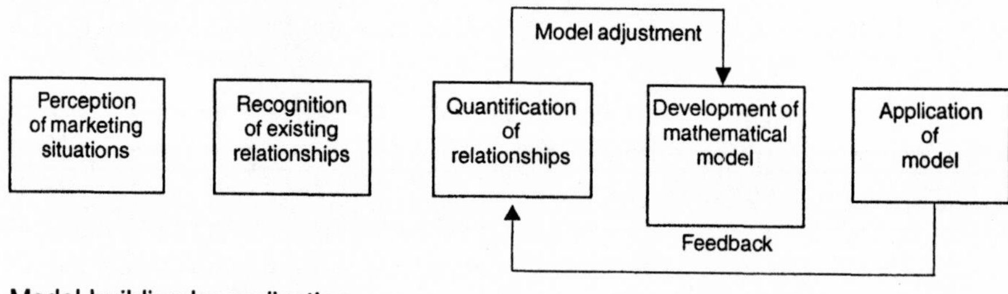

Model building by realization:

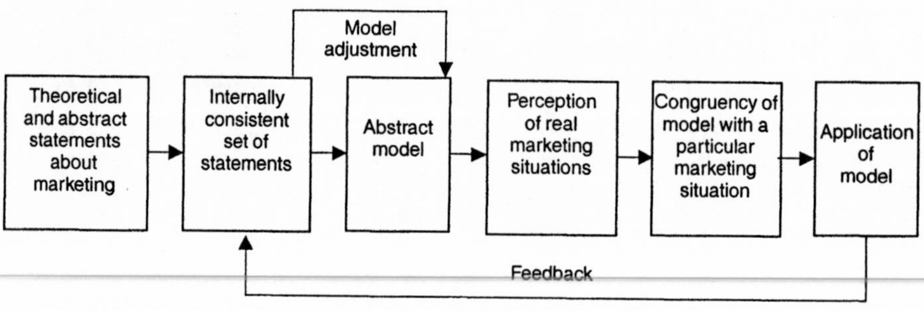

3. Differentiate between *marketing* research and *market* research. Can both result in possible publications for scholarly journals in marketing? Should they? Would marketing practitioners enjoy reading a journal that was exclusively devoted to results of *market* research studies? Would academicians? Is *marketing* research impractical?
4. Many of the articles in the *Journal of Marketing Research* (*JMR*) can be classified as very quantitatively sophisticated profit/micro/normative in content. At the same time, *JMR* is often criticized as being too scientific. Are the preceding two statements contradictory? Is the discipline called management science a *science*? Could it possibly

be a science? Is marketing *management* a science? Is accounting a science? *Could* accounting be a science?

5. Table 1.1 purports to be a classificational schema that encompasses the entire scope of marketing. Examine several issues of the *Journal of Marketing* and the *Journal of Marketing Research.* Determine which articles fall into which categories. Can some fall into several categories simultaneously? Conduct the same procedure for the chapters and major issues in a marketing textbook. Whenever an article, chapter, or issue cannot be classified satisfactorily, propose a modification of the schema to accommodate it.
6. What is the optimal combination of cells and topics in Table 1.1 for a basic course in marketing? A marketing management course? A marketing research course? MBA courses? Ph.D. courses? What were your criteria for optimality?
7. Why is it important to differentiate the *discovery* of theories and laws from the *justification* of theories and laws? Are the processes of discovery different in marketing than they are in the physical sciences? Should they be different?
8. Why is the "is marketing a science?" issue important? Does it have implications for the kind of research that is done in marketing? For how marketing is taught? For the standards for acceptance or rejection of manuscripts by the marketing journals? For marketing practitioners?
9. Why is the "broadening the concept of marketing" issue important? What are the implications of this issue for the areas in Question 8?
10. This chapter began with an epigraph that quoted the Greek philosopher Epictetus. What is the relevance of the epigraph to the body of the chapter?
11. Bartels (1970) proposes that seven axioms comprise his metatheory:

    a. Theory proceeds from a concept of its subject and should be consistent with it.
    b. Theory is built upon basic concepts derived from the concept of the subject and from related disciplines.
    c. By subdivision of basic concepts, their range and qualities may be shown in intraconcept differences.
    d. Concepts in a dependent-independent relationship are the bases of explanation or prediction.
    e. Theory based on presumed relationships is valid to the degree that those relationships have generality.
    f. As theory bears the mark of the marketing theorist, individuality and diversity are normal characteristics of theory.

g. All theories of a discipline, however diverse, should be embraceable, implicitly or explicitly, in a general theory, either by grouping or synthesis.

Evaluate this metatheory. Is it a *logic* of discovery? Should it be evaluated entirely in the context of discovery? Which of the statements are normative, and which are positive?

12. Some marketers believe that marketing is an art, not a science. Others have observed that marketing people have been neither good artists nor good scientists. Finally, some have pointed out that truly great scientists have also been great artists, because genius in both science and art emanates from the taking of great care. Evaluate these positions. Be sure to define carefully what you mean by "art," "science," "artist," and "scientist." (Turn to the epigraph at the beginning of chapter 6 for another point of view.)
13. Some writers believe that a necessary condition for scientific progress is that scientists must ask important questions. This position emphasizes the importance of the logic of discovery because no matter how good our process of validation, if the question is trivial, nothing can save it. Evaluate this position. How does one separate "important" questions from "unimportant" questions? Does current research in consumer behavior ask important questions? Does research in channels of distribution? Can the answers to "trivial" questions sometimes *become* important?
14. "If science is the body of knowledge obtained by methods based on observation, then painting is a science because it is based on observation." Evaluate.
15. Myers, Greyser, and Massy (1979) decry the lack of "problem-oriented" research in marketing. Examine the last two volumes of the *Journal of Marketing* and the *Journal of Marketing Research*. What percentage of the articles were "problem oriented?" What are the factors that influence the kinds of research that academicians will pursue? Which of these factors encourage and which discourage the pursuit of "problem-oriented" research?
16. "Studying the exchange process is the province of economics, not marketing. That [the exchange process] is the whole purpose of supply and demand analysis." Evaluate.
17. In "discovery-oriented" consumer research, Wells (1993) provides five guidelines for improving consumer research:

    1. "Leave home." That is, move from brand purchase to more important marketing decisions.

2. "Forsake mythodology." That is, abandon the views that:

    a. Students are consumers
    b. Lab represents environment
    c. Statistical significance is substantive significance
    d. Correlation equals correction
    e. Limitations mentioned go away

3. "Reach out." That is, involve business, government, foundations, and other academic disciplines in research.
4. "Start small—stay real." That is, do not reach for abstract universal theories. Ask: "So what?" Be relevant.
5. "Research backward." That is, start with how research will be implemented by asking "Who would care if I found X?"

Which of these lie in the context of discovery? Which lie more in the context of justification? Which of the five do you agree/disagree with? Why?

NOTES

1. As I discuss in Hunt (2001b), the overall philosophy underlying my work embraces (1) the importance of critical discussion in knowledge development, (2) the view that civility in critical discussion is a virtue, (3) a proscription against ad hominem discourse, (4) a proscription against sophistry, (5) a respect for reason and evidence, (6) the view that clarity in scholarship is a virtue, (7) the belief that critical pluralism is desirable, and (8) the view that, of all the "isms" in the philosophy of science, scientific realism seems to make the most sense.

2. Some of the observations of Professor Kotler (1972a) were apparently extemporaneous because they were not included in his published paper.

3. Every generation of marketing students needs to be reminded that hostility to marketing activities and institutions is as ancient as marketing itself. Thus, Plato (1942, p. 271) has Socrates say, "In well-ordered states, [retail traders] are commonly those who are the weakest in bodily strength, and therefore of little use for any other purpose."

4. See: Mindak and Bybee 1971; Farley and Leavitt 1971; Zikmund and Stanton 1971; Carmen 1973; Robin 1974.

5. See: Lazer 1969; Dawson 1971; Aaker 1971; Kangun 1972; Webster 1974; Moyer 1972; Wish and Gamble 1971; Goble and Shaw 1975; Gist 1971; Lazer and Kelly 1973.

6. See: Rudner 1966; Salmon 1963; Kyburg 1968; Hempel 1966; Bergmann 1957.

7. See: Rudner 1966, p. 5; Salmon 1963, p. 10; Bergmann 1957, p. 164; Kyburg 1968, p. 5.

2 ON THE MARKETING DISCIPLINE

For here we are not afraid to follow truth wherever it may lead, nor to tolerate error so long as reason is left free to combat it.

—Thomas Jefferson on the founding of the University of Virginia

Chapter 1 explored the nature and scope of marketing and the nature of science, and developed the Three Dichotomies Model as a taxonomical framework to examine both marketing and science. This chapter continues the introductory material, first, by exploring the nature of the marketing *discipline*. Second, using as an analytical tool the Three Dichotomies Model, it will focus on the nature of marketing *research*. Third, with respect to marketing research, this chapter addresses the issue of why marketing's major journals are devoted almost exclusively to studies using quantitative, rather than qualitative, methods.

2.1 ON MARKETING AS . . .

What *kind* of discipline is marketing? Many writers claim that marketing is an applied discipline. Others opine that marketing is a professional discipline. Customarily, writers claiming that marketing is an applied or professional discipline make the further claim that marketing is *not* an academic discipline, and, therefore, marketing is misguided when it focuses on either basic research or research that is not (relatively immediately) useful to the marketing practitioner.

So what kind of discipline is marketing? One answer, and an answer that serves as a good starting point for analysis, would be: "Marketing is a discipline that is housed within colleges or schools of business, which are themselves housed within universities." Recalling Levitt's (1960) classic work on the importance of identifying the business of *firms*, the "university discipline" answer suggests that we need to explore first the "business" of universities. The business of this societal institution, I argue, strongly influences the business of our discipline. Our analysis here will follow closely the views in Hunt (1992b).

2.1.1 . . . A University Discipline

Universities, I suggest, are in the knowledge "business." Specifically, universities warehouse, retail, and manufacture knowledge. Universities store or "warehouse" knowledge by means of libraries. They disseminate or "retail" knowledge through their teaching function. They produce or "manufacture" knowledge through research. Other institutions are also in the knowledge business, for example, public libraries, elementary and secondary schools, trade schools, corporate training programs, and corporate research and development departments. However, these institutions all differ significantly from universities.

Whereas public libraries focus on the needs of the general public, university libraries focus on the needs of scholars. Whereas trade schools provide skills-oriented training, highly context-specific knowledge, and certificate programs leading to craft occupations, universities provide "higher" education (generally), context-free knowledge, and degree programs that either (a) constitute a general, liberal education with no specific occupational emphasis or (b) lead to employment in a professional occupation. Similarly, whereas corporate research is primarily oriented toward developing new products and services for the corporation (knowledge for profit's sake and the benefit—at least the proximate benefit—of the corporation), university research is primarily oriented toward basic research that contributes to our inventory of knowledge (knowledge for knowledge's sake and the benefit of society at large).

Surprisingly, many academicians are unaware that only recently have university faculty assumed the role of producers of knowledge. Although Western universities trace to the founding of institutions such as Oxford and the University of Paris in the thirteenth century, for their first 600 years, university professors were limited to *professing*. That is, they taught the knowledge that was produced by the ancient Greeks, was lost to Europe after the fall of the Western Roman Empire in the sixth century, and was rediscovered (compliments of the Arabs—thank you very much) in the thirteenth century. The professorial scholarship of the university "scholastics" in the Middle Ages did not build on, improve, or extend the ideas found in ancient manuscripts. Rather, by emphasizing hermeneutics, scholarship was restricted to interpreting the works of the ancient Greeks, particularly those of the canonical triumvirate: Aristotle, Ptolemy, and Galen.

The Scientific Revolution (roughly 1550 to 1700 A.D.) was a necessary precursor for the rise of the modern university ("modern" here being identified with the university's role in producing knowledge). Scientists (then called "natural philosophers") in the seventeenth century formed a new method of producing knowledge by conjoining the emphasis on critique, speculation, and reason they found in Plato's method of "critical discussion" with (a) the strong emphasis on careful observation and syllogistic logic that they saw in Aristotle, (b) the powerful tool of mathematics, as had been emphasized in the ancient works of Pythagoras, and (c) the use, where possible, of experimentation to arbitrate disputes, as was being forcefully argued by their contemporary, Galileo. Science and its method developed, it should be stressed, not because of the influence and support of universities, but despite their hostility and vigorous opposition. Universities in the seventeenth century were uniformly sectarian and science threatened religion's authority.[1]

By demonstrating that new knowledge could be produced by method, rather than revealed by authority, revelation, or mystical experience, science made possible the "grand compact" underlying the 1810 founding of the University of Berlin. The mission of this first "modern" university was to focus on graduate education (the Ph.D.) and research. It was to be "the workshop of free scientific research," according to its founders. To Berlin's faculty, the German state granted academic freedom (*akademische Freiheit*), that is, the privilege of conducting research free from the dictates of both church and state. From Berlin's faculty, the state demanded a commitment to the ideal of objective knowledge. That is, in exchange for faculty being independent from the pressures of political and religious groups, academic research at Berlin was to be unbiased as to religious and political points of view:

> The German professor . . . made it a rule to refrain from participation in politics for fear it would make an opportunist of him, which in the end would be bound to distort his disinterested pursuit of truth. If he kept his academic skirts clear of political bias, the state was more likely to respect the objectivity of his research. (Brubacher and Rudy 1976, p. 315)

For society, the objectivity of university research would guarantee its trustworthiness; university research could be *relied* on. Within the short span of a few decades, the University of Berlin became extraordinarily prominent. Gradually, the "grand compact" spread to other German universities, making them world leaders in education, particularly science education. It then spread to other European universities, and, in the latter half of the nineteenth century, it crossed the Atlantic.

At the beginning of the nineteenth century, American universities were patterned after Oxford and Cambridge. Accordingly, they were loose collections of colleges that (a) were sectarian, (b) offered only undergraduate and masters degrees, (c) focused on classical instruction in the humanities, and (d) lacked both academic freedom and a research mission. In the 1800s, scores of American educators traveled to Germany to earn the new, research-oriented, Ph.D. degree.[2] They returned to become presidents of many American universities and to promote graduate education, research, and the values underlying the grand compact: academic freedom and objective knowledge. At the same time, the various state legislatures, many strongly encouraged by the Morrill Act of 1862, were chartering state universities. These distinctly American institutions were products of both European influences and the emerging American culture's emphasis on religious freedom, free speech, pragmatism, and egalitarianism. Thus, these universities were nonsectarian, were free or charged only a modest tuition, had a research mission, and had a broad range of undergraduate, graduate, and professional programs—including engineering and agriculture. (In contrast, engineering and agriculture were thought to be improper subjects for university education in Europe and were relegated to the so-called technical institutes—where many reside today.) Because of the powerful strain of pragmatism inherent in American culture, the state universities were to offer instruction and conduct research (as well as to provide service through "extension") in the "practical" subjects of engineering and agriculture. This paved the way in the next century for another practical subject, business, to be taught at the university level.

By 1900, the system of higher education in the United States was largely in place, and a pluralistic system it was. With over a thousand colleges and universities, public and private, sectarian and nonsectarian, competition was intense. Also by 1900, industrialization and mergers had led to the rise of large corporations, and, with them, a need for professional corporate managers. The old apprenticeship system for business education and training was woefully inadequate for these large, complex institutions. If engineering is appropriate for university education, why not business?

The world's first university-housed business school was established at the University of Pennsylvania in 1881 as the result of a $100,000 grant from a Mr. Joseph Wharton. It was followed by schools at the Universities of Chicago and California in 1898, at Dartmouth, Wisconsin, and New York University in 1900, and at Northwestern, Pittsburgh, and Harvard (the first exclusively graduate business school) in 1908. Growth in business education was slow, but steady, in the first six decades of the twentieth century. By 1965, business schools' 63,000 undergraduate degrees and 6,600 masters degrees represented 12.8 percent and 5.9 percent, respectively, of all such degrees granted in the United States. By 1995, approximately 20 percent and 23 percent of undergraduate and masters' degrees, respectively, were awarded to business students.

Why the rapid growth in business education's market share since 1965? The precipitating event was the publication of the "Foundation Reports," authored by Gordon and Howell (1959) and Pierson (1959). These reports found business education, particularly at the undergraduate level, to be a veritable wasteland. Rather than being intellectually demanding, analytically rigorous, science-based, and professional/managerial, these reports found business courses, programs, and faculty to be intellectually shallow, "seat-of-the-pants," anecdotally based, and craft/vocational. Business schools' responses to the "Foundation Reports," as documented by Hugstad (1983), were to raise admissions standards and require (and integrate into business courses) more mathematics, statistics, computer science, economics, and behavioral science. These changes dramatically improved business education, making it more attractive to students and employers.

In short, the steep rise in business education's market share in the 1970s, 1980s, and 1990s resulted, first and foremost, from its producing a superior academic "product." In fairness, however, it must be admitted that the dramatic decline in the standards and quality of education provided by business's "competition" in the late 1960s and 1970s also contributed to the market share gain. The attack on reason, civility, and tolerance in universities in the late 1960s is chronicled by Brubacher and Rudy:

> The most shortsighted limits to academic freedom in this period were posed by university students themselves. Some tried not only to "shut it down" by strikes, arson, and "trashing," but to shout it down as well. By stirring up noisy commotions they disrupted unpopular speakers on university platforms and unpopular professors in their classrooms. Worse yet they forced physical confrontations with the police when summoned to restore order to the campus, thus supplanting reason with force in the very citadel of reason. Sometimes motivated by theories of anarchism and nihilism they showed an anti-intellectualism that was anything but conducive to the open mind. (Brubacher and Rudy 1976, p. 328)

Although all areas in universities suffered when riotous students in the 1960s replaced reasoned discussion with violence and intimidation as the preferred method for effecting change, the liberal arts suffered most. For them, the 1960s were an "unmitigated disaster" (Bloom 1987, pp. 320, 357). In the name of "openness," "student's rights," "equality," and "relevance," liberal arts standards deteriorated, grade inflation spiraled out of control, the core curriculum was abolished, studies in pop culture replaced classical instruction, political activism replaced scholarship, and a form of dogmatic skepticism/nihilism replaced truth: "On the portal of the humanities is written in many ways and many tongues, 'there is no truth—at least here'" (Bloom 1987, p. 372). Thus, at the very same time that business schools were becoming more professional, analytical, scholarly, and ideas-oriented, that is, more "liberal" in the classic sense of the word, the liberal arts were embracing a dogmatic illiberalism. As business education was improving, liberal arts education was self-destructing. As business education became more attractive to students, liberal arts became less attractive.

The preceding discussion of the "business" of the university enables us to address: "What kind of business is the marketing discipline in?" We begin with an examination of marketing as an applied discipline.

2.1.2 . . . An Applied Discipline

When marketers claim that marketing is an applied discipline, and, therefore, academics should restrict themselves to applied research (instead of, as they mockingly put it, "pushing back the frontiers of knowledge"), what kind of research do they have in mind? Consider the following research question: How should the Jones Toy Company allocate its advertising budget among the various media to reach its primary target market, children under twelve years of age? Referred to as "consulting research" when done by academics, answering this kind of research question implies applying existing knowledge to the solution of a firm's specific corporate problem. If "applied" research means consulting research, should marketing academics restrict themselves to these kinds of projects?

There are three reasons, closely related, why marketing academics should not restrict themselves to doing just consulting research. First, because consulting research does not, except by accident, add to new knowledge (in that it just applies existing knowledge), the knowledge base of the discipline would stagnate at its current level. This would, most assuredly, not be in the best interests of marketing students and practitioners (present or future). Second, because marketing is housed within university schools (and colleges) of business, our discipline has an obligation, a duty, to adhere to all three elements of the university's core mission, that is, retailing, warehousing, and producing knowledge. Our responsibility to conduct original research that contributes to the corpus of marketing knowledge stems not—as our discipline's critics derisively contend—from the ego need of "seeking the respect of our liberal arts colleagues." Our responsibility stems from our duty to respect, abide by, and support the university's core mission, a mission that is of utmost importance to our society.

As a third reason, recall that Day and Wensley (1983) proposed that the marketing discipline should adopt a more strategic orientation and urged the acceptance of a set of research priorities that emphasized marketing's role in the development of corporate, sustainable, competitive advantage. In his decade-later retrospective on marketing's lack of contribution to the "strategy dialogue," Day (1992, p. 328) laments: "Within academic circles, the contribution of marketing . . . to the development, testing, and dissemination of strategy theories and concepts has been marginalized during the past decade." Indeed, he points out that "Academics outside of marketing pay little attention to marketing literature or theory." Moreover, he believes, "The prognosis for marketing—based on the present trend and past behavior of other disciplines—is not encouraging." The question is: *Why has marketing made so few original contributions to the "strategy dialogue" over the past decade?* Our answer to this question, drawing on the analysis in Hunt (1994b), provides further grounds for questioning the consulting oriented, "applied discipline" view.

As a result of being an author, a reviewer, a section editor, a proceedings editor, and a journal editor, I have read the reviews of well over 1,000 manuscripts for both marketing and nonmarketing journals (such reviews being written by both marketing and nonmarketing referees). These reviews reflect the norms of several disciplines' "gatekeepers." Consistent with nonmarketing reviewers and nonmarketing journals, marketing referees (quite appropriately) want to know the nature and extent of a manuscript's contribution to marketing's literature. However, quite inconsistent with nonmarketing reviewers and nonmarketing journals, marketing reviewers often react quite negatively when a manuscript offers a genuinely original contribution to knowledge. Criticisms such as "where is the precedent?" and "where is the authority?" are, in my experience, disproportionately prominent in reviews by marketing referees. Indeed, marketing authors have been known to cite nonmarketing researchers for authority even when, strictly speaking, the marketing author has made an original nonmarketing contribution. Marketers making genuinely original contributions to knowledge often do so at their peril.

Why are original contributions to knowledge punished by marketing journal referees? I suggest that this sorrowful situation has come about, at least in part, as a result of marketers defining our discipline as an applied discipline. That is, the notion that marketing is an applied discipline implies for many journal reviewers that marketing's "job" is to take concepts, frameworks, and theories from other "more basic" disciplines and then apply them to marketing. Stated succinctly, the norm is "new to marketing, but not new elsewhere." With such a norm, the absence of original contributions to the strategy dialogue (or any other dialogue) is unsurprising. Also unsurprising is the lack of attention that our journals receive from nonmarketing academics. If original contributions to knowledge are systematically screened from our literature, why should others pay attention to our literature?

In summary, marketing should not be viewed as an applied discipline. That is, marketing should not be viewed as being *solely* interested in the kind of market research questions as that presented in the Jones Toy advertising example. Viewing marketing as an applied discipline contributes to (1) stagnating marketing's knowledge base at its current level, (2) abrogating our discipline's obligation to adhere to all three elements of the university's core mission, that is, retailing, warehousing, and producing knowledge, and (3) marginalizing our discipline by other academic disciplines. In short, viewing marketing as an applied discipline is pernicious. Therefore, many writers contend that, because marketing is a profession, the marketing discipline is a professional discipline and our responsibility, our only responsibility, is to produce knowledge that *can* be, has the *potential* to be, applied by marketing practitioners.

2.1.3 . . . A Professional Discipline

Myers, Massy, and Greyser (1980) strongly encourage the marketing discipline to focus, not on consulting research, but on "problem-oriented" research, for "if marketing knowledge over the long run is to be considered 'effective,' it should contribute something to improved decision making or other aspects of marketing management practice in the industrial sector" (p 145). Such research, as discussed in Section 1.1, would attempt to find general solutions to general classes of practitioner problems. In Myers's words:

> Marketing is a "professional discipline" and not an "academic discipline." Marketing academicians should recognize that the overall importance of research and knowledge development in this field, over the short-run or long-run, is to improve marketing practice and decision-making, and, in general, to advance the state of knowledge useful to the profession. (Myers 1979, p. 62)

Peters (1980, p. 5) agrees: "Marketing scholars are beginning to view marketing as a professional discipline as contrasted to an academic discipline." Viewing the discipline this way, he argues, will encourage marketing faculty to do more applied research, consulting, textbook writing, continuing education teaching, and business community service. Giving these activities major credit in tenure and promotion would then help close the "marketing professor—practitioner gap" (p. 4). Likewise, Simon (1994, p. 29) holds that "marketing science is an applied discipline that should help to improve business practice." Similarly, Enis (1986, pp. 2, 3) contends: "We are in the business of providing rigorous, relevant, managerial education. . . . We should see ourselves as professional educators, in league with medical, legal, and engineering educators, preparing and renewing professional managers." Westing puts it this way:

> Our goal should be to try to make business more proficient and efficient—and this in not an unworthy goal. It is similar to the goals of engineering, law, medicine, pharmacy, agriculture, and education. We are all professional disciplines, rather than academic disciplines. . . . We should content ourselves with borrowing from basic disciplines and concentrate on applications which will enable business to do its job better and cheaper. (Westing 1977, p. 16)

> [Marketing is] not a discipline. Economics is the discipline of study in business. . . . So I would predict that if we continue down the road we are going, we would end up having lost the allegiance of our clients—the business people—without gaining the

> acceptance of our colleagues in the universities. . . : [We should] try to be good professional schools rather than try to be something we aren't and can't be, and that is academic scholars trying to push back the frontiers of knowledge. (Westin 1979, p. 53)

The "marketing is a professional discipline" argument appears to be: (1) there are two kinds of university disciplines, those that are professional and those that are academic; (2) academic disciplines, for example, physics, economics, psychology, and history, conduct basic research that contributes to knowledge; (3) professional disciplines, for example, law, medicine, and engineering, restrict themselves to borrowing knowledge from academic disciplines and applying it for the benefit of their practitioner clients; (4) marketing is a professional discipline, and, therefore, (5) marketing academics should restrict themselves to applying knowledge from academic disciplines such as economics, psychology, anthropology, sociology, mathematics, and statistics for the benefit of their clients, marketing practitioners.

The standard reply to the preceding argument goes something like this: "marketing academics should continue to conduct 'basic research' and not restrict themselves to 'problem-solving' research because the history of science tells us that, even though much research at the time it is conducted appears to be nonrelevant to solving practical problems, it ultimately becomes highly relevant."[3] Although there is merit to the "standard reply," I suggest it suffers because it tacitly accepts most of the premises of the "professional discipline" argument. Some of these premises are highly suspect and others are demonstrably false.

First, it is simply false that academics in professional disciplines restrict themselves to "applying" knowledge from "academic disciplines." Legal scholars draw somewhat on areas such as philosophy, history, and the social sciences. Yet, it would be ludicrous to maintain that legal scholarship, as reflected in their journals, is accurately described as "applied" philosophy, history, and social science. Rather, legal scholars explore (primarily) the positive question of what kind of legal system *do* we have and the normative question of what kind of legal system *should* we have? Similarly, the engineering disciplines draw heavily on physics, chemistry, mathematics, and statistics. Yet, the engineering scholarship in their journals contains original contributions to engineering knowledge, not just "applied" physics, and the like. Likewise, medical research, as published in journals such as the *New England Journal of Medicine*, goes significantly beyond just being "applied" biochemistry, cell biology, and microbiology—it independently contributes to our knowledge of diseases, their cures, and so forth.

Second, just as marketing practitioners are clients of marketing scholars and their research, lawyers, physicians, and engineers are certainly clients of legal, medical, and engineering scholars. Yet, it is simply false that legal, medical, and engineering research efforts are exclusively (or even primarily) guided by, focused on, or for the benefit of, the interests—especially the pecuniary interests—of lawyers, physicians, and engineers. To understand why this is the case requires an understanding of what constitutes a professional occupation.

The literature on the nature of professional occupations is enormous.[4] Having the same etymological root, just as professors profess, so do members of professions. What do members of professions claim when they *profess*? Foremost, they profess to have mastered an esoteric body of knowledge based on systematic theory that requires formal, advanced education and is useful in solving certain problems of their clients. By virtue of their professed superior knowledge, professionals can, if they choose to do so, take advantage of their clients. Consequently, the underlying values embodied in the organizational cultures of all professional associations—such values customarily formalized in codes of ethics—emphasize the responsibility of professionals to avoid conflicts of interest in servicing the genuine needs of their clients. Lacking professionals' knowledge, clients must be able to trust them. In exchange for status, authority, and autonomy (enforced by self-regulation), the social contract between society and the professions requires that professionals act in a fiduciary manner toward their clients.

The preceding discussion enables us to better understand the nature of research in schools of law, medicine, and engineering. These schools are truly *professional* schools. Just as consumer goods' manufacturers view wholesalers and retailers as intermediate customers for their goods, schools of law, medicine, and engineering view practicing lawyers, physicians, and engineers as "intermediaries." They are intermediate clients for legal, medical, and engineering scholarship. The ultimate client for a truly professional discipline is always society and its needs. For law, it is society's need for a just legal system. For medicine, it is society's need for health care. For engineering, it is society's need for buildings, bridges, highways, and machines that are safe, functional, efficient, and economical. And for marketing? I suggest it is society's need for high quality products and services that are reasonably priced, responsibly promoted, and conveniently available.

The "marketing is a professional discipline" argument got off to the wrong start with its initial premise that there are two kinds of university disciplines, professional and academic. It is true that (1) some disciplines in the academy are closely related to recognized professions; for example, law and medicine; (2) many disciplines are closely related to vocations aspiring to be professions; for example, marketing, management, finance, social work, and journalism; (3) other disciplines are less closely related to any specific occupation, for example, psychology and chemistry; and (4) still others are almost totally unrelated to any specific occupation, for example, English, history, sociology, and philosophy. Nevertheless, it is equally true that *all* university disciplines are "academic": we are *all* "members of the academy." As such, we are all responsible for all three elements of the university's core mission: retailing, warehousing, and producing knowledge. With regard to knowledge production, we are all responsible for upholding the "grand compact" of academic freedom for objective knowledge.

In 2000, the American Marketing Association launched its Professional Certified Marketer Program, which furthers the professionalization of marketing. Yet, it is still safe to say that none of the various and remarkably heterogeneous occupations associated with marketing, that is, sales, advertising, brand/product management, marketing research, retail management, wholesale management, distribution management, and marketing management, has reached (or been accorded by society) the status of "profession."[5] Nonetheless, most marketers desire that all marketing practice become more *professional* (just as many of those who believe that no part of marketing is a science nonetheless often see benefits in marketing becoming more *scientific*). On similar grounds, we can conclude that marketing is, or should aspire to be, a professional discipline that is closely related to the occupations constituting marketing practice. However, the *implications of marketing being a professional discipline are almost exactly the opposite of what marketing's critics contend.*

First, as members of the academy, we have a responsibility to respect, uphold, and abide by the university's core mission, that is, retailing, warehousing, and producing knowledge. Second, we must uphold its "grand compact" with society, that is, in exchange for academic freedom, we must strive for objective knowledge. Third, as a professional discipline we have a responsibility to keep in mind that society is the ultimate client of the knowledge we produce and marketing practitioners are intermediate clients. More generally, marketing research on "what kind of marketing system do we have?" and "what kind of system should we have?" must be emphasized for us to discharge our responsibilities as members of a professional discipline in the university.

2.1.4 . . . A Set of Responsibilities

With marketing being viewed as a university discipline that aspires to be a professional discipline as a foundation for our analysis, marketing can be viewed from the perspective of "deontological philosophy."[6] In this view, marketing can be considered as a set of responsibilities, duties, or obligations. I start with our ultimate client, society.

To Society. To society, marketing academics owe the pursuit of original contributions to objective knowledge, that is, truth. Society, in exchange for the extraordinary privilege of academic freedom, has the right to insist on objective, trustworthy knowledge. Is such knowledge possible? (Although "is" does not imply "ought," "ought" does imply "can.") In the 1960s and 1970s, the works of writers such as Hanson (1958), Kuhn (1962), and Feyerabend (1970) implied that, because of the "theory ladenness" of language and perception, objective knowledge was impossible. However, philosophy of science scholarship in the 1980s revealed that, as long as objectivity is not confused with OBJECTIVITY, that is, the objectivity of an infallible "god's-eye-view," nor truth confused with TRUTH, that is, infallible truth, objective knowledge is both possible and desirable. Hanson, Kuhn, and Feyerabend (among scores of others) were simply wrong. In brief, because "percepts," as distinguished from "data," are in a very important sense both theory-free and substantially veridical, observations can be used to objectively test theories.[7] Indeed, rather than preventing objectivity, the "theory-informity" of observation enables science to be objective. When scientists and their communities are not objective, they lack the will, not the means.

Also to society, we have a duty to turn out graduates who are technically competent to take their places in their chosen profession, marketing. Technical competence produces productive citizens, and it is the productivity of a society's citizens that determines its standard of living. But technical competence is not enough. We owe to society graduates who are ethically responsible. Our graduates must realize that they have responsibilities not only to themselves and their companies ("ethical egoism") but to other important societal stakeholders.

Finally, we owe to society graduates whose education is such that, as citizens, they can identify, understand, reflectively evaluate, implement, and support the core cultural values of our country, as embodied most prominently in the principles underlying its founding documents. Thus, marketing graduates must be liberally educated, not just technically competent and socially responsible.

To Students. To our students, marketing academics owe the kind of education that will prepare them for entry, middle, and upper-level positions in marketing. Moreover, students should understand their society and marketing's role in that society. Therefore, as marketing professionals, they should be capable of recognizing their own responsibilities to society and responding to them. Our students' career responsibilities imply for us the duty to construct programs of instruction that emphasize both the "micro" and "macro" dimensions of marketing. Referring now to the Three Dichotomies Model, the scope of marketing programs should span all eight cells of the scope of marketing, not just the two micro-normative ones.

The kind of education just discussed and advocated places on us a continuing, derivative duty to learn. Staying abreast of the literature, both academic and trade, is obligatory. Translated to the specific courses we teach, the duty to learn implies a responsibility to revise. Sometimes "old yellow notes" contain timeless truths that bear repeating semester after semester. Regretfully often, however, such notes contain only analyses of yesterday's hot topic, yesterday's faddish issue, or yesterday's solution to yesterday's problem.

Finally, we owe our students an obligation to listen. That is, our clients' expressed needs must serve as input for marketing programs and pedagogy. However, we also have a complementary duty: we must resist the temptation to obey. As professionals, just as physicians cannot allow patients to prescribe their own medicine, we—mindful of our fiduciary relationship with students—must also rely on our best professional judgment as to appropriate marketing programs, courses, and pedagogy.

To Disadvantaged Students: A Special Responsibility. The phrases "land of opportunity" and "American dream" have long been applied to the United States. Indeed, even with our nation's problems, of which there are many, each year millions of people of all races, creeds, and nationalities—many in desperation—seek a new start here. Why does the United States continue to be a nation of immigrants, instead of emigrants?

It is well known that, compared with the rest of the world, the United States has an extraordinarily fluid socioeconomic structure. Studies document not only the numerous anecdotes of "rags to riches," but also those of "riches to rags." For example, the Survey Research Center at the University of Michigan has, since 1968, been continuously tracking the fortunes of a panel, comprised of 5,000 American families and their descendants, that is representative of the total U.S. population (Duncan 1984). Its findings on economic mobility are striking. If we use a seven-year time period as a base, the findings imply that almost half of all families whose incomes put them in the bottom quintile at the beginning of the period will move up at least one quintile. Similarly, *more* than half of those families whose incomes place them in the top quintile in the beginning will move *down* at least one quintile. "Being on top"—unlike in rigidly structured societies—is no guarantee of "staying on top." Moreover, the results concerning intergenerational economic mobility are equally striking. More than half of all children born to families in the lowest quintile will advance at least one quintile above their parents and more than half of all children born to families in the highest quintile will drop at least one quintile (Hill et al. 1985). Neither economic success nor failure is determined by accident of birth. Indeed:

> Income mobility in the top income quintile was as great as it was at the bottom. . . . Family income mobility is pervasive at all income levels. In all, nearly one-quarter (23.1 percent) of the sample moved at least two quintile positions in either direction, about three-eighths (36.8 percent) moved at least one, and only two-fifths (40.1 percent) of the population remained in the same relative income position. . . . Only

> about two-thirds of the individuals living in families with cash incomes below the poverty line in a given year were still poor in the following year, and only one-third of the poor in a given year were poor for at least eight of the ten prior years. (Duncan 1984, pp. 14, 60)

What does income mobility have to do with business education and marketing? Plenty. It is axiomatic that one cannot ascend any ladder until one is on it. For a society to maximize the opportunity for every person to ascend the socioeconomic ladder, it must first enable people to get *on* the ladder. Business education, particularly undergraduate business education, I suggest, is an important and effective mechanism for many disadvantaged young people to "get on the ladder."

For those young people born to upper-income families, "getting on the ladder"—if they choose to do so—is relatively easy. As they grow up, they naturally acquire the social skills (among them, how to dress, sit, stand, gesture, talk, and groom themselves) commensurate with corporate America. Furthermore, through family and friends they have all the contacts in corporate America necessary for at least starting a prosperous career. Indeed, such fortunate youths often view universities as places where they can "find themselves."

Though undergraduate business programs service the entire spectrum of society, when compared with the liberal arts, a greater share of our students comes from the lower socioeconomic strata. In particular, undergraduate youths from "blueblood" families in the social register seldom major in business. Indeed, undergraduate education in business is not even permitted (needed?) at most prominent, elite, private universities (and a few public universities emulating their private cousins). In short, students from the less affluent portions of our society turn by the hundreds of thousands each year toward undergraduate business education as a vehicle for "getting on the socioeconomic ladder."[8] Thus, business education contributes significantly toward the ideal of equal opportunity for all and the "American dream."

To Practice. To marketing practice, marketing academics owe a continuing supply of technically competent, socially responsible graduates as new entrants to the marketing profession. Also, because "problem-oriented" (Myers, Massy, and Greyser 1980) research makes a legitimate and important kind of contribution to marketing knowledge, a significant portion of our knowledge production efforts should be of this genre. The results of such research should be communicated to marketing practitioners by appropriate means and should also find their way into our lectures, textbooks, and other instructional materials. Similar to our obligation to listen to students, we should seek the input of marketing practitioners about the kinds of problems that our problem-oriented research should address. Indeed, research that claims to be managerially relevant should be managerially relevant.

Doing research that educates the public about the social value of marketing activities and marketing institutions is also a responsibility we have to marketing practice. There has never been a book entitled *Does Finance Cost Too Much?* or *Does Management Cost Too Much?* or *Does Accounting Cost Too Much?* As we know, however, there was a famous study that was financed by the Twentieth Century Fund entitled *Does Distribution Cost Too Much?* (Stewart, Dewhurst, and Field 1939). This should tell us something about our discipline and our role in helping the general public understand it.

Even people who customarily evaluate issues in a thinking, logical, and rational manner seem incapable of approaching cognitively, logically, and rationally the subject of marketing, particularly the advertising component of marketing. People seem to put their minds "on hold" at the very mention of marketing. It is worth remembering that L.D.H. Weld (1882–1946), one of the founding fathers of the marketing discipline, was called before a special committee of the Minnesota legislature to explain why he taught what the legislature considered "dangerous doctrines" (Cowan 1960). As we know, he was only pointing out that marketing intermediaries have a positive role to play in the marketing of agricultural products and are not there to exploit anyone, let alone, the farmer. We should also be mindful that only very recently (and by very narrow margins in the United States Supreme Court) have the courts held that professional associations cannot forbid their members to advertise. For over 100 years, the American Bar Association and the American Medical Association were saying to us, their clients, "trust our members." At the same time, they were claiming that their members could not be trusted to engage in advertising because they would engage in advertising that was misleading and deceptive. Think of incongruity here. If the American Bar Association and American Medical Association did not themselves trust their members to be honest *communicators* about their services, why should society trust the members of these associations to be honest *providers* of said services?

The preceding notwithstanding, the marketing discipline should not play the role of professional apologist for products of shoddy quality, for genuinely misleading or deceptive advertising, for collusive pricing, or for coercive practices in distribution channels. To *good* marketing practice, we have a responsibility to research, expose, and publicize *bad* marketing practice. We should be at the forefront in researching questionable marketing practices, not standing at the sidelines.

To the Academy. To the academy as a societal institution, marketing academics have a responsibility for supporting and furthering its core mission of retailing, warehousing, and producing knowledge, while upholding the university's implied contract with society, that is, objective knowledge for

Table 2.1

The Truth Continuum

Dogmatic Skepticism (TRUTH)	Humean Skepticism (truth)	Fallibilism (truth)	Dogmatism (TRUTH)
• Academic Skepticism	• Logical Positivism	• Scientific Realism	• Vulgar Absolutism
• Solipsistic Skepticism	• Logical Empiricism	• Critical Realism	• Scientism
• Relativism	• Critical Rationalism	• Critical Pluralism	• Fundamentalism
• Idealism	• Falsification	• Naturalism	• Theocracy
• Subjectivism	• Instrumentalism		• Maxism
• Constructionism			• Nazism
• Deconstructionism			• Facism
• Neo-Marxism			
• Critical Theory			

Source: Hunt (1992a). Reprinted by permission of the American Marketing Association.

academic freedom. Therefore, our responsibilities to the academy entail developing the four cells comprising the positive, science "half" of marketing. As developed in Chapter 1, marketing science is the behavioral science that seeks to explain transactions, that is, exchange relationships. It is particularly interested in those exchange relationships involving buyers and sellers.

We also have a duty to adhere to the academy's core values. Paramount among these values are respect for reason, for evidence, and for reason applied to evidence. The fact that all knowledge-producing methods are fallible implies an intellectual openness, a civility toward alternative views. The fact that all, genuinely rival, alternative views can be compared and evaluated by reason, evidence, and the application of reason to evidence, implies the rejection of the relativistic thesis that, because of "incommensurability," all alternative views are equally good, equally bad, equally trustworthy, equally untrustworthy, equally true, equally false."[9]

Our responsibilities to the academy for objective knowledge can be illustrated by means of Table 2.1, which shows a continuum of perspectives on truth. At the extreme right we find various kinds of dogmatism. Dogmatists not only know that truth is findable, but that they have found the one and only TRUTH, unequivocally, certainly, or surely, and their TRUTH is not to be questioned. At the extreme left we find the TRUTH of dogmatic skepticism. Dogmatic skeptics claim to have incorrigibly, certainly, surely found the one and only TRUTH. Their TRUTH is that there is no truth to be found. Humean skepticism and fallibilism are two positions, among possible others, between the extremes of dogmatism and dogmatic skepticism. Both extremes are to be avoided:

> There are two threats to reason, the opinion that one knows the truth about the most important things and the opinion that there is no truth about them . . . the first asserts that the quest for truth is unnecessary, while the second asserts it is impossible. (Bloom 1990, p. 18)

2.1.5 Conclusion on the Nature of the Marketing Discipline

So, what kind of discipline is marketing? Marketing is a university discipline that aspires to be a professional discipline and that, accordingly, has responsibilities (a) to society, for providing objective knowledge and technically competent, socially responsible, liberally educated graduates, (b) to students, for providing an education that will enable them to get on and move up the socioeconomic ladder and prepare them for their roles as competent, responsible marketers and citizens, (c) to marketing practice, for providing a continuing supply of competent, responsible entrants to the marketing profession and for providing new knowledge about both the micro and macro dimensions of marketing, and (d) to the academy, for upholding its mission of retailing, warehousing, and producing knowledge, its contract with society of objective knowledge for academic freedom, and its core values of reason, evidence, openness, and civility.

2.2 ON THE NATURE OF MARKETING RESEARCH

What is the nature of marketing research? Historically, the American Marketing Association defined marketing research as the "systematic gathering, recording, and analyzing of data about problems relating to the marketing of goods and services." In 1987 the Board of Directors of the AMA approved the following definition:

> Marketing research is the function which links the consumer, customer, and public to the marketer through information—information used to identify and define marketing opportunities and problems; generate, refine, and evaluate marketing actions; monitor marketing performance; and improve understanding of marketing as a process. Marketing research specifies the information required to address these issues; designs the method for collecting the information; manages and implements the data collection process; analyzes the results; and communicates the findings and their implications. (Bennett 1988, p. 115)

Several academic members of the Board of Directors, after vigorous debate, voted against the definition, believing it to be too managerial in orientation.

Definitions are "rules of replacement" (Hempel 1970, p. 654). That is, a definition means that a word or group of words (the definiens) is proposed to be truth-functionally equivalent to the word being defined (the definiendum). *Good* definitions exhibit inclusivity, exclusivity, differentiability, clarity, communicability, consistency, and parsimony. That is, good definitions should (1) include all phenomena that should be "taken in," (2) exclude all phenomena that should be left out, (3) differentiate the definiendum from other (often closely related) terms, (4) clearly define the term, (5) communicate well the term's meaning to its intended audience, (6) be consistent with the meanings of other important terms, and (7) be no longer than necessary to accomplish criteria 1–6.

The purpose of this section, following closely the analysis in Hunt (1987), is to explore the *inclusivity* of the AMA definition of marketing research. That is, to what extent does the definition include all the activities and phenomena that marketers would *want* to be labeled "marketing research?" In doing so we shall generate six prototypical research questions in marketing, examine the characteristics of these research questions, and inquire whether research conducted about these questions would be properly called "marketing research" under the new definition. It is hoped that this procedure will shed light on whether the new definition is properly inclusive.

2.2.1 Research Questions in Marketing

Table 2.2 displays six prototypical research questions that researchers commonly explore when they contend they are doing "marketing research." Although each question examines the same substantive area (advertising), the kinds of research projects designed to explore these questions will vary greatly. The table categorizes each research question according to the Three Dichotomies Model and (1) identifies whether such research is primarily conducted by practitioners or academicians, (2) indicates whether such research would be publishable, (3) states the proximate (immediate) purpose or objective of the research, (4) shows the ultimate potential value or consequences (intended or unintended) of the research, and (5) indicates whether the research would be considered "marketing research" under the new AMA definition.

Research Question (1). The first research question was used as an example in section 2.1.2. It asks: "How should the Jones Toy Co. allocate its advertising budget among the various media to reach its primary target market, children under twelve years of age?" A research project addressing this question would be profit/micro/normative, because it takes the perspective of an individual firm and attempts to provide specific guidance for its marketing problem. Academicians in their consulting activities sometimes develop research projects to answer this kind of question. However, the overwhelming majority of these projects are done by practitioners, be they "in-house" marketing researchers or those in marketing research agencies. This kind of project is labeled "market research" in section 1.1, called "problem-solving" research by Myers, Massy, and Greyser (1980), and referred to as "applied" research by countless others.

Table 2.2

Prototypical Research Questions in Marketing

Research question	Category[a]	Primary researchers[b]	Publication of knowledge[c]	Proximate purpose[d]	Ultimate potential value	Consistency with AMA definition
1. How should the Jones Toy Co. allocate its advertising budget among the various media to reach its primary target market, children under twelve years of age?	Profit/micro/ normative	Practitioners	No	Better decisions for a firm	Firm productivity Societal productivity	Yes
2. How should firms *in general* allocate their advertising budgets among the various media in an optimal fashion?	Profit/micro/ normative	Academicians Consulting firms	Yes	Better decisions for firms in general	Firm productivity Societal productivity	No
3. To what extent does television advertising in general shape children's beliefs about products and consumptions?	Profit/micro/ positive or Profit/macro/ positive	Academicians	Yes	K.f.K.S.[e]	Firm productivity Societal productivity Better public policy Better informed citizenry	No
4. To what extent is television's shaping of children's beliefs about products and consumption injurious to society?	Profit/micro/ normative	Academicians	Yes	K.f.K.S.[e]	Socially responsible firms Better public policy Better informed citizenry	No

5. To what extent should the federal government restrict or regulate the amount of content of advertising directed at children?	Profit/micro/ normative	Academicians	Yes	Better public policy	Firm productivity	No
6. What are the best research methods to explore questions one through five?	Not applicable	Academicians	Yes	Better research	Firm productivity Societal productivity Socially responsible firms Better public policy Better informed citizenry	No

Source: Adapted from Hunt (1987). Reprinted by permission of the American Marketing Association.

[a]Using the "Three Dichotomies Model."

[b]Emphasis on "primary." That is, it is recognized that on occasion practitioners, consulting firms, and academicians conduct all kinds of research.

[c]The immediate objective of the inquiry.

[d]In scholarly journals such as the *Journal of Marketing* and the *Journal of Marketing Research.*

[e]"Knowledge for Knowledge's Sake."

The results of a research project directed at question (1) would in general not be publishable in journals such as the *Journal of Marketing* or the *Journal of Marketing Research.* These journals have adopted the value system of scholarly journals, which requires manuscripts to make some new contribution to marketing knowledge that is *generalizable* to some extent. Therefore, research projects that simply *apply* existing marketing knowledge to the solution of a firm's problem would be unacceptable.

In researching question (1), the immediate objective of the researcher is to help the manager make a better decision, thereby increasing the firm's productivity. That is, better decisions increase the firm's efficiency and/or effectiveness, and, as a consequence, increase productivity in the sense of resource-advantage theory (Hunt 2000b; Hunt and Morgan 1995, 1996, 1997). However, the consequences do not necessarily stop there. Society also benefits because increases in individual firm productivity can lead to greater efficiency/effectiveness for society as a whole.

A research project designed to explore question (1) would obviously fit comfortably within the AMA definition. This is the type of research that is routinely and regularly conducted by corporate marketing research departments and marketing research agencies. What might surprise some people is the fact that this is precisely the kind of marketing research project that is most often conducted by marketing academicians.

There are no accurate figures on the total number of marketing professors, even in the United States, let alone the world. Nevertheless, given that there are approximately 1,300 four-year institutions offering bachelor's degrees in business in the United States and about 700 such institutions offering a major in marketing, an estimate of 5,000 marketing academicians in four-year institutions would not seem unreasonable (*Peterson's Annual Guide to Four-Year Colleges 2000*). Again, although no "hard" numbers are available, probably 90 percent of the 5,000 marketing academicians do almost *exclusively* these kinds of "consulting" research projects. Many marketers, both practitioners and academicians, seem to believe that the remaining 10 percent should *also* focus exclusively on consulting research. Put another way, to what extent should *any* marketing academician explore research questions similar to questions (2) through (6), and to what extent should such projects be considered "marketing research"?

Research Question (2). The second research question asks: "How should firms in general allocate their advertising budgets among the various media in an optimal fashion?" Like research question (1), question (2) is also profit/micro/normative. However, question (2) calls for research that attempts to generate a procedure or model to solve a particular class of marketing problem. The procedure or method would presumably be applicable across many firms in many different contexts. Such context-free research is conducted primarily by academicians and consulting firms. To the extent that practitioners conduct these kinds of projects, the results of such studies are generally held to be proprietary in nature and not disseminated to the larger marketing community. Consulting firms also tend to keep such studies proprietary.

Unlike research projects directed toward question (1) that focus on a particular firm, projects directed at question (2) attempt to improve the decision making of firms *in general* in a particular decision area. Like question (1), the ultimate consequences are higher levels of productivity for both firms and society. Given that the procedure or model developed by the researcher makes a significant "enough" contribution to marketing knowledge and is perceived to be generalizable across contexts, the results of such a project would be potentially publishable in *JM* and/or *JMR*.

Research projects directed at addressing questions such as question (2) are what Myers, Massy, and Greyser (1980) call "problem-oriented" research. Consistent with the objectives of the Marketing Science Institute, they recommend that marketing academicians focus more of their attention on these kinds of research projects. On the other hand, writers such as Anderson (1983), Arndt (1985), Hirschman (1987), Holbrook (1987), and many others (especially in the consumer behavior area of marketing) believe that academic marketing researchers spend too much of their time working on "problem-oriented" research and that too much of our journal space is devoted to reporting the results of such projects. Curiously, the proposed AMA definition of marketing research would seem to exclude research projects directed at these kinds of questions from being considered "marketing" research. This anomaly would appear to be either an error of interpretation on my part or a gross oversight on the part of the definitions committee. (Surely, the committee did not want to exclude "problem oriented" research.)

Research Question (3). The third research question asks: "To what extent does television advertising in general shape children's beliefs about products and consumption?" Research projects directed at this question would be either profit/micro/positive or profit/macro/positive, depending on the nature of the specific research design. Such projects are almost exclusively the province of academicians and would be considered "basic" marketing research by Meyers, Massy, and Greyser (1980) or "pure" consumer research by Holbrook (1986). The results of such research projects would be potentially acceptable for publication in *JM*, *JMR*, the *Journal of Macromarketing*, the *Journal of Public Policy and Marketing*, and the *Journal of Consumer Research*.

The proximate purpose of such "basic" research projects is "knowledge for knowledge's sake." Ultimately, the results of such projects might be useful in guiding decision makers in their efforts to determine the "best" solutions to research questions like (1) and (2), thus impacting on firm and societal productivity. Likewise, such research efforts might be useful to government officials in their efforts to develop better public policy. (Please note that better public policy may also be in the best interests of firms.) Finally, the results of such research projects may simply result in a better informed citizenry.

Marketing practitioners routinely decry the emphasis on basic research projects (like number 2) by marketing academicians, and this negative attitude toward such research may be responsible for the apparent exclusion of these research projects from the official AMA definition. Many marketing academicians share practitioners' disdain for any research that does not have a predictable, observable, relatively direct benefit to marketing management (Enis 1986; Parasuraman 1982; Peters 1980; Westing 1979). For example, Meyers, Massy, and Greyser propose that "although much basic research in marketing is generated for 'its own sake,' the Commission's view was that if marketing knowledge over the long run is to be considered 'effective,' it should contribute something to improved decision making or other aspects of marketing management practice in the industrial sector" (1980, p. 145). Similarly, Parasuraman contends that "the *raison d'etre* for any marketing theory is its potential application in marketing practice" (1982, p. 78).

In contrast, consistent with the view articulated in section 1.7.5, there have always been academicians and practitioners advocating the legitimacy and desirability of basic research in marketing. The *Journal of Marketing* in its first few decades published *primarily* basic research. In fact, the very first article in the very first issue of *JM* examined whether the interests of the consumer were being well served by the Agricultural Adjustment Administration (Anderson 1936). Decades ago, Levy called for splitting the "basic" side of marketing from its "applied" side, referring to the former as "marcology" (1976). Similarly, Anderson (1983, p. 27) has called for more basic research, pointing out that "it is clear that marketing must be more concerned with the pursuit of knowledge as knowledge."

Most interestingly, while the Definitions Committee of the AMA was busy drafting a definition of marketing research that excluded basic research efforts, another AMA committee was specifically recognizing the legitimacy of such research. The special task force on the development of marketing thought noted that research in marketing has many "clients" and identified the following five "audiences of marketing knowledge" (Monroe et al. 1986, p. 8):

1. managers of enterprises ("practitioners")
2. educators/teachers, scholars, and students
3. public policy makers
4. special interest groups (includes hostile groups such as consumer interest groups, as well as supportive groups)
5. consumers (all of us)

As with many large institutions, the "left hand" seems oblivious or indifferent to the "right."

Research Question (4). The fourth research question asks: "To what extent is television's shaping of children's beliefs about products and consumption injurious to society?" Research projects directed at this question would be profit/macro/normative, conducted almost entirely by academicians, and publishable in journals such as *JM* and the *Journal of Macromarketing*.

Research projects directed at answering this question are pursued "for the sake of knowledge." Some commentators contend (or their works tend to imply) that the knowledge generated by such a project should not influence marketing management decisions (Friedman 1970; Levitt 1958). Others believe that such information should be used by "socially responsible" managers (Gray 1968; Morell 1956). In any respect, such knowledge might result in better public policy and, of course, a better informed citizenry. Although "better public policy" would seem to be in the best interests of *all* marketing practitioners, and socially responsible decisions are definitely an objective of at least *some* (Wood, Chonko, and Hunt 1986), this kind of research project would, again, not be "marketing" research under the new definition.

Research Question (5). The fifth research question asks: "To what extent should the federal government restrict or regulate the amount or content of advertising directed at children?" Efforts directed at answering this question would be categorized as profit/macro/normative, conducted almost exclusively by academicians, and potentially publishable in the *Journal of Marketing*, the *Journal of Macromarketing*, and the *Journal of Public Policy and Marketing*.

The proximate purpose of research conducted here would be the same as its ultimate value: better public policy. Please note that such research efforts could be significantly informed by the results of projects designed to answer questions (3) and (4). Also, note that this kind of research would not be, officially, "marketing research" according to the definition.

Research Question (6). The sixth research question asks: "What are the best research methods to explore questions (1) through (5)?" Research directed at this question cannot be classified within the Three Dichotomies Model because the model focuses on substantive rather than methodological issues. Research efforts dealing with methodological issues on a fundamental or philosophical level (such as scientific realism vs. relativism) would potentially be publishable in the *Journal of Marketing*. Similarly, research efforts on research techniques (such as factor analysis, multidimensional scaling, etc.) would potentially be publishable in the *Journal of Marketing Research*. Historically, the *Journal of Marketing Research* has devoted between 50 percent and 60 percent of its pages to the development of better marketing research techniques. The emphasis on what is considered by many to be "esoteric" research techniques has been criticized by practitioners and academicians. For example, Arndt (1985) claims that our discipline suffers from "instrumentitis" as a result of undue emphasis on research techniques.

The proximate purpose of methodological research efforts is better research on *all* marketing research problems. To the extent that better methods are used in the conduct of marketing research, all the clients of marketing knowledge are better served. Nevertheless, research on methodological issues would appear not to be "marketing" research as per the definition.

2.2.2 Conclusion on the Nature of Marketing Research

Is the current AMA definition of marketing research *properly* inclusive? Quite obviously, the definition specifically addresses only one of the preceding prototypical marketing research questions, that is, research directed at solving a specific firm's marketing problem. Research directed at providing new knowledge for solving general *classes* of marketing management problems, or for providing *basic* knowledge that might be *ultimately* useful in solving marketing management problems, or for informing public-policy decisions, or for addressing the interests of society in having a well-informed citizenry do not seem to find a "home" within the new definition.

The preceding notwithstanding, there is a good argument that the new definition is in fact properly inclusive. Clearly, the definition was never meant to be a good definition of marketing research in *all* its aspects. Rather, the purpose of the definition was to articulate for students and the public at large what practitioner marketing researchers actually do (or ought to do) in corporate and agency research organizations. This is obviously the case when words like "the function" are used in the definition. Recall that good definitions exhibit not just inclusivity, but communicability as well. The definition, it may be argued, communicates well with its intended audience.

Rather than changing the *definiens* to make it include a broader array of research issues under the rubric of marketing research, it would be simpler and just as appropriate to change the *definiendum*. That is, rather than change the *definition*, we could delimit the construct being *defined*. We could clearly state that we are defining marketing research of the "problem-solving" or "applied" variety. Changing the first part of the first sentence in the definition to read: "Marketing research is the function *within the firm* that links the consumer . . ." would succinctly accomplish this objective.

Definitional issues aside, our discussion explicitly and implicitly raises numerous fundamental questions about research in the marketing academic discipline. To what extent should marketing academicians focus exclusively on consulting research (should the 10 percent join the 90 percent)? To what extent should more marketing academicians be encouraged to conduct scholarly research (should the 90 percent be encouraged to join the 10 percent)? What are the institutional mechanisms that encourage/discourage research of a consulting/scholarly nature? Should specific institutional mechanisms be developed to encourage/discourage more research of a consulting/scholarly nature?

The view here is that marketing academicians should not do just consulting research—the 10 percent should not join the 90 percent. Rather, we should encourage more scholarly research—the 90 percent should be encouraged to become more professionally active in scholarly activities. There are numerous institutional mechanisms that tend to encourage consulting research and discourage scholarly research. Furthermore, changes in these institutional mechanisms would be desirable from the perspective of both marketing practitioners and academicians alike. The myopic view of the American Marketing Association's definition of marketing research represents a small, but potentially significant, institutional mechanism discouraging scholarly marketing research. It should be changed.

2.3 ON MARKETING'S AVERSION TO QUALITATIVE METHODS

The label "qualitative methods" is often applied to research approaches that, in contrast to those labeled "quantitative," do not employ the tools of mathematics and statistics. The "qualitative" label is often used to describe approaches such as naturalistic inquiry (Belk, Wallendorf, and Sherry 1989), humanistic inquiry (Hirschman 1986), ethnographic methods (Sherry 1983), historical methods (Fullerton 1987; Lavin and Archdeacon 1989), semiotics (Holbrook and Grayson 1986; Mick 1986), literary explication (Stern 1989a, 1989b), and existential-phenomenological methods (Thompson, Locander, and Pollio 1989).

Since the early 1980s, scores of researchers have been advocating qualitative methods for studying marketing. Yet, except for the *Journal of Consumer Research*, most articles in major marketing journals do not use qualitative methods. It would certainly appear that qualitative approaches could make important contributions to marketing knowledge. As yet, however, their contributions have been infrequent. This section examines reasons for marketing's aversion to qualitative methods and begins by examining the nature of scholarly journals.

2.3.1 The Nature of Scholarly Journals

The objective of all research is to produce *knowledge*, or (more epistemologically modest) knowledge claims. Every university discipline has an extant body of knowledge and all scholarly journals associated with academic disciplines evaluate manuscripts according to whether each submitted manuscript contributes to, or extends, the extant body of knowledge as judged by a jury of one's peers. Essentially, the process of evaluating manuscripts for a scholarly journal involves answering three questions: (1) What is the nature of the purported contribution to knowledge of the manuscript? (2) What is the extent of the purported contribution to knowledge? (3) Is the purported contribution to knowledge *genuine*?

The first evaluative question categorizes the purported contribution. Does the manuscript fall within the domain of the journal? Each journal defines (loosely or tightly) its domain. For the *Journal of Marketing*, for example, the major question is whether a manuscript submission is truly in the area of *marketing*, or whether it is more appropriate for a general management journal or a sociology journal, or some other journal. Many articles submitted to marketing journals are rejected because they are viewed by editors and reviewers as outside the domain of *marketing*.

The second question, identifying the *extent* of the purported contribution, is actually a composite of three subquestions. First, to what extent is the purported contribution to marketing knowledge new? That is, has the contribution been previously reported in the literature? The second aspect of the extent criterion concerns whether, in the judgment of the reviewers, the contribution is "large enough" to warrant publishing in the journal. Sometimes this criterion is known as the contribution-to-page-length ratio criterion. The third aspect of the extent criterion has to do with the value of the contribution. Will the manuscript be valuable in encouraging further research? Does the manuscript have value for decision makers? Does the manuscript have value for government policy?

In addition to the nature of the contribution and the extent of the contribution, the third criterion of the manuscript review process for scholarly journals evaluates the *genuineness* of the contribution. How do we know that the knowledge claims in the manuscript are true, or trustworthy, or verified, or confirmed, or (in philosophy of science terms) that they have "high epistemic warrant?"

2.3.2 Three Reasons for the Aversion

Applying the criteria for evaluating manuscripts provides several potential reasons for the aversion to qualitative methods. First, many qualitative research projects, though conducted by marketers, have been viewed by reviewers and editors as outside the domains of their respective journals. This is especially likely to be the case for those reviewers—of whom there are many—who view marketing as an applied discipline whose only client is marketing managers. It is also especially likely for projects adopting Marxist and neo-Marxist approaches, for reviewers are likely to recommend that reports of such projects belong in journals specifically devoted to, for example, Marxist economics.

A second reason for the aversion is the problem of the contribution-to-page-length ratio. In particular, ethnographic studies often require many pages to report results in an adequate manner. The page limitations of a typical journal article may be too short to permit authors the full development of their contributions to marketing knowledge. For many such studies, monographs are required.

Third, with regard to the "genuine" criterion, many journal reviewers equate "mathematics and statistics" with "science." Strongly influenced by neoclassical economics, which has adopted mathematics as its language of discourse, many reviewers summarily reject nonmathematical, nonstatistical works as being nonscientific and nonmeritorious. Such sophomoric reviewers, of course, are sorely misguided. They do exist in abundance, however, and are influential "gatekeepers."

There is a fourth reason for the aversion, and it also has to do with whether the contribution is genuine. Specifically, it concerns how advocates of qualitative methods have argued for their approaches. Given the philosophical nature of this reason, it requires elaboration.

2.3.3 The Fourth Reason: The "Standard Argument"

Early advocates argued for qualitative methods using what might be called the "standard argument." The argument can be succinctly summarized in six assertions:

1. All disciplines have paradigms, and, because paradigms are incommensurable, objective choice between competing paradigms is impossible.
2. There is one paradigm that is dominant in marketing.
3. The dominant paradigm in marketing is "positivism" (logical positivism or logical empiricism), which implies the use of quantitative methods, functionalism, the adoption of realism, reifying unobservables, the search for causality, and the assumption of determinism.
4. As a result of the writings of Kuhn, Hanson, and Feyerabend, among others, by the 1970s, the philosophy of science had abandoned positivism, and, therefore, marketing's dominant paradigm is discredited or passé.
5. Upon the abandonment of positivism, the philosophy of science embraced relativism, constructionism, and subjectivism.
6. Therefore, marketing should accept qualitative methods (e.g., naturalistic inquiry, humanistic inquiry, historicism, ethnography, postmodernism, critical theory, semiotics, semiology, deconstructionism, Marxism, and feminism) because (a) marketing's dominant paradigm has been discredited and (b) qualitative methods embrace the

"new" philosophy of science, that is, relativism, constructionism, and subjectivism.

The problem with the "standard argument" for qualitative methods is that, of the five premises, four (1, 2, 3, and 5) are false and the remaining one (4) is misleading. As a result, the argument degenerates into obfuscation, obscurantism, and what is referred to by Coyne (1982) as "postmodernist epistobabble." In this section, space limitations dictate that I can only sketch the major objections to the five premises and point readers toward literature discussing the objections in detail.

Premise (1). Writers use the term "paradigm" in numerous ways. (Kuhn [1962] himself used the term in twenty-one different ways.) The most common conception in today's philosophy of science is that a paradigm consists of (1) a knowledge content, for example, a theory and its concepts, (2) a methodology, that is, a procedure by which knowledge is to be generated, and (3) an epistemology, that is, a set of criteria for evaluating knowledge claims. For Kuhn (1962, p. 108), the three components constitute a unified, interdependent whole: in learning a paradigm, the scientist acquires theory, methods, and standards together, usually in an inextricable mixture. Thus construed, disciplines probably have "paradigms." But, no interpretation of paradigm *incommensurability* has ever been put forth that can justify the claim that choice between genuinely rival paradigms, that is, paradigms that make conflicting claims, cannot be made on objective grounds (Hunt 1989a, 1991a). The conclusion of Hintikka is typical: "The frequent arguments that strive to use the absolute or relative incommensurability of scientific theories as a reason for thinking that they are inaccessible to purely scientific (rational) comparisons are simply fallacious" (1988, p. 38). Premise (1) is false.

Premise (2). Laudan reviews the history of science and finds the complete absence of dominant paradigms: "Virtually every major period in the history of science is characterized both by the coexistence of numerous competing paradigms, with none exerting hegemony over the field, and by the persistent and continuous manner in which the foundational assumptions of every paradigm are debated with the scientific community" (1977, p. 74). Just as it is in other disciplines, there is no dominant paradigm in marketing (Hunt 1991a, b). In fact, marketing has historically been an extraordinarily open discipline, borrowing—often indiscriminately—methods, theories, and concepts from everywhere. Premise (2) is false.

Premise (3). Positivism does not imply quantitative methods (Phillips 1987); nor does it imply either scientific realism (Manicas 1987) or functionalism (Hunt 1994c); nor does it imply that researchers should search for causal relations (Manicas 1987); nor does positivism assume that theories must be deterministic (Suppe 1977); nor can research guided by positivism reify unobservables (Hunt 1989b; Levin 1991). If positivism does not imply these things, what does it imply? In order to provide a philosophy that, among other things, could accommodate the indeterminacy of quantum mechanics (the "Copenhagen interpretation"), the positivists (1) adopted formal logic as a methodology for studying science, (2) rejected the scientific realist view that unobservable concepts can be *real*, (3) believed that science should avoid metaphysical concepts and rely exclusively on observables, (4) viewed "cause" as an unobservable, metaphysical concept that is at best superfluous to science and at worst a source of great mischief, and (5) viewed functionalism as highly suspect. Furthermore, because they believed that science should restrict itself to knowledge with *certainty*, the positivists (6) adopted Humean skepticism. For them, inductive reasoning was problematic or impermissible. Premise (3) is false.

Premise (4). Many of the tenets of positivism have, indeed, been discredited, but the influence of Kuhn, Hanson, and Feyerabend has been exaggerated. Moreover, the attacks on "positivistic science" are often just an attack on science, *per se*. As Levin puts it:

> Logical positivism was the most self-critical movement in the history of philosophy. Every major objection to positivism was proposed by positivists themselves or associates on work on problems set by positivism, all in the scientific spirit of seeking truth. It is particularly unfortunate that the technical failure of particular positivist doctrines is so often used . . . to cover an attack on clarity and science itself. (Levin 1991, pp. 63, 64).

Premise (4) is misleading.

Premise (5). Although philosophy of science did flirt with the relativism, constructionism, and subjectivism of Kuhn and Feyerabend in the 1960s, by the 1970s, most philosophers of science had adopted some version of scientific realism, even though, as Leplin (1984, p. 1) puts it, "Scientific realism is a majority position whose advocates are so divided as to appear in a minority." To understand why philosophy of science turned away from relativism, constructionism, and subjectivism, we need to explore briefly each of these "isms."

"Relativism" is a term of art from philosophy. All genuine forms of relativism have two theses: (1) the relativity thesis that something is relative to something else and (2) the nonevaluation thesis that there are no objective standards for evaluating *across* the various kinds of "something else" (Siegel 1987). With the preceding in mind, we can define several forms of relativism, constructionism, and subjectivism:

1. *Cultural relativism* holds that (a) the elements embodied in a culture are relative to the norms of that culture, and (b) there are no objec-

tive, neutral, or nonarbitrary criteria to evaluate cultural elements across different cultures.

2. *Ethical relativism* holds that (a) what is ethical can only be evaluated relative to some moral code held by an individual, group, society, or culture, and (b) there are no objective, impartial, or nonarbitrary standards for evaluating different moral codes across individuals, groups, societies, or cultures.
3. *Rationality relativism* holds that (a) the canons of correct or rational reasoning are relative to individual cultures, and (b) there are no objective, neutral, or nonarbitrary criteria to evaluate what is called "rational" across different cultures.
4. Conceptual framework-relativism holds that (a) knowledge claims are relative to conceptual frameworks (theories, paradigms, world views, or *Weltanschauungen*), and (b) knowledge claims cannot be evaluated objectively, impartially, or nonarbitrarily across competing conceptual frameworks.
5. *Constructionism* (alternatively spelled "constructivism") is the same thing as *reality relativism*, which holds that (a) what comes to be known as "reality" in science is constructed by individuals relative to their language (or group, social class, theory, paradigm, culture, world view, or *Weltanschauung*), and (b) what comes to count as "reality" cannot be evaluated objectively, impartially, or nonarbitrarily across different languages (or groups, etc.).
6. *Subjectivism* is the thesis that there is something basic to the human condition—usually something about human perception and/or language—that categorically prevents objective knowledge about the world.

Although philosophy of science flirted with relativism, constructionism, and subjectivism in the 1960s, by the 1970s, most philosophers of science had adopted some version of scientific realism (Suppe 1977).

To understand why relativism, constructionism, and subjectivism are minority views within the philosophy of science, consider how these "isms" would respond to the following questions. Question (1): "Does the sun revolve around the earth or does the earth revolve around the sun?" Conceptual framework relativism, for example, Kuhn (1962), answers: "First I must know whether you subscribe to the paradigm of Copernicus or Ptolemy, for these paradigms—like all paradigms—are incommensurable and, therefore, there is no *truth* to the matter independent of the paradigm you hold." And subjectivism, with great exasperation, responds: "Because scientists see what their theories and paradigms tell them is there, the theory-ladenness of observation tells us that an *objective* answer to your query is impossible."

Question (2): "Was Great Britain morally *right* in leading the drive in the nineteenth century to abolish slavery in cultures throughout the world?" Relativism responds: "Because slavery is a cultural element that cannot be evaluated independently of the norms of the culture within which it exists, no judgment on this matter can be made—to apply one's own norms elsewhere is simply cultural ethnocentrism." Question (3): "Should Great Britain work toward the abolition of the few remaining states, for example, Mauritania (Masland et al. 1992), where slavery continues to exist?" Answer: "See response to previous question." Question (4): "Did the Holocaust occur?" Answer: "Because the Holocaust is a 'constructed' reality (Lincoln and Guba 1985, p. 84), just one of many 'multiple realities,' the Holocaust's occurrence or nonoccurrence cannot be objectively appraised independent of the world view of a particular social grouping or culture."

Question (5): "Is a culture that is tolerant of individuals from other cultures preferable to a culture that oppresses everyone outside the dominant culture?" Answer: "Although the predisposition toward tolerance is a cultural element that varies widely across different cultures, no judgment can be made across cultures as the moral superiority of tolerant versus intolerant cultures." Question (6): "Should an academic discipline be open to the views of those outside the discipline?" Answer: "Although it is true that different academic disciplines differ in their relative openness to the views of outsiders, no judgment can be made across disciplines as to the relative desirability of such openness."

It should be easy now to understand why relativism, constructionism, and subjectivism are minority views in the philosophy of science. Relativism does not imply a constructively critical stance toward knowledge claims, nor does it imply acknowledging that the knowledge claims of science are fallible. Relativism implies nihilism—the belief that we can never have genuine knowledge about anything. Relativists, incoherently, *know* that no one else can ever know anything. Furthermore, relativism does not imply a tolerant stance toward outside ideas and other cultures; it implies *indifference* to the norm of tolerance. Moreover, relativism does not imply ethical sensitivity; it implies ethical impotence. Finally, subjectivism does not caution science to work at minimizing bias; it maintains that the human condition makes the very idea of objectivity a chimera. Therefore—like truth—objectivity should be abandoned.

In contrast, most scientists and philosophers of science not only adopt fallibilism and realism, but also hold in high regard the ideals of truth and objectivity. Modern philosophy of science recognizes that there is nothing in the nature of human perception, nothing in the nature of human language, nothing in the nature of "paradigms" that makes true theories and objective knowledge to be—in principle—impossible. (Indeed, the fact that each and every one of our theories *may* be wrong does not imply that they necessarily *must* be wrong.)

2.3.4 Conclusion on the Aversion to Qualitative Methods

In conclusion, reasons for the aversion to qualitative methods in marketing include difficulties with meeting the domain requirement, the contribution-to-page-length problem, and the existence of sophomoric reviewers. In addition, a major reason is the "standard argument" used by advocates of qualitative methods. As long as advocates begin their analyses with (1) the ritual of bashing what they misleadingly call "positivism" (i.e., science and/or quantitative methods) and (2) adopting relativism, constructionism, and subjectivism, then (3) reviewers are likely to view qualitative studies as untrustworthy. That is, they are likely to reject qualitative research projects as failing the criterion of genuineness. However, there appears to be no reason why qualitative researchers must use the standard argument or that the output of qualitative research cannot be worthy of trust. The goal of the adoption of qualitative methods—a goal I share with many marketers—would be furthered by abandoning the standard argument.

QUESTIONS FOR ANALYSIS AND DISCUSSION

1. Westing (in Ferrell et al. 1979) claims that marketing academia is "moving farther and farther away from our clients who are the businessmen of the country." What is a "client?" Is marketing academia "moving farther away?" Westing claims that marketing is a professional discipline like medicine. Are the "clients" of medical schools the practicing physicians or people who are sick? Does marketing have any *other* clients? Who are they, and how would these clients influence the nature of the market discipline? Is society in general a client?
2. Westing (in Ferrell et al. 1979) claims that "we are not a discipline. Economics is the discipline of study in business." Further, he observes that economics is the "mother science of marketing." He then proposes that the application of economics to marketing has been largely unsuccessful because "economics has never paid much attention to demand creation" and the theory of pricing was not "much of a contribution to the field." Evaluate the consistency of these views. What does the concept "mother science" imply?
3. Many writers claim that "marketing is a professional discipline, not an academic discipline." Others refer to marketing as an "applied" rather than a "basic" discipline. Are these positive or normative statements? Differentiate among these kinds of disciplines. What are the consequences for marketing teaching and research if it is a professional or academic or applied or basic discipline? What is the nature of the marketing discipline?

4. A colleague once observed:

> Economics, not marketing, is the professional discipline because economics is much more of a profession than marketing. After all, there are far more professional economists than professional marketers, and economics has far more professional status.

   Evaluate.

5. Peters (in Ferrell et al. 1979) suggests that the "fast-track research schools are influencing the other types of schools so that everyone now, or almost everyone, is setting up 'publish or perish' requirements." Do you agree? Estimate the total number of colleges and universities that teach marketing. What percentage of faculty do you think really "publish or perish?" Estimate the number of faculty that teach marketing. Now estimate the percentage of faculty who have published one or more journal articles in *JM*, *JMR*, or *JCR* in the past three years. Does this suggest that there must be a whole lot of perishing going on?
6. Peters (in Ferrell et al. 1979) indicates that his school gives "credit for unpublished, applied research studies if they truly make a contribution to the applied area of the discipline." What is an "applied research study?" If such a study is unpublished, how could one decide whether it makes a contribution or not? What does "make a contribution" mean?
7. Myers, Greyser, and Massy (1979) believe that:

> The objectives of knowledge generation in our field should be to improve marketing management practice. Thus, even basic research if it is to be considered "effective" should, over the long run, contribute something to improved decision-making or other aspects of management practice. (1979, p. 21)

   Evaluate. Before research is undertaken, what clues are there that a piece of research would "over the long run" contribute to management practice? How long is the "long run?"

8. Myers, Greyser, and Massy (1979) conclude:

> What the commission in effect rediscovered in the management science/model-building area was a reaffirmation of what many model-builders themselves have long believed—comparatively few firms or practicing management people seem to be using their models. (1979, p. 22)

   Why is this the case? Is it reasonable to expect line managers extensively to use sophisticated marketing models?

9. Accounting practitioners have historically been very generous in supporting academic accounting departments. Marketing practitioners

provide very little support to academic marketing departments. Why is this the case? What steps could be undertaken by marketing academia to encourage marketing practitioners to be more supportive?

10. Differentiate between the study of consumer behavior and the study of buyer behavior. Is consumer behavior a subset of marketing? Is buyer behavior? Ought they to be? What were your criteria for inclusion/exclusion?
11. All of academia (not just marketing and business schools) is currently under siege from taxpayers, legislators, and even university officials to be *more productive* and *more relevant*. Apparently, many groups are no longer willing to accept semester credit hours taught, articles and books published, and community service rendered as adequate indicators of productivity.

    a. Develop a set of productivity measures that would satisfy the critics of academe.
    b. To what extent are your measures consistent or inconsistent with traditional measures?
    c. Which stakeholders of universities would be better served by your measures? Which ones worse served? Why?

12. The AMA "task force" (Monroe et al. 1988) identifies five "constituencies of marketing knowledge":

    (1) academics and students
    (2) practitioners
    (3) policy makers
    (4) special interest groups
    (5) customers/consumers

    This chapter discusses four "clients" of marketing:

    (1) society
    (2) students
    (3) practice
    (4) academy

    Do the "constituencies of marketing knowledge" differ from the "clients of the marketing discipline?" Defend the view that Monroe et al. (1988) and the book are consistent. Now attack this view. What is your philosophy on this issue? Why?
13. A student has commented: "The analysis of relativism, constructionism, and subjectivism [in section 2.3.3] is totally unnecessary. Because it is *obvious* that relativism has no merit, one need not develop

arguments against it." Evaluate the student's comment. If you agree that "it is obvious," why did (and do) so many researchers use the "standard argument?" If you disagree that "it is obvious," why did the student make the comment?

14. Paul Meehl at a conference on social science and metatheory states the following:

> It was agreed that logical positivism and strict operationism won't wash . . . the last remaining defender of anything like logical positivism was Gustav Bergman, who ceased to do so by the late 1940s. Why then the continued attack on logical positivism and its American behaviorists' near-synonym "operationalism?" My answer to this is unsettling but, I think, correct. Our conference on social science came about partly because of widespread dissatisfaction about the state of the art, and we have always been more introspective methodologically than the physicists and biologists, who engage in this kind of thing only under revolutionary circumstances. My perhaps cynical diagnosis is that one reason the conference members spend needless time repeating that logical positivism and simplistic operationalism are incorrect views of scientific knowledge is that this relieves scientific guilt feelings or inferiority feelings about our disciplines. It is as if somebody said, "Well, maybe clinical psychology isn't up to the standards of historical geology or medical genetics, let alone theoretical physics; but we need not be so fussy about our concepts and empirical support for them because logical positivism, which was so stringent on that score, is a nefarious doctrine and we are no longer bound by it." (Meehl 1986, pp. 315–16)

Evaluate the thesis of Meehl. To what extent does it apply or not apply to marketing?

15. "Many critics claim to attack positivistic science. However, because most of science is not 'positivistic' in any true sense of the term, such critics are actually attacking science itself." Evaluate this thesis.

NOTES

1. For example, as late as 1874, the Catholic University in Ireland refused to allow science to be taught (Gieryn 1983).

2. Oxford and Cambridge at the time still admitted only Anglicans and were not yet research oriented. Oxford granted its first Ph.D. in 1917, fifty-six years after Yale granted the first Ph.D. in the United States. Between 1815 and the outbreak of the World War I, over 10,000 American students earned degrees at German universities, half of them at the University of Berlin (Brubacher and Rudy 1976, p. 175).

3. This seems to be the argument of Myers, Massy, and Greyser (1980, p. x), when, among other things, they discuss scholarly research as "basic fuel."

4. For an introduction, see Lynn (1965), Vollmer and Mills (1966), and Moore (1970). For an excellent summary related to management as a profession, see Osigweh (1986).

5. It is worth noting that medicine and law have a single, dominant occupation associated with them and even accounting has only two: the CPA and the corporate accountant. The radical heterogeneity of marketing occupations poses a unique difficulty for those wanting "marketing" *per se* to be a profession. Indeed, the "marketing manager" as customarily described in marketing textbooks, constitutes a distinct minority as to numbers of people engaged in marketing occupations.

6. All moral philosophies can be categorized as either deontological (which focus on the inherent rightness/wrongness of behaviors) or teleological (which focus on the amount of good or bad embodied in the consequences of behaviors). See Hunt and Vitell (1986, 1992) for a theory of ethics embracing both deontological and teleological philosophies.

7. See Hunt (1992a) for a brief review of science and objectivity. See Hunt (1993, 1994a, 2003) for more extensive analyses.

8. Engineering is, of course, the other popular major for getting on the socioeconomic ladder. MBA programs also have this role, but there is less evidence that MBA programs *disproportionately* serve those from lower socioeconomic strata.

9. If two, genuinely rival, alternative views, for example, two theories or paradigms, are "incommensurable," then, by definition, their relative merits cannot be evaluated. Consequently, each view must be considered equally good, equally bad, equally trustworthy, equally untrustworthy, equally true, or equally false, because, if a judgment can be made that one alternative view is superior to its rival, then the two views are commensurable, not incommensurable.

3 THE MORPHOLOGY OF EXPLANATION

Science has not the monopoly of truth but only the monopoly of the means for checking truth and enhancing it.

—Mario Bunge

The term *explanation* plays a prominent role in all kinds of scientific inquiry. Although the observation, description, and classification of phenomena are important in science, the *explanation* of phenomena remains the *sine qua non* of science; without explanation, there is no science. As will be shown later, the systematic explanation of phenomena is a logical requirement for the scientific *understanding* of phenomena.

Ernest Nagel (1961, p. 15) suggests that "the distinctive aim of the scientific enterprise is to provide systematic and responsibly supported explanations." However, terms such as *systematic*, *responsibly supported*, and *explanation* are remarkably compressed concepts, and much of this monograph will be devoted to unpacking them. The objective of this chapter is to unpack the concept of explanation. That is, how does one go about explaining the occurrence of some phenomenon? What general characteristics do all satisfactory explanations have? How can various explanations be evaluated? Are some explanations better than others? Before turning to these questions, the next section will explore the purpose of explanations in marketing.

3.1 EXPLANATIONS IN MARKETING

Carl Hempel (1965a, p. 334) suggests that scientific explanations should be viewed as scientific answers to "why" questions. Why did phenomenon X occur? Phenomenon X occurred because. . . . Thus, marketers might want to know: Why have the sales of product X been decreasing rapidly? Why do newspapers charge lower rates to local advertisers than to national advertisers? Why did budget motels enter the lodging industry in the 1970s? Why do people purchase particular brands of detergents? Possible explanations for these "why" questions might involve, in turn, the product life cycle, price sensitivity, the "wheel of retailing," and a consumer behavior model. These specific marketing explanations will be evaluated in detail in the next chapter. At this point, we need only emphasize that marketing research is vitally concerned with explaining marketing phenomena and that answers to "why" questions usually serve as precursors to "what will happen if" questions. For example, if one can explain why people buy particular detergents, one can predict "what will happen if I produce a particular brand of detergent."

A model is any structure that purports to *represent* something else (Rigby 1965, p. 109). Aeronautical engineers use miniature models of airplanes to represent full-sized airplanes in wind-tunnel tests. A road map is a model of a highway system. *Mathematical* models use mathematical symbols to represent certain characteristics of phenomena. A poem is a kind of *verbal* model using words to represent phenomena. A photograph or statue is an *iconic* model that *looks like* what it is supposed to represent. Most marketing models are *verbal* models, although mathematical and statistical models are becoming more common. All theories are models because (as Chapter 7 will reveal) all theories purport to represent some aspects of real-world phenomena. However, the converse is not true: all models are not theories, in that many models will not have all the requisites of theoretical constructions. *An explanatory model is any generalized procedure or structure that purports to represent how phenomena are scientifically explained.*

Subsequent sections of this chapter will analyze six different kinds of explanatory models: deductive-nomological explanations, deductive-statistical explanations, inductive-statistical explanations, statistical relevance explanations, pattern explanations, and functionalist explanations. These various kinds of explanatory models are structurally dissimilar. That is, they employ fundamentally different kinds of logic and evidence to explain phenomena. Before analyzing and comparing them, we need to develop some normative criteria for evaluating the adequacy of purportedly explanatory structures.

3.2 CRITERIA FOR EVALUATING EXPLANATORY MODELS

Generally, most philosophers of science agree that to seek an answer as to why a phenomenon occurred is to show at least that, given some antecedent conditions, the phenomenon was somehow *expected to occur.* Thus, any explanation of the decreased sales of a product must show that, given certain conditions, one would have *expected* the decreased sales. If one seeks to explain the growth of budget motels, one must show that, given certain other phenomena, the growth of budget motels could be *expected.* So the first criterion is that any model that purports to be explanatory must somehow show that the phenomenon to be explained was expected. Three other normative criteria seem equally appropriate for assessing the explanatory adequacy of a model. Explanatory models should be *pragmatic, intersubjectively certifiable,* and have *empirical content.*[1]

Pragmatism, the second criterion, can best be illustrated with an example. Suppose a particular analysis logically *precluded* Newton's laws of motion as qualifying as explanatory. Because Newton's laws are prime examples of what would almost universally be considered explanations in the sciences, simple pragmatism would suggest that the analysis was too restrictive and that we should go back to the drawing board. Thus, *pragmatism* dictates that models incorporating devices structurally similar to Newton's laws should be considered explanatory. More generally, models of explanatory structures should be in accord with scientific practice.

The third criterion provides that explanations, like all scientific knowledge, must be objective in the sense of being *intersubjectively certifiable.* That is, different investigators (hence, *intersubject*) with different opinions, attitudes, and beliefs must be able to check the logic and make observations or conduct experiments to determine the truth content of the purported explanation. The intersubjectively certifiable criterion implies that *explanatory structures must be testable.* For example, one criticism of cognitive dissonance theory in social psychology is that the proponents of dissonance theory generally find results favorable to the theory; whereas nonbelievers in dissonance theory generally find no evidence to support the theory. That is, cognitive dissonance researchers have had problems in attempting to intersubjectively certify dissonance theory.

The fourth criterion requires explanations to have *empirical content.* Not only must an explanation be testable, it must be *empirically* testable. This rules out so-called purely analytic explanations, where statements are true, not by recourse to empirical (real-world) phenomena, but just because of the way terms are defined. There is something uncomfortable about the claim that one can explain the high market share of a brand by pointing out that more people buy it than any other brand. Such explanations would be purely analytic: true by definition alone. Explanations using extraempirical statements are also ruled out by the empirical content criterion. As Lambert and Brittan (1970, p. 26) point out, "Appeals to God's will, for instance, although satisfying to many people, are not generally held to be explanatory; that the Lisbon earthquake occurred because God willed it is not really an assertion open to scientific investigation."

The preceding criteria do not exhaust the possibilities. However, they do appear to be a minimal set of desirable attributes for scientific explanations. Given these criteria, we can begin exploring the structure of various explanatory models.

3.3 DEDUCTIVE-NOMOLOGICAL EXPLANATION

The classical model of explanation is the deductive-nomological (D-N) model. Suggested by Hempel (1965a, p. 335), the terms literally mean "to deduce from laws." The D-N model, referred to as hypothetic-deductive (Kaplan 1964, p. 10; Brodbeck 1968, p. 385), covering law (Dieks 1980), and, simply, deductive (Kaplan 1964, p. 336), is classical in the sense that early philosophers such as Hume (1911) and Kant (1783/1968) implied the D-N model in their writings when referring to explaining phenomena. For example, in discussing the nature of science, Kant (1783/1968, p. 18) refers to "the laws from which reason explains the facts." Rigorous explication of the D-N model has been developed by Stallo (1960), Campbell (1952), Cohen and Nagel (1934), and Hempel (1965a).

The deductive-nomological model of explanation has the following structure:

$$\left.\begin{array}{l} C_1, C_2, \ldots C_k \\ L_1, L_2, \ldots L_r \end{array}\right\} \quad \text{Explanans } S$$
$$\overline{\qquad\qquad E \qquad\qquad} \} \quad \text{Explanandum}$$

The $C_1, C_2, \ldots C_k$, refer to the characteristics or facts of the particular situation, and the $L_1, L_2, \ldots L_r$ refer to certain laws of strictly universal form. These laws state that *every* time some particular set of phenomena ($C_1, C_2, \ldots C_k$) occurs, then some other phenomenon (E) will also occur. Together, the characteristics and the laws jointly make up the explanans. The explanans deductively implies (this is the meaning of the solid horizontal line) the explanandum E, which represents the phenomenon to be explained. The D-N model suggests that to explain a phenomenon scientifically is to deductively subsume the phenomenon under a set of laws, and, therefore, to show that the phenomenon could be *expected to occur* (Cohen and Nagel 1934, p. 397). Note that in the D-N model, *if* the explanans is true, then the explanandum *must* be true because the laws are of strictly universal form. That is, the laws state that *every* time characteristics $C_1, C_2, \ldots C_k$ occur, then E must occur.

A simple example of D-N explanation should make the model clearer. Why does a cube of ice with dimensions 1 foot x 1 foot x 1 foot float in water? The characteristic facts are that the cube of ice weighs approximately 56.2 pounds and that a cubic foot of water weighs approximately 62.4 pounds. Archimedes' principle states that a body in a fluid will displace an amount of that fluid equal to the weight of the body and that the fluid will exert an upward force on the body equal to the weight of the displaced fluid. Also, Newton's first law of motion states (essentially) that every time the result of all the forces acting on a body equals zero, the body will remain at rest. The characteristics (the weight of ice versus the weight of an equal volume of water) in conjunction with the principle/law (Archimedes' and Newton's) logically imply (predict) that the cube of ice will float in the water.

Many explanations of why ice floats in water will mention Archimedes' principle but neglect to explicitly state Newton's law. A logician would refer to such explanations as *enthymemes* (or elliptical explanations [Hempel 1965a, p. 414]) because one of the laws necessary to deduce the explanandum was suppressed or skipped over. Enthymemes are common in scientific discourse.

The D-N model of explanation certainly satisfies the four criteria in section 3.2 for evaluating purportedly explanatory structures. The classical explanations of the sciences are unquestionably consistent with it. If the terms have empirical content (refer to real-world phenomena), then the model assures us that the explanation will be testable (at least testable in principle), which means that the explanation will be intersubjectively certifiable. The beauty of the D-N structure is that the explanandum is a logical consequence of the explanans, which greatly simplifies empirical testing. To the extent that the explanandum is verified by empirical observation, evidence is provided that reality is actually isomorphic (structurally similar in essential respects) with the proposed explanans. Thus, *scientific understanding* of the real world is increased. Some philosophers of science accept only the D-N model as satisfactorily explanatory (Donagan 1966, p. 132). This tunnel view of explanation is too restrictive, as our analysis of statistical explanations will show.

3.4 STATISTICAL EXPLANATION

Statistical explanation differs markedly from deductive-nomological explanation. Fundamentally, whereas D-N explanations employ only laws of strictly universal form, all statistical explanations contain at least one law in the probabilistic or statistical form:

$$P(G, F) = r$$

The law states that "the probability of G, given F, is r." An interpretation of this law suggests that in the long run the expected proportion of those cases of F that are also G is r.

We say an interpretation of the statistical law because there are basically three different theories of probability: mathematical probability, relative frequency, and subjective probability (Kaplan 1964, p. 225). Some familiarity with these three theories is necessary to analyze the basic nature of statistical explanations.

3.4.1 Theories of Probability

Roughly speaking, mathematical probability is an *a priori* notion, in which probabilities can be assigned to events without observation of the frequencies with which those events actually occur. To mathematical probability advocates, the probability of an event is determined simply by dividing the number of "favorable" cases of an event by the total number of all alternatives, provided that all cases are equally likely (equipossible). Therefore, the probability of throwing an "ace" with a "fair die" is 1/6 because there are six equally likely alternatives, of which an "ace" is one. The major problem with mathematical probability is that not all statistical situations are *a priori* deterministic. Thus, enter the relative frequency advocates.

The relative frequency approach also divides events into favorable and unfavorable cases, but it does so on the basis of actual observation of historical data rather than *a priori* judgment. Here the desirability or necessity of equipossible events vanishes. What is the probability that Jones Steel Company will get the next order from Smith? Because Smith historically has given Jones 20 percent of all their steel orders, the probability is 0.2. Unfortunately, there often is no sound basis for assuming that past frequencies will continue into the future, as there is for mathematical probability, and, also, many events *have* no historical frequencies. What is the probability of total nuclear war next year? What is the probability that Joseph Parker will get a Ph.D.? Now enter the subjectivists.

The subjectivists claim that if the statement "Nuclear war is more likely during crisis periods than during detente periods" has meaning, then ascribing probability numbers to phrases such as "more likely" might prove a useful enterprise. For example, a group of scientists in the 1970s estimated a probability of 0.5 that total nuclear war would break out before the year 2000. Obviously, a probability of that kind could not be estimated from either historical frequency or mathematical *a priori* reasoning. (Equally obvious is the fact that the phenomenon did not occur.) In the nuclear war example, the term *probability* stands for the subjective degree of belief or certitude concerning the occurrence of an event, rather than its historical frequency. Although initially viewed with horror by traditional statisticians, by the 1960s, the so-called Bayesian approach to probability had gained widespread respectability because of its admitted usefulness (Schlaifer 1959).

The preceding discussion of the theories of probability is meant to be suggestive rather than exhaustive. Each theory is useful, given a particular kind of problem. However, the notion of statistical explanation that follows presumes a mathematical or relative frequency interpretation of probability.

3.4.2 Statistical Explanation and the Social Sciences

Gustav Bergmann (1957) points out that statistical laws and statistical explanations gain in importance when our knowledge is imperfect because we do not know all of the variables that influence the phenomenon to be explained. Although the terms *perfect* and *imperfect* may have unfortunate connotations, the basic notion seems reasonable. May Brodbeck amplifies the view by succinctly stating the reasons why statistical explanation has such importance in the social sciences.

> Without some abstraction or selection from all the possibilities the world presents[,] there can be no science at all. By their very nature scientific laws describe only certain features of the kinds of things or events they hold to be connected. How much can safely be ignored depends upon the way things are. . . . To say, in consequence, that abstraction is all very well for the physical sciences but will not do for the study of man and society is the counsel of desperation; that is, no solution at all. The social scientist, striving to merit the honorific half of that title, settles for something less than perfection. . . . The use of the statistical concept [in the physical sciences] marks our ignorance of all the influencing factors, a failure in either completeness or closure or, usually, both. Similarly, the social scientist, deliberately selecting for study fewer factors than actually influence the behavior in which he is interested, shifts his goal from predicting individual events or behaviors to predicting a random variable, that is, to predicting the frequency with which this kind of behavior occurs in a large group of individuals possessing the circumscribed number of factors. This is the price. The reward, of course, is that instead of helplessly gazing in dumb wonder at the infinite complexity of man and society, he has knowledge, imperfect rather than perfect, to be sure, but knowledge not to be scorned nonetheless, of a probability distribution rather than of individual events. After all, while we might much prefer to know the exact conditions under which cancer develops in a particular person, it is far from valueless to know the factors which are statistically correlated to the frequency of its occurrence. (Brodbeck 1968, pp. 293–94)

It is important to differentiate clearly between the assertion that some explanations are statistical in form and the assertion that, because no scientific explanation is *known* to be true, all scientific explanations are only more or less *probable*. This would be confounding the nature of the structure of explanations with the quantity and quality of the evidence in support of those explanations. As Hempel points out, "The distinction between lawlike statements of strictly universal form and those of probabilistic form pertains, not to the evidential support of the explanation in question, but to the claims made by them: roughly speaking, the former attribute (truly or falsely) a certain characteristic to all members of a certain class; the latter to a specified proportion of its members" (1965a, p. 379).

A similar confusion sometimes surrounds the terms *deduction* and *induction* as they relate to statistical explanation. As we shall see in the following section, not all statistical explanations are inherently inductive (i.e., some are deductive). Likewise, not all inductive processes are inherently statistical.

3.4.3 Deductive-Statistical Explanation

In the deductive-statistical model (D-S) the explanandum *E* is deduced from the explanans in exactly the same fashion as in the D-N model; that is, the phenomenon to be explained is a logical consequence of the explanans. Therefore, if the explanans is true, then the explanandum must be true. If the explanandum is false, then the explanans is false. However, the explanandum may be true and the explanans false. The reader is advised to review the preceding three statements as many times as is necessary to see that they are logically true.

The D-S explanatory model can best be illustrated by an example. Assume the following definitions and statistical laws:

C_1 = Purchasing agent *J* sees no difference between the offerings of suppliers *X* and *Y*.
C_2 = Purchasing agent *J* desires to split his orders between suppliers *X* and *Y* approximately evenly.
C_3 = Purchasing agent *J* does not want his suppliers to become complacent.
C_4 = Purchasing agent *J* decides to flip a fair coin to decide which supplier gets each order.
C_5 = Successive tossings of the coin are "independent."
O_k = Supplier *k* gets an order.
O_k* = Supplier *k* gets two orders in succession.
SL_1 = $P(O_k, C_1 \cdot C_2 \cdot C_3 \cdot C_4) = 0.5$. The probability of *k* getting any order is a statistical law with probability 0.5, given C_1, C_2, C_3, and C_4.
SL_2 = $P(m + n) = P(m) \times P(n)$. This is a statistical law that if two events, *m* and *n*, are independent, then the probability of both events occurring $(m + n)$ equals the probability of *m* times the probability of *n*.

The schema for a deductive-statistical explanation can now be formed:

$$\left.\begin{array}{l} C_1, C_2, C_3, C_4, C_5 \\ SL_1, SL_2 \end{array}\right\} \text{Explanans } S$$

$$\overline{P(O_k{}^*, S) = 0.25} \quad \} \text{ Explanandum } E$$

The D-S model states that, given S (the characteristics C_1, C_2, C_3, C_4, and C_5 and the two statistical laws SL_1 and SL_2), the probability that supplier k will get two orders in succession is precisely 0.25 (that is, 0.5×0.5). Just as in the D-N model, the explanandum is a deductive, logical consequence of the explanans.

Note that the explanandum in the example is a statement in statistical form. This is important and no accident. *The D-S model can explain only other statistical laws; the only statements that are deductive, logical consequences of statistical laws are other statistical laws.* Section 3.4.4 will demonstrate that *all other* kinds of explananda are inductively inferred from the explanans and not strict logical consequences of the explanans.

The D-S model is reasonably consistent with our normative criteria for explanations in section 3.2. If the terms in the explanandum have empirical counterparts, the D-S model is intersubjectively confirmable by empirical testing. That is, we can observe real-world phenomena to determine whether the explanandum actually occurs. Many of the classical explanations in genetics are fundamentally of the D-S variety. Likewise, the decomposition of radioactive materials in physics (the "half-life" statistical laws) can be used to explain other statistical laws. Nevertheless, most statistical explanations in the social sciences are not D-S in nature. Most statistical explanations are *inductive*, not *deductive.*

3.4.4 Inductive-Statistical Explanation

Unlike with the D-S and D-N models, with the inductive-statistical (I-S) model, the phenomenon to be explained is *not* a logical consequence of (is not necessarily implied by) the explanans. In the I-S model the explanans only confers a certain likelihood that the phenomenon will occur.

To put I-S into schematic form, we need to add two items to the example in section 2.4.3:

$O_k{}^{**}$ = Supplier k gets at least one order in the next ten orders.

SL_3 = $P(O_k{}^{**}, C_1 \cdot C_2 \cdot C_3 \cdot C_4 \cdot C_5 \cdot SL_1 \cdot SL_2) = 1 - (0.5)^{10} = 0.999 \ldots$ The statistical law that the probability of supplier k getting at least one order in the next ten orders is extremely high, given $C_1 \ldots C_5$ and SL_1 and SL_2.

Following Hempel's (1965a, p. 383) procedure, the schema for the inductive-statistical explanation can now be formed:

$$\begin{array}{ll} C_1, C_2, C_3, C_4, C_5 & \\ & \} \text{ Explanans } S \\ SL_1, SL_2, SL_3, & \\ \hline\hline & \text{[it is very likely that]} \\ O_k^{**} & \text{Explanandum } E \end{array}$$

Given that the circumstances ($C_1 \ldots C_6$) and the appropriate statistical laws (SL_1, SL_2, SL_3) are true, O_k** is *very likely* to occur. Instead of a single line indicating that O_k** is deductively subsumed under the explanans, we show a double line indicating that the explanans only confers *inductive* support to O_k**. The conclusion E is not a logical consequence of the premises S in the sense that it is possible for E not to occur and the premises still be true. That is, the negation of E does not logically imply the negation of S.

An Evaluation of I-S Explanatory Model. Evaluating the I-S model via the criteria of section 3.2 reveals substantial conformity. For example, "Why were 51 percent of all babies born last year in General Hospital male?" This phenomenon would classically be explained by the use of an I-S model referring to certain statistical laws in genetics. The model also makes predictions of a sort, thus making the model testable, and, hence, intersubjectively confirmable. Finally, the explanans would lead one to *expect* the explanandum to occur.

Three problems sharply demarcate the fundamental differences between the D-N and I-S explanatory models. First, consider the consequences of testing a particular D-N model.

Test 1

D-N model K implies A.
A is false.

D-N model K is false.

Test 2

D-N model K implies B.
B is true.

D-N model K is supported.

Test 3

D-N model K implies B_1, B_2, B_3, B_4.
B_1, B_2, B_3, B_4 are true.

D-N model K is strongly supported.

Test 1 shows that *if* D-N model K does imply A (i.e., if our logic is correct) and if A is in fact false (i.e., if our measurements are accurate), then all or some part of model K is false. The D-N model is *falsifiable* in a very strong sense because the D-N model incorporates laws of strictly universal form. The laws in the D-N model state that every time certain circumstances prevail, then some phenomenon will occur. Therefore, if we observe the required circumstances, and if phenomenon A does *not* occur, there exist only three possibilities: (1) there has been an error in logic (model K does not really imply that A will occur); (2) there has been an error in measurement (the characteristics $C_1 \ldots C_k$ were not present, or phenomenon A occurred but the measurements did not detect it); or (3) all or part of model K is false. So, the researcher must check the logic, check the measurements, and then draw the appropriate conclusions.

Now examine Tests 2 and 3 of the D-N model. Note that it is never appropriate to conclude that a particular D-N explanation is true. Rather, repeated empirical testing can only inductively confer more or less empirical *support* or corroboration that a particular D-N explanation is true.

Now examine the consequences of testing a particular I-S model:

Test 1

I-S model J suggests A.
A is false.

I-S model J is not supported.

Test 2

I-S model J suggests B.
B is true.

I-S model J is supported.

Test 3

I-S model J suggests B_i, B_2, B_3, B_4.
B_1, B_2, B_3, B_4 are true.

I-S model J is strongly supported.

I-S model J suggests (makes more or less very likely) that if certain circumstances occur, then phenomenon A will occur. Empirical Test 1 shows that, in fact, A does *not* occur; that is, A is false. Once again, just as with the D-N model, the researcher should check both the logic and the measurements. However, in contrast with the D-N model, if the logic and measurements are found to be correct, the researcher cannot claim that I-S explanation J is false. Rather, because of the statistical nature of the laws in model J, the researcher can only conclude that the model is *not* supported. An example may serve to clarify the preceding observation.

Consider the I-S example previously discussed in this section that had the statistical law $SL_3 = P(O_k{**}, C_1 \ldots)$. The law suggests that $O_k{**}$ (getting at least one order in the next ten orders) is very likely to occur. Suppose we observe that O_k** does *not* occur; X fails to get a single order ten times in succession. The apologist for the I-S model might say, "Isn't that just my luck? Every time *I* test a model, the observation winds up in the tail of the distribution!" Or the researcher might ascribe the poor results to "noisy data." The preceding implies a fundamental difference between D-N and I-S explanations: I-S *models are fundamentally not falsifiable.* Further, if falsifiability is a reasonable normative criterion for explanatory models, then I-S models cannot be considered *explanatory.* This is exactly the conclusion of those holding what is here labeled the "strict deductivist" position.

Is there another sense of the word *falsifiable* that might admit I-S explanations? Yes, there is. Consider the following test:

Test 4

I-S model J suggests A_1, A_2, A_3, A_4.
A_1, A_2, A_3, A_4 are all false.

It is very likely that I-S model J is false.

Test 4 shows that a whole series of observations have failed to support I-S model J. This might be considered very strong evidence that model J is probably false and could be called the *weak falsifiability criterion.* In the previous example, if X loses forty orders in a row, this is strong evidence that the underlying statistical law in model J is false.

If strict falsifiability is demanded, then I-S models cannot be deemed satisfactory explanations. If a weak falsifiability criterion suffices, then I-S models should be considered acceptable explanations. Is the weak falsifiability criterion justified? I believe the answer is yes. Even Hempel (1965a), the strict deductivist, finally moved toward the acceptance of statistical explanations as explanatory. If weak falsifiability were rejected, then almost all explanations in marketing and other social sciences would also have to be rejected. As will be shown in Chapter 6, almost all the laws (hence, all the explanations) in the social sciences are basically statistical in nature.

The second problem of the I-S model concerns how to ascertain the amount of inductive support that the premises confer upon the conclusion; for example, in Test 4, precisely what do we mean by the phrase "it is very likely that?" What is needed is a system of *inductive logic* to quantify the amount of inductive support, and this has been an intractable problem for centuries. Carnap's (1962) system of inductive logic suggests that for simple I-S models with only one statistical law, the likelihood of (degree of inductive support for) the occurrence of an event is the statistical probability of the event. Therefore, because SL_1 and SL_2 combine to form SL_3 in the previous example, the structure would be:

$$\frac{\begin{array}{l} C_1, C_2, C_3, C_4, C_5 \\ SL_3 \end{array}}{O_k^{**}} \quad [r = 0.999\ldots]$$

Unfortunately, Carnap's system has not been extended to more complicated statistical systems with multiple statistical laws. *The degree of inductive support that a series of statistical laws confers upon the occurrence of an event remains unresolved except where all the laws can be compressed into a single law.*

The third problem with the I-S model concerns its ambiguity (Hempel 1965a, p. 394). Consider the following I-S argument:

C_1 = Jones is a Scottish-American.
C_2 = Jones drinks alcoholic beverages.
SL_1 = 90 percent of all Scottish-American drinkers drink Scotch.
════════════════════ [very likely]
Jones drinks Scotch.

However, suppose the following premises are also true:

C_3 = Jones is a Southerner.
SL_2 = 90 percent of all Southerners who drink do *not* drink Scotch.
════════════════════ [very likely]
Jones does not drink Scotch.

The preceding two arguments (whose premises we assume to be true only for expository purposes) yield contradictory conclusions. It is psychologically uncomfortable to note that *ex post* we can always find a model consistent with the observation. If Jones is observed drinking Scotch, the I-S model builder says, "Aha, he drinks Scotch because he is a Scottish-American." And if Jones is observed drinking bourbon, the I-S model builder says, "Indeed, as I always said, very few Southerners drink Scotch."

Carnap (1950, p. 211) suggests resolving the ambiguity problem with *the requirement of total evidence*: "In the application of inductive logic to a given knowledge situation, the total evidence available must be taken as a basis for determining the degree of confirmation." Similarly, Hempel (1968) proposes *the requirement of maximal specificity*: "In formulating or appraising an I-S explanation, we should take into account all the information . . . which is of potential explanatory relevance to the explanandum event" (1968, p. 118). (See Cooke [1981] for an evaluation of this criterion.) The criterion implies that an acceptable statistical explanation of why Jones drinks Scotch must be based on a statistical law using as a reference class the most narrowly defined class that our total evidence suggests as relevant. In this case we need a statistical law concerning the proportion of Scottish-American Southerners who drink Scotch. Using any other reference class may yield poor results.

3.5 ARE LOGICAL EMPIRICIST MODELS OF EXPLANATION ADEQUATE?

Suppe (1977) has observed that the logical empiricist treatment of science has been subject to significant and sustained attack. In particular, the "received view" concerning the nature of scientific theories and explanations has been assaulted, and Suppe (1977, p. 619) concludes that "the last vestiges of positivistic philosophy of science are disappearing from the philosophical landscape." Therefore, he proposed, "Positivism truly belongs to the history of the philosophy of science, and its influence is that of a movement historically important in shaping the landscape of a much-changed philosophy of science" (Suppe 1977, p. 632). The purpose here is to review and evaluate the attacks on the logical empiricist models of explanation. Both the deductive-nomological model and the inductive-statistical model will be examined.

3.5.1 Is the D-N Model Dead?

Attacks on the D-N model have generally been prefaced by showing that some "explanation" may "fit" the D-N model and yet be regarded as unsatisfactory by most people. A well-known illustration is the "flagpole" explanation proposed by Bromberger (1966) and discussed by Suppe:

> Using geometric optics, we can form a law of coexistence which correlates the height of a flagpole, the angle of the sun to the horizon, and the length of the shadow cast by the flagpole. Using this law and initial conditions about the height of the flagpole and the sun's angle, we can explain the length of the shadow in accordance with the D-N model. However, if we take our initial conditions as being the length of the shadow and the sun's angle, using the law the D-N model allows us to (causally!) explain the height of the flagpole. But only the former case is a genuine explanation, the latter being spurious; since the D-N model sanctions both as genuine, the D-N model is defective. (Suppe 1977, p. 621)

Bromberger (1966) concludes that only explanations that employ causal laws can be satisfactory. Similarly, Jobe (1976) uses examples such as Ohm's law and concludes that satisfactory D-N explanations must use "genuine laws of nature." Finally, Brody (1972, p. 20) uses the following illustrations (adapted from Aristotle):

(A) a. The planets do not twinkle.
b. All objects which do not twinkle are near the Earth.
c. Therefore, the planets are near the Earth.

(B) a. The planets are near the Earth.
b. All objects near the Earth do not twinkle.
c. Therefore, the planets do not twinkle.

Brody proposes that both (A) and (B) are "acceptable" D-N explanations but that only (B) *should* be considered as explanatory. He concludes that "a deductive-nomological explanation of a particular event is a satisfactory explanation of that event when, besides meeting Hempel's requirements, its explanans essentially contains a description of the cause of the event described in the explanandum" (Brody 1972, p. 23).

The preceding attacks are persuasive. To suggest that "lack of twinkling" *explains* the distance of the planets from the Earth clearly will not do, just as the length of women's hemlines will not *explain* stock market purchases. In other words, as will be shown in section 4.1, predictive adequacy is not sufficient for explanatory adequacy.

The position here is that any *satisfactory* explanation must contain in its explanans some mechanisms or laws or lawlike generalizations that are *purportedly* causal (see section 4.2 for more on causality). This position coincides with the views of advocates of *scientific realism*, the closest thing today to a "school" to supersede logical empiricism. For example, the realists Keat and Urry (1975, p. 13) point out that the D-N model fails "to distinguish between providing the grounds for expecting an event will occur, and explaining *why* it will occur." Nevertheless, scientific realism should be viewed less as a *replacement* for logical empiricism and more as the next most reasonable step for philosophy of science, because both movements share substantial common ground:

> Both share a general conception of science as an objective, rational enquiry which aims at true explanatory and predictive knowledge of an external reality. . . . First, the idea that scientific theories must be objectively assessed by reference to empirical evidence. This evidence is such that all scientists who are competent, honest, and lacking in perceptual deficiencies can agree upon it, though not necessarily with total certainty. Second, there is the idea that there are "objects," in the broadest sense of the term, which exist independently of our beliefs and theories about them. . . . This means a rejection of the view that scientific theories determine that reality, rather than make genuine discoveries about it. . . . Both hold that there are general standards of scientificity, of what counts as an adequate explanation, of what it is that we must try to achieve by scientific theories, of the manner in which empirical evidence should be used to assess their truth or falsity, and so on. Whilst disagreeing about what these standards are, both believe that they exist. . . . They are external and universal standards, independent of particular, substantive theories and explana-

> tions, and applicable to all periods in the historical development of science. (Keat and Urry 1975, p. 44)

Curiously, Hempel himself, in his early work on the D-N model, ascribed a role for causal mechanisms (1965c, p. 250). However, his later works dropped the requirement (1965a, pp. 351–54). Dropping any reference to causal mechanisms from the D-N model resulted from the desire of the logical positivists and their successors, the logical empiricists, to expunge all metaphysical concepts from their analyses. And, because causality can never be *conclusively* verified, it was considered too metaphysical. What the logical empiricists never completely realized (or never could bring themselves to admit) is that if the *conclusive verification* criterion were applied to all concepts in science, the domain of scientific inquiry would be dangerously close to an empty set!

Is the D-N model dead? Not at all. The basic structure of the model still stands. The attack discussed in this section simply reveals that the model is not restrictive enough. The D-N model should be modified to require the specific inclusion of purportedly causal mechanisms, entities with causal powers, or causal laws in the explanans.

3.5.2 Is the I-S Model Dead?

Leading the charge against the I-S model have been Salmon (1971), Jeffrey (1966), and Greeno (1966). Recall that both the D-N and I-S models of explanations are, fundamentally, *arguments.* That is, premises (the explanans) and a conclusion (the explanandum) are joined by a "therefore." With the D-N model the *premises* deductively imply or entail the conclusion. With the I-S model the premises suggest the conclusion with "high probability." Salmon, Jeffrey, and Greeno deny that explanations are arguments, leading Suppe (1977, p. 623) to conclude that "one will have to give up the requirement that statistical explanations are 'correct' arguments. . . . The important point is that Hempel's I-S model is defective, hence by implication so is his D-N model" (Suppe 1977, p. 623).

If explanations are not arguments, what are they? Salmon (1971) proposes the "statistical relevance" (S-R) model of explanations. By this account, an explanation "is an assembly of facts statistically relevant to the explanandum regardless of the degree of probability that results" (Suppe 1977, p. 623). Note that the S-R model violates the "high probability" requirement of the I-S model.

Writers cite numerous examples of satisfactory explanations that do not accord a high probability to the explanandum. Three examples can illustrate the procedure: (1) Half-life laws can be used to explain the emission of an electron from a radioactive substance where the probability of the electron emission at the time is very low. (2) The fact that a person gets lung cancer is often explained by noting that the person smokes two packs of cigarettes per day, even though only a small percentage of cigarette smokers contract cancer. (3) Finally, an injection of penicillin may legitimately be thought to explain why a patient gets a rash even though only a few patients have this reaction. These kinds of examples have led writers to propose that "it is not the high probability conferred on the explanandum which makes an account explanatory, but rather the specification of a so far unnoticed factor which changes this probability to a value which differs from the value ascribed to it on the basis of the information that was available before the explanation had been given" (Kruger 1976, p. 131).

However, the S-R model does not propose that *any* assembly of facts will qualify as explanatory, only an assembly of those facts that are *relevant*; and most analyses of the model have been directed at separating the "relevant" from the "irrelevant." Criteria such as "homogeneous reference classes" and "screening-off relations" have been proposed to help solve the problem of separating "causal" relevance relations from "merely" statistical relevance relations. We shall not evaluate these issues here. Interested readers should consult Shrader (1977) and Meixner (1979) for reviews. The purpose here is to evaluate the following line of reasoning implied by advocates of the S-R model:

1. S-R explanations are adequate.
2. S-R explanations are *not* arguments.
3. I-S explanations are arguments.
4. Therefore, I-S explanations and, by implication, D-N explanations are defective.

To evaluate whether S-R explanations are adequate, consider the S-R explanation "cigarette smoking causes lung cancer in a person." Suppose scientists someday discover a "cancer gene" such that 50 percent of all the people who have this gene will ultimately contract cancer. Suppose further research yields the finding that "98 percent of all people who smoke two packs of cigarettes daily *and* have the cancer gene will ultimately develop lung cancer." Note that the "98 percent" statistical generalization enables one to *explain* the incidence of lung cancer by way of an I-S explanation, because 98 percent would provide "high probability."

The preceding example enables us to draw several conclusions. First, *if* the original cigarette S-R explanation is "adequate," then the 98 percent I-S explanation *must* be adequate, because the 98 percent I-S explanation contains all the information of the S-R explanation and *more*. Further, if adequacy is considered a relative concept, then no one would dispute that the 98 percent I-S explanation is *better than* the S-R explanation. (See Watkins [1984], pp. 239–401 for more.)

Second, the fact that the 98 percent I-S explanation is *better* than the S-R explanation suggests that the goal of all scientists employing S-R explanations should be to upgrade these explanations to I-S types. Third, if the goal of scientists should be to upgrade S-R explanations (which are not arguments) to I-S types (which are all arguments), one cannot claim that I-S explanations are "defective" because they are arguments. *If anything, S-R explanations are defective because they are not correct arguments.*

Are S-R explanations adequate? If "adequate" is construed as "useful," then the answer must be yes. It is certainly useful to know that although only a small percentage of smokers will contract lung cancer, heavy smokers are five to ten times more likely to develop lung cancer than are nonsmokers. However, as a goal for developing explanations of phenomena, S-R explanations are *inadequate* because they should be viewed as intermediate explanations directed toward the development of I-S explanations or D-N explanations. The original "cigarette" S-R explanation was "adequate" only because it was the best that science could provide at the time. This is as it should be, because all explanations must be evaluated given our knowledge base at a point in time (Gardenfors 1980).

In an analysis similar to the one here, Strevens (2000) evaluates the view that the size of a probability makes no difference to the quality of a probabilistic explanation and Salmon's (1984, p. 388) statement that any view to the contrary is an "anachronistic carryover" from Laplacean determination. Using explanatory practices in statistical mechanics, Strevens concludes that, "although low probabilities may have some explanatory power, the explanatory power of high probabilities is much greater" (p. 367). Indeed, although "hard core" critics of logical empiricism continue to cite Salmon's work as evidence of the inadequacies of the D-N and I-S models, Salmon's most recent work has, essentially, abandoned the S-R model. He has adopted—as does this work—a realist view of scientific explanation. Salmon writes:

> It seemed obvious at the time [of writing the 1971 book] that statistical relevance relations had some sort of explanatory power in and of themselves. As I have said repeatedly throughout this [1984] book, that view seems utterly mistaken. . . . Their fundamental import lies in the fact . . . that they constitute evidence for causal relations. (Salmon 1984, pp. 191–92)

In conclusion, the logical empiricist models of explanation remain the most viable models available for explaining phenomena. This is not to say that there are no unresolved issues with respect to the models. The D-N model should be made *more* restrictive by requiring causal mechanisms, entities with causal powers, or causal laws in the explanans. The I-S model should be made *less* restrictive by relaxing the "high-probability" requirement and recognizing that sometimes the best that science can provide at a point in time is an "explanation" of the S-R variety. Nevertheless, these modifications neither suggest that the basic logical empiricist models of explanation are "fundamentally defective" nor that the S-R model should be the goal of science, as Salmon himself now admits.

3.6 THE PATTERN MODEL

The pattern model (P-M) purportedly constitutes a fifth distinctive kind of explanation (in addition to the D-N, D-S, I-S, and S-R models). Abraham Kaplan (1964), an advocate of the pattern model, views P-M explanations as extremely important in the methodology of the behavioral sciences. Kaplan defines and discusses the pattern model:

> Very roughly, [in the pattern model] we know the reason for something when we can fit it into a known pattern . . . something is explained when it is so related to a set of other elements that together they constitute a unified system. We understand something by identifying it as a specific part in an organized whole . . . in the pattern model we explain by instituting or discovering relations . . . These relations may be of various different sorts: causal, purposive, mathematical, and perhaps other basic types, as well as various combinations and derivatives of these. The particular relations that hold constitute a pattern, and an element is explained by being shown to occupy the place that it does occupy in the pattern. . . .
>
> The perception that everything is just where it should be to complete the pattern is what gives us the intellectual satisfaction, the sense of closure, all the more satisfying because it was preceded by the tensions of ambiguity. (Kaplan 1964, pp. 332–35)

Is the P-M explanatory? Does it meet the normative criteria set forth in section 3.2? Certainly, many so-called explanations in the behavioral sciences and marketing simply show how the phenomenon fits into a distinctive pattern; thus, pragmatism favors the pattern model. Also, many of the concepts employed in pattern explanations have empirical content; that is, their terms have empirical referents. As we shall see, however, the criterion of *intersubjective confirmability* poses problems for P-M explanations. The potential for the intersubjective confirmability of pattern models can be best explored by analyzing an example of a P-M explanation by Kaplan:

> According to the pattern model, then, something is explained when it is so related to a set of other elements that together they constitute a unified system. We understand something by identifying it as a specific part in an organized whole. There is a figure consisting of a long vertical straight line with a short one branching upwards

> from it near the top, and a short curved line joining it on the same side near the bottom; the figure is meaningless until it is explained as representing a soldier with fixed bayonet, accompanied by his dog, disappearing around the corner of a building (the curved line is the dog's tail). We understand the figure by being brought to see the whole picture, of which what is to be explained is only a part. (Kaplan 1964, p. 333)

Is the preceding P-M explanation intersubjectively certifiable? To analyze it, let's designate the soldier-with-dog P-M explanation as *J*. Consider now a second P-M explanation, *K*, for the figure in Kaplan's example. Pattern model *K* proposes that the figure actually is a dead tree with small branches at the top and the bottom. Which explanation is correct? If two subjects perceive different patterns that encompass the same phenomenon, what objective criteria can be used to confirm one pattern over the other? Kaplan (1964) mentions "intellectual satisfaction" as a criterion. But intellectual satisfaction is an irretrievably individual phenomenon. Model *K* may be more intellectually satisfying to me, whereas model *J* may be more intellectually satisfying to you. A criterion such as familiarity suffers from the same weakness. A familiar pattern to a Western European might be totally unfamiliar to an East Asian.

The intersubjective confirmability criterion for the D-N, D-S, and I-S models is overcome via empirical testing. All of these models employ laws that make predictions that are susceptible to testing. Choosing between rival explanatory constructions can be accomplished by examining multiple tests of the models where the rival constructions predict different outcomes. At present, there are no similar "tests" for pattern models. *Therefore, the pattern model fails the criterion of intersubjective confirmability and cannot be considered as having explanatory power.*

It can be shown that all of the examples discussed by Kaplan either (1) fail the intersubjective confirmability criterion or (2) are actually D-N explanations in disguise. Kaplan discusses a P-M to explain thunder: "[A] bolt of lightning heats the air through which it passes, which then expands, disturbing the air around it and thus setting up sound waves" (1964, p. 334). This particular pattern model has explanatory power *only* because it presumes some lawlike relationships: (1) lightning heats air; (2) heated air expands; (3) expanding air will disturb surrounding air; and (4) disturbed air creates sound waves. That D-N explanations will have "patterns" is undoubtedly true, but that *patterns alone* have explanatory power is an entirely different assertion.

The true value of pattern models may lie, not in the context of justification (with the notion of explanation), but rather, in the context of discovery. Because explanatory schemata frequently have distinctive patterns and because these patterns may be consistent across different kinds of phenomena, the theorist searching for tentative explanations might start by first looking for a familiar pattern. Kaplan (1964, p. 332) himself admits that "the pattern model may more easily fit explanations in early states of inquiry."

3.7 FUNCTIONALIST EXPLANATION

No one even remotely familiar with the social sciences can avoid being exposed to functionalism, and the advocates of functionalism as a distinct methodology are legion (Radcliffe-Brown 1952; Malinowski 1944; Merton 1938; Parsons 1949; Stinchcombe 1968). Some students of marketing, notably the late Wroe Alderson (1957; 1965), have also taken up the functionalist banner. Is functionalist explanation fundamentally different from other forms of explanation? First, we should note that functionalism belongs in the general class of philosophical inquiry known as *teleology* (literally, the study of purposes). No one would deny that much animal and human behavior is purposive, leading analysts such as Taylor (1967), Grene (1976), and Wright (1977) to conclude that the explanation of human behavior may be irreducibly teleological. Others, such as Utz (1977) and Clark (1979), propose that all purportedly teleological explanations can be recast as D-N or I-S explanations (as in section 3.7.2). The most prominent of the teleologically oriented writers have been the functionalists.

Despite the popularity of functionalism, there are tremendous logical difficulties with functionalism and functional explanation. First, despite all the writings on functionalist methodology, the meanings of the terms *function*, *functional*, and *functional explanation* lack both specificity and universal consensus, even among advocates of functionalism. Before analyzing the basic logic of functional explanations, we must first explore the different usages of the term *function*.

3.7.1 Uses of the Terms *Function* and *Functional Explanation*

Ernest Nagel (1961, p. 522) suggests that functionalists use the term *function* in at least six different ways. These different usages alone account for substantial confusion in functionalist literature, and four of them seem particularly appropriate for our analysis.

1. The first use of the term *function* is when it simply signifies the dependence or interdependence between variables; that is, X is a function of Y. For example, "the incidence of purchase of major brand gasoline is a function of the generalized self-confidence of the subjects." However, such lawlike locutions are precisely the kinds of statements that are found in nonfunctionalist approaches. Hence, if

the entire functionalist procedure were so construed, then functionalism could not be considered a distinctive mode of inquiry. That is, functionalist explanations would not be different from other kinds of explanations.

2. Biologists and others use the term function to refer to certain organic processes ("vital functions") such as reproduction and respiration that are considered indispensable for the continued life of the organism or the maintenance of the species. Similarly, in anthropology, Malinowski asserts that "in every type of civilization, every custom, material object, idea, and belief fulfills some vital function" (1936, p. 132). Thus, functionalists sometimes use the term *function* as synonymous with "indispensable role."
3. A third use of the term signifies some generally recognized use or utility of a thing. "The function of a salesperson's call report is to transmit intelligence," or "the function of advertising is to create sales." However, if all uses of the term *function* were confined to relatively simple assertions about the intended use of certain phenomena, then functional explanations would be weak, if not impotent.
4. Finally, the term *function* often signifies the contribution that an item makes or can make toward the maintenance of some stated characteristic or condition in a given system to which the item is assumed to belong. *Thus, functional analysis seeks to understand a behavior pattern or a sociocultural institution by determining the role it plays in keeping the given system in proper working order or maintaining it as a going concern* (Hempel 1959, p. 277). If functionalism is to lay claim to being a distinct method of inquiry, it will do so on the basis of this final interpretation of function.

This last view of functions and functional explanation (which we shall adopt and analyze) seems reasonably consistent with Wroe Alderson:

> Functionalism is that approach to science which begins by identifying some system of action, and then tries to determine how and why it works as it does. Functionalism stresses the whole system and undertakes to interpret the parts in terms of how they serve the system. Some writers who are actually advocates of functionalism prefer to speak of the holistic approach because of emphasis on the system as a whole. (1957, p. 16)

Similarly, Radcliffe-Brown discusses his version of functionalism:

> [In] social life, if we examine such a community as an African or Australian tribe, we can recognize the existence of a social structure. Individual human beings, the

> essential units in this instance, are connected by a definite set of social relations into an integrated whole. The continuity of the social structure, like that of an organic structure, is not destroyed by changes in the units. Individuals may leave the society, by death or otherwise; others may enter it. The continuity of structure is maintained by the process of social life, which consists of the activities and interactions of the individual human beings and of the organized groups into which they are united. The social life of the community is here defined as the *functioning* of the social structure. The *function* of any recurrent activity, such as the punishment of a crime, or a funeral ceremony, is the part it plays in the social life as a whole and therefore the contribution it makes to the maintenance of the structural continuity. (1952, p. 179)

Last, Malinowski presents his view of functionalism:

> [Functionalism] aims at the explanation of anthropological facts at all levels of development by their function, by the part which they play within the integral system of culture, by the manner in which they are related to each other within the system, and by the manner in which this system is related to the physical surroundings. . . . The functional view of culture insists therefore upon the principle that in every type of civilization, every custom, material object, idea, and belief fulfills some vital function, has some task to accomplish, represents an indispensable part within a working whole. (1936, p. 132)

Although we shall adopt the fourth interpretation of the term *function* for analytical purposes, a caveat is warranted. A proper evaluation of any author's functionalist theoretical construction requires the reader to consider carefully how the author uses the term *function.* Not only do different authors use the term differently, but also individual authors (perhaps unknowingly) slip back and forth in their usage of the term. This can create considerable problems for anyone attempting to analyze functionalist explanations.

3.7.2 Preliminary Problems of Functional Explanation

Before we attempt a formal analysis of functional explanation, two minor issues need resolving.[2] One logical requirement for *causal* explanations (see Chapter 4 for a discussion of causality) is temporal sequentiality: If *A* is supposed to cause *B*, then *A* must occur before *B* in time. Functionalist explanations, like all teleological explanations, make liberal use of the concepts "goals" and "purposes." Because goals and purposes refer to *future* events, does this not ascribe causal efficacy to future events? That is, does this not mean that future phenomena can cause present phenomena? For example, can the goal of an increased market share (a future event) *cause* a firm to increase advertising effort and have explanatory power? Is this not contradictory? The reader will note that a simple resolution to this apparent contradiction lies in the manner of phrasing. Future events do not cause or explain present actions; the *desire* for a future event may cause or explain present actions. Here, the desire temporally precedes the behavior that one seeks to explain, and the apparent contradiction dissolves.

A similar teleological problem confronts the user of explanations of this sort: "The chameleon has the ability to change its skin color in order to blend in with its varying backgrounds, thus protecting it from natural enemies." The phrase "in order to" signifies a teleological emphasis in the explanation. However, using Darwinian theory, such covertly teleological explanations can be entirely avoided. A skeletal outline of such an explanation might include statements along these lines: (1) An early mutant lizard had the ability to change colors. (2) This ability increased the likelihood of its survival and the survival of those of its progeny that also carried the mutant gene. (3) Over time, the proportion of the species carrying the mutant gene rose due to "survival of the fittest." Note that no reference to purposive or teleological factors is required. Most such covertly teleological explanations can be recast in other, nonteleological, forms. Similarly, some purportedly functionalist explanations can also be recast. These two minor problems resolved, we are now in a position to explore the formal logic of functional explanation.

3.7.3 The Logic of Functional Explanation

The best way to evaluate the logic of functional explanation is to (1) present a classical functional explanation in the fourth sense of the term *function*, (2) dissect the explanation so as to lay bare its logical structure, and (3) evaluate that structure. Malinowski's well-known explanation of the function of mourning in primitive cultures provides just such a typical illustration:

> The ritual despair, the obsequies, the acts of mourning, express the emotion of the bereaved and the loss of the whole group. They endorse and they duplicate the natural feelings of the survivors; they create a social event out of a natural fact. Yet, though in the acts of mourning, in the mimic despair of wailing, in the treatment of the corpse and in its disposal, nothing ulterior is achieved, these acts fulfill an important function and possess a considerable value for primitive culture.
>
> What is this function? The death of a man or a woman in a primitive group, consisting of a limited number of individuals, is an event of no mean importance. The nearest relatives and friends are disturbed to the depth of their emotional life. A small community bereft of a member, especially if he be important, is severely mutilated. The whole event breaks the normal course of life and shakes the moral foundations of society. The strong tendency on which we have insisted in the above description: to give way to fear and horror, to abandon the corpse, to run away from the village, to destroy all the belongings of the dead one—all these impulses exist, and if given way to would be extremely dangerous, disintegrating the group, destroying the material foundations of primitive culture. Death in a primitive society is, therefore, much more than the removal of a member. By setting in motion one part of the deep forces of the instinct of self-motivation, it threatens the very cohe-

> sion and solidarity of the group, and upon this depends the organization of that society, its tradition, and finally the whole culture. For if primitive man yielded always to the disintegrating impulses of his reaction to death, the continuity of tradition and the existence of material civilization would be made impossible. (Malinowski 1954, p. 52)

What is the basic structure of the preceding functional explanation? Basically, the structure is as follows:

Functional Model 1

1. At some time *t*, a system *s* (a primitive society) is in state *k* (proper working order).
2. The class of systems *S* (primitive societies) of which *s* is a member must have condition *n* (group cohesiveness and solidarity) in order to maintain state *k* (proper working order).
3. Phenomenon *j* (death of a member) has negative effects on condition *n* (group cohesiveness and solidarity).
4. If characteristic *c* (mourning and other acts of bereavement) were present in system *s* at time *t*, then *c* would counter the effect of *j* and condition *n* would be satisfied.
5. Therefore, statements 1 through 4 explain why characteristic *c* is present in system *s* at time *t*.

Several observations on the morphology (structure) of Functional Model 1 (FM1) are apparent. First, FM1 shows that functional explanations belong to a class of explanations called *homeostatic* or *equilibrating*. FM1 suggests that there are certain preferred states in the system (e.g., survival) and that if the existence of these preferred states is threatened (e.g., by a death), the system will adopt certain mechanisms to return to these preferred states, Thus, FM1 is an equilibrating model of explanation.

Second, the FM1 explanatory structure incorporates certain laws or lawlike statements. Note the verb "must have" in statement 2, the phrase "has negative effects on" in statement 3, and the verb "would counter" in statement 4. All of these statements can be construed as having essentially lawlike form (see Chapter 5). Statement 5, the explanandum, is thus derived from statements 1 through 4 (the explanans) in precisely the same way as in the D-N, D-S, and I-S explanatory models. *Therefore, FM1 is neither a fundamentally different kind of explanation nor a different methodology. To the extent that it is an explanation at all (see next paragraph), FM1 is a special case of deductive-nomological or statistical explanation where certain of the lawlike statements involve homeostatic mechanisms.*

Third, as Hempel (1959) has observed, the explanandum (statement 5) in FM1 is not a logical consequence of the explanans (statements 1 through 4). Statement 4 essentially provides that *if c* were present, then condition *n* would be satisfied; that is, *c* is sufficient for *n*. However, what is required is a statement of the following variety: *if n* is to be satisfied, then *c* must be present; that is, *c* must be necessary or indispensable for *n*. Logicians would refer to this logical error as affirming the consequent (Salmon 1963, p. 27). This fallacy can be illustrated by the following incorrect syllogism:

All people are mortal.
Fido is mortal.

Fido is a person.

Note that the preceding syllogism and FM1 have the same structure. *Therefore, the host of functional explanations that have the basic structure of FM1 are logically false—the premises do not imply the conclusion.*

Because there are almost no circumstances where a characteristic *c* is functionally indispensable for condition *n*, can a form of functional explanation by salvaged? Is it possible to reconstruct a functional model that both captures the essence of functionalism, and, at the same time, is logically correct? Functional Model 2 (FM2) attempts to do just that. Note that although statements 1 through 3 are identical to those of FM1, statements 4 and 5 are different.

Functional Model 2

1. At some time *t*, a system *s* (a primitive society) is in state *k* (proper working order).
2. The class of systems *S* (primitive societies) of which *s* is a member must have condition *n* (group cohesiveness and solidarity) in order to maintain state *k* (proper working order).
3. Phenomenon *j* (death of a member) has negative effects on condition *n* (group cohesiveness and solidarity).
4. Set *C* is the set of all sufficient items that, if any one were present in the system *s*, would counter phenomenon *j* and maintain condition *n* and thus system state *k*.
5. Therefore, statements 1 through 4 explain why some item in set *C* will be in system *s* at time *t*.

A functional explanation such as FM2 can now predict only that some item in the set *C* will occur. When sociologists Merton (1968, p. 106) and Parsons

(1949, p. 58) discuss *functional equivalents*, they are in our terms exploring the nature of set *C*. Thus salvaged, constructing sound functionalist explanations, though such constructions constitute valuable contributions to science, is no small task. The job of identifying the complete set of functional alternatives and then tying the set into functionalist lawlike generalizations is seldom achieved. All too often, functional explanations of phenomena degenerate into one or more of the following: (1) *ad hoc ex post* rationalizations of why some phenomenon has occurred, (2) pseudo-explanations that are empirically empty, (3) logically fallacious explanations, or (4) hopelessly circular explanations, such as:

(a) Why does *X* do *Y*?
(b) Because *X* has goal *J*, and
(c) *Y* leads to the satisfaction of goal *J*.
(d) Therefore, *X* does *Y*.
(e) How do you know *X* has goal *J*?
(f) Because *X* does *Y*!

These observations have led many analysts of functionalism to believe that the major importance of functionalism lies not in the context of justification but in the context of discovery (Kaplan 1964, p. 365; Rudner 1966, p. 109; Hempel 1959).

3.7.4 Functionalism in the Context of Discovery

The claim that functionalism has a unique *methodology* implies that the *logical apparatus* for confirming or falsifying functional explanations, theories, and laws is distinct from the logical apparatus used in other branches of scientific inquiry. As discussed in Chapter 1, the methodology (as contrasted with the techniques) of a discipline concerns the very bases or criteria on which to test the truth content of the discipline's claims about knowledge. On the other hand, the assertion that the importance of functionalism for the social sciences lies primarily in the context of discovery implies that functionalism may have heuristic value to scholars searching for fundamental relationships among social phenomena. Presumably, Robert Bartels was suggesting that marketers adopt a functionalist "set" in his "theory of social initiative."

> Different societies attain similar ends (in relative measure) by different means. The level of technology, the values of the group or nation, even the relative importance attached to economic, intellectual, religious, or leisure activity are factors which must be considered in interpreting the marketing process and institution of a people. *Ecological orientation, in other words, is the starting point in marketing analysis.* (Bartels 1968, p. 32, italics added)

Under what circumstances might adopting a functionalist perspective be desirable for a researcher? Arthur Stinchcombe (1968, p. 80) has proposed these criteria, "Whenever we find *uniformity of the consequences* of action but *great variety of the behavior causing those consequences*, a functional explanation in which the consequences serve as causes is suggested." He (1968, p. 82) has further proposed several situations in which the researcher should consider functional explanations: (1) If, when subjects experience increased difficulty in achieving their goals, they increase their activity, functional explanations are indicated. (2) If a variety of explanations or purposes, or inadequate and inconsistent purposes, are offered by people behaving to explain their behavior, a functional explanation is indicated. (3) If it is known that some causal process is operating that selects patterns of behavior according to their consequences, a functional explanation is indicated. That is, when we know that processes are selecting out certain functional behavior, it is strategic to look for those functions in any bit of behavior that we find in that selective context.

In the context of discovery, the value of functionalism is primarily an empirical question: Is it likely that adopting a particular perspective or mode of exploration will lead to the discovery of new knowledge? The study of discovery, though always viewed as extraordinarily important for understanding science, has historically been viewed as lying in the domain of the psychology or sociology of science rather than in the domain of the philosophy of science. If we are to evaluate the scientific worth of functionalism on the basis of the quantity and quality of scientific knowledge that a functionalist "set" generates, then the jury on functionalism is still out in both marketing and the other social sciences. As Mahner and Bunge put it:

> To conclude, social functionalism can be barren or fruitful. It will be barren if it only restates Doctor Pangloss's thesis that we live in the best of all possible worlds: that in which everyone maximizes his or her expected utilities. But it will be fruitful if it analyzes social systems and attempts to discover what makes them tick—that is, their mechanisms. (Mahner and Bunge 2001, p. 90)

3.8 SUMMARY AND CONCLUSIONS

Explanations play a crucial role in scientific inquiry. A major task of science is to explain the phenomena that constitute its basic subject matter. In general, explanations are scientific answers to *why* questions. Any proposed explanation of a phenomenon must at least (1) show that somehow the phenomenon was expected to occur, (2) be intersubjectively certifiable, and (3) have empirical content. Generalized procedures or structures that purport to show how phenomena can be explained are called explanatory models. Of the six purportedly explanatory models that have been examined, only the deductive-nomological (D-N), deductive-statistical (D-S), and inductive-statistical (I-S) models meet the criteria for satisfactory explanations. All three kinds of explanations, it should be noted, should contain causal mechanisms, entities with causal powers, or causal laws in their explanans. The pattern model (P-M) fails the intersubjectively certifiable criterion, and functionalist explanations, to the extent that they are satisfactory explanations at all, are simply special cases of deductive-nomological explanations or statistical explanations. The greatest value of functionalism probably lies in the context of discovery rather than justification.

QUESTIONS FOR ANALYSIS AND DISCUSSION

1. Zaltman et al. (1973)—drawing upon Harvey (1969)—suggest two alternative routes to scientific explanation—one by Bacon and one by Harvey. The "Baconian" route has the following order: (1) perceptual experiences; (2) unordered facts; (3) definition, classification, measurement; (4) ordered facts; (5) inductive generalizations; (6) laws and theory construction; and (7) explanation.

   The "Harvey" route has this order: (1) perceptual experiences; (2) image of real-world structure; (3) *a priori* model; (4) hypotheses; (5) experimental design; (6) data; (7) verification procedures; (8) laws and theory construction; and (9) explanation. Both (7) and (8) feed back into (2).

   Are these two different *models* of explanation? What are the essential differences between these models? Do the models fall within the scope of the logic of justification or the logic of discovery? Which model is superior? Why?
2. Find three other definitions of the term *model in* the marketing literature. How do the perspectives of these definitions differ from the perspective presented here? Would the other definitions allow someone to distinguish among models and laws, theories, explanations, and hypotheses? Would a road map be a *model* using these other definitions? If not, would you rather choose to declare (1) that a road map is not a model or (2) that the definition of the term *model* is inadequate? Evaluate the usefulness of the varying perspectives on models.
3. How does an explanation of some phenomenon differ from an explanatory model?
4. What phenomena does marketing science seek to explain? Assess the current "state of the art" of our ability to explain each phenom-

enon you identify. Which phenomena do we seem to be making the most progress in explaining?

5. Find an explanation of some phenomenon in the marketing literature. Evaluate the nature, adequacy, and usefulness of the explanation.
6. Succinctly summarize the nature of the D-N, D-S, and I-S models of explanation. What are the essential differences among these models? Does *induction* play any role at all in the D-N and D-S models?
7. The notion of *Verstehen* suggests that the only way to understand and explain some human process is to be a *participant* in that process (Abel 1948). For example, only women could (or should) teach women's studies courses. Only marketing practitioners could possibly understand marketing phenomena. Would such a procedure and such knowledge pass the *intersubjectively certifiable* criterion?
8. Are explanations in marketing a *means* or an *end*, or both? That is, *why* are we interested in "why" questions? Would your answer depend on who you are, that is, a practitioner, student, or academician?
9. From the works of Wroe Alderson (1957; 1965), select what purports to be a *functionalist* explanation of some marketing phenomenon. Evaluate the adequacy of this explanation.
10. How does requiring explanations to be *falsifiable* differ from requiring them to be *confirmable*? Why are confirmability and falsifiability important?
11. In analyzing the work of Wroe Alderson, Hostiuck, and Kurtz state:

    > Functionalism, for example, is mostly an analytical-conceptual schema. But, there is increasing evidence that it may also qualify as a theoretical structure. It is a "systematically related set of statements" that certainly includes "some lawlike generalizations." The aspects of "empirical testing" may admittedly have to wait for further developments in qualitative analysis. (Hostiuck and Kurtz 1973, p. 150)

    Evaluate their conclusion.
12. It is often suggested that to explain a phenomenon is to make the "unfamiliar become familiar." Is *making familiar* a necessary condition for explanation? Is it sufficient? Is it desirable?
13. Louch (1979, p. 284) proposes that "when we say that a man . . . kills his father because he has been cut out of the will . . . we are offering [an explanation of a case that does] not require the support of general or theoretical statements." How satisfactory is this explanation, given the fact that only an infinitesimal fraction of all children who are cut out of their parents' wills subsequently kill their parents? What were your implicit or explicit criteria for "satisfactory"?

NOTES

1. Lambert and Brittan (1970, p. 26) have an excellent discussion of normative criteria for evaluating explanations.

2. The analysis that follows in this section draws to varying degrees on the writings of Ernest Nagel (1961, pp. 520–34), Richard Rudner (1966, pp. 84–111), and Carl Hempel (1959).

4 EXPLANATION: ISSUES AND ASPECTS

Whenever we propose a solution to a problem we ought to try as hard as we can to overthrow our solution rather than defend it. Few of us, unfortunately, practice this precept; but other people, fortunately, will supply the criticism for us if we fail to supply it ourselves.

—Karl R. Popper

The purpose of this chapter is to explore certain issues in explanation and to evaluate several marketing explanations. The issues include the interrelationships among prediction, explanation, and scientific understanding. The nature of causal explanations will be explored, and the ways in which explanations are incomplete will be investigated. The fundamental explananda of marketing science are next proposed. The chapter concludes with a formal analysis of four different explanations in marketing: a product life cycle explanation, a consumer behavior explanation, a price discrimination explanation, and a wheel of retailing explanation.

4.1 EXPLANATION, PREDICTION, AND RETRODICTION

Does having an acceptable explanation for a phenomenon imply that we could have predicted it? That is, does being able to explain market share imply that we could have predicted market share? Conversely, does being able to predict market share imply that we can explain it? The issue has relevance to marketing because many marketing theorists apparently believe that explanation and prediction are not systematically interrelated. Robert Bartels (1970, p. 9) suggests, "Explanation, however, rather than prediction is generally the objective of theory in the social and behavioral sciences." Likewise, Luck, Wales, and Taylor (1970, p. 4) believe that explanation does not imply prediction. However, Green, Tull, and Albaum (1988, p. 4) maintain that "the functions of marketing research include *description* and *explanation* (which are necessary for *understanding*), *prediction*, and *evaluation* . . . [which are] necessary for effective (1) *planning* of future marketing activity, (2) *control* of marketing operations in the present, and (3) *evaluation* of marketing results." Hempel (1965a, p. 367) refers to the issue at hand as the thesis of structural identity or structural symmetry: "*(1) Every adequate explanation is potentially a prediction, and (2) every adequate prediction is potentially an explanation.*" Let's explore each half of the thesis, in turn. (See also Hunt 1991a, pp. 280–82)

4.1.1 Explanations as Potential Predictions

To writers such as May Brodbeck and Karl Popper, the thesis of structural identity seems to be not an issue but a fact. First, Brodbeck:

> Prediction has the same logical form as explanation. In predicting something as yet unknown, we deductively infer it from particular facts and laws that are already known. This deductive tautological connection among statements also shows why observations confirm or refute hypotheses. If a prediction inferred from a set of premises turns out to be true, then the generalization is further confirmed. If it turns out to be false, then we know that either the generalization or the individual fact used in making the prediction *must* be false. Because we are less likely to be mistaken about individual facts, in most cases the failure of a prediction means that the generalization is thereby refuted.
>
> It makes no difference whether the premises are statistical or deterministic, as nonstatistical generalizations are called. If they are deterministic, we may predict an individual event; if they are statistical, only statements about classes of events may be either explained or predicted. (Brodbeck 1968, pp. 9–10)

Popper (1960, p. 133) comes to similar conclusions concerning the basic way in which explanations, predictions, and testing are interrelated. He suggests that explanations, predictions, and testing do not differ in logical structure. Rather, the differences are related to what is considered *known* or *given* and what is considered *unknown* or to be *uncovered*. With *explanation*, certain phenomena are known and what is to be uncovered are the laws and theories that can explain the phenomena. For example, if we know that many consumers are brand loyal, our task in marketing may be to *explain* their brand loyalty by uncovering certain laws and theories. With *prediction*, certain laws and theories are known, and we wish to apply our scientific knowledge by predicting certain phenomena. For example, if certain laws and theories concerning brand loyalty are known, a marketing practitioner may apply these constructions to predict the characteristics of consumers who might be brand loyal to his particular product. Finally, with *testing*, certain laws and theories are proposed, and we compare the actual phenomena with the phenomena that the laws and theories predicted would occur. To the extent that the laws and theories predict correctly or incorrectly (that is, the test results are positive or negative), we have corroborative or noncorroborative evidence that the real world is actually constructed as our laws and theories would suggest.

To Brodbeck and Popper, every explanation implies an *ex post facto* prediction. Thus, the explanation-implies-prediction argument is:

The E-P Argument

(a) The explanation of phenomenon X at time t_n implies that
(b) *if* person A had been present at time t_{n-2}, and
(c) *if* A had known circumstances $C_1, C_2, C_3, \ldots C_k$, and
(d) *if* A had applied laws $L_1, L_2, L_3, \ldots L_j$,
(e) *then* A could have predicted that X would occur at time t_{n-1},
(f) therefore, all explanations are potentially predictive.

Careful examination of the premises (statements [a] through [d]) of the E-P argument shows them to be true. All of the models that do explain phenomena—the D-N, D-S, and I-S models—are consistent with the premises. Models that do *not* explain phenomena, such as the pattern model, are *not* consistent with the premises of the E-P argument. Finally, the conclusions (statements [e] and [f]) of the E-P argument do seem to be logically implied by the premises. Therefore, we must conclude that the E-P argument is true: every adequate explanation is potentially a prediction. That is, if we could not have predicted the occurrence of a phenomenon, we cannot now satisfactorily explain it.

The preceding discussion provides insight into a common circumstance in the social sciences and marketing. Someone creates a model or theory. A critic evaluates the model and concludes that it is not empirically testable because the model has no predictive capacity. The apologist for the model then claims, "The fact that my model makes no predictions is irrelevant because my purpose is to *explain* the phenomenon, not predict it!" In light of this analysis, the apologist's defense becomes vacuous because *all adequate explanations must have predictive capacity.*

Dubin (1969) struggles at length with his "power paradox," and although he refers to *understanding* rather than *explanation*, the issue is similar to the thesis of structural identity. He (1969, p. 17) states the power paradox in terms of a question: "Why is it that we can create models of social behavior that are powerful in contributing to understanding, without providing, at the same time, precision in prediction?" Because Dubin uses the term *model* as synonymous with our term *theory*, we can reconstruct the premises and conclusions of Dubin's paradox for analysis:

(a) Many social science theories do not provide precision in prediction.
(b) Many of these same theories contribute powerfully to understanding.
(c) The preceding seems paradoxical.

Many marketing theorists believe that their theories and models contribute to the understanding of marketing phenomena, while, at the same time, admitting the lack of predictive power of their theories. Bettman and Jones (1972) evaluated several models of consumer behavior, including those proposed by Farley, Ring, and Nicosia. After observing the lack of predictive power of many of these models, they conclude, "The main use of these models may lie in attempting to understand behavior rather than predict it" (1972, p. 556). Can we understand behavior without being able to predict it? Perhaps an analysis of Dubin's power paradox will shed light on the issue.

Because paradoxes are created by humans, not nature, we should explore whether the premises ([a] and [b]) of the paradox are true. Even a casual observer of the social sciences would conclude that *a* is true; many social science and marketing models and theories do not predict. However, is *b* true? Do these nonpredictive models contribute powerfully to understanding? The answer depends on the meaning of the term *understanding*. Bunge (1967b, p. 31) suggests that two usages are common, (1) *intuitive understanding* and (2) *scientific understanding*. Intuitive understanding of a phenomenon suggests that we are *psychologically comfortable* or *familiar* with the phenomenon. Scientific understanding of a phenomenon implies, at least, that we can *scientifically explain* the phenomenon. Now, intuitive understanding does not imply scientific understanding; many people are psychologically comfortable with a rainbow but cannot explain how rainbows occur. Also, intuitive understanding is inescapably individual in kind. Phenomena that may be psychologically comfortable to one person (e.g., thunder) may be psychologically uncomfortable to another person. Therefore, just as we found with the pattern model (section 3.6), intuitive understanding fails the criterion of being intersubjectively confirmable and cannot be considered as a part of scientific knowledge.

Clearly, Dubin does not mean *understanding* in the intuitive sense, but rather, in the scientific sense. However, because scientific understanding (in order to be intersubjectively confirmable in the context of section 3.2) implies explanatory power, and because explanatory power implies being potentially predictive, *the power paradox disappears. Premise* (b) *is false; marketing and other social science theories that do not predict do not make powerful contributions to (scientific) understanding.*

What does it mean, however, to claim that a theory "does not predict" or that it "lacks precision" in prediction? Consider, for example, the following five levels of prediction:

(1) *X* and *Y* may or may not be related.
(2) *X* and *Y* are related.
(3) *X* and *Y* are positively (or negatively) related.
(4) *X* and *Y* are related at $r = k \pm e$.
(5) *X* and *Y* are related, in the presence of *M*, *N*, . . . , at $r = j \pm e$.

Clearly, theories that predict at level (5) have greater precision than those at level (4), and so forth. That is, the five levels (of which there obviously can be others) are ordinally ranked. Equally clearly, most social science researchers would (a) be pleased with level (5) and (b) view level (1) with disdain. However, what about levels (2) through (4)? Meehl (1990, p. 204) argues that levels (2) and (3) are unacceptable because "everything correlates to some extent with everything else." Similarly, Bass (1995) maintains that (2) and (3) are unacceptable. The view here is that, though levels (4) and (5) are worthy goals, level (3), but not (2), has sufficient precision to warrant a claim of increasing scientific understanding.

4.1.2 Predictions as Potential Explanations

The second half of the thesis of structural identity asserts that every adequate prediction is potentially an explanation. The case favoring the second half of the structural identity thesis usually rests on this kind of argument:

The P-E Argument

(a) The prediction that phenomenon *X* will occur at time t_{n+1} means that
(b) *if* person *A* observes certain circumstances $C_1, C_2, C_3, \ldots C_k$ at time t_n, and
(c) *if* *A* applies laws $L_1, L_2, L_3, \ldots L_j$ at time t_n,
(d) *then* *A* can predict that *X* will occur at time t_{n+1},
(e) furthermore, if *A* waits until time t_{n+1}, and
(f) *if* *A* observes that phenomenon *X* occurs,
(g) *then* *A* can explain phenomenon *X* by reference to statements (b) and (c).
(h) Therefore, all adequate predictions are potential explanations.

Many people who readily accept the explanation-implies-prediction argument totally reject the prediction-implies-explanation argument. Critics claim that they can predict the business cycle by measuring the length of hemlines on women's skirts, but no reasonable person would argue that women's hemlines *explain* business cycles. Similarly, one can accurately predict the birth-rate in Oslo, Norway, by observing the temperatures of the sidewalks in Madison, Wisconsin, but reasonable people would not claim to *explain* the former by the latter.[1]

The critic's claim can be supported and the P-E argument broken by attacking statement (c), "if *A* applies laws $L_1, L_2, L_3, \ldots L_j$ at time t_n." Are there statements that can be used to make accurate predictions but that are not *laws*? Because the subject of "laws" is the topic for Chapter 5, the treatment here will be extremely brief. However, consider the following statement: "All desks in room 201 that have the initials S.D.H. also have the initials S.E." The statement has universal form (all *X* are *Y*) and can generate a prediction of a sort; that is, if you go to room 201, and if you find any desk with S.D.H. on it, you will also find S.E. on it. Nevertheless, such statements are not properly considered *laws*, but rather, are *accidental generalizations*. Therefore, because accidental generalizations have predictive capacity, and because explanations must contain laws, and because accidental generalizations are not laws, *the P-E argument is false.* Contrary to the thesis of structural identity, *all adequate (accurate) predictions are not potential explanations.*

The conclusion that the P-E argument, the second subthesis of structural symmetry, is false is consistent with scientific realism but contrary to logical empiricism. For example, Hempel (1965a) reviews criticisms similar to those developed here, and, though acknowledging their force, states simply that the P-E argument must "be regarded here as an open question" (p. 376). The reason why Hempel and other logical empiricists could not deny the second subthesis in the symmetry argument was that they were firmly committed to the logical positivist view that the concepts "cause" and "causal" were metaphysical and superfluous to science, that is, they were firmly committed to the Humean view of causality. For example, Brodbeck (1962, p. 250) defended the thesis of structural symmetry by noting that critics had adopted the "causal idiom" and that the truth-content of "statements like '*C* is the cause of *E*' is problematic."

4.1.3 Are Explanations and Predictions Potential Retrodictions?

Although the terms *explanation* and *prediction* are familiar words in common English, the term *retrodiction* belongs strictly to the scientific vocabulary. The term *retrodiction* as used by Ryle (1949, p. 124) implies making inferences about the past on the basis of present observations. Hempel (1965d, p. 173) and Hanson (1963, p. 193) use the term *postdiction* to imply the same procedure.

Note the significant difference between retrodiction and both explanation and prediction. With explanation, the phenomena that do the *explaining* occur in time before the phenomenon to be explained. Likewise, with prediction, the phenomena that do the *predicting* antecede the phenomenon to be predicted. In contrast, with retrodiction, the phenomena that accomplish the *retrodicting* occur *after* the phenomenon to be retrodicted.

An example of retrodiction should show how it differs from both explanation and prediction. Carbon-14 dating of objects classically illustrates the retrodiction of when an animal died. By measuring the amount of carbon 14 contained in the bone structure of a deceased animal and by employing certain (statistical) laws concerning radiocarbon decay, the date when the animal died can be *retrodicted* within an accuracy of ±50 years (Blanchard et al. 1972, p. 315). Thus, retrodiction has this formal structure:

(a) Certain circumstances $C_1, C_2, C_3, \ldots C_k$ are observed (e.g., the amount of carbon 14 in the bones of a deceased animal), and
(b) certain laws $L_1, L_2, L_3, \ldots L_j$ (e.g., laws governing radiocarbon decay) are then applied to
(c) *retrodict* the occurrence of some past phenomenon (e.g., date of death) that anteceded $C_1, C_2, C_3, \ldots C_k$.

Must we be able to retrodict in order adequately to explain or predict? Hanson (1963, p. 193) argues affirmatively: "Every prediction, if inferentially respectable, must possess a corresponding postdiction [retrodiction]." Unfortunately, Hanson uses as his model for explanatory adequacy certain models such as Newtonian mechanics that are deterministic in a very strong sense. That is, the relationships in the models are reversible with respect to their time variables. Hanson confuses necessary conditions with sufficient conditions. Many very useful explanations need only show that condition C_1, $C_2, C_3, \ldots C_k$ are *sufficient* to predict X. Retrodiction requires that conditions $C_1, C_2, C_3, \ldots C_k$ were *necessary* for X to occur; that is, X could not have occurred without $C_1, C_2, C_3, \ldots C_k$ also occurring. It is one thing to be able to predict that certain circumstances will be sufficient to assure the early demise of a new product. It is an entirely different thing to be able to take a dead product and retrodict the circumstances that killed it. Although retrodiction would be a desirable characteristic of any model, neither explanatory nor predictive adequacy implies the ability to retrodict.

4.2 CAUSAL EXPLANATIONS

Are all explanations *causal*? Can an explanation be adequate and yet noncausal? The paradox of causation: although the term *cause* is widely used in both everyday language and scientific language, for centuries the notion of *causality* has steadfastly resisted definitive explication.

In everyday language we ask, "Why did the window break?" And we are satisfied with the explanation: "*Because* little Jimmy threw a ball into it!" Also, "What caused the house to burn down?" "Little Jimmy caused it by playing with matches." Likewise, physical scientists remain comfortable with assertions such as, "the force of gravity *causes* the missile to fall to the earth" and "the rays of the sun *cause* the ice to melt." Marketers seem comfortable with statements such as, "lack of promotion caused the product to fail" and "high prices caused the recent sales decline." However comfortable both laymen and scientists are with the terms *cause* and *causal explanation*, the next section shows how methodologically troublesome the notion of causality has been.

4.2.1 The Notion of Causality

Exactly what is meant by the assertion "*X* causes *Y*," and precisely what kinds of evidence can be gathered to support the assertion? In particular, the fundamental problem of causation is: *What evidence can empirically or logically separate the assertion* "X *causes* Y" *from the assertion* "X *and* Y *occur regularly in the same pattern*"? Perhaps the best place to start would be with a review of some historical perspectives on causation.

Most of the perspectives on causation invoke two common themes. To illustrate the first theme, in 1840 William Whewell (1840/1968, p. 67) suggested that "by cause we mean some quality, power, or efficacy by which a state of things produces a second state." He then espoused his version of the law of universal causation:

> We assert that "Every event must have a cause": and this proposition we know to be true not only probably, and generally, and as far as we can see; but we cannot suppose it to be false in any single instance. We are as certain of it as of the truths of arithmetic or geometry. We cannot doubt that it must apply to all events past and future, in every part of the universe, just as truly as to those occurrences which we have ourselves observed. (Whewell 1840/1968, p. 67)

Although not necessarily subscribing to the law of universal causation, modern-day adherents to scientific realism believe that causation must involve the powers and capacities of things. As discussed in Chapter 1, scientific realism holds that "the long-term success of a scientific theory gives reason to believe that something like the entities and structure postulated by the theory actually exists" (McMullin 1984, p. 26). The realists Harré and Madden discuss causal powers:

> The proper analysis of the ascription of a power to a thing or material (and, with some qualifications, also to a person) is this:
>
> "*X* has the power to *A*" means "*X* will (or can) do *A*, in the appropriate conditions, *in virtue of its intrinsic nature.*"

> In ascribing powers to people, "can" must be substituted for "will." Whether he will or no has to be explained by considerations other than the extrinsic conditions for action. It is the reference to the nature of the potent thing that marks the difference between the ascription of powers and of mere dispositions. (Harré and Madden 1975, p. 86)

Harré and Madden then maintain that their analysis leads to two important points:

> 1. To ascribe a power to a thing or material is to say something specific about what it *will* or *can do*, but it is not to assert any specific hypotheses about the nature of that thing. To ascribe a power to a thing asserts only that it can do what it does in virtue of its nature, whatever that is. It leaves open the question of the exact specification of the nature or constitution in virtue of which the thing, person, or material has the power. It leaves it open to be discovered by later empirical investigation, should that prove to be possible.
> 2. But to ascribe a power is to say that what the thing or material does or can do is to be understood as brought about not just by the stimuli to which it may be subject or the conditions which it finds itself in, i.e., by extrinsic conditions, but in some measure by the nature or constitution of that thing or material, i.e., by intrinsic conditions. (In a sense the ascription of a power is a schema for an explanation of the manifestation of the power.) (Harré and Madden 1975, p. 87)

William Stanley Jevons (1968, p. 140) illustrates the second theme: "A cause is defined as the necessary or invariable antecedent of an event, so that when the cause exists, the effect will also exist or soon follow." A modern version of this kind of analysis is the "INUS condition" proposed by Mackie (1965). INUS stands for "insufficient-necessary-unnecessary-sufficient." He (1965, p. 257) proposes that "*A* is an INUS [causal] condition of a result *P* if and only if, for some *X* and some *Y*, (*AX* or *Y*) is a necessary and sufficient condition of *P*, but *A* is not a sufficient condition of *P* and *X* is not a sufficient condition of *P*." That is, a cause may be an insufficient but necessary part of a condition that is itself unnecessary but sufficient for the result. As Sosa (1975, p. 4) has pointed out, an INUS condition is very little different from a condition which is, *ceteris paribus*, sufficient. Bagozzi proposes that many of the causal relations proposed by marketers are INUS conditions and offers the following example:

> As an example, let us examine the claim sometimes made by marketers that brand image (measured by the brand name) affects the perception of quality. When marketers make this claim they are not saying that the brand image is a necessary cause or condition for the attribution of quality. One may judge a product as high or low in quality without knowing the brand. Similarly, marketers are not claiming that the brand image is sufficient for the perception of quality since one must at least attend to, be aware of, and evaluate the brand name before such an attribution can be made.

> Rather, the brand image may be regarded as an INUS condition in that it is an insufficient but necessary part of a condition that is itself unnecessary but sufficient for the result. Many of the causal relations investigated by marketers are of this sort. (Bagozzi 1980, pp. 17–18)

Therefore, by "*X* causes *Y*" writers usually mean that "*X* has the power to produce *Y*," or "*X* is an invariable antecedent of *Y*," or "*X* is *necessary* for *Y*," or "*X* is *sufficient* for *Y*." But how can we *know* that "*X* has the power to produce *Y*" or any of the other conceptualizations of cause? What are the kinds of evidence or criteria? So far, we have synonyms for *cause* but no objective criteria. In short, what are the necessary and sufficient conditions to enable one to label a relationship *causal*? Many philosophers of science have attempted to generate the necessary and sufficient conditions for causality, including J.S. Mill with his canons of induction.

The logical positivists and logical empiricists believed that "cause" was a metaphysical concept that could (and should) be avoided. Thus, following the position of Hume, Kyburg (1968, p. 236) questions whether the concept of "cause" is "of scientific interest" and Brodbeck (1968, p. 672) contends that "as we learn more about the laws of temporal processes, the notion of cause tends to be eliminated." Similarly, Dubin states:

> Empirically relevant theory in the social sciences is built upon an acceptance of the notion of relationship rather than the notion of causality. . . . The *operations* by which we test [a] relationship between theoretically predicted values and empirical values differ in *absolutely no respect* whether we label the relationships among units of a model as *laws of interaction* or as *causal laws* . . . . The temptation is strong to interpret sequential laws of interaction as though they were causal in structure. This gratuitous assumption of causality adds nothing to social science, however much it satisfies psychological needs. (Dubin 1969, pp. 91, 94, 106)

So the term *causation* is firmly ensconced in common English and the technical languages of both the social and physical sciences. At the same time, sufficient conditions to apply the term (at least with certainty) do not exist. Therefore, Dubin and other "Humeans" suggest throwing the term out. To do so, I argue, would be to commit the "philosophers' fallacy of high redefinition." First used by Edwards (1951) in his analysis of Bertrand Russell's doubts on induction and used later by Harré (1986) and me (Hunt 1990), this is the fallacy of redefining a concept (e.g., scientific knowledge, truth, falsity, objectivity, causality, or progress) in such a manner (e.g., must be "known with certainty" or "known with probability *p*") that the concept cannot be realized, and then lapsing into relativism, nihilism, or skepticism. Instances of the philosophers' fallacy abound in marketing. For example, Anderson (1986, p. 163) claims that theories cannot be falsified because their falsity "can never be known with certainty." Furthermore, "science is a process without a goal" because "there is no *guarantee* that it progresses toward anything—least of all toward 'truth'" (Anderson 1983, p. 22, emphasis added). Popper's theory is faulty because "it is impossible to *conclusively* refute a theory" (Anderson 1983, p. 21, emphasis added). Because science cannot conclusively show that it produces "objective absolute meanings," then "all meanings" in science "are subjectively determined," and, therefore, "science is subjective" (Peter and Olson 1983, pp. 120–1). Although proponents of such views put them forth as supposedly implying relativism, subjectivism, and irrationalism in science, such innocuous claims imply nothing other than that science is fallible.

4.2.2 Evidence for Causation

Much better than throwing "causality" out or lapsing into relativism, would be an attempt to set forth certain *necessary* or *minimal* conditions for causality. This procedure could at least point out some patently noncausal explanations. *Pragmatically speaking, we may refer to causal explanations as those explanations that employ nonspurious, theoretically supported, sequential laws in their explanans.* Using the preceding definition as a guide, we can identify four criteria for classifying an explanation as causal.

1. *Temporal sequentiality.* If changes in factor *A* are to be used to explain causally factor *B*, then the occurrence of the changes in *A* must precede in time the occurrence of changes in *B*. That is, *A* and *B* must be related by a *law of successon.* Not all laws are laws of succession (see Chapter 6). Many laws, such as Boyle's law of gases, are *laws of atemporal coexistence*; they show a relationship that must be realized and contain no time variable.

The notion of temporal sequentiality suggests that if the introduction of additional salespeople is to be considered a *cause* of increased sales, then the salespeople must be added before the observed increase in sales. Similarly, if a new volume discount policy is to be considered a *cause* of better channel relations, then the discount policy must precede in time the improved channel relations. However, the direction of the sequentiality of phenomena is not always intuitively obvious. Though it was presumed for years that attitude changes preceded behavior changes, research shows that behavior changes often precede attitude changes (Fishbein and Ajzen 1972; Ray 1973).

2. *Associative variation.* If factor *A* is a cause of factor *B*, then changes in the level or presence of factor *A* must be systematically associated with changes in the level or presence of factor *B*. Although it is true that "correlation does not imply causation," the observation that two factors are systematically as-

sociated (correlation being a measure of the degree of this association) is evidence *in support of* causation. Conversely, the *absence* of association is very strong evidence that the two factors are *not* causally related. If market shares are caused by advertising, then we could expect to find differences in market shares systematically associated with differences in the quantity or quality of advertising.

3. *Nonspurious association.* If *A* causes *B*, then there must be no factor Z that, if introduced into the explanation, would make the systematic association between *A* and *B* vanish. If one diligently explores for other factors, that is, other possible causes, that might possibly have resulted in changes in *B* and can find no such factors, then this evidence supports the assertion that the association between *A* and *B* is a true causal relationship rather than a spurious one.

The nonspurious criterion emphasizes the tremendous scientific value of experimental research designs as opposed to nonexperimental designs. Although definitions of "experimental design" differ, most experimental designs either systematically exclude from the research setting, or carefully monitor and control, factors other than the independent variable (the one purportedly doing the *causing*) that might influence the dependent variable (the one being *caused*). To discount the possibility that other factors cause changes in *B* becomes much more difficult in *nonexperimental* designs. Causal imputations in marketing are particularly likely to fail the nonspuriousness criterion because most research in marketing has traditionally relied upon nonexperimental designs. Many important research questions simply do not lend themselves to experimental manipulation of the independent variables.

4. *Theoretical support.* The fourth criterion suggests that well-conformed theories can be used to support the assertion that *A* causes *B*. That is, if *A* causes *B* is consistent with theory *X*, and if theory *X* has been successfully used to explain other phenomena, then theory *X* provides theoretical support for the assertion that *A* causes *B*.

Suppose someone says, "The length of women's skirts *causes* our market share to rise or fall." Suppose further that an examination of the evidence reveals (1) the general rising of women's skirts has preceded the rising of marketing shares, (2) the correlation between the two factors has been very strong, and (3) no third factor can be found that makes the correlation vanish. That is, the evidence accords with the temporal sequentiality, associative variation, and nonspuriousness criteria. Clearly, most people would *still* view as ridiculous the claim that "the length of women's skirts *causes* market share." The causal claim in question is ridiculous precisely because it has no theoretical support; that is, it does not fit into all the other things we know about factors associated with the lengths of skirts and market share.

The criterion of theoretical support must not be pushed too far. Poor Galileo paid a heavy price because his notions concerning the movements of celestial bodies did not fit with the theological belief that the Earth was the center of the universe. Also, recall that Einstein's theory of relativity did not fit with Newtonian mechanics. Nevertheless, the burden of proof must lie with the proposer of new, nonfitting truth-claims.

Many marketing researchers advocate the so-called *Granger conditions* as a means of testing for causal relationships. Jacobson and Nicosia (1981), using the techniques of Granger (1969), Sims (1972), and Pierce and Haugh (1977), explored for causal relationships between advertising and various measures of aggregate demand. Bass and Pilon (1980) used similar techniques to evaluate their time-series model of market share behavior. Granger's definition of causality suggests that a variable *X* is causally related to *Y* if we are better able to predict *Y* by using all of the available variables, including *X*, than by using the same set of variables without *X*. Using this definition, Granger, Sims, and Pierce and Haugh propose a wide range of specific tests. These tests are cross-correlational in nature and use time-series data. All of the tests use as evidence of causality what is referred to here as "temporal sequentiality" and "associative variation."

Other marketing researchers are vigorously pursuing the structural equation approach to causal modeling. Originally conceptualized by Bock and Borgman (1966) and later developed by Joreskog (1968, 1973), structural equation modeling ("SEM") uses, among others, the maximum likelihood method for estimating parameters. Bagozzi (1980) introduced the approach in marketing and used it to explore for causal relationships between performance and satisfaction among industrial salespeople. Bentler (1990), Bollen (1989), Fornell (1983), Rigdon (1995), and Rigdon and Ferguson (1991), among others, develop the approach. Major advantages of SEM include the ability to control for measurement error; an enhanced ability to test the effects of experimental manipulations; the ability to test complex theoretical structures; the ability to link micro and macro perspectives; and more powerful ways to assess measure reliability and validity (MacKenzie 2001).

The use of the concepts *cause* and *causation* remain and should remain in marketing. Indeed, the search for true causal relationships is central to the mission of marketing science. However, we must never delude ourselves into believing that we can ever know any causal relationship with certainty. Purportedly causal relationships are always only more or less probable, and we should always diligently explore the possibility that the relationships are actually spurious. The very essence of science is that all statements are tentative and subject to change and revision on the basis of future evidence.

4.3 EXPLANATORY INCOMPLETENESS, EXPLANATION CHAINS, AND INFINITE EGRESS

All explanations are incomplete in a fundamental way: something is always left unexplained. Phenomenon K (e.g., the path of a celestial body) is explained by subsuming it under laws L_1 and L_2 (Newtonian mechanics). But the critic rightly complains that L_1 and L_2 are unexplained. The theorist responds that L_1 and L_2 can be explained by subsumption under L_3 and L_4 (Einstein's Special Theory of Relativity), and the critic demands the explanation chain of L_3 and L_4. The theorist stops his *explanation chain* at the most basic lawlike statements known at the time (Einstein's general theory of relativity), prompting the critic to note that the explanation is still incomplete.

Since all explanatory structures involve potentially infinite regresses of the preceding variety, explanations are incomplete in this sense. Thus, the critic's point must be admitted. Fortunately, the problem poses no insurmountable conceptual barrier when placed in proper perspective. Surely, no one would seriously propose that in order to explain *anything* we must explain *everything.* Such nihilism would place ludicrous requirements on scientific explanations in light of the admitted usefulness of explanations that involve potentially infinite regresses. In addition, the admission that the most basic laws underlying explanations are left unexplained must be clearly differentiated from the assertion that the basic laws are *unsupported.* Even though the basic laws at the end of the explanation chain may be unexplained by other laws, there may well exist tremendous empirical support for the veracity of the laws.

4.3.1 Marketing Explanation Chains

Explanation chains abound in marketing. For example, many studies in consumer behavior, at least implicitly, employ variants of the A-P-I-B chain:

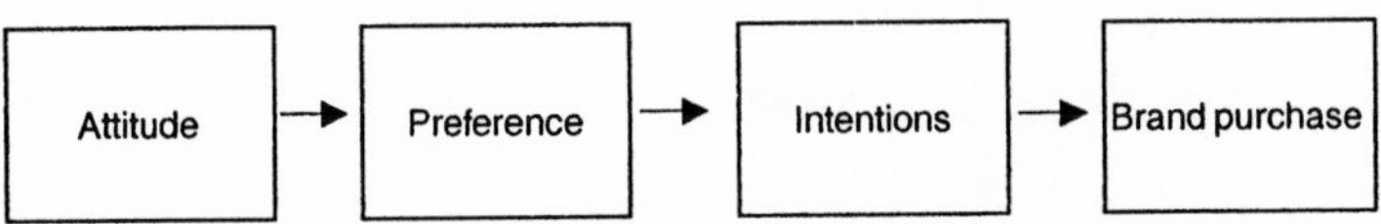

The chain implies that attitude can be used to explain preference and preference can be used to explain intentions, and, thus, intentions can be used to explain brand purchase. The chain can be stated even more simply by starting at the other end. Consumers are more likely to purchase brands they intend to buy than brands they do not intend to buy; consumers are more likely to intend to buy brands they prefer than brands they do not prefer; finally, consumers are more likely to prefer brands toward which they have a favorable attitude than brands toward which they do not have a favorable attitude.

Bunge (1967b, p. 29) has suggested that explanation chains be evaluated according to their explanatory depth. Some explanation chains remain at a shallow, superficial, or trivial level, even though they involve several stages. Other explanations seem deep, relying on profound or fundamental lawlike statements. Returning to the A-P-I-B chain, there is something intellectually disquieting about its depth. The chain seems to regress no further than a seemingly superficial level. Now consider the "multiattribute" chain:

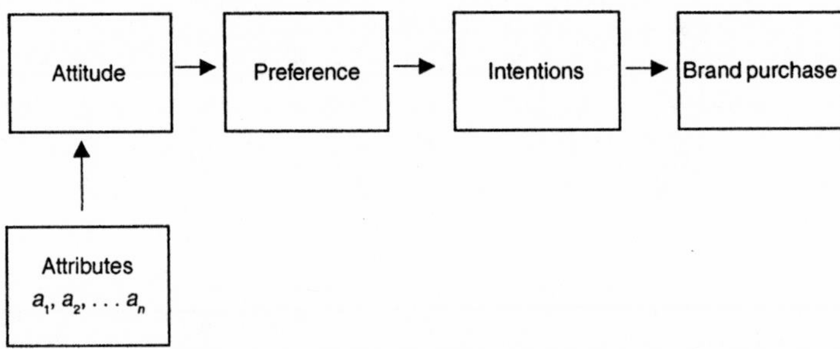

The multiattribute chain goes one step further by showing the attributes that form attitudes. Therefore, it is deeper and more satisfactory than A-P-I-B.

How deep must an explanatory chain go to reach respectability? Even chains as shallow as A-P-I-B have found usefulness in short-range predictions (explanations) of the purchase of consumer durables (Katoma 1960). Unfortunately, the A-P-I-B chain is usually of limited usefulness to practitioners because it is not deep enough to provide most marketers with guidance as to *how* and *where* to *influence* the chain. Marketers contend, "Don't tell me that people who have a favorable attitude toward my brand are likely to purchase it; tell me what factors that I control can influence attitude!" Therefore, from the marketing practitioners' perspective, the respectability of an explanatory chain is directly proportional to the guidance it gives marketers in their attempts to influence the chain. In contrast to the A-P-I-B chain, the multiattribute chain is useful to practitioners attempting to influence the chain because it specifies attributes that can be influenced.

From the marketing academician's perspective, the issue of how deep an explanatory chain must be for *scientific respectability* is also ambiguous. Such academic norms are essentially set by peer group consensus. These norms are strongly influenced by the editors and reviewing staffs of the major professional journals. Consequently, different journals have (widely) different norms.

4.4 OTHER FORMS OF EXPLANATORY INCOMPLETENESS

Besides the problem of the infinite regress of explanation chains, numerous other ways in which explanations may be incomplete have been suggested. Three in particular seem worthy of note: enthymemes, partial explanations, and what Hempel (1965a, p. 424) refers to as explanation sketches.

4.4.1 Enthymemes

Many explanations are incomplete in that they are elliptically formulated; the logician refers to these as *enthymemes* (Lambert and Brittan 1970, p. 29). To be elliptically incomplete implies that certain necessary statements or laws are skipped over or suppressed in the explanation. The person offering the explanation presumably *assumes* that the reader will either consciously or unconsciously fill in the missing statements. Most narrative explanations are elliptically formulated because both writer and reader would perceive fully articulated explanations as tedious and unnecessary. This form of incompleteness is usually harmless enough, provided the writer is certain that the reader can fill in the explanation with the appropriate statements. Refer to the structural analysis of the consumer behavior explanation later in this chapter for an illustration of an enthymeme (see section 4.7.1).

4.4.2 Partial Explanations

Often a proposed explanation is *partial* in the sense that the explanation does not explain why *k* occurred, but only that some phenomenon of type *G* occurred and that *k* is a subclass of *G*. For example, using the construct "generalized self-confidence," it might be possible to explain why a person purchased a "major brand" of gasoline but not which *specific* brand. Recall that FM2 in section 3.7.3 was a partial explanation, and, in this sense, incomplete. Naturally, we would prefer all explanations to be complete, but the importance of partial explanations should not be minimized.

4.4.3 Explanation Sketches

The last form of explanatory incompleteness is suggested by the term *explanation sketch.* Here, the proposed explanation is neither *elliptically* formulated nor is it *partial* in the sense of the previous section. An explanation sketch implies that only a general outline of the explanation is offered. ("Here are some variables that might be related to brand preference.") Explanation sketches need substantial elaboration and development before they can qualify as complete explanations.

Explanation sketches probably belong more in the context of discovery than in the context of justification. They are meant to suggest fruitful areas of inquiry for researchers exploring the phenomena in question. Most explanations in both marketing and other social sciences may come closer to being explanation sketches than to being fully articulated explanations.

4.5 THE FUNDAMENTAL EXPLANANDA OF MARKETING

If the distinctive aim of science is to explain phenomena, what phenomena does marketing theory attempt to explain? That is, what are the fundamental explananda of marketing science? Alternatively, what are the fundamental "dependent variables" of marketing science? Consistent with the perspective of most marketing theorists (Alderson 1965; Bagozzi 1974; Kotler and Levy 1969a), this writer has proposed that the basic subject matter of marketing is the exchange relationship or transaction. The discipline of marketing has its normative or "applied" side, which is not science. The positive or "basic" side houses the science of marketing. *Therefore, marketing science is the behavioral science that seeks to explain exchange relationships.* Given this perspective of marketing science and adopting the customary (albeit somewhat arbitrary) convention of designating one party to the exchange as the "buyer" and one party as the "seller," the fundamental explananda of marketing can be logically derived. The four sets of fundamental explananda (FE) of marketing science (Hunt 1983a) are:

- FE1. The behaviors of buyers directed at consummating both individual and ongoing exchanges.
- FE2. The behaviors of sellers directed at consummating both individual and ongoing exchanges.
- FE3. The institutional framework directed at consummating and/or facilitating both individual and ongoing exchanges.
- FE4. The consequences for society of the behaviors of buyers, the behaviors of sellers, and the institutional framework directed at consummating and/or facilitating both individual and ongoing exchanges.

The first set of fundamental explananda indicates that marketing science seeks to answer this question: *Why do which buyers purchase what they do, where they do, when they do, and how they do?* The "which buyers" seeks to explain why certain buyers enter into particular exchange relationships and others do not. The "what" indicates that different buyers purchase different product/service mixes. The "where" is the institutional/locational choice of buyers. That is, why do some buyers purchase at discount department stores and others at full-service department stores, and why do some buyers purchase in neighborhood stores and others in shopping centers? The "when" refers to the timing decisions of buyers. Why do buyers purchase differently at different stages in the family life cycle? Finally, the "how" refers to the processes that consumers use in making their purchasing decisions. That is, what are the identifiable stages in consumer decision making? The "how" also refers to any organizational systems that buyers develop to accomplish the purchasing task, for example, the sharing of buying responsibilities among various members of the household.

The second set of fundamental explananda of marketing concerns the behaviors of sellers. As Lutz (1979, p. 5) has pointed out, "It has been extremely unfortunate that the vast bulk of theory-based behavioral research in marketing has been on consumer behavior." He then concludes that "if we truly believe that exchange is the fundamental building block of marketing, then we have virtually ignored (in a scientific sense) the behavior of the party selling to the consumer." The guiding question is, *Why do which sellers produce, price, promote, and distribute what they do, where they do, when they do, and how they do?* The "which" points out that not all sellers participate in all exchanges. The "what" seeks explanations for the kinds of products produced, prices charged, promotions used, and distributors employed. The "when" seeks explanations for the timing of the behaviors of sellers. The "where" refers to the locations chosen by sellers to do business. The "how" refers to the processes involved and to the organizational frameworks developed by sellers when they engage in exchange relationships.

The third set of fundamental explananda suggests that marketing science seeks answers to these questions: Why do which kinds of institutions develop to engage in what kinds of functions or activities to consummate and/or facilitate exchanges, when will these institutions develop, where will they develop, and how will they develop? The "which" points out that not all kinds of institutions participate in the consummation and/or facilitation of all kinds of exchanges, and seeks to identify the kinds of institutions and "what" specific kinds of activities (functions) will be performed by each. The "when" refers to the evolution or changing of the kinds of institutions over time and "where" these changes will take place. The "how" refers to the processes that bring about these institutional changes.

As used here, the term *institution* refers both to the intermediaries that either take title to goods or negotiate purchases or sales, such as wholesalers and retailers, and to purely *facilitating* agencies such as those that are solely engaged in transportation, warehousing, advertising, or marketing research. As suggested by Arndt (1981b, p. 37), marketing institutions can also be considered as sets of norms, that is, as "sets of conditions and rules for transactions and other interactions." Note that the study of *marketing systems* can be considered the study of collections of interacting marketing institutions and the norms that guide them. In short, the third set of explananda seeks to explain the nature and development of all kinds of marketing systems.

The fourth set of fundamental explananda concerns the consequences of marketing for society. The guiding question is, Why do which kinds of behaviors of buyers, behaviors of sellers, and institutions have what kinds of consequences for society, when they do, where they do, and how they do? The "which" directs the theorists to focus on specific kinds of behaviors and/or institutions and explain "what" kinds of consequences these behaviors or institutions will have for society. Again, the "when" refers to the timing of the consequences and the "where" focuses on those on whom the consequences will fall. For example, will the consequences fall disproportionately on the disadvantaged members of society? Finally, the "how" focuses on the processes and mechanisms by which various parts of society are impacted by marketing activities. The study of the kinds of consequences discussed here is generally subsumed under the term macromarketing. The preceding four sets of explananda are proposed to be fundamental in the sense that every phenomenon that marketing science seeks to explain can ultimately be reduced to a phenomenon residing in one of the four sets.

4.6 A PRODUCT LIFE CYCLE EXPLANATION

As samples of "why" questions in marketing, section 3.1 asked (1) why the sales of product *X* have been decreasing rapidly; (2) why consumers purchase particular brands of detergents; (3) why budget motels entered the hotel/motel industry in the 1970s; and (4) why newspapers charge lower rates to local advertisers than to national advertisers? This section and the three subsequent sections will offer typical marketing explanations of these phenomena and then systematically explore the underlying structure of the explanations.

Why are the sales of product X decreasing rapidly? A marketing explanation of this phenomenon might include reference to the product life cycle (PLC) concept. The product life cycle suggests that products go through four stages: introduction, growth, maturity, and decline. During the introductory stage, sales increase very slowly and profits are usually negative. During the growth stage, the product catches on and both sales and profits increase rapidly. At the maturity stage, sales begin to level off and profits start a gradual decline. Finally, both sales and profits decrease precipitously during the decline stage. *The decrease in sales of product X can be explained by noting that X is in the decline stage of its life cycle where rapidly decreasing sales and profits are to be expected.*

Product life cycle explanations of the preceding variety frequently turn out to be vacuous. The crucial part of the explanans is the statement "*X* is in the decline stage," because this statement carries the burden of explaining the decreasing sales. Yet, how do we know that "*X* is in the decline stage"? Kotler (1972c, p. 436) has observed that "the stages, if stages there are, [of the product life cycle] are too variable in length to permit a prediction of when the next one will occur." Since the lengths of the stages are too variable, the primary factor determining the stage of the life cycle is sales. But the explanans then turns into a *tautology* or an *analytic* explanation because if the level of sales determines the stage of the life cycle, then the stage in the life cycle cannot be used to explain the level of sales. Unless and until the product life cycle can be refined to the point where the stages can be identified independent of the sales variable, the life cycle concept will remain impotent and void of explanatory power.

Recognizing the essentially tautologous nature of the product life cycle, Tellis and Crawford (1981) have developed a substitute notion, the product evolution cycle (PEC). Drawing upon the theory of biological evolution, they propose that sales are an evolutionary function of three motivating forces: market factors, managerial effectiveness, and government mediation. Unlike the PLC, the PEC does not assume that sales is a function of time. Rather, the evolution of sales proceeds within the dimension of time. The evolution proceeds in the direction of greater efficiency, greater complexity, and greater diversity. The PEC would appear to resolve some of the troublesome tautological problems of the PLC.

4.7 A CONSUMER BEHAVIOR EXPLANATION

The next explanation attempts to answer the question "*Why do consumers purchase particular brands of detergents?*" Engel, Kollat, and Blackwell (1973) present a model of habitual decision-process behavior, and, in a section entitled "Using the Model to Explain Consumer Behavior," they provide an explanation for detergent purchasing:

> Laundry detergents generally are purchased on the basis of habit rather than extended problem solving. A problem is recognized when the housewife runs out of detergent, and her decision usually calls for purchase of a preferred brand on her next visit to the grocery store. There is no need to engage in conscious weighing of alternatives or external search for information. The situation changes, of course, when a significant new product comes on the market, but innovations of that magnitude are a rarity in this industry.
>
> Survey results showed that women evaluate a detergent on the following bases: (1) cleaning ability (96 percent), (2) low suds (54 percent), (3) safety to colors (48 percent), (4) whitening and brightening ability (44 percent), (5) price (31 percent),

and (6) fresh smell (20 percent). In addition to these evaluative criteria, 86 percent favored a powdered form and 60 percent preferred to use warm water. Several major brands were found to rate highest on these criteria, with Tide being the dominant favorite. These ratings of brand attitude closely paralleled market shares. The result is strong loyalty toward one or two preferred brands and only relatively small incidence of permanent brand switching. If the housewife does switch, it tends to be a temporary action to take advantage of a price reduction.

Those who were interviewed, for the most part, evidenced satisfaction with their present alternative. Postdecision evaluation, therefore, seldom takes place. (Engel, Kollat, and Blackwell 1973, pp. 66–67)

4.7.1 A Reconstruction of the Explanation

The explanation provided by Engel, Kollat, and Blackwell uses a narrative format that is pedagogically appropriate for a textbook but makes evaluation difficult. The following reconstruction (1) captures the essence of the explanation, (2) shows specifically how the explanation relates to the model, and (3) lends itself more readily to structural analysis and evaluation.

(a) Most people do not engage in conscious weighing of alternatives or external search for information when purchasing detergents.

(b) Therefore, for most people, and except for unusual circumstances, the purchase of detergents can be classified as habitual in nature.

(c) Therefore, the habitual decision-process behavior model can be applied to the purchasing of detergents.

(d) The *stimulus* occurs when the housewife runs out of detergent.

(e) The *evaluative criteria* for detergents (surveys show) are in rank order of most often mentioned to least often mentioned: (1) cleaning ability, (2) low suds, (3) . . .

(f) Additional evaluative criteria suggest that 86 percent of women prefer detergent in powder form, and 60 percent prefer to use warm water (survey results).

(g) The model suggests that the components of *attitude* are the evaluative criteria. That is, people are likely to *prefer* brands that they *rate highly* on specific attributes considered *important* in that generic product.

(h) The model suggests that people are more likely to purchase brands they prefer (favorable attitude) than brands they do not prefer.

(i) Therefore, the model suggests that people are likely to purchase brands rated highly on the evaluative criteria.

(j) Therefore, the preceding suggests that, with high likelihood, the ratings of each brand on the evaluative criteria should match closely with the market share of each brand.

(k) Survey results show that ratings of brand attitude closely parallel market shares.

(l) This explains the market shares of different brands of detergents.

The preceding reconstruction, which attempts to accurately summarize the underlying logic of the explanation, shows in graphic relief the different kinds of statements in the explanatory structure. Taken in order, statement (a) is an *assumption* that probably could be validated empirically if challenged. Statement (b) is *classificatory*; however, the underlying classificatory schema is not given explicitly. Therefore, determining the acceptability of the classificatory schema is not possible. Statement (c) is a *logical* classificatory statement. Given (b), then (c) must be true. Statement (d) is another assumption that probably could be empirically verified, if necessary. Statements (e) and (f) are both *observation* statements; here the authors bring in "real-world" evidence. The next three statements contain the heart of the explanation; (g), (h), and (i) are the *laws* or *lawlike* statements that carry the brunt of the explanation. Statement (j) is a *hypothesis* suggested by the preceding arguments. Finally, (k) is an *observation* sentence and (i) is the *explanandum*, or conclusion.

4.7.2 Structural Analysis of the Explanation

What is the basic form of the explanation? As reconstructed, the nature of the lawlike statements (g), (h), and (i) makes the explanation inductive-statistical. The qualifier, "with high likelihood," in (j) suggests an I-S model. The conclusive test, however, is the following question, "Can (k) be false and (j) still be true?" The answer must be yes; even with no measurement error, a nonrepresentative sample might give us the wrong results.

The reconstruction also shows that the original narrative explanation was an *enthymeme* (elliptical); some necessary statements were skipped over or suppressed. For example, the logical equivalent of statement (h) was suppressed. Although often heuristically unimportant, the suppression of premises can frequently impede analysis.

Next, note the *teleological* character of the explanation. That is, the lawlike generalizations are heavily purposive in kind. Statements (g), (h), and (i) suggest that the brand purchase decision is purposive to the extent that people seek brands that they perceive will correspond most closely to their evaluative criteria.

Consider the depth of the explanation chain. The most basic statements in the chain concern components of the evaluative criteria that are product-specific, for example, cleaning ability and low suds. These components are presumably under the control of the detergent firms. Therefore, the explanation attempts to explain a phenomenon (market share) by relying on factors (cleaning ability, etc.) that potentially enable the firm to *influence* the explanation chain. This suggests that, pragmatically speaking, the explanation is respectably deep.

An examination of causal considerations casts a shadow on the pragmatics of the explanation. The explanation implies that a firm might increase its market share by changing its product and promotion along lines suggested by the evaluative criteria. This presumes that changes in the evaluative criteria will cause subsequent changes in purchase and market share. However, the *temporal* sequence in this instance may be counterintuitive. Studies suggest that the "real" causal chain may be the reverse: changes in purchase (market share) cause subsequent changes in the evaluative criteria. Therefore, policy decisions based on such explanations may prove faulty.

Finally, consider the underlying habitual decision-process behavior (H-D-P-B) model. Many of the concepts in the model are not explicitly included or discussed in the explanation, for example, personality, information, experience, income, culture, and family. What was the role of the H-D-P-B model in generating the explanation? Essentially, the H-D-P-B model provided numerous constructs that fit together in a theoretical manner and that the authors suggest might be useful in explaining habitual purchase behavior. The *users* of the model then select several constructs as potentially explanatory.

4.8 A PRICE DISCRIMINATION EXPLANATION

Firms often engage in price discrimination; they charge different prices to different customers for the same product or service. Theaters charge different prices for adults than they do for children. Universities charge brilliant students less than average students by providing scholarships. For the services provided by the federal government, wealthier citizens are charged more than poorer citizens because the income tax rate is progressive. The same phenomenon occurs in newspaper advertising. *Why do newspapers charge lower rates to local advertisers than to national advertisers?* The late Julian Simon states one possible explanation:

> *Factual problem.* It is an observed fact that newspapers charge lower advertising rates to local retailers than to nationally advertised brands of goods. To explain why they do is a research problem.
>
> *Assumptions.* We *assume*, first, that businessmen (newspaper owners, in this case) will charge that price to each group of people that will result in *maximum profit.* (This is the "economic man" assumption.) . . . Second, we *assume* that businessmen know how groups of customers (retailers and national advertisers) react to various prices. (This is the "perfect knowledge" assumption.) . . .

Deduction. We *deduce* that, if one customer group is *less sensitive* to a price increase than another group is, it will be profitable to charge a higher price to the less sensitive customer. (This can be shown with a standard logical chain of economic deduction.) . . .

Hypothesis. We then hypothesize that, if the deduction is correct, the newspaper publishers believe that national advertisers are less sensitive to price changes. This hypothesis can be tested by finding out what the newspaper advertisers believe about the relative sensitivity of local and national advertisers. A questionnaire study found that publishers do indeed believe that national advertisers are less sensitive to price changes and thus confirmed the hypothesis. (Simon 1969, p. 38)

Simon's proposed explanation is well formed, succinct, and rigorous. It thus requires little elaboration or analysis. Some of the terminology differs in minor ways from the present treatment. For example, his *factual problem* would be our *explanandum*; this is the phenomenon to be explained. His *assumptions* would be our *laws*, insofar as these are generalized statements that do most of the explaining. The term *assumption* carries unfortunate connotations in the social sciences, such as "cannot be tested," "should not be tested," and "need not conform to reality." Because formal analysis of axioms and assumptions will be deferred to the next chapter, we need here only observe that few terms have been so thoroughly abused in the social sciences as have the terms *assumption* and *axiom.* They should definitely be labeled "handle with care."

A final observation concerning Simon's excellent explanation of newspaper price discrimination focuses on his *hypothesis* section. Simon deduces certain predictions that should occur *if his explanation is correct.* He then tests these predictions. Thus, Simon provides a graphic illustration of what it means to require explanations to be empirically testable and intersubjectively verifiable.

4.9 A WHEEL OF RETAILING EXPLANATION

The 1970s saw the successful rise of so-called budget motels in the lodging industry. These motels lacked many of the amenities (room service, bellhops, chandeliers, and posh wallpaper) but featured very low prices for rooms. *Why was the introduction of budget motels such a successful retail innovation?* A marketing explanation might involve the wheel of retailing, first proposed by McNair (1958).

Stanley Hollander's (1960/1969) conceptualization of the wheel of retailing holds that new types of retailers "usually" enter the market as low-status, low-margin, low-price operators. Gradually, they acquire more elaborate establishments and facilities with both increased investments and higher operating costs. Finally, they mature as high-cost, high-price merchants, vulnerable to newer types who, in turn, go through the same pattern.

A wheel explanation of budget motels would start with the observation that the original motels began as cabins along the highways. They were low-cost, low-margin, low-price, and emphatically low-status operations. Over time, motels added many services and upgraded their facilities to the point where the distinguishing features between motels and hotels were difficult to find. Concomitant with the added services and upgraded facilities were increases in costs and prices. Therefore, the entry of budget motels can be explained by demonstrating that it is another instance of the wheel of retailing.

The wheel constitutes a form of inductive-statistical explanation because of the claim that new retailers "usually" enter the market. Hollander acknowledges that *not all* new retailers enter as low-cost, low-margin, and so on. Vending machine retailing, department store branches, and convenience stores are retail institutions whose entries did not conform with the wheel notion. Unfortunately, no one has been able to suggest the particular conditions that must prevail for new retail institutions to enter in accordance with the wheel.

Essentially, the wheel attempts to explain the entry of budget motels by demonstrating that the history of the motel industry is consistent with an *empirical regularity* (see Chapter 5) observed in other industries, that is, the upgrading of services and facilities, and, therefore, the increasing of costs and prices. The explanation seems incomplete because it does not explain *why* the motel industry continually increased services, facilities, costs, and prices. Perhaps, integrating the wheel notion with the theory of competition for differential advantage might make the explanation more complete.

4.9.1 The Wheel of Retailing and Competition for Differential Advantage

The economist J.M. Clark (1954, 1961) promulgated a theory of "effective competition" that stressed the concept of "differential advantage" (see section 9.3). Clark held that new firms or institutions enter an industry when they believe they will have some differential advantage over existing firms in serving some subset of customers. Competition consists of a series of initiatory moves by some firms to gain a differential advantage and of subsequent countermoves by rivals to neutralize that advantage. Alderson captures the essence of the concept:

> Every business firm occupies a position which is in some respects unique. Its location, the product it sells, its operating methods, or the customers it serves tend to set it off in some degree from every other firm. Each firm competes by making the most of its individuality and its special character. It is constantly seeking to establish some competitive advantage. Absolute advantage in the sense of an advanced method of operation is not enough if all competitors live up to the same high standards. What is important in competition is differential advantage, which can give a firm an edge over what others in the field are offering. (Alderson 1957, p. 101)

We can now attempt to integrate the wheel of retailing into the theory of competition for differential advantage.[2]

1. All new retail institutions enter the market because the participants perceive that they will have some form of differential advantage over existing retail forms. The basis for differential advantage may be some innovation that yields greater convenience in location to certain customers (e.g., vending machines), speedy service (e.g., fast-food restaurants), low prices (motels), or some other benefit to a subset of potential customers. The particular differential advantage of early motels, when competing against hotels, was both convenient locations along the highway and low prices. Motels were low cost, low price, and low status, and they competed primarily against existing *hotels.*

2. The number of motels increased rapidly as a large segment of the market desired both convenient locations away from downtown areas and the low prices. As the number of motels increased, the nature of competition changed from motel versus hotel to motel versus motel. That is, the primary thrust of competition for motels changed from trying to lure customers from hotels to trying to lure customers from *other motels.* Then, individual motels began to seek some differential advantage over other motels.

3. Price reductions are the form of differential advantage that would be neutralized most easily and quickly. Therefore, the upgrading of services and facilities would be the most common means used to gain differential advantage. For example, most motels followed this progression: no television, pay television, free television, color television, cable color television. Each motel attempted to neutralize the differential advantage of its competitors by matching its competitors' services and facilities.

4. Therefore, over time the motel industry gradually increased its costs, margins, and prices. The motel industry thus became a tempting target for budget motels stressing low costs, margins, and prices.

The preceding integration of the wheel with competition for differential advantage shows why the wheel must state that new types of retailers *usually* enter as low cost, low price, and so on. There is no basis for supposing that *all* new forms of retailing would seek low price as their basis for differential advantage. In addition, the revised structure appears testable, at least in principle. In particular, the generalization that as a new form of retailing matures, the thrust of competition will change in the directions noted seems amenable to empirical confirmation. Finally, integrating the wheel of retailing into the theory of competition for differential advantage has made the explanation of the phenomenon of budget motels substantially deeper and more complete.

The theory of competition for differential advantage, as initiated by Clark and further developed by Alderson, would seem to be a viable alternative to neoclassical perfect competition theory. Yet, the theory lay fallow for decades. This situation changed with the development of resource-advantage ("R-A") theory (Hunt 2000b; Hunt and Morgan 1995, 1996, 1997). Indeed, "resource-advantage theory draws more strongly from differential advantage theory than from any other research tradition" (Hunt 2000b, p. 63). (See Chapter 9 for more on R-A theory.)

4.10 SUMMARY AND CONCLUSIONS

This chapter has explored a variety of issues concerning explanation and has used the tools developed so far to analyze several explanations of marketing phenomena. The thesis of structural symmetry was examined and found to be half correct: all adequate explanations of phenomena must be potentially predictive. However, all adequate predictions of phenomena are not necessarily adequate explanations because predictions can be made without the use of lawlike generalizations. And lawlike generalizations are necessary for the scientific explanation of phenomena. Furthermore, the ability to *retrodict* phenomena is *not* a necessary condition for explanation.

The relationships among scientific *understanding*, *explanation*, and *prediction* were explored via an analysis of Dubin's power paradox. The paradox disappears upon the realization that prediction is necessary for explanation and that explanation is necessary for understanding. Therefore, models and theories in marketing that do not explain and predict do not contribute to scientific understanding.

The epistemologically troublesome notions of causality and causal explanations were shown to be problematic with respect to generating *sufficient* conditions for classifying an explanation as *causal.* However, various kinds of evidence can be introduced to *suggest* that a particular relationship or explanation is causal. These include temporal sequentiality, associative variation, nonspurious association, and theoretical support.

All explanations are incomplete in one way or another. In principle, all explanations involve an explanation chain and are, therefore, incomplete. Some explanations are incomplete because they are enthymemes, that is, they skip over or leave out some premise. Some explanations are better termed partial explanations or explanation sketches.

The product life cycle was explored as an explanatory device and found to lack explanatory power. A consumer behavior model was found to be useful in the context of discovery. Simon's price discrimination explanation was found to be well formed and illustrated how explanations can be empirically testable. Finally, the wheel of retailing was integrated into the theory of competition for differential advantage and used to explain the phenomenon of budget motels.

QUESTIONS FOR ANALYSIS AND DISCUSSION

1. Summarize the thesis of structural symmetry. Why have so many marketing and social science theorists been reluctant to accept the conclusion that every acceptable explanation is a potential prediction?
2. Find an instance in the marketing literature where the author has used the term *cause*, and evaluate the appropriateness of the author's usage. What criteria, either explicit or implicit, did the author use to justify his causal assertion? Evaluate those criteria.
3. Can there be any such thing as a "final explanation" of any marketing phenomenon?
4. Find an example of an explanation chain in the marketing literature. Is it acceptably deep? Evaluate the explanation.
5. How do enthymemes, partial explanations, and explanation sketches differ? Are there other ways in which explanations can be incomplete?
6. This chapter found the product life cycle to be explanatorily impotent. If this is so, why does the product life cycle receive so much attention in the marketing literature? Is the attention justified?
7. The explanation of marketing phenomena is the cornerstone of research in marketing. Yet, the term *explanation* does not appear in the index of most prominent marketing research texts. How can this paradox be reconciled?
8. Empirical studies frequently cite the coefficient of determination (R^2), and they discuss the percentage of the dependent variable "explained" by the independent variable(s). When used in this context, why is the term *explained* usually enclosed in quotation marks?
9. What does it mean to propose that all marketing phenomena can "ultimately be reduced" to one of the four sets of fundamental explananda? Chapter 1 proposed that one dimension of macromarketing is the "consequences of society for marketing systems." Could this dimension be "reduced?" Go through a recent issue of *JMR*. See whether all of the dependent variables can be "reduced." If not all of them can, what additional fundamental explananda are required?
10. Bagozzi (in Hunt 1983b) suggests that marketing researchers want to understand and control marketing behavior. He contends that "both objectives—understanding and control—rest fundamentally on the identification and analysis of causal relationships." Could understanding not come about simply through the use of regularity relationships? Similarly, could control not come about by way of regularity relationships? Evaluate.

11. Chapter 4 identifies four criteria for classifying explanations as potentially causal: (1) temporal sequentiality, (2) associative variation, (3) nonspurious association, and (4) theoretical support. John Stuart Mill—discussed by Bagozzi in Hunt 1983b—suggests the methods of agreement, difference, residues, and concomitant variation. Compare and contrast these two sets of criteria.

NOTES

1. Yes, it can be done. The sidewalk temperature in Madison is correlated with the ambient temperature in Madison. The latter is correlated with the ambient temperature in Oslo. The temperature in Oslo is related to the rate of conception in Oslo (higher in winter). QED.

2. This analysis parallels in part the integration of the wheel into the concept of intertype competition; see Bucklin (1972, p. 120 ff).

5 THE MORPHOLOGY OF SCIENTIFIC LAWS

Several kinds of statements about behavior are commonly made. When we tell an anecdote or pass along a bit of gossip, we report a single event—what someone did upon such and such an occasion. . . . These accounts have their uses. They broaden the experience of those who have not had firsthand access to similar data. But they are only the beginnings of a science. The next step is the discovery of some sort of uniformity.

—B.F. Skinner

Commentators (e.g., Brodbeck 1968, p. 673) on the history of science have found that the notion of descriptive or scientific laws evolved from the older conception of prescriptive or normative laws. The earliest laws were normative commandments that asserted rules for proper (moral) conduct: "Thou shalt not kill." Whether these normative laws were sanctioned by the established church or civil government, or frequently both, all people were universally obliged to obey them. From this genesis, the term law has been extended to descriptive regularities in science because these, too, apply "universally" to all phenomena. However, at that point the similarity ends. Normative laws prescribe what people ought to do; scientific laws in human behavior describe what people actually do.

When a citizen fails to *obey* a normative law, the appropriate authorities may invoke sanctions, for example, excommunication, public humiliation, failing the marketing theory course, imprisonment, flogging, or even death. As conspirators find out in antitrust cases, when a marketer disobeys a governmental normative law such as "Thou shalt not conspire to fix prices," both fines and imprisonment may ensue. On the other hand, the consequences of finding behaviors that "disobey" a descriptive or scientific law suggest a reexamination of the law in question rather than punishment. If behaviors do not follow the law, then either the law should be rejected or the conditions under which the law is believed to be true should be modified. When the term *law* is used in this book, we refer to scientific laws and not normative laws.

Both normative laws and scientific laws should be carefully distinguished from normative decision rules or normative decision models. Normative decisions rules or models prescribe the most appropriate courses of action to follow in order to attempt rationally to achieve some stated objective. Thus, linear programming can provide a set of normative decision rules for optimally allocating the advertising budget among the various media. As a second example, consider the marketing concept. Note that it is not a *concept* in the normal sense of the term. Rather, it is a philosophy of doing business based on a set of three normative decision rules: (1) firms should be customer oriented; (2) all marketing activities of the firm should be integrated; and (3) profit rather than sales should be the orientation of the firm. Although many normative decision rules are nothing more than crude *rules of thumb*, some are firmly based on scientific laws. Bunge (1967b, p. 132) suggests that normative decision rules that are based or founded on some set of scientific laws be referred to as *grounded rules.* In summary, normative laws prescribe what people *morally* or *legally* ought to do; normative decision rules or models prescribe what people ought to do rationally to achieve some stated objective; scientific laws in human behavior describe what people actually do.

This chapter concerns the morphology of scientific laws and their role in scientific inquiry. First, we shall explore the role of laws in marketing research; then, we shall provide some criteria for separating lawlike generalizations from ordinary conversational generalizations and evaluate some marketing lawlike generalizations.

5.1 ROLE OF LAWS IN MARKETING RESEARCH

Laws and lawlike statements play vital roles in marketing inquiry. As indicated in Chapter 3, the development of laws in marketing is a requirement for explaining marketing phenomena. All of the models discussed in Chapter 3 that have explanatory power (deductive-nomological, deductive-statistical, and inductive-statistical) explain phenomena by deductive or inductive subsumption under lawlike generalizations. That is, we can *explain* the market shares of various detergents by showing that the shares are consistent with certain lawlike statements relating brand purchases with the components of brand attitudes (section 4.7). In addition to explaining marketing phenomena, lawlike statements in marketing facilitate the *prediction* of marketing phenomena. All models that can provide satisfactory scientific explanations of *past* marketing phenomena must be potentially capable of predicting future marketing phenomena; or, as Chapter 4 indicated, all satisfactory explanations are potential predictions. The laws in the models provide the predictive power.

Taken together, the ability systematically to explain marketing phenomena and the ability to predict marketing phenomena lead to the *scientific understanding* and *control* of marketing phenomena. If, by employing certain laws, marketers can predict the consequences of changing certain resources under their control, then they have at least some ability to *control* the system. Thus, the intellectual goal of all scientific endeavor is scientific understanding, and the pragmatic consequence of scientific endeavor is increased control over man's environment.

The next section will discuss the basic form of laws, that is, generalized conditionals. Also, some distinctions will be made concerning laws, lawlike generalizations, and principles. One caveat prefaces our discussion: the term *law* is another slippery term (like the term *explanation*) that seems intuitively clear at first glance but provides stout resistance to rigorous analysis.

5.2 THE FIRST CRITERION: GENERALIZED CONDITIONALS

All laws specify a relationship in the form of a generalized conditional.[1] *Conditional* implies some kind of "if-then" relationship. Thus, a common basic form is: "Every time *A* occurs, then *B* will occur." Or, in slightly more developed form, "For any *x*, if *x* is *A*, then *x* is *B*" (or, alternatively, "All *A* are *B*"). For example, "All consumers who systematically avoid purchasing private label merchandise are low in generalized self-confidence." Note that this statement can be recast in generalized conditional form: "For any *x* (consumer), if *x* is *A* (systematically avoids purchasing private label merchandise), then *x* is *B* (low in generalized self-confidence)." Not all statements of generalized conditional form constitute laws. In particular, we have previously suggested that *accidental generalizations*, although having the form of generalized conditionals, are not laws.

Confusion continues concerning the requirement that all laws must specify a relationship in the form of a generalized conditional. Consider the interesting article by Sheth and Sisodia (1999) entitled "Revising Marketing's Lawlike Generalizations." They argue that (1) marketing is a context-driven discipline, (2) the context for marketing is changing radically due to electronic commerce, market diversity, new economics, and coopetition, (3) as marketing academics we need to question and challenge well-accepted lawlike generalizations in marketing. Their Table 2 identifies twelve entities that they consider to be "old" lawlike generalizations that should be changed: (A) retail gravitation, sales and distribution channels, intermediary-based advertising and promotion, (B) diffusion of innovation, product life cycles, and brand loyalty, (C) market segmentation, customer satisfaction, and market-driven orientation, and (D) market share, generic competitive strategies, and vertical integration.

Kerin and Sethuraman (1999) provide a commentary on the Sheth and Sisodia article. First, they discuss the criteria for considering an entity to be a lawlike generalization. They argue for the following four criteria: (1) generalized conditionals, (2) empirical support, (3) systematic integration into a coherent scientific structure or framework, and (4) insight/importance. They then evaluate the twelve entities that Sheth and Sisodia maintain are lawlike generalizations that should be challenged and conclude:

> We believe nine of the twelve generalizations do not qualify as lawlike generalizations. The product lifecycle is probably a tautology (see Hunt 1983b, p. 131). Others [e.g., generic competitive strategies] are normative statements or decision rules that prescribe a course of action to achieve some end. . . . Market-driven orientation is an organizational philosophy, not unlike the marketing concept. Four of the purported generalizations—physical distribution channels, location-based advertising, marketing segmentation, and, to some extent, vertical integration—represent current or conventional marketing practice or strategy. No discernable conditional lawlike statements are offered in their support. Thus, they fail the first requirement for a lawlike generalization. (Kerin and Sethuraman 1999, p. 103)

Agreed, "It may very well be that our progress and status as a discipline in the twenty-first century will be gauged by our success or failure in . . . the quest for lawlike generalizations that explain and facilitate the prediction of marketing phenomena" (Kerin and Sethuraman 1999, p. 104). Also agreed, Sheth and Sisodia provide some interesting thoughts as to topics in marketing that warrant reconsideration due to electronic commerce, market diversity, the new economics, and "coopetition." However, confusing *lawlike generalizations* with concepts, normative decision rules, strategies, and conventional wisdom detracts from their argument.

After an examination of principles, laws, and lawlike generalizations, the criteria for according lawlike status to statements will occupy the rest of this chapter. Confusion often arises concerning the differences among the following concepts: "principles," "laws," and "lawlike generalizations." First, let's differentiate between laws and lawlike generalizations. Lawlike generalizations (or "lawlike statements" or "lawlike propositions") are statements in generalized conditional form that fulfill all the criteria of laws but have not yet been tested and confirmed or corroborated.[2] Although the subject of criteria for corroboration (or confirmation) of laws and theoretical constructions will be extensively investigated in Chapter 7, a few preliminary observations can be made here. To say that a lawlike statement is highly confirmed, or corroborated, or believed to be true, is different from saying that it is absolutely true, or true-with-certainty, or "True" (with capital "T"). (See section 1.1 and Hunt [1990] for further discussion on this issue.) Therefore, we do not require lawlike statements to be "True" to be a law. Rather, we require them to be highly confirmed or corroborated by the evidence, which gives us reason to believe them to be true or isomorphic with the real world.

A second distinction is between laws and principles (sometimes referred to as "high-level laws," "most fundamental laws," or, simply, "Laws" with an uppercase "L"). The distinction is largely honorific. In any discipline a *law* becomes a *principle* when it is widely held to be of extreme significance or importance to that discipline and when the evidence corroborating it is overwhelming. Thus, we have the Law of Demand in economics, the First Law of Thermodynamics in physics, and Weber's Law in psychology.

For example, Simon (1969, p. 38, his emphasis) seems to have blurred the distinction between *law* and *principle*: "If an empirical test of the hypothesis confirms the hypothesis, the generalization might be called a *law*, provided that the finding is sufficiently *important*." The unfortunate consequences of this confusion have led many writers to decry the absence of *laws* in the behavioral sciences when what they have really observed is the absence of *principles* (or *Laws* with uppercase "L") in those areas. Berelson and Steiner (1964) have documented a host of reasonably well-supported generalizations worthy of being called *laws* in the behavioral sciences. Kincaid defends both the possibility and existence of laws in the social sciences. Indeed, he finds that "parts of the social sciences produce laws, evidence, and explanations quite similar in form to those of evolutionary biology and ecology" (1990, p. 58). And in marketing, Bass and Wind (1995), identify over three dozen generalizations that (at least potentially) qualify as lawlike.

As examples of generalizations that at least potentially qualify as lawlike in marketing, Blattberg, Briesch, and Fox (1995) offer the following in the area of promotions: (1) Temporary retail price reductions substantially increase sales. (2) Higher market share brands are less deal elastic. (3) The frequency of deals changes the consumer's reference price. (4) The greater the frequency of deals, the lower the height of the deal spike. (5) Display and feature advertising have strong effects on item sales. In the area of reference price research, Kalyanaram and Winer (1995) propose the following: (1) Reference prices have a consistent and significant impact on consumer demand. (2) Internal reference prices utilize past prices as part of the consumer's information set. (3) Consumers react more strongly to price increases than to price decreases. In the area of consumer choice, Meyer and Johnson (1995) offer: (1) Subjective attribute valuations are a nonlinear reference-point dependent, function of the corresponding objective measure of the attribute. (2) The algebraic integration rule that best describes how valuations are integrated into overall valuations is a multiplicative-multilinear function that recognizes an overweighting of negative attribute information. (3) Overall valuations of an option are linked to choices by a function that recognizes the proximity or similarity of the option to others in the set. In the area of market entry, Kalyanaram, Robinson, and Urban (1995) propose: (1) For mature consumer and industrial goods, there is a negative relationship between order of market entry and market share. (2) For consumer packaged goods, the entrant's forecasted market share divided by the first entrant's market share roughly equals one divided by the square root of order of market entry.

5.3 THE SECOND CRITERION: EMPIRICAL CONTENT

What kinds of statements that have the basic form of generalized conditionals should be characterized as *lawlike*? Alternatively, what criteria should be applied to distinguish lawlike statements from nonlawlike statements? One extremely desirable criterion is that *all lawlike statements must have empirical content* (Lambert and Brittan 1970, p. 38). The empirical-content criterion rules out both nonsense statements and strictly analytical statements. An example of a nonsense generalized conditional might be: "All marketing maloglops are high priced." Clearly, according lawlike status to such statements would be patently ridiculous since maloglops are nonexistent.

Much more important than just ruling out nonsense laws, the empirical-content criterion also excludes strictly analytical statements from being considered lawlike. Before discussing the importance of excluding strictly analytical statements, we need to distinguish between two basic kinds of statements: analytic and synthetic.

Consider the following two statements: (1) marketing activities consume a large portion of the consumer's dollar; and (2) either marketing activities consume a large portion of the consumer's dollar, or marketing activities *do not* consume a large portion of the consumer's dollar. Both statements are true, yet they are true for different reasons. The first statement is known to be true because of studies conducted by Reavis Cox (1965), Harold Barger (1955), Louis P. Bucklin (1978), and others. That is, statement 1 is known to be true only after we examine the facts in the real world. Such statements are called *synthetic* (Bergmann 1957). Conversely, statement 2 is true no matter what the real-world facts are. Statement 2 is true because it makes no assertion about the real world: it does not say anything at all! Such statements are called *purely analytic*, and, strictly speaking, they are true only because of the order and nature of the logical terms (such as *either* and *or*) and the way in which they define certain descriptive terms (such as *marketing*). True analytic statements are *tautologies,* and false ones are *contradictions.*

Bergmann (1957, p. 27) suggests that in tautologies the descriptive words appear only vacuously; that is, the truth content of tautologies is independent of the descriptive words. Therefore, to show that statement 2 is really tautological, we need to define the descriptive words:

p = marketing activities
q = consume a large portion of the consumer's dollar

As constructed, statement 2 then merely asserts that "either p is q, or p is not q." We could then insert any descriptive terms for p or q that we desire, and the statement would still be true. Therefore, the descriptive terms in statement 2 appear only *vacuously.* A similar reconstruction of statement 1 will reveal it to be a synthetic statement. (Try it!)

So the *empirical-content* criterion successfully weeds out strictly analytic statements from lawlike statements because we want our laws to "say something" about the real world. We want lawlike statements to be empirically testable. However, the analytic/synthetic distinction may not always be as clear-cut as has been implied. Consider this assertion: "No consumer can be brand loyal to more than one brand at a time in the same product class." The statement is certainly a generalized conditional of the form "*If* for any *X*, if *X* is a consumer, and if she is loyal to brand *A*, and if brands *A* and *B* are in the same product class, *then* she cannot at the same time be loyal to brand *B*." Does the statement pass the empirical content criterion for being considered lawlike? Is the statement analytic or synthetic?

Whether the brand-loyalty assertion is analytic or synthetic depends primarily on how brand loyalty is defined. Consider the following definition: "Consumer *X* is considered to be brand loyal to brand *A* if, and only if, the consumer purchases over 50 percent of his/her requirements of the product class from brand *A*." Given this definition, the brand-loyalty assertion is obviously analytic, because it would be mathematically impossible for a consumer to purchase in excess of 50 percent of his/her requirements from brand *A* and at the same time purchase over 50 percent from brand *B*. Therefore, given this definition, the "brand-loyalty" generalization would fail the empirical-content criterion.

On the other hand, Tucker (1964) suggests denoting consumers as brand loyal if they make three successive choices of the same brand. Consider the following sequence of purchases over a twelve-month period:

CBAAACABBBAB

Using Tucker's definition, the consumer would be brand loyal to *both* brands *A* and *B* during the same twelve–month period, and the assertion that a consumer will be brand loyal to only one brand in a single time period becomes synthetic, not analytic. That is, with the revised definition, it is now *possible* to show that the brand-loyalty generalization is empirically false. Therefore, the statement would pass the *empirical content* criterion.

Halbert (1965, p. 66) maintained that many of the generalizations in the marketing literature seem to be "either tautologies, truisms, or so overly general that they are of very limited use in developing marketing science." As one example, Halbert points out a generalized statement by Jastram (1955): "If it appears to be profitable to plan advertising at all, there will be some one rate of outlay for which it will be most profitable to plan." Readers should decide for themselves whether the statement is a tautology.

In his "theory of social initiative," Robert Bartels (1968, p. 32) states, "Society, not the business entrepreneur, is the basic undertaker of all activity." Is this analytic or synthetic? Would it pass or fail the empirical-content criterion for lawlikeness? As previously illustrated, the key depends on how certain terms (such as *basic undertaker*) are defined, and, unfortunately, Bartels provides no definitions. However, because innumerable "basic" activities do seem to be undertaken by business entrepreneurs, *if* the statement is intended to be synthetic, it is probably false. Therefore, there would probably be a strong temptation to define the term *basic undertaker* in such a way that the truth content of the statement would be assured. Consequently, to the extent that the statement is synthetic, it is probably false. And to the extent that the statement is analytic, it will fail the empirical-content criterion. In either case, the statement should not be considered lawlike.

5.4 THE THIRD CRITERION: NOMIC NECESSITY

The previous discussion suggests that lawlike statements must have (1) the basic form of generalized conditionals and (2) empirical content. The third criterion states that *all purportedly lawlike statements must possess nomic* (nō'mĭk) *necessity* (sometimes referred to as "nomological universality" or "nomic universality"). The purpose of the nomic-necessity criterion is systematically to prevent *accidental* generalizations from being considered laws. Nomic necessity implies that the occurrence of some phenomenon *must* be associated with some other phenomenon; the relationship cannot be, simply, by *chance.* The classic illustration of an accidental generalization has been provided by Nagel (1961, p. 52): "All the screws in Smith's current car are rusty." Note that the statement is a generalized conditional with empirical content. Nevertheless, few people would like to accord lawlike status to such a generalization precisely because it somehow seems to describe an *accidental* relationship.

As Rescher (1970b, p. 103) has observed, although there is widespread agreement that scientific laws involve a necessity that transcends simple accidental regularity, the issue of explicating what exactly is meant by nomic necessity remains a major problem. A few examples of generalizations might help to clarify the issue. Consider the following five generalizations: (1) all the coins in my pocket are half-dollars; (2) all products produced by Procter and Gamble are distributed through supermarkets; (3) all products with the trade name Maxwell House have a coffee base; (4) two cities attract retail trade from an intermediate town in the vicinity of the breaking point (where 50 percent of the trade is attracted to each city) in direct proportion to their populations and in inverse proportion to the square of the distances from the two cities to the intermediate town (Converse 1949, p. 379); and (5) in any survey, the percentages of people who express intentions to purchase a brand are directly proportional to the square roots of the percentages of informants who currently use the brand (Ehrenberg 1971, p. 34).

Note that all five of the statements in the previous paragraph are generalized conditionals of the "all *A* are *B*" variety and that all five have empirical content. Nevertheless, most scholars would find it intellectually disquieting to accord lawlike status to the first three and would be more than willing to consider the last two as suitable candidates for lawlike status. (Remember, this does not necessarily mean that we have enough empirical evidence to consider [4] and [5] to be *laws* but only that they pass muster for consideration as *lawlike.*) Intuitively, the generalizations embodied in the first three statements seem qualitatively different, more *accidental*, than those embodied in the last two. But precisely how do we analytically (rather than intuitively) separate accidental from nonaccidental generalizations? The answer lies in the fact that *generalizations exhibiting nomic necessity have a kind of hypothetical power that is different from that of accidental generalizations.*

The major purposes of scientific laws are to explain and predict phenomena. To accomplish these tasks, laws must have the power to generate hypotheses such as "If phenomenon *X* occurs, then phenomenon *Y* will occur." To demonstrate that accidental generalizations lack hypothetical power, consider the following statements:

A. If this coin (which is not in my pocket) were placed in my pocket, it would be a half-dollar.
B. If this product (which is not labeled Maxwell House) were labeled Maxwell House, then it would have a coffee base.
C. If this automobile were produced by Procter and Gamble (which it is not), it would be distributed through supermarkets.

Statements A, B, and C are all called *counterfactual conditionals* because the premises of the statements are not true.[3] That is, the premises are "counter to the facts": The coin is not in my pocket, the product is not labeled Maxwell House, and the automobile is not produced by Procter and Gamble.

Referring to the five generalizations, none of the first three generalizations support their respective counterfactual conditionals. No reasonable person would believe that statements A, B, and C were true *even though* he or she knew that generalizations (1), (2), and (3) were true. The generalization "All the coins in my pocket are half-dollars" does *not* support (i.e., give someone good reason to believe) statement A. The generalization "All products with the trade name Maxwell House have a coffee base" does *not* support statement B. Finally, the generalization "All products produced by Procter and Gamble are distributed through supermarkets" does not support statement C because there is nothing to prevent Procter and Gamble from distributing a product through another channel of distribution if it chooses to do so. The Procter and Gamble generalization (like the others) thus lacks the element of *must.* Alternatively, the Procter and Gamble generalization lacks the nomic necessity required of genuine lawlike statements because it lacks the *hypothetical power* to support counterfactual conditionals. As the next paragraph will show, genuine lawlike statements will exhibit nomic necessity by supporting counterfactual conditionals.

Consider the following statements:

D. If city *K* had four times the population of city *J* (*K* actually has only twice the population of *J*), then city *K* would double the percentage of retail trade that it draws from intermediate city *I.*

E. If the usership of brand *X* had been 16 percent (it actually was only 4 percent), then in this survey the percentage of people who expressed an intention to purchase brand *X* would have doubled.

Note, once again, that both D and E are counterfactual conditionals like A, B, and C. However, this time the generalizations *can support* their respective counterfactual conditionals if in fact the generalizations accurately represent the real world (a strictly empirical question). That is, generalization 4, "Two cities attract retail trade from an intermediate town. . . ," can support statement D if generalization (4) accurately depicts the real world. Similarly, generalization (5) can support statement E. *Therefore, in order for a statement to be considered lawlike, our third criterion is that it must exhibit nomic necessity, which rules out accidental generalizations. Accidental generalizations can be identified by their lack of hypothetical power as evidenced by their inability in principle to support counterfactual conditionals.*

5.5 THE FOURTH CRITERION: SYSTEMATIC INTEGRATION

The analysis thus far has shown that lawlike statements have the form of generalized conditionals that have empirical content and exhibit nomic necessity. The final requirement provides that *all purportedly lawlike statements must be systematically integrated into a body of scientific knowledge.* Stated negatively, a simple empirical regularity (even a well-confirmed one) is not a lawlike generalization. An empirical regularity does not qualify as a lawlike statement until it is systematically integrated into a coherent scientific structure or framework.

An empirical regularity is a statement summarizing observed uniformities of relationships between two or more concepts or variables. That empirical regularities should not be classified as lawlike until they have found a niche in a systematic framework has been observed both by philosophers of science and by theoreticians. Lambert and Brittan (1970, p. 45) suggest, "What leads us to reject the red sky in the morning/rain in the afternoon as a law, is that it is an isolated assertion having no apparent theoretical ramifications." Kaplan (1964, p. 92) believes that a "nomic generalization must be derivable from other laws, that is, play a part in scientific theory. Otherwise, we obtain what might be called an empirical generalization rather than a law." Merton (1968, p. 149) lamented that the literature in sociology abounds with isolated propositions that have not been assimilated into sociological theory. And Bass (1995, p. G8) admonishes marketing researchers to incorporate empirical generalizations into lower level and higher level theories because such an incorporation leads to "low level explanation" and "high level explanation." Finally, Rescher plainly states the systematically integrated criterion:

> An empirical generalization is not to be viewed as fully adequate for explanatory purposes until it can lay claim to the status of a law. Now a law is not just a summary statement of observed-regularities-to-date; it claims to deal with a universal regularity purporting to describe how things inevitably are: how the processes at work in the world must invariably work, how things have to happen in nature. Such a claim has to be based upon a stronger foundation than any mere observed regularity-to-date. The *coherence of laws* in patterns that illuminate the "mechanisms" by which natural processes occur is a critical element—perhaps the most important one—in furnishing this stronger foundation, this "something more" than a generalization of observations. An "observed regularity" does not become a "law of nature" simply by becoming better established through observation in additional cases; what is needed is *integration* into the body of scientific knowledge. (Rescher 1970b, pp. 15–16)

The requirement that generalizations must be systematically integrated with other statements in the total corpus of knowledge points out the importance of theories. Because theories are systematically related sets of statements that include some lawlike generalizations, theories provide a crucial mechanism for according lawlike status to empirical regularities and other isolated propositions. As Barwise (1995, p. G31) argues, empirical generalizations in marketing should be "explained by, or at least linked in some way with theory."

Consider Ehrenberg's (1971, p. 33) "duplication of viewing" (hereafter referred to as "D-V") relationship: $d_{ts} = kr_t r_s \pm 1$. Ehrenberg was interested in determining what percentage of the audience would be duplicated if *X* percentage of the population viewed a television program on Monday night and *Y* percentage of the population viewed a program on Tuesday night. This information, of course, would be of great value to potential sponsors of the programs. Ehrenberg suggested that a wide range of empirical conditions support the relationship $d_{ts} = kr_t r_s \pm 1$, where:

d_{ts} = the audience (in rating points) that is duplicated at two times, *s* and *t*, on two different days of the week
r_t = the rating of the program at time *t*
r_s = the rating of the program at time *s*
k = a constant

Is the D-V relationship an empirical regularity, or is it a lawlike generalization? Certainly, the relationship is in the basic form of a generalized conditional and it also has empirical content. Ehrenberg indicates that several hundred cases examined support the relationship. However, if the D-V relationship is to be considered a lawlike statement, it must be *systematically integrated* into a body of scientific knowledge, and Ehrenberg provides no clues as to how the relationship fits existing knowledge. Actually, it appears to run *counter to* known "facts" about television viewing. For example, we "know" that different kinds of television programs attract different kinds of viewers, and that similar kinds of programs attract similar kinds of viewers. Nevertheless, the D-V relationship would lead one to conclude that the duplication of audience between a western on Monday and a western on Tuesday would be identical to the duplication between the same western on Monday and a Wednesday documentary on the political situation in Brazil (provided that the appropriate ratings are the same). On the other hand, the notion that similar programs draw similar audiences suggests that the duplication between the two westerns would be greater than the duplication between the western and the documentary. Therefore, the D-V relationship runs counter to our existing body of knowledge about television viewing.

Headen, Klompmaker, and Rust tested the D-V law in the United States. They conclude:

> The authors attempted to examine the major conclusions of Goodhardt and Ehrenberg in terms of a national sample of U.S. data. The basic conclusions are that, because of the differences between the U.S. and U.K. media environments, the simplifying assumptions of Goodhardt and Ehrenberg (i.e., the use of only within- and between-channel *K*-values) cannot be used if accuracy is desired. For example, because of

> the longer broadcast day in the U.S., duplication patterns should take into account the daypart in which audience flow patterns are being studied. Also, whereas, there seems to be no program-type loyalty in the U.K., the authors' results show positive evidence of this phenomenon. (Headen, Klompmaker, and Rust 1979, p. 340)

Is the D-V relationship a lawlike generalization? The previous analysis suggests that it is not. The D-V relationship (to the extent that it is true) is an empirical regularity because (a) it has not been systematically integrated into a body of knowledge about television viewing and (b) it actually contradicts a well-corroborated existing body of knowledge. It is important to note that classifying the relationship as an empirical regularity in no way disparages the importance or value of the discovery (if it is true). Requiring a relationship to be systematically integrated into a body of knowledge in order to be considered lawlike is one way of ensuring that we focus on the scientific explanation of phenomena (answering "why" questions), not simply the prediction of phenomena. And, we have found, prediction does not imply explanation.

In contrast to the D-V relationship, consider the sources of price reliance proposed by Shapiro (1973). He investigated the phenomenon of consumers using the price of a product as an indicator of the perceived quality of the product. He found that the tendency of consumers to rely heavily on price (price reliance) as an indicator of quality was a generalized mental construct, an attitude or trait. He found that some people seemed price reliant regardless of the product under consideration and that some people were not price reliant. Shapiro then tested hypotheses regarding the relationships that determined the existence of price reliance. Both personal and situation-specific factors were examined. Among the relationships tested were:

1. Price reliance increases as the *credibility* of the source of price information increases.
2. Price reliance increases as the *perceived risk* in the purchasing situation increases.
3. Price reliance increases as the *specific self-confidence* of the consumer decreases.

Shapiro empirically tested these relationships (and others) and found corroborative evidence.

Are these determinants of price reliance to be considered empirical regularities or lawlike statements? They do have the basic form of generalized conditionals, and they do have empirical content—both requirements for lawlike status. However, are the observed relationships systematically integrated into a body of scientific knowledge? An affirmative reply seems justified. Shapiro demonstrates that all three relationships logically flow from the previous theoretical and empirical work of Bauer (1960, 1965, 1967a, 1967b), Brody and Cunningham (1968), and Cox and Bauer (1964). Therefore, in contrast to Ehrenberg's duplication of viewing relationship, the determinants of price reliance relationships should be accorded lawlike status. Note that this does not necessarily imply that the price reliance relationships are *laws.* Lawlike statements become laws only after substantial empirical corroboration. What is meant by "substantial empirical corroboration" is a subject for Chapter 7, where we discuss the criteria for confirmation of lawlike and theoretical constructions.

The criterion that statements must be systematically integrated into a coherent body of knowledge in order to be considered lawlike raises some potentially dangerous problems, the most obvious of which is conservatism. There is no question but that the *systematic integration* criterion casts a conservative bias on scientific inquiry—newly discovered relationships that do not fit into some overall framework may, unfortunately, be automatically categorized as "spurious." Some observed regularities may then not receive the careful attention and further exploration that they deserve. Similarly, the systematically integrated requirement may be drastically distorted. Rescher speaks to this problem:

> The law must certainly fit into *some* pattern, but this need not of course necessarily be *the presently accepted* pattern. It is a convenient but unwarranted step to condemn the unfamiliar as unscientific, and to bring to bear the whole arsenal of scientific derogation (as "occult," "supernatural," "unscientific") that one sees, for example, orthodox psychologists launch against parapsychology.
>
> But the fact that the requirement of coherence [systematic integration] for explanatory laws can be abused does not show that it should not be used. (Every useful instrument can be misapplied.) And, of course, the proper use of this requirement must always be conditioned by reference to the primary requirement of correspondence—the evidence of tested conformity to fact. (Rescher 1970b, pp. 16–17)

Therefore, although researchers in marketing should require their lawlike statements to fit systematically into some larger framework, we must consciously avoid either ignoring "nonfitting" empirical regularities or rejecting them because they do not fit into some currently accepted framework or theory.

5.5.1 Role of Empirical Generalizations

The preceding section should not be interpreted as in any way minimizing the importance of empirical generalizations. Unquestionably, empirical generalizations or empirical regularities play a prominent role in science. As noted previously, empirical regularities may become lawlike statements after they are systematically integrated into a body of scientific knowledge. A second prominent role of empirical generalizations lies within the *context of discovery*. Undoubtedly, the observation of empirical regularities by scientists is a frequent stimulus for scientific inquiry, research, and the discovery of corroborated lawlike generalizations.

For example, Edward Jenner's development of a vaccine for smallpox can be cited as an instance of an empirical regularity leading to the discovery of scientific knowledge (Hopkins 1983; Fenner and White 1976). Jenner observed that, although almost the entire population of eighteenth-century England at one time or another had smallpox, milkmaids almost never had smallpox. This observed empirical regularity sparked his scientific curiosity and led him to observe that milkmaids did contract a mild disease known as cowpox. He theorized that, somehow, the contraction of cowpox kept the milkmaids from being susceptible to smallpox. Thus, an observed empirical relationship led directly to the ultimate discovery of a vaccine for smallpox. The process that led Jenner to develop a smallpox vaccine illustrates the frequently important role that empirical regularities play in the context of discovery.

It would appear that some of the work of early synthesizers of marketing thought was spurred by observed empirical regularities. In recounting the origins of Arch W. Shaw's marketing writings, Joseph C. Seibert (in Bartels 1962) comments:

> Mr. Shaw's intellectual curiosity led him to devote a great deal of his time to the discovery of [business systems] and brought him conferences with leaders of many different types of industries. The outstanding discovery of these meetings, to Mr. Shaw, appeared to be the uniformity of procedures in spite of the variety of products produced and the outward differences of the separate organizations. (Bartels 1962, p. 234)

In the preceding case, the development of Shaw's concepts can be traced to his observation of an empirical regularity concerning the similarity of business systems across various different kinds of industries and products.

A final caveat on the role of empirical generalizations seems desirable. We must carefully distinguish between asserting that observing empirical regularities may often be a first step toward establishing lawlike relationships and asserting that the *only* way or at least the *best* way to discover lawlike relationships is to first observe some empirical regularities. Unfortunately, the latter assertion seems to be implied in much recent marketing literature. Consider the perennial debate on the best process for scientific progress in marketing. Obviously, science progresses through a process that includes both empirical work and the development of theory. One view has it that the best way to proceed is first to develop empirical generalizations from sets of data, then to search for and/or create theories that might explain the empirical generalizations, then return to investigating the empirical generalizations in terms of the theory proposed, and so forth. Such a procedure might be illustrated as E→T→E→T. . . . A second process would be to develop a theory, then empirically test the theory, then modify the theory to reflect the empirical testing, then test the revised theory, and so forth. Such a process might be modeled as T→ E→ T→ E. . . . Ehrenberg (1994, 1995) is the strongest, most articulate, and most consistent advocate of ETET. Most marketing researchers, however, follow the TETE route. As argued by Bass (1995, p. G12), "Empirical does not always preceed Theory, and thus Ehrenberg's schema [ETET] excludes TETE. The distinction is important because the theory may have other empirical applications beyond the immediate empirical generalization." Similarly, Rossiter (1994, p. 117) argues that, contra-Ehrenberg, "Many theories in marketing *are* tested extensively" (italics in original). He provides several examples of theories that have been thoroughly tested and are generally considered to be success stories in marketing research. These examples include the Fishbein model of multi-attribute attitude formation, information overload theory, the elaboration likelihood model, and the attitude-toward-the-ad theory.

The view here, as discussed in Chapter 1, is that it is certainly possible that lawlike statements may be discovered by first amassing data on many different variables and then continuously sifting the data through ever more sophisticated mathematical and statistical sieves. However, to state that this is the *only* procedure or even the most preferable procedure seems totally unwarranted.

5.6 SUMMARY

We are now in a position to build a comprehensive framework for principles, laws, and lawlike statements. This framework is illustrated in Figure 5.1, which suggests that all statements that purport to be of lawlike form must specify a relationship in the form of a *generalized conditional.* Common examples of generalized conditionals are: "All instances of *A* are also instances of *B*," and "Every time *X* occurs, then *Y* will occur."

In order for a generalized conditional statement to be a *lawlike generalization* or, alternatively, a lawlike statement, it must (a) have empirical content, (b) exhibit nomic necessity, and (c) be systematically integrated into a body of scientific knowledge. The empirical-content criterion successfully weeds out strictly analytic statements, tautologies, and nonsense generalizations from being considered lawlike. The nomic-necessity criterion serves the useful purpose of distinguishing lawlike statements from accidental generalizations such as "All products with the trade name Maxwell House have a coffee base."

Figure 5.1 **Laws and Lawlike Statements**

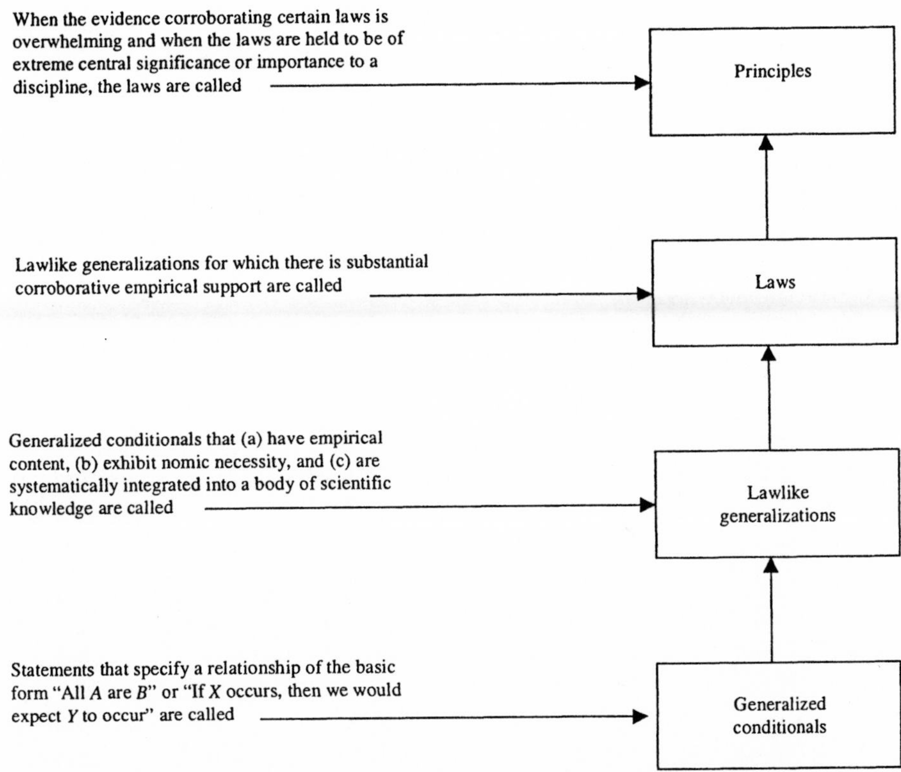

Source: Hunt (1991a). Reprinted by permission of the author.

Finally, the systematic integration criterion enables us to differentiate lawlike statements from strictly empirical regularities. Empirical regularities have been shown to play an important role in the context of scientific discovery.

Lawlike generalizations become *laws* when a substantial body of corroborative empirical evidence has been developed. Exactly what is meant by a "substantial body of corroborative empirical evidence" will be the topic of Chapter 7. Finally, a law becomes a *Principle* or *Law* (note uppercase "L") when the evidence corroborating the law is overwhelming and the law is held to be of extreme significance or importance to the scholars in a particular discipline.

QUESTIONS FOR ANALYSIS AND DISCUSSION

1. A "perfect system" for playing blackjack would destroy the game of blackjack, which would therefore render useless the "perfect system."

Similarly, the discovery of marketing "laws" would be self-defeating. Evaluate.

2. John D.C. Little (1970) suggests that good normative decision models should be: (a) simple, (b) robust, (c) easy to control, (d) adaptive, (e) complete on important issues, and (f) easy to communicate with. Should normative decision models, like scientific laws, be required to be empirically testable? If no, why not? If yes, how would you empirically test a normative decision model? Is the distinction between normative decision models and scientific laws a useful one? How about the distinction between normative laws and normative decision models?
3. Evaluate the statement: "It is curious that marketing practitioners disclaim any interest in marketing laws because every time they make a strategic decision, they must rely either explicitly or implicitly on a presumed marketing law."
4. Alderson's (1957, p. 424) principle of postponement "requires that changes in form and identity occur at the latest possible point in the marketing flow; and changes in inventory location occur at the latest point in time." Is this a principle, law, lawlike generalization, empirical regularity, theory, or what? Is it empirically testable?
5. Suppose Congress, in its infinite wisdom, passed a law making it illegal for Proctor and Gamble to distribute products through any channel other than supermarkets. Would the generalization "All products produced by Proctor and Gamble are distributed through supermarkets" then pass the nomic necessity criterion?
6. Schwartz (1965, p. 8) suggests, "A law is a former theory which over time, and for the geographic area to which it is supposed to apply, has been demonstrated to yield perfectly accurate predictions each time it is used." Evaluate the usefulness of this conceptualization of law. Why did Schwartz insert his "geographic area" qualifier but not others (e.g., he could have qualified his conceptualization with reference to a particular culture or industry)?
7. Economic theory is sometimes criticized because its lawlike statements are supposed to be true only *ceteris paribus*. The phrase *ceteris paribus* is seldom found in the physical science or marketing literature. What does *ceteris paribus* imply? Is it a "defect" in economic theory? Should the physical sciences use it more often? Should marketing? Could the use of *ceteris paribus* be abused? How?
8. If the distinction between laws and principles (or Laws) is strictly honorific, is it therefore, unimportant?
9. Ehrenberg (1971, p. 32) suggests that "the *validity* of a scientific law

depends only on its range of empirical generalization, i.e., on the different conditions for which it is known to hold or not to hold, as shown by direct observation and analysis." Evaluate this perspective of *validity.* Does the concept of *ceteris paribus* relate to Ehrenberg's statement?

10. Evaluate the following argument:

    a. No purely analytic statement can be a lawlike generalization (such statements fail the empirical content criterion).
    b. The statement "2 + 2 = 4" is purely analytic.
    c. All mathematical statements have a basic form similar to "2 + 2 = 4."
    d. Therefore, all statements in mathematics are purely analytic.
    e. Since no analytic statement can be lawlike, no mathematical statement can be lawlike.
    f. All theories contain lawlike generalizations.
    g. Therefore, mathematics contains no theory.
    h. All sciences must contain theory.
    i. Therefore, mathematics is not a science.
    j. Mathematicians will dislike statement i.

11. "The nomic necessity criterion is really only requiring that laws be theoretically supportable because it is really theories that enable us to 'support' counterfactual conditionals." Evaluate.
12. Bunge (1961, p. 260) proposes that "a proposition is a law statement if and only if it is *a posteriori* (not logically true), general in some respect (does not refer to unique objects), has been satisfactorily corroborated for the time being in some domain, and belongs to some theory (whether adult or embryonic)." Evaluate.
13. Is empirical evidence alone necessary and sufficient for according the status of law to a generalization? Is it necessary but not sufficient? Is it sufficient but not necessary? Is it neither necessary nor sufficient?

NOTES

1. For excellent discussions of laws, see Nagel (1961, pp. 47–73); Hempel (1965c, p. 264 ff); Lambert and Brittan (1970, p. 37 ff); Kaplan (1964, p. 84 ff); and Bunge (1961).

2. Many writers use the term *confirmed* instead of the word *corroborated.* Popper (1959, p. 251 ff) suggests that confirmed, more than corroborated, is likely to indicate that the lawlike statement is known to be absolutely true, which is not a requirement for a law.

3. The classic treatment of counterfactual conditionals is in Goodman (1965). For a good review and articulation of counterfactuals, see Lange (1999). For a good discussion of counterfactual conditionals in marketing, see Gaski (1985).

6 SCIENTIFIC LAWS: ISSUES AND ASPECTS

Don't tell me our problem lies in prediction. No doubt it will remain our greatest weakness. But prediction runs parallel to explanation: the two problems are really the same one. And the better we are able to explain what has happened, the better we shall be able to predict what will.

—George C. Homans

The previous chapter examined the basic nature of laws and lawlike statements. Lawlike statements were found to be generalized conditionals that (a) have empirical content, (b) exhibit nomic necessity, and (c) are systematically integrated into a body of scientific knowledge. Laws are lawlike generalizations for which there is substantial corroborative support. The challenge of the present chapter will be to explore the various kinds of scientific laws and to examine certain issues relating to them. First, we shall explore how different kinds of laws incorporate time as a variable, and, thus, examine equilibrium laws, laws of atemporal coexistence, laws of succession, and process laws. Second, we shall systematically inquire into the nature of, and the proper role for, axioms or "assumptions" in theory construction. Third, lawlike statements will be shown to differ as to their extension and universality. In this context we shall examine singular statements, existential statements, statistical laws, and universal laws. Finally, the importance of carefully delimiting the extension of laws will be discussed, along with an evaluation of an extension of Weber's law and the so-called psychophysics of prices controversy.

6.1 THE TIME ISSUE

One way of exploring the various kinds of laws and lawlike statements is to analyze the manner in which the time dimension is handled. Figure 6.1 shows four kinds of laws that differ with respect to the time dimension: process laws, laws of succession, laws of atemporal coexistence, and equilibrium laws.

Some very powerful lawlike statements not only explicitly incorporate time variables to facilitate the prediction of *future* phenomena but also permit the retrodiction of *past* phenomena. Bergmann (1968, p. 416) refers to these powerful statements as *process laws*. Following Hempel (1965a, p. 352), lawlike statements that incorporate time-dependent relationships and allow the prediction of future phenomena but not the retrodiction of past phenomena can be called *laws of succession*. In contrast with process laws and laws of succession, *laws of atemporal coexistence* do not specifically incorporate time as a real variable at all. Finally, certain kinds of laws of atemporal coexistence state relationships that occur only when the system is "at rest." Such statements are called *equilibrium laws* (Brodbeck 1968, p. 417). The next sections will systematically explore and elaborate on the unique characteristics of each of the previously mentioned kinds of laws that differ with respect to the time dimension. First, let's start with an analysis of laws of equilibrium.

6.1.1 Equilibrium Laws

Equilibrium laws are laws of atemporal coexistence stating that certain specified relationships in a particular system will be true only if the values of the variables are not changing over time; that is, the system must be at rest. Thus, the basic form of such laws is:

$$Y_{t(e)} = f\,[X_{t(e)}]$$

That is, specified values of *Y* are associated with specified values of *X* only when the system is at a point in time *e* when *X* and *Y* are not changing (the definition of equilibrium).

Conventional demand theory analysis prescribes that, at *equilibrium*, the consumer will purchase the particular combination of goods *X* and *Y* where the marginal rate of substitution of good *X* for good *Y* equals the ratio of the price of *X* to the price of *Y*. The marginal rate of substitution shows the rate at which consumers are willing to substitute *X* for *Y*, and the price shows the rate at which they can substitute *X* for *Y*. Note that the relationship holds only if the system is at equilibrium. Of equal importance for demand theory, the converse is true: if the relationship does not hold, the system is not at equilibrium.

Equilibrium laws, of course, play an important part in neoclassical economics. They are also important in the scheme of science proposed by functionalists. As discussed in Chapter 3, functional analysis seeks to understand a behavior pattern or sociocultural institution by determining the role it plays in keeping the given system in "proper working order" (an equilibrium kind

Figure 6.1 **Laws and the Time Variable**

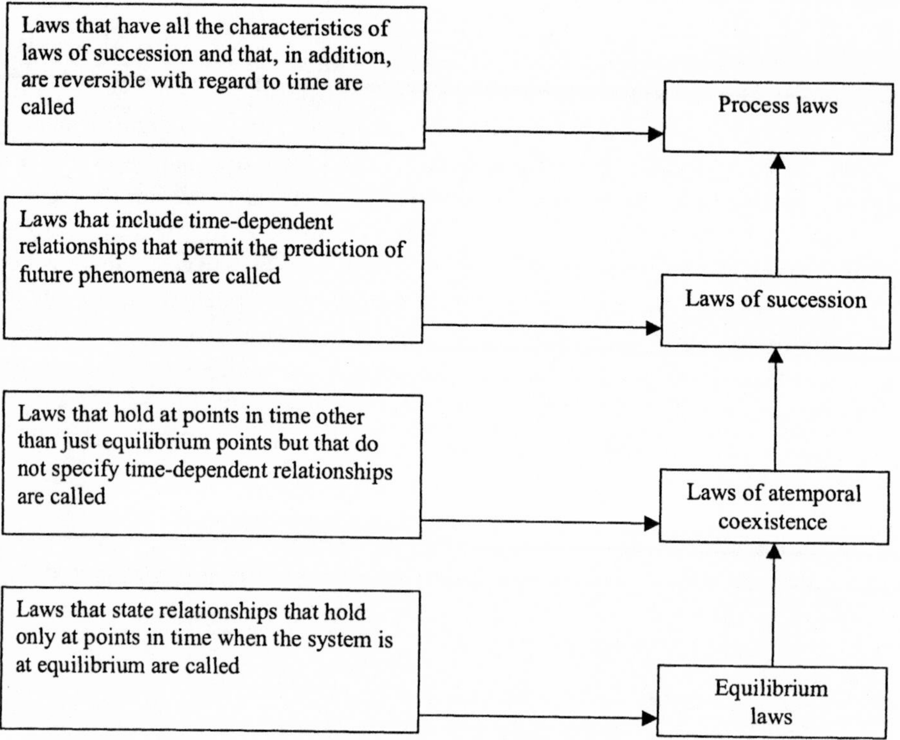

Source: Hunt (1991a). Reprinted by permission of the author.

of notion) or maintaining it as a going concern (Hempel 1965b, p. 305). Alderson, as a functionalist, suggested that marketers recognize that there are three different levels of equilibrium in organized human activities:

> First, there is market equilibrium which pertains to the network of external relations among organized behavior systems. Secondly, there is an organizational equilibrium which is a form of internal balance within an individual system. Finally, there is the more embracing concept of ecological equilibrium pertaining to the adjustment between a society and its environment. (Alderson 1965, p. 304)

Other marketing theorists have also extolled the virtues of viewing the markets for products as illustrations of equilibrating systems. Lawrence C. Lockley (1964, p. 39) unequivocally advocates this position:

> The concept of an equilibrium is a universal natural concept. The populations of fish and food tend to reach an equilibrium in each stream or body of water. The action of

> osmosis brings about an equilibrium between separated bodies of liquids. Human populations tend to reach a point of equilibrium in terms of their sources of support. Whatever organization of natural phenomena we consider, we see a tendency for forces ultimately to come to rest in an equilibrium.
>
> Strangely, this same tendency is apparent in the marketplace. Consider the case of staple foods (as will be discussed in more detail later) offered in cans. Some products are promoted by food packers as nationally advertised brands and some offered by wholesalers or retailers as private brands. Many years ago, when canned foods were relatively new in the market, some of the well-advertised brands had a disproportionate share of the market. But as time has passed, there seems to have developed a sort of rough equilibrium in this field, an equilibrium which is only temporarily upset by special promotional efforts.
>
> This same type of equilibrium is present, actually or incipiently, among competitors in many individual consumer markets. Men's shoes, household mechanical appliances, breakfast cereals, soaps and detergents, and bed sheets and blankets illustrate the tendency toward equilibrium. Among dentifrices, for example, the advertising, the point-of-purchase promotional material, the package design, the product formulation, and the channels of distribution have come to be about the same. Share of the market may have reached a point of stability. In the absence of any marked modification of these forces, we may have an excellent illustration of a market equilibrium. (Lockley 1964, p. 39)

Lockley then goes on to show how the notion of equilibrium led to the conceptualization of several lawlike statements, including the principle of *drift*. "There will always be a tendency for merchandise to drift down from a 'specialty' to a 'shopping' to a 'convenience' goods classification. This is another way of saying of course that an equilibrium tends to be reestablished as soon as it is disturbed" (1964, p. 44).

Is the principle of drift an equilibrium law? The answer must depend on whether the stated relationship has time as a real variable and whether the relationship holds only at an equilibrium position. Clearly, time *does appear* as a real variable in the principle of drift, insofar as we can restate the principle as, "There will always be a tendency *as time passes* for merchandise to drift . . ." To state that an equilibrium will appear is not the same thing as specifying certain lawlike relationships that will hold *at equilibrium.* It is the latter requirement that separates equilibrium laws from laws of succession. Therefore, to the extent that the principle of drift is lawlike, it should be considered as a kind of law of succession.

A caveat seems desirable here concerning equilibrium laws and equilibrating systems. Students of marketing should carefully distinguish between (1) the assertion that there exist equilibrium laws concerning marketing phenomena and (2) the assertion that all (or even most) marketing processes and systems are inherently equilibrating (i.e., marketing systems universally tend toward the establishment of equilibrium positions). Note that statement (1) is a positive existential statement (see section 6.3.2) that, in principle, can be verified by finding examples of equilibrium laws in marketing. However, statement (2) appears to have an essentially metaphysical quality. The usefulness of believing in statement 2, as Lockley appears to do, may lie more in the context of discovery. Therefore, the appropriate question would be, "To what extent has the belief that marketing processes are inherently equilibrating led to the discovery of well-supported lawlike statements?" If this is truly the appropriate question, then there would appear to be insufficient evidence either to accept or reject the assertion that marketing systems universally or even commonly tend toward the establishment of equilibrium positions. Indeed, resource-advantage theory, argued to be a general theory of competition in section 9.4 and to be *toward* a general theory of marketing in section 9.5, maintains that competition is *disequilibrating*.

6.1.2 Laws of Atemporal Coexistence

The previous section explored one specific type of coexistence law, that is, equilibrium laws. Now, all equilibrium laws are laws of atemporal coexistence, but not all laws of atemporal coexistence are equilibrium laws. That is, many laws of atemporal coexistence state relationships that occur at points in time other than just equilibrium positions. Therefore, the basic form of laws of atemporal coexistence would be:

$$Y_t = f(X_t)$$

Specified values of Y at any time t are associated with specified values of X at the same time t.

Bergmann (1957, p. 102) refers to all laws of atemporal coexistence as *cross-sectional laws* and states that "cross-sectional [law] is taken from the metaphor that considers a state a temporal cross-section of a process. Such laws state functional connections obtaining among the values which several variables have at the same time."

Dubin takes a slightly different position on atemporal coexistence laws. Identifying these laws as *categoric laws*, Dubin says:

> The recognition of a categoric law of interaction is facilitated by noting that its typical form employs the words *is associated with*. Synonyms for this phrase serve, of course, to provide the same identification. . . . Categoric laws are symmetrical. It does not matter whether one or the other of the units comes first in the statement of the law. Thus, "juvenile delinquency and broken homes are positively related" is identical with "broken homes and juvenile delinquency are positively related." The symmetry of categoric laws is emphasized, for this fact buttresses that a law of interaction is not a statement of causality. What, indeed, is the meaning of cause if

> the units *juvenile delinquency* and *broken homes* can be interchanged without restriction in the law of interaction between them? (Dubin 1969, pp. 100–1)

Dubin then goes on to admonish the reader to avoid jumping to the conclusion that the broken-home condition preceded in time the juvenile delinquency, and, therefore, *caused* it.

Dubin's caveat merits the scrutiny of marketing students. Caution must be exercised when attempting to infer the temporal sequence of a relationship from data that are strictly cross-sectional or associative. For example, there may be a strong temptation to infer that high advertising expenditures cause high sales. Such an inference may be unwarranted if the supportive data are cross-sectional because it is common knowledge that many firms set their advertising budgets at specified percentages of sales. Thus, the data may equally support either of the two assertions "advertising causes sales" or "sales cause advertising." There are numerous instances where the temporal sequentiality of the relationships remains in doubt. Are changes in attitude lawfully related to subsequent changes in purchase behavior? Or, are changes in purchase behavior lawfully related to subsequent changes in attitude? Or, does the relationship go in both directions depending on the situation? The major conclusion to be drawn from the preceding discussion would appear to be: if the data used to test lawlike statements are cross-sectional (i.e., all data are drawn from the same time period), adopt the agnostic position of treating any corroborated or confirmed lawlike statements as *laws of coexistence* rather than *sequential laws* or *causal laws*. By adopting this agnostic position the researcher will, it is hoped, remain alert to the possibility that the actual direction of the temporal sequence may be opposite to intuition.

However, though scientists have the luxury of the agnostic position with respect to the causal direction in laws, managers and policy makers do not. Consider again Dubin's "juvenile delinquency-broken home" law of interaction. Whether the relationship is juvenile delinquency→ broken homes or broken homes→ juvenile delinquency impacts on policy in terms of the temporal order of possible corrective actions. Should the emphasis of policy be to prevent broken homes in order to reduce juvenile delinquency or to curb juvenile delinquency, and, thus, to prevent broken homes? For policy makers, choices must be made. Why did Dubin—a social scientist—not recognize specifically (or even acknowledge) that not all stakeholders of science have the luxury of the agnostic position? The answer is that he was so strongly influenced (as were the logical positivists and empiricists) by Humean skepticism. Thus, the rule is: the scientist *qua* scientist may/should be agnostic on causal direction; the scientist *qua* advocate or consultant may not and/or should not be agnostic; the policy maker and manager *cannot* be agnostic.

6.1.3 Laws of Succession

The preceding sections have discussed the two kinds of laws that do not include time as a real variable. *Laws of succession*, however, provide that specified values of one or more variables will be succeeded in time by specified values of one or more other variables (Hempel 1965a, p. 352). Dubin (1969, p. 100) refers to such laws as *sequential laws*, and Kaplan (1964, p. 109) uses the term *temporal laws*. The basic form of such laws is:

$$Y_{t+n} = f(X_t)$$

One extremely useful perspective for evaluating laws of succession is to examine the *level of specificity* of the time variable in the proposed relationships. Varying degrees of specificity are found in the relationships in marketing models and theories. Many marketing theorists only minimally specify the time variable in their theoretical constructions. Others are much more explicit in identifying which variables are hypothesized to influence other variables over time.

Consider the Engel, Kollat, and Blackwell (1973) model of consumer behavior. The authors, in their discussion, often do not explicitly state which relationships are time-dependent and which are not. There is little doubt about some of the proposed relationships. For example, the authors clearly imply that changes in exposure precede changes in attention, preceding changes in comprehension and retention. But what about the relationships among these constructs: attitude, evaluative criteria, and personality? What is the proposed temporal sequence of changes in these constructs? Possibly the authors mean to propose that these relationships be considered laws of atemporal coexistence. The ambiguity results from the minimal specification of the time variable. Unfortunately, many marketing models only minimally specify the time-dependent relationships. Sometimes, the implied time-dependent relationships are intuitively clear; at other times, they are not.

Next, consider the "hierarchy of effects" model investigated by Palda (1966) and based on the cognitive-affective-conative sequence of psychological states proposed by Lavidge and Steiner (1961). As stated by Terrence O'Brien (1971, p. 284), the hierarchy of effects model consists of three statements:

1. Awareness influences attitude over time, and the relationship is expected to be positive.
2. Attitude influences intention to purchase over time, and the relationship is expected to be positive.
3. Intention influences actual purchase over time, and the relationship is expected to be positive.

Note that the time-dependent relationships are specified: changes in awareness precede changes in attitude, which precede changes in intention. O'Brien (1971, p. 289) then tested the relationships using the method of cross-lagged correlations on panel data on 636 housewives and concluded that the results basically supported the hierarchy predictions. The point of the illustration is that when the time-dependent relationships are unambiguously specified, the process of empirical testing is facilitated.

Although the hierarchy of effects model is superior to many marketing models in specifying the time-dependent relationships, it is far from optimal in this regard. Note that the hierarchy of effects model states that changes in awareness precede changes in intention. However, the model does *not* specify the length of time between these expected changes. A few marketing models are very specific in identifying the time dimension. The Nicosia model of consumer behavior is one such model. The equations composing Nicosia's linear model and his explanation follow:

1. $dB(t)/dt = b[M(t) - \beta B(t)]$
2. $M(t) = mA(t)$
3. $dA(t)/dt = a[B(t) - \alpha A(t)] + cC(t)$
4. $C(t) = C$

Specifically, Equation 1 says that the time rate of change in the level of buying of a certain brand by a consumer of a certain type is directly proportional to the difference $[M(t) - \beta B(t)]$. Equation 2 states a dependence of motivation M upon attitude A. Then, Equation 3 says that the time rate of change in level of attitude is directly proportional to the difference $[B(t) - \alpha A(t)]$ plus a constant multiple of the advertising level C. Finally, the level of C is defined by Equation 4 to be constant with respect to time (Nicosia 1966, p. 209).

Thus, the nature of the time-dependent relationships is very clearly specified in the Nicosia model. Once again, this should greatly facilitate testing the model. However, this should not be interpreted as meaning that the entire model is easily testable. Severe measurement and parameter estimation problems exist with the Nicosia model. In evaluating the falsifiability of the Nicosia model, Zaltman, Pinson, and Angelmar (1973, p. 108) conclude that "one can even fear that no test of the model will be possible without a significant alteration of its very nature."

6.1.4 Process Laws

Up to this point, we have considered equilibrium laws, laws of atemporal coexistence, and laws of succession, and how each of these kinds of laws incorporates the time variable. However, laws of succession are not the final way to deal with time. Bergmann (1968, p. 416) uses the term process law to refer to lawlike statements that have all the characteristics of laws of succession and, in addition, are reversible with regard to time. Laws of succession enable one to predict future phenomena; process laws enable one to both predict future phenomena and retrodict past phenomena. This is the meaning of "reversible with regard to time." Thus, if we know the position and velocity of a planet at a single instant in time, the laws of Newtonian celestial mechanics enable us not only to predict the position and velocity of the planet in the future but also to retrodict the position and velocity of the planet at points of time in the past.

As the reader will note, process laws are very powerful kinds of statements. To the best of the writer's knowledge, at present there exist no examples of process laws in marketing. This should not be too depressing because, in fact, there probably exist no examples of process laws in any of the social sciences. The development of process laws, and, hence, the accumulation of what Bergmann calls "process knowledge," would still be a useful goal or ideal point for marketing and the social sciences, even if the objective were never to be reached.

6.2 AXIOMS, FUNDAMENTAL LAWS, AND DERIVATIVE LAWS

Few issues in the methodology of the social sciences have spawned as much controversy as the nature of, and the proper role for, axioms or "assumptions" in scientific inquiry. The debate has been especially lively in economics, with Friedman, Samuelson, and other writers expressing sharp differences of perspective.[1] Although all of the major issues in the so-called Friedman-Samuelson debate cannot be specifically evaluated at this point, two aspects of the controversy are appropriate here: (1) What are axioms or assumptions? and (2) What does it mean to say that "the axioms of a theory are assumed to be true?"

To appreciate the nature and role of axioms in scientific inquiry requires some elaboration of the notions of *fundamental laws* versus *derivative laws*. Hempel (1965c, p. 267) suggests that all lawlike statements in any theory can be categorized as either fundamental or derivative. The set of derivative laws in a theory consists of all those laws that can be deduced from other laws *in the same theory*. Thus, Kepler's laws concerning the motions of planets can be deduced or derived from the more fundamental Newton laws. In marketing, the "square root law," which states that to double the attention-getting power of an advertisement the size of the advertisement must be increased fourfold, can be derived from the more fundamental Weber's law (Meyers and Reynolds 1967, p. 13).

The fundamental laws of a theory are those that (1) are used to deduce other laws and (2) cannot themselves be deduced from other laws in that same theory. The fundamental laws of a theory are the axioms of that theory, and the derived laws are often called theorems. As Bergmann (1957, p. 131) has observed, "The laws of a theory are deduced from its axioms."

Two observations need emphasizing with regard to fundamental versus derivative laws. First, laws that are fundamental (axioms) in one theory can be derived (theorems) in some other theory (Bunge 1961, p. 268). For example, Newton's laws are fundamental in Newtonian mechanics but are derived laws vis-à-vis Einstein's theory of relativity. This implies that the categorization of fundamental versus derived is *theory specific*. Second, for some theories there may be a choice between which laws should be considered fundamental and which should be considered derived. Consider a hypothetical theory composed of five laws, L_1, L_2, L_3, L_4, and L_5. One construction of the theory may consider L_1 and L_2 to be fundamental, since they can be used to derive L_3, L_4, and L_5. On the other hand, a rival construction may consider L_1 and L_3 to be fundamental and use them to derive L_2, L_4, and L_5. In such cases, the theorist has a choice of which statements should be considered as fundamental.

So, if the axioms of a theory are the fundamental laws of the theory, what does it mean to assert that "the axioms of a theory are *assumed* to be true?" Unfortunately, the preceding assertion seems often to be interpreted as meaning either that the axioms *should not* be empirically tested to see whether they are consistent with reality or that the axioms cannot be so tested. Nothing could be further from the truth! The selection or recognition that certain lawlike statements in a theory are fundamental, and, thus, to be called "axioms," convey to them no privileged sanctuary from the criterion that all purportedly lawlike statements must be empirically testable. Empirically testing the axioms of a theory is both possible and desirable. The assertion that the axioms are assumed to be true does not mean that the axioms are assumed to be true *empirically*. Rather, the axioms of a theory are assumed to be true *analytically*.

Understanding the difference between assuming that axioms are true empirically and assuming that axioms are true *for strictly analytical purposes* is crucial for clearing up many of the misconceptions about the proper role of axioms in theory construction and evaluation. Therefore, what does the phrase "for strictly analytical purposes" imply? Recalling our distinction between fundamental and derivative laws, the statement that axioms are assumed to be true for strictly analytical purposes implies that we assume axioms to be true *only* for the purpose of generating derivative laws and other statements. Therefore, "for strictly analytical purposes" comprises the following kinds of processes: "if these statements (the axioms) are true or false, then the following statements (theorems or hypotheses) are true or false." The preceding discussion can be summarized by noting that we assume that axioms are true for the purpose of *constructing* theory rather than for the purpose of *evaluating* theory.

6.2.1 Bridge Laws

One set of derivative laws deserving special attention is *bridge laws*, or what Hempel refers to as *bridge principles*:

> [Bridge laws] indicate how the processes envisaged by the theory are related to empirical phenomena with which we are already acquainted, and which the theory may then explain, predict, or retrodict. . . . Without bridge principles, as we have seen, a theory would have no explanatory power. . . . Without bridge principles, the internal principles of a theory would yield no test implications, and the requirement of testability would be violated. (Hempel 1966, pp. 72–75)

Bridge laws, then, are derivative laws that "bridge the gap" between the general laws in any particular theory and the specific classes of empirical phenomena under investigation. Sometimes when researchers refer to the "guiding hypotheses" or even "hypotheses" of their research, they are implicitly referring to bridge laws.

An example will better serve to illustrate the nature and function in theory of fundamental laws, derivative laws, and bridge laws. The marketing implications of Leon Festinger's (1957) theory of cognitive dissonance provide an excellent vehicle for illustrating these concepts. Before discussing the lawlike statements in Festinger's theory, four definitions are necessary:

Definition 1. Cognitions are the bits of knowledge one has about himself, about his behavior, and about his surroundings.

Definition 2. Two cognitions are in a dissonant state if, considering these two alone, the obverse of one cognition would follow from the other.

Definition 3. Two cognitions are consonant if one cognition does follow from the other.

Definition 4. Two cognitions are irrelevant if one cognition implies nothing at all concerning the other.

With the preceding four definitions in mind, the core of the theory of cognitive dissonance can be stated in terms of three *fundamental lawlike* (FL) statements:

FL_1: After a decision is made, there may exist dissonant or "nonfitting" relations among cognitive elements.

FL_2: The existence of dissonance gives rise to pressures to reduce the dissonance and to avoid increases in dissonance.

FL_3: Dissonance can be reduced by (a) changing one or more of the cognitive elements, (b) adding new consonant elements, and (c) decreasing the importance of the elements in the dissonant relations.

Scores of dissonance theorists have used these fundamental lawlike statements to generate derivative laws. While conducting research on appliance purchases, the present writer (1970) used the fundamental laws of dissonance theory to derive the following bridge laws (BL):

BL_1: Consumers will experience cognitive dissonance after the decision to purchase a major appliance.

BL_2: If retailers provide information to recent purchasers of major appliances, and if the information reassures the consumers that they made wise decisions, then the information will assist the consumers in their efforts to reduce cognitive dissonance.

The first bridge law can be derived from the set of fundamental laws on the basis that the purchase of a major appliance would be an important decision for consumers. Furthermore, consumers would have dissonant cognitions because it is unlikely that the chosen brand model would be rated the best on all relevant characteristics, for example, style, color, and price. The second bridge law follows from the notion that the post-transaction reassurances provided to the consumer would be perceived as adding consonant cognitions, which is one method for reducing the dissonance of the consumer. Note that both bridge laws enable the researcher to span the gap between the general relationships in the fundamental laws and the specific relationships in real-world phenomena.

The writer then used the preceding bridge laws, a sample of 152 recent purchasers of refrigerators, and an experimental research design to test, among other things, the following *research hypothesis*: the subjects who received the post-transaction reassurances will have lower perceived dissonance scores (i.e., will be less dissonant) than the subjects in the control group. The results of the study provided modest support for the research hypothesis, and, therefore, the underlying bridge laws, and, finally, the entire theory in general.

All research that purports to test some theoretical construction will employ bridge laws. They may be either explicitly stated or implicitly implied. The more explicitly the bridge laws are stated, the less chance there is that the researcher will make a logical error. Often the hypotheses that are actually tested in a research project are not derivable from the theory that is supposedly being evaluated, simply because the researcher has not specifically stated the bridge laws. Such research is useless at best and misleading at worst.

In summary, Figure 6.2 shows that the fundamental laws or axioms of a theory (1) are used to deduce other laws and (2) cannot themselves be deduced from other laws in that same theory. Axioms are not assumed to be true empirically; rather, they are assumed to be true for the analytical purpose of deriving other statements. The derivative laws in a theory are deduced from the fundamental laws. Bridge laws are derivative laws that bridge the gap between the general laws of a theory and the specific classes of phenomena under investigation. As the cognitive-dissonance example illustrated, bridge laws are needed to derive the research hypotheses for testing purposes. Researchers often do not specifically state the bridge laws, and, instead, jump directly from other more general derived laws or even fundamental laws to the directly testable research hypotheses. Such procedures run the risk of testing research hypotheses that cannot in fact be derived from the set of lawlike statements that comprises the theory.

6.3 EXTENSION AND UNIVERSALITY

Bunge (1961, p. 266) suggests that both lawlike and nonlawlike statements should be categorized by their extension or range. The *extension* of a statement consists of the set of all possible objects (past, present, and future) covered by the statement. The work of Weitz (1981) illustrates the importance of carefully delineating the extension of theories and propositions. Weitz reviews the research that has been conducted on salesperson performance using variables such as sales behaviors, behavioral predispositions, and salesperson capabilities. He concludes that past research results were contradictory or inconclusive in part because the researchers were attempting to uncover universal characteristics or behaviors that would be predictive of performance over too wide a range of situations. That is, the researchers were seeking generalizations with an *extension* that was unlikely. Weitz (1981, p. 91) then suggests a contingency framework for sales effectiveness based on the following basic postulate: "The effectiveness of sales behaviors across customer interactions is contingent upon or moderated by (a) the salesperson's resources, (b) the nature of the customer's buying task, (c) the customer-salesperson relationship, and interactions among (a), (b), and (c)."

Knowledge of the extension of a statement is valuable both because statements differing in extension have different roles in theory construction and because statements differing in extension vary with respect to their confirmability and falsifiability. *Confirmable* means the extent to which a

Figure 6.2 **Fundamental and Derivative Laws**

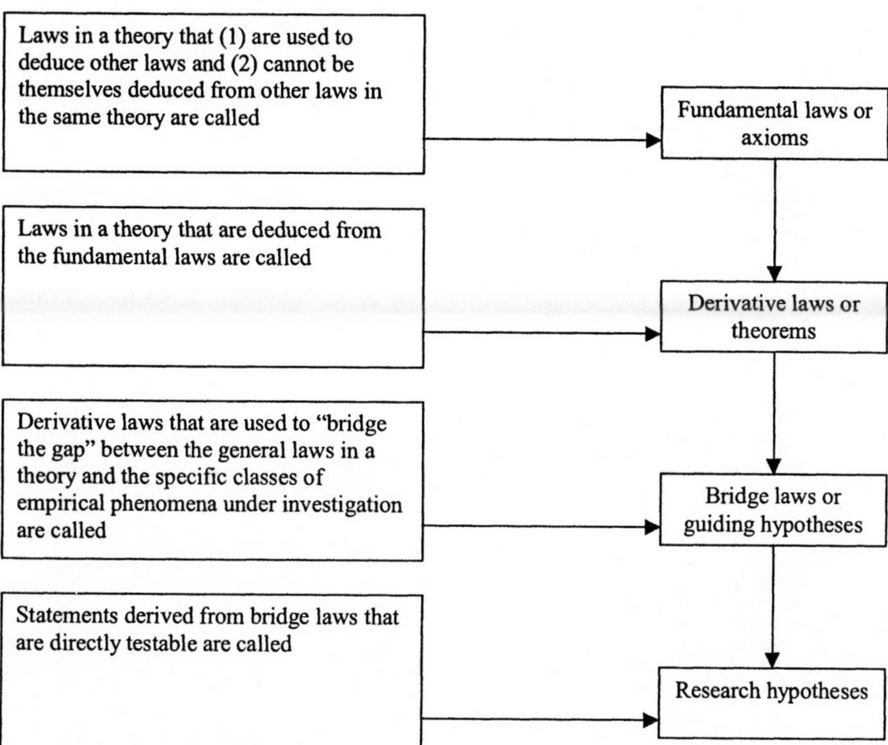

Source: Hunt (1991a). Reprinted by permission of the author.

statement is capable of being shown to be empirically true; that is, does the statement accurately describe the real world? *Falsifiable* means the extent to which a statement is capable of being shown to be empirically untrue; that is, how conclusively can we show that the real world is not arranged in accordance with the statement? As will be demonstrated, not all statements that are confirmable are at the same time falsifiable. Likewise, some statements are falsifiable but not confirmable; some are *neither* confirmable nor falsifiable. Others are only *weakly* confirmable or falsifiable. We shall restrict the discussion to four basic kinds of statements that have differing degrees of extension: singular statements, existential statements, statistical laws, and universal laws.

6.3.1 Singular Statements

Singular statements, sometimes referred to as particular (Popper 1959, p. 27) or observation (Hempel 1965b, p. 103) statements, extend only to specific phenomena that are bound in time and space. Singular statements are never lawlike statements because they do not have the form of generalized conditionals, which is a basic requirement for any statement to be considered lawlike. Singular statements play a crucial role in the confirmation or validation of theories and laws because the research hypotheses that are used to test theories and laws are usually singular statements.

The research hypothesis concerning cognitive dissonance discussed in the preceding section is illustrative of singular statements in marketing research: "The subjects who received the post-transaction reassurances will have lower perceived dissonance scores (i.e., will be less dissonant) than the subjects in the control group." That the statement is singular is evident from the fact that it refers to specific subjects in specific groups and specific scores taken at identifiable points in time. The dissonance hypothesis also shows the tremendous value of singular statements in testing theories. The statement is (a) derived from dissonance theory and (b) both confirmable and falsifiable. If the actual data show that the dissonance scores of the subjects in the experimental group are lower than the scores of the subjects in the control group, then the hypothesis (singular statement) is *confirmed*. Because the hypothesis is derived from the theory, the confirmation of the hypothesis is evidence in support of dissonance theory; that is, it *corroborates* (or tends to confirm) dissonance theory. Conversely, if the data show the opposite results, then the hypothesis is *falsified*, and, thus, we have evidence noncorroborative of dissonance theory. It is in this sense that singular statements are generally both confirmable and falsifiable, and, consequently, play such a vital role in theory validation.

6.3.2 Existential Statements

Existential statements are statements that propose the existence of some phenomenon. "There exist products that have life cycles." "People have psychological needs." "The abominable snowman exists!" All of the previous statements are existential in basic form. Even though their extension is greater than that of singular statements, note that existential statements are not lawlike because they do not have the form of generalized conditionals.

Zaltman et al. (1973, p. 66) suggest that all existential statements are purely confirmable but not falsifiable. To illustrate their point they cite Martilla (1971, p. 173) as an example of an existential statement: "There are opinion leaders in industrial firms." The position taken here is that, although all existential statements are purely confirmable, only those statements whose extension or range is unqualified or unbounded are not falsifiable. Qualified or bounded existential statements are both confirmable and falsifiable. Zaltman's example is actually a bounded existential statement, and, hence, is capable, at least in principle, of being falsified. That is, there is a bounded or finite number of industrial firms. Therefore, one could, in principle, examine the entire set of industrial firms and potentially falsify the statement "There are opinion leaders in industrial firms." Contrast the preceding with the unqualified existential statement, "There are opinion leaders." Finding a single opinion leader would confirm the statement, but, because of the unbounded extension of the statement, it is not falsifiable.

In attempting to explore the foundations of consumer behavior, Tucker (1967, p.134) asserted two "propositions":

Proposition 1. Someone goes through some process and acquires something with some effect.

Proposition 2. Someone uses something in some way with some effect.

These "propositions" are in reality unqualified existential statements, and, thus, are confirmable but not falsifiable. The first proposition can be confirmed as true if one can discover a single person who has gone through some process and acquired something with some effect. Nevertheless, no possible research design could possibly show the statement to be false.

The primary role of these "propositions" and other existential statements in marketing research is probably heuristic. For example, if one adopts the existential belief that there exist lawlike relationships among marketing phenomena, then one may attempt to discover the relationships. On the other hand, if one holds firmly the belief that the relationships among marketing phenomena are nonlawlike, then why conduct research? It is precisely in this context that the belief or nonbelief in existential statements plays a heuristic role in research.

6.3.3 Statistical Laws

The nature and form of statistical laws were first broached in the evaluation of various methods of scientific explanation in Chapter 3. Laws of basically statistical form gain prominence when there are a large number of variables (many of which are often unknown) that influence the phenomenon to be explained or predicted. Therefore, the exact specification of the relationship between changes in the phenomenon to be explained or predicted and any other single variable is thwarted by other variables. Under such conditions, theoreticians frequently rely on statistical laws that state an indeterministic relationship between variables. Such lawlike statements have substantially greater extension than either singular statements or existential statements because statistical laws *do* have the form of generalized conditionals. That is, the relationships implied in statistical laws extend to a far greater number of objects and phenomena than do singular or existential statements.

Kaplan (1964, p. 97) refers to one particular subset of statistical laws as *tendency* laws. Such laws state that there *tends* to be a relationship, usually rather loosely specified, between two variables. Commentators on laws in marketing would probably agree that *most of the lawlike statements in marketing are (explicitly or implicitly) tendency laws.* For example, the generalizations discussed in section 5.2 are tendency laws. Other examples of tendency laws in marketing include: "Opinion leaders [tend to] meet more salesmen than nonleaders" (Schiffman and Gaccione 1974, p. 50). "Brand loyalty [tends to vary] directly with perceived satisfaction with the old brand" (Newman and Werbel 1973, p. 406). "Lower income consumers [tend to] prefer credit contracts that include the lowest monthly payments" (Walker and Santer 1974, p. 73). "The greater the cost of the product considered, the greater the tendency for two or more family members to be involved in the decision process" (Granbois 1971, p. 196). A final illustration: "Audiences tend to expose themselves selectively to those messages which best fit their existing predispositions or inclinations" (Bogart 1962, p. 53).

Unlike singular statements, tendency laws (like all statistical laws) are neither *strictly* confirmable nor *strictly* falsifiable. To illustrate this, consider how one would test the "opinion leader" statement mentioned in the previous paragraph. The procedure would probably involve obtaining a sample of opinion leaders and nonleaders and then measuring their respective contact with salesmen. No matter how strong the relationship found, the evidence would never be *conclusive* in favor of or against the "opinion leader" statement. If the data contradicted the statement, defenders could always claim that the data base was too small, or was biased, or that the data were "contaminated" or "noisy." For example, Farley and Ring (1970, p. 435) found very low coefficients of determination in their test of the Howard-Sheth theory of buyer behavior. They then postulated that "noisy data" was the problem, rather than the low explanatory power of the theory.

If, on the other hand, the results of a research project *supported* the "opinion leader" statement, attackers could claim that the observed relationship was "spurious" and that the relationship could disappear with a larger sample or a different kind of test. Therefore, tendency laws are neither *strictly* confirmable (i.e., able to be proved conclusively true) nor *strictly* falsifiable (i.e., able to be proved conclusively false). Rather, test results can be shown to be either *consistent* or *inconsistent* with the tendency law in question, and, thus, *corroborative* or *noncorroborative.*

Observations of the preceding kind lead many scholars to debunk the whole notion of statistical laws. Bunge suggests that this would be a mistake:

> Some die-hard classical determinists claim that stochastic statements do not deserve the name of law and are to be regarded, at their best, as temporary devices. This anachronistic view has no longer currency in physics, chemistry, and certain branches of biology (notably genetics), especially ever since these sciences found that all molar laws in their domains are stochastic laws deducible (at least in principle) from laws concerning single systems in conjunction with definite statistical hypotheses regarding, e.g., the compensation of random deviations. Yet the prejudice against stochastic laws still causes some harm in psychology and sociology, where it serves to attack the stochastic approach without compensating for its loss by a scientific study of individuals. (Bunge 1967a, p. 336)

The preceding advice by Bunge is also wise counsel for marketing. Tendency laws have played, do play, and will continue to play a central role in marketing theory. The fact that such laws are only *weakly* confirmable and *weakly* falsifiable should be no cause for methodological alarm.

There are other kinds of statistical laws besides tendency laws, the most prominent of which is the *probability* law. Recall that the relationship between the variables in a tendency law is usually very loosely specified. In contrast, the relationship between the variables in a probability law is clearly specified in the form of a probability or relative frequency statement:

$$P(G, F) = r$$

That is, the probability of event G, given that event F has occurred, is r. Or, alternatively, in the long run, the proportion of cases of F that are also G is r. "The probability of throwing an 'ace' given a 'fair die' is 1/6." The reader may want to review the section on theories of probability in Chapter 3 at this point.

Although, as Popper (1959, p. 189) has pointed out, probability laws are not falsifiable, they are in general more powerful than tendency laws precisely because the relationships between the variables are more clearly specified. This increases their predictive and explanatory power, and thus their susceptibility to empirical testing and corroboration.

Probability laws are less common in marketing than tendency laws because the existence of a probability law between two variables presupposes that the other variables that influence the process interact either in a random manner or at least in a consistent way with the phenomenon in question. That is, the law that the probability of throwing an ace with a fair die equals 1/6 presupposes that such factors as initial velocity and the direction of the throw, which do in fact influence the results of each single toss of the die, will be randomly distributed over time. Therefore, the factor determining the probability of an ace on any throw will be the geometry of the cube. The lack of probability laws in marketing can be ascribed to the fact that in most marketing processes the other variables that might influence the phenomenon in question do not exert random or consistent interactions over time.

The work of Bass (1969, p. 215 ff) on the rate of diffusion of innovations illustrates a probability law in marketing. Bass classified the initial purchasers of new consumer durable goods into innovators and imitators, where the latter group included early adopters, the early majority, the late majority, and laggards. From the basic notion that imitators are primarily influenced in their purchase of durables by other buyers, Bass proposed the following probability law: "The probability that an initial purchase will be made at *T*, given that no purchase has yet been made, is a linear function of the number of previous buyers." Bass then tested his probability law on purchasers of eleven consumer durable goods and found substantial corroborative support. The reader can satisfy himself that the Bass proposition is in fact a probability law by observing that it has the basic form $P(G, F) = r$. In this case, the probability r is a linear function of the number of previous buyers rather than a simple constant.

The probability law proposed by Bass, like many statistical laws, is perhaps more significant for what it excludes than for what it includes. The law excludes certain variables from playing significant roles in determining the rate of purchase of new durable goods. For example, one might propose *a priori* that different levels of advertising would influence the rate of purchase. However, since this variable is not explicitly included in the relationship, then, *if the probability law is true*, we must conclude that either (a) advertising does not influence (or only minimally influences) the rate of purchase or (b) advertising influences the rate of purchase, but it does so in a consistent manner across different products. In the latter case, advertising would be *implicitly* incorporated in the probability statement.

6.3.4 Universal Laws

Laws of *strictly universal form* take the form of universal generalized conditionals and constitute the prototypes of all laws. Universal laws state: "Every time *A* occurs, then *B* will occur," or "All *A* are *B*," or "For any *x*, if *x* is an instance of *A*, then *x* is an instance of *B*." Note that universal laws do *not* simply state that "*B* exists," as would an existential statement. Neither do they state that "*B* tends to be associated with *A*," as would a tendency law. Nor do universal laws state that "the probability of *B* happening, given *A*, is *r*," as would a probability law. Because laws of strictly universal form extend to all instances of *A*, they have greater extension than singular statements, existential statements, or statistical laws.

The tremendous power of universal laws lies in their being falsifiable in a very strict sense. As Popper (1959, p. 69) has observed, laws of universal form can be alternatively expressed as negative existential statements or "there-is-not statements." An example from Newtonian mechanics will illustrate this point. Newton's third law of motion states that for every action there is a reaction equal in magnitude and opposite in direction. Note that this law can be stated alternatively as a negative existential statement, "There exists *no* action for which there is *not* a reaction equal in magnitude and opposite in direction." All laws of strictly universal form can be similarly reconstructed as negative existential statements.

As previously discussed, positive existential statements are strictly confirmable. That is, to confirm the statement "Opinion leaders exist," one need only find a single opinion leader. Similarly, negative existential statements are strictly falsifiable. The negative existential statement "Opinion leaders do not exist" can be falsified by finding a single opinion leader. *Therefore, because all universal laws can be alternatively expressed as negative existential statements, all universal laws are strictly falsifiable.*

Universal laws have greater explanatory and predictive power than statistical laws. Recall that the deductive-nomological (D-N) model of scientific explanation, discussed in Chapter 3, has the following structure:

$$\left.\begin{array}{l} C_1, C_2, \ldots C_k \\ L_1, L_2, \ldots L_k \end{array}\right\} \quad \text{Explanans } S$$

$$\overline{E \qquad\qquad\qquad} \Big\} \quad \text{Explanandum } E$$

In this model, the characteristics (C_1, C_2 . . .) of the situation and the strictly universal laws (L_1, L_2, . . .) deductively imply the phenomenon to be explained, *E*. Thus, the D-N model explains the occurrence of a phenomenon *E* by invoking a universal law stating that certain antecedent circumstances C_k are invariably followed by phenomenon *E* and then noting that circumstances C_k had, indeed, occurred.

The most common form of statistical explanation is the inductive-statistical (I-S) model:

$$\left.\begin{array}{l} C_{1i}, C_2, \ldots C_k \\ SL_1, SL_2, \ldots SL_k \end{array}\right\} \quad \text{Explanans } S$$

$$\overline{\overline{\qquad\qquad\qquad}} \quad \text{[it is very likely that]}$$

$$E \qquad \Big\} \quad \text{Explanandum } E$$

In the I-S model of explanation, unlike the D-N model, the phenomenon to be explained is not a logical, deductive consequence of the explanans. The I-S model states that, given circumstances C_k and certain statistical laws SL_k, then it is *very likely* that E would have occurred (or would tend to occur). Because the laws are statistical, not universal, the explanandum E is not a logical consequence of the premises S, in the sense that even if E does not occur, S could still be true. Therefore, universal laws have greater explanatory power than statistical laws, and a structurally similar argument could be developed to demonstrate that they have greater predictive power as well.

As Leone and Schultz (1980, p. 12) point out, "There are no universal laws in marketing." In this regard, marketing does not differ from the other social or behavioral sciences, none of which contain laws of strictly universal form (Kaplan 1964, p. 97). The previous statements do not mean that theorists in marketing (or the other behavioral sciences) never state their lawlike generalizations in universal form. Rather, even though some theorists *state* their lawlike generalizations in universal form, they expect their readers to *interpret* the laws statistically. Readers should ask themselves the following question when they confront any lawlike generalization that is stated in strictly universal form: "Would the theorist be willing to accept the conclusion that his law is false if he were shown the results of a *single experiment* where the law did not predict correctly and where the theorist was convinced that there were neither methodological nor observational errors in the experiment?" If the answer to this question is affirmative, then the theorist truly wants his law to be interpreted in a strictly universal manner, insofar as the essence of this question is whether the law being examined is *strictly falsifiable*. Strict falsification is a requirement of all laws of truly universal form. However, most theorists would probably reply in the negative to the previous question and then defensively retort, "Don't take my words so literally!"

We may conclude that no existing laws in marketing have the form of strictly universal, generalized conditionals. Indeed, some would take the position that marketing phenomena (like other behavioral phenomena) are *inherently* indeterministic, and, thus, the best that can ever be accomplished will be laws of basically statistical form.[2] *If* marketing phenomena were assumed to be inherently indeterministic, this should not be intellectually discomforting to marketing researchers. Although strictly universal laws have greater explanatory and predictive power than statistical laws, in many situations statistical laws perform quite adequately.

6.4 SUMMARY AND CONCLUSIONS

This chapter has attempted to explore the extension and universality of both lawlike and nonlawlike statements. The reader may wish to consult Figure 6.3,

Figure 6.3 **Extension and Universality**

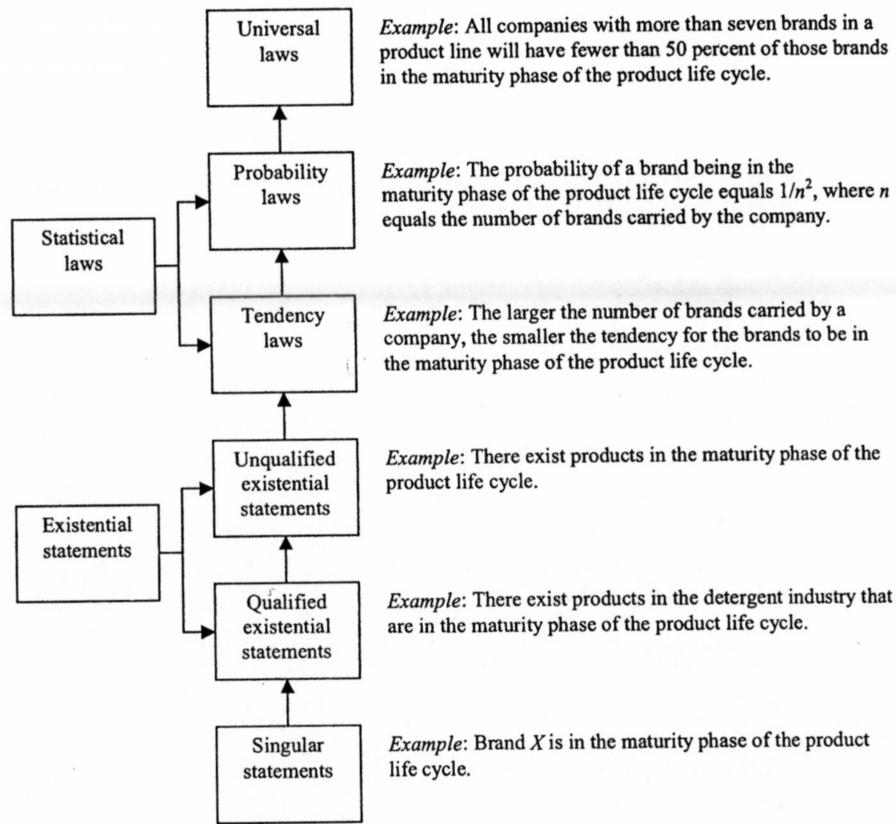

Source: Hunt (1991a). Reprinted by permission of the author.
Note: All examples are hypothetical and are for illustrative purposes only.

which delineates the various kinds of statements that have differing extension and gives hypothetical examples of each kind. The examples were specifically constructed so that each would involve the common construct of the "maturity phase of the product life cycle." Singular statements have the least extension of all statements because they refer to specific phenomena that are bound in time and space. Singular statements are both strictly confirmable and strictly falsifiable. Thus, their primary role in research lies in the *testing* of laws and theories. Existential statements propose the existence of some phenomenon. Bounded or qualified existential statements are both confirmable and falsifiable, whereas unqualified existential statements are confirmable but not strictly falsifiable. Tendency laws are a kind of statistical law stating that two variables tend to vary together in a systematic way. Most lawlike statements in marketing are tendency laws. Probability laws are a genus of statistical law where the relationship between two variables is clearly specified in the form of a probability or relative frequency statement. Both tendency laws and probability laws are neither confirmable nor falsifiable. Universal laws state a relationship between two variables in the form of a strictly universal generalized conditional. Such laws have the greatest extension and universality and are falsifiable but not strictly confirmable.

6.5 PROBLEMS IN EXTENSION: THE PSYCHOPHYSICS OF PRICES

The previous sections have attempted to classify various kinds of statements according to their differing extension. The extension of a statement was defined as the set of all possible objects (past, present, and future) covered by the statement. That is, to what is the statement referring: apples, oranges, attitudes, or preferences? A careful delimitation of the extension of statements is essential to systematic, scientific inquiry. Unfortunately, the marketing discipline as an applied area of investigation has been awash with lawlike statements that have been borrowed from other disciplines and then extrapolated to fit marketing problems. This extrapolation often extends the lawlike statement far beyond its legitimate domain or "universe of discourse." To illustrate the problems of questionable extension or extrapolation, we shall consider some of the issues raised by the so-called psychophysics of prices and Weber's law controversy.

Kamen and Toman (1970) used preference behaviors of consumers concerning various pricing combinations of major branded gasolines and independent branded gasolines to attempt to test their "fair price" theory versus Weber's law. The research sparked critical comments by Monroe (1971) and by Gabor et al. (1971) and a reply by Kamen and Toman (1971). Although many issues were raised during the controversy, only the issue of the extension of Weber's law will be explored here.

The crux of the fair price theory of Kamen and Toman (hereafter referred to as K-T) is that consumers have specific notions about what constitutes a fair price for a product and that when the actual price exceeds this fair price, consumers will take courses of action in an attempt to maintain the fair price. Thus, for their gasoline data, K-T suggest:

> According to the "fair price" theory, as the price of major brand gasoline exceeds the perceived fair price, more and more motorists will turn to the Independents. Thus, suppose that the price difference between Majors and Independents is two

> cents. This theory would predict that when the price of gasoline is high—for example, 42 cents for Majors and 40 cents for Independents—more people would be attracted to the Independents than when the price of gasoline is low—for example, 28 cents for Majors and 26 cents for Independents. This prediction is exactly opposite to the one inferable from Weber's Law. (Kamen and Toman 1970, p. 27)

K-T thus imply that the following *bridge law* is inferable from Weber's law: when the price of gasoline is high, more people will be attracted to the majors than to the independents than when the price of gasoline is low, if the same price *differential* is maintained at both price levels. Since K-T's results supported that fair price prediction, the major issue is whether their bridge law was a valid inference from Weber's law. That is, can Weber's law be extended to cover K-T's concepts in the predicted relationship?

First, a review of Weber's law and its original extension seems desirable. All participants in the controversy agree that Weber's law states:

$$\Delta I / I = K$$

where ΔI equals the smallest increase in the intensity of a stimulus that will be just noticeably different from the previous intensity of the stimulus, I equals the original intensity of the stimulus, and K equals a constant that varies according to the nature of the stimulus. Substantial research has confirmed that the relationship *extends* to the following stimuli: pressure, visual brightness, lifted weights, tone, smell, and taste (Berelson and Steiner 1964, p. 96). K-T (1971, p. 253) concede that they have extrapolated Weber's law beyond its original extension but claim that their extrapolations are consistent with the current marketing literature. They cite Engel, Kollat, and Blackwell for the following example:

> Assume, for example, that a price increase of $1 is to be put into effect. That increase would be highly apparent on a 50-cent item, whereas it probably would escape detection on an $80 item. (Kamen and Toman 1970, p. 27)

Are K-T just testing current and reasonable extensions or extrapolations of Weber's law? To this issue we now turn.

The original extension of Weber's law concerned people's ability to discriminate between different intensities of selected stimuli (smell, taste, etc.). The marketing literature, like the above quotation from Engel, Kollat, and Blackwell, has extended Weber's law to a different stimulus, that is, *price.* K-T, on the other hand, have extended Weber's law beyond the current literature in at least two other respects.

The literature has retained the notion of discriminability (note that Engel et al. use the phrases "highly apparent" and "escape detection"). K-T extend

Weber's law to *consumer preferences* instead of *discriminability*. K-T (1971, p. 253) recognize that they have done this but provide no logic to justify the extension. Perhaps the logic exists, but it was not presented. K-T (1971, p. 253) state that "any price difference is discriminable" and that "there simply is no JND (just noticeable difference) for price." These statements seem curious in light of K-T's own research, which appears to indicate that some price changes for some people were not discriminable. To wit, K-T's following paragraph is presented:

> An opportunity for a cleaner validation study arose a little less than a year after general gasoline price levels rose slightly over one cent in the same 24 markets mentioned previously. Approximately 1,500 motorists, randomly selected from city directories, were interviewed by telephone on their reactions to the price increase. Approximately 47 percent believed that the general gasoline price level went up during the past year, 2 percent believed that it went down, 44 percent that it remained the same, and 7 percent did not know or failed to answer this question. (Kamen and Toman 1970, p. 34)

In any respect, even if it were true that all price changes were discriminable, this would be insufficient reason to extend Weber's law from *discriminability* to *preferences*. To repeat, there may be a logic available to justify extending discriminability to preference, but K-T did not present it.

The third major extension of Weber's law by K-T concerns the notion of ΔI, the *differential*. In the original extension of Weber's law, the differential referred to different intensities of the *same stimulus* (smell, taste, etc.). However, the differential that K-T refer to is different intensities of *different stimuli*. That is, the K-T differential is the difference in price between major branded gasoline and independent gasoline (not a difference for the same gasoline). Once again, K-T provide no logic to show that this is a reasonable extension.

In summary, K-T extended the original version of Weber's law (1) to a different stimulus (price), (2) from discriminability to preferences, and (3) from different intensities of the same stimulus to different intensities of different stimuli. Taken in total, and without any justifying logic, these extensions (especially [2] and [3]) seem unwarranted because they so drastically alter the basic statement of the law. The "fair price" theory of K-T is intriguing; K-T's research is interesting; and their data base is sound. Unfortunately, it is difficult to see what any of their results have to do with Weber's law. They certainly did not test Weber's law in any meaningful sense of the word *test*. It is hoped that, if the "psychophysics of prices" controversy has done nothing else, it has underscored the tremendous importance of carefully delimiting the extension of lawlike statements. One must always stop to ask, "What is this statement really saying?" Also, "To which kinds of circumstances and situations does this statement apply, and to which does it not?"

QUESTIONS FOR ANALYSIS AND DISCUSSION

1. "Models are really the bases for marketing theories since they are the *axioms* on which marketing theories are founded" (Lazer 1962). Evaluate the view that models are axioms.
2. Find a theory or model in the marketing literature. Determine which statements purport to be lawlike. How do the statements handle the time dimension? Examine the extension of the statements.
3. Laws are "hypotheses that are empirically corroborated to a degree regarded as satisfactory at a certain point in time" (Zaltman, Pinson, and Angelmar 1973, p. 71). To what extent is this perspective consistent or inconsistent with the treatment presented herein?
4. All lawlike statements have empirical content. Any statement that has empirical content can be empirically tested. Any statement that can be empirically tested can be shown to be true or false. Therefore, all lawlike statements can be shown to be empirically true or false. Evaluate.
5. Alderson (1965, p. 345) proposed "a research agenda for functionalism" that included 150 falsifiable propositions. "For a proposition to be falsifiable, it must make a flat assertion with no authority behind it except its apparent consistency with other propositions that have already been accepted into the body of theory." Further, "a proposition is not falsifiable, or testable, if it has been hedged and qualified until it is almost certainly true under some circumstances." Analyze a sample of Alderson's propositions. What kinds of lawlike statements are they? What is their extension? To what extent are they *falsifiable*?
6. "As the degree of extension of a lawlike generalization increases, its accuracy of prediction will decrease." Evaluate.
7. Pinson et al. take great issue with the term *lawlike generalization*:

   > The term "lawlike generalization" . . . is not commonly used in the philosophy of science literature. Instead, most authorities use the term "lawlike statement." . . . The reason for preferring the term "lawlike statement" over "lawlike generalization" relates to the redundance of the latter term [because] a minimum necessary condition of any scientific statement proposed as lawlike is that it can be a universal generalization. (Pinson et al. 1972, p. 67)

   Evaluate the charge made by Pinson et al. Are all generalizations *lawlike*? Are all lawlike statements *universal*?
8. Lockley (1964, p. 48) proposes the following tendency law in marketing, which he calls the principle of nonprice competition: "For products for which product or marketing differentiation becomes dif-

ficult, there will be an increasing tendency toward nonprice competition, and the extent of nonprice competition will tend to be in proportion to the size and resources of the competing vendors." Does this imply that for products for which differentiation is *easy* there will be a *decreasing* tendency for nonprice competition? Evaluate.

9. The channels of distribution literature often discusses the notions of power and conflict. A major problem has been to get an adequate definition of conflict. The following two perspectives are typical: (1) "The term conflict refers neither to its antecedent conditions, nor to individual awareness of it, nor certain affective states, nor its overt manifestations, nor its residues of feeling, precedent, or structure, but to all of these taken together as the history of a conflict episode" (Pondy 1967, p. 319). (2) "Conflict in our scheme refers to overt behavior arising out of a process in which one unit seeks the advancement of its own interests in its relationship with others" (Schmidt and Kochon 1972, p. 363).

   Are these *definitions* of conflict, *explanations* of conflict, *lawlike generalizations* involving conflict, or what? Is it possible for a statement to be both a lawlike generalization and a definition at the same time? How useful would the two preceding perspectives be in conducting research on conflict in channels of distribution?

10. Is it possible to have a set of nontrue theorems that are derived from a set of true axioms? Does your answer differ depending on whether the axioms were universal or statistical in nature?

NOTES

1. See: Friedman 1953; Samuelson 1963, 1964, 1965; Garb 1965; Machlup 1964; Lerner 1965; Masey 1965; Nagel 1963; Blaug 1980.

2. The reader should be analyzing all statements by now and should recognize that this statement is falsifiable but not strictly confirmable. Can the statement be alternatively constructed as a negative existential statement?

7 THE MORPHOLOGY OF THEORY

Once upon a time two explorers came upon a clearing in the jungle. In the clearing were growing many flowers and many weeds. One explorer says, "Some gardener must tend this plot." The other disagrees, "There is no gardener." So they pitch their tents and set a watch. No gardener is ever seen. "But perhaps he is an invisible gardener." So they set up a barbed-wire fence. They electrify it. They patrol with bloodhounds. (For they remember how H.G. Wells's The Invisible Man *could be both smelt and touched though he could not be seen.) But no shrieks ever suggest that some intruder has received a shock. No movements of the wire even betray an invisible climber. The bloodhounds never give cry. Yet still the Believer is not convinced. "But there is a gardener, invisible, intangible, insensible to electric shocks, a gardener who has no scent and makes no sound, a gardener who comes secretly to look after the garden which he loves." At last the Sceptic despairs, "But what remains of your original assertion? Just how does what you call an invisible, intangible, eternally elusive gardener differ from an imaginary gardener or even from no gardener at all?"*

—A.G.N. Flew

This chapter will attempt to explicate the nature and role of theory in scientific inquiry and research. After discussing various perspectives on the concept of theory, a consensus conceptualization of theory will be offered. A review of some basic misconceptions of the nature of theory will show that, as a result of these misconceptions, marketing theory has taken a "bum rap." The body of the chapter will be devoted to developing in some detail the full import of the three key ideas embodied in the consensus conceptualization of theory. First, let's explore some perspectives on the notion of theory.

7.1 THE NOTION OF THEORY

What constitutes a theory? Is the term *theory* synonymous with *law*? How does a *theory* of *X* differ from an *explanation* of *X*? How do theories differ from hypotheses? Is a theory simply a model? Strangely enough, although *theory* would have to rank high among the most abused terms in marketing, there is probably more unanimity among philosophers of science as to what constitutes a theory than there is agreement among them concerning the nature of laws and explanations. This is not to say that there is a universal consensus concerning the nature of theoretical constructions. Rather, different uses of the term *theory* in philosophy of science are more apparent than real, more superficial than substantive, as a representative sample of perspectives will demonstrate.

Kaplan (1964, p. 297) defines theory thus: "We may say to start with that a theory is a system of laws. But the laws are altered by being brought into systematic connection with one another, as marriage relates two people who are never the same again." Similarly, Bergmann (1957, p. 31) notes, "If there has to be a formula again, one might say that a theory is a group of laws deductively connected." Blalock suggests:

> It has been noted that theories do not consist entirely of conceptual schemes or typologies but must contain lawlike propositions that interrelate the concepts of variables two or more at a time. Furthermore, these propositions must themselves be interrelated. (Blalock 1969, p. 2)

Bunge is much more specific and detailed in his description of theory:

> In ordinary language and in ordinary metascience "hypothesis," "law," and "theory" are often exchanged; and sometimes laws and theories are taken to be the manhood of hypotheses. In advanced science and in contemporary metascience the three terms are usually distinguished: "law" or "law formula" designates a hypothesis of a certain kind—namely, non-singular, non-isolated, referring to a pattern, and corroborated; and "theory" designates *a system of hypotheses, among which law formulas are conspicuous*—so much so that the core of a theory is a system of law formulas. In order to minimize confusions we will provisionally adopt the following characterization: A set of scientific hypotheses is a scientific theory if and only if it refers to a given factual subject matter and every member of the set is either an initial assumption (axiom, subsidiary assumption, or datum) or a logical consequence of one or more initial assumptions. (Bunge 1967a, p. 381; italics added)

In his classic work *The Logic of Scientific Discovery*, Popper (1959, p. 59) metaphorically suggests that *theories* are "nets to catch what we call 'the world': to rationalize, to explain, and to master it. We endeavor to make the mesh finer and finer." Braithwaite (1968, p. 22) believes that "a scientific theory is a deductive system in which observable consequences logically follow from the conjunction of observed facts with the set of the fundamental hypotheses of the system." Finally, the marketing theoretician Wroe Alderson (1957, p. 5) proposes that a "theory is a set of propositions which are consistent among themselves and which are relevant to some aspect of the factual world."

Although the previous perspectives on theory differ, a careful examination will reveal that the differences are noteworthy primarily for their superficiality. Note how often these similar terms and phrases are repeated: "system of laws," "systematic connection," "interrelated lawlike propositions," "set of scientific hypotheses," "factual subject matter," "group of laws," and "deductively related." All of these key concepts can be incorporated into a consensus definition of theory, which will serve as the focal point for this chapter and which was originally proposed by Richard S. Rudner:

> Definition: A theory is a systematically related set of statements, including some lawlike generalizations, that is empirically testable. The purpose of theory is to increase scientific understanding through a systematized structure capable of both explaining and predicting phenomena. (Rudner 1966, p. 10)

Much of the rest of this chapter will be devoted to fully explicating the import of this conceptualization of the nature and role of theory. In the process we will show that a full articulation of the three key criteria of theory—(1) it is systematically related, (2) it includes lawlike generalizations, and (3) it is empirically testable—will demonstrate that this conceptualization can be truly described as consensus. Concurrently, we will show that the correct application of the three key criteria will both systematically *exclude* all constructions that should not be given the status of *theory*, and, at the same time, will systematically *include* all constructions that should be referred to as theories. However, before we proceed further, a brief analysis of theoretical misconceptions will reveal that careless usage of the term *theory* has resulted in much mischief in marketing.

7.2 MISCONCEPTIONS OF THEORY

No marketing academician would dispute this assertion: the term *marketing theory* is often viewed with disfavor by both marketing students and marketing faculty. Few criticisms in academia are more damning than "This course is too theoretical!" A suggested opening gambit for a course in marketing theory is to ask the students to try to think of another course they have had that they disliked because it was "too theoretical." The instructor then begins to probe the students to determine exactly what each meant when he or she thought some particular course was *too theoretical*. After some discussion the students' criticisms begin to center on four recurring themes:

1. The too theoretical course was difficult to understand.
2. The too theoretical course was conjectural rather than factual. ("That's just a theory, not a fact.")

3. The too theoretical course was not related to the real world.
4. The too theoretical course was not practical enough. ("It's all right in theory but not in practice.")

Although the complaint that *too theoretical* courses are difficult to understand is often justified, this complaint should be met with sympathy and compassion, but not with alarm. Theories often deal with abstract concepts and complicated relationships, and, thus, they may be difficult to comprehend. Simplicity is a desirable characteristic of theory, but reality is often complex and theoretical constructions used to explain reality must often be complex. However, the theory presented in courses is sometimes difficult to understand because of the theorist's obtuse and nonlucid manner of writing, rather than because of the inherent difficulty of the theoretical relationships. Even great theorists (such as J.M. Keynes) have often expressed their ideas in a manner susceptible to great variance in interpretation. While discussing Wroe Alderson's theoretical constructions, Hostiuck and Kurtz (1973, p. 141) note that "the authors have heard even recognized scholars of marketing groan at the mere mention of Alderson and intimate that they never really understood him." Perhaps it is just too much to expect a creative theorist to present his theoretical constructions lucidly, but a nonlucid articulation of a theory will make students groan that it is difficult to understand and will also retard the testing and future development of the theory.

The second complaint states that too theoretical courses are *conjectural* rather than *factual*. One characteristic of the scientifically immature mind is to be uncomfortable in the presence of uncertainty. True scientists are always ready to revise their beliefs in the light of fresh evidence. The really important issues in any discipline are always conjectural rather than factual. To recognize that consumers' preferences are shifting toward smaller automobiles is useful, but the real challenge is to develop theories, which by their very nature will be conjectural, to explain past shifts in consumer preferences and to predict future shifts. Likewise, knowing that distribution channels are now shorter is less useful than theorizing *why* they are now shorter and attempting to predict what will happen to the length of distribution channels in the future. Although theories must be empirically testable (hence, not "purely conjectural"), because of the nature of any theory's constituent lawlike generalizations, a theory can never be *confirmed* in the same sense that simple descriptive or singular statements can be confirmed. Nevertheless, except for people who just like to read telephone books or census data, the most interesting issues in a discipline are usually more conjectural than factual.

The charges that the content of courses is "not related to the real world" or is "not practical" are serious indeed. In fact, these charges are perhaps the most common and serious of all the charges that are made against theoretical courses. *The resolution of these charges lies in the realization that all purportedly theoretical constructions must be empirically testable and must be capable of explaining and predicting real-world phenomena.* Two conclusions immediately follow: (1) All purportedly theoretical constructions *must* be related to the real world. (2) All purportedly theoretical constructions *must* be practical, because the explanation and prediction of real-world phenomena must rank high on any list of practical concerns. Rather than "it is all right in theory but not in practice," the truth of the matter is that *if it is not all right in practice, it cannot be all right in theory*! Courses filled with complex mental gymnastics (often couched in mathematical terms) that have no relevance to the real world and no explanatory or predictive power are not *too theoretical* at all. On the contrary, such courses are completely devoid of theoretical content.

Unfortunately, all too many marketing students and academicians have tended to bestow the term *theory* on locutions that are nothing more than obtuse armchair philosophy or mathematical mental gymnastics with no explanatory or predictive power. It is little wonder that the label "too theoretical" has truly become an epithet. One of the objectives of this book is to challenge marketing theorists to cull out the obtuse armchair philosophy and to ensure that their purportedly theoretical constructions are empirically testable and have explanatory and predictive power. For too long, marketing theory has taken a "bum rap" because it has been awash in nontheoretical constructions masquerading as theory.

In summary, since the real world is often complex, the theoretical constructions with which we attempt to explain reality will often be complex. Because by their very nature theories cannot be conclusively shown to be *true* (in the sense that a singular statement can be shown to be true), theories are, of necessity, *conjectural*. But the most important issues (such as explanation and prediction) in any discipline are always of the conjectural variety. Finally, the notion that *theoretical* and *practical* are at opposite ends of a continuum is false. Any construction that purports to be a theory must be capable of explaining and predicting real-world phenomena. And the explanation and prediction of phenomena are eminently *practical* concerns. With these misconceptions of theory disposed of, we can now turn our attention to the three criteria distinguishing theoretical from nontheoretical constructions.

7.3 THE "SYSTEMATICALLY RELATED" CRITERION

So, a theory is a *systematically related* set of statements, including some lawlike generalizations, that is empirically testable. This section will explore two basic questions: (1) Why should the statements in a theory be required to be systematically related? (2) In what precise way should the statements in a theory be systematically related? Rudner provides one response to the first question:

> We are all familiar with the view that it is not the business of science merely to collect unrelated, haphazard, disconnected bits of information; that it is an ideal of science to give an *organized* account of the universe—to connect, to fit together in relations of subsumption, the statements embodying the knowledge that has been acquired. Such organization is a necessary condition for the accomplishment of two of science's chief functions, explanation and prediction. (Rudner 1966, p. 11)

Robert K. Merton addresses the same issue in sociology:

> [A] miscellany of . . . propositions only provides the raw materials for sociology as a discipline. The theoretic task, and the orientation of empirical research toward theory, first begins when the bearing of such uniformities on a set of interrelated propositions is tentatively established. The notion of directed research implies that, in part, empirical inquiry is so organized that if and when empirical uniformities are discovered, they have direct consequences for a theoretic system. (Merton 1968, p. 149)

The view taken here is that we require theories to contain systematically related sets of statements in order to increase the *scientific understanding* of phenomena. To understand scientifically the occurrence of a phenomenon requires more than simply being able to explain and predict it using *isolated* lawlike generalizations. In addition, we must be able to show how the statements used to explain and predict a phenomenon are incorporated into the total body of scientific knowledge. The view that the *systematically related* criterion represents a consensus position can be supported by a careful examination of the previously cited perspectives on theory. For example, Kaplan mentions "systematic connection," Bergmann talks about "deductively connected," Blalock requires "interrelated propositions," and Braithwaite discusses a "set of fundamental hypotheses." Therefore, all of these writers allude to what we are calling the systematically related criterion.

The second question asks, "In *what precise way* should the statements in a theory be systematically related?" As Dubin (1969, p. 16) has observed, simply to have a collection of propositions is not necessarily to have a theory. The propositions or statements in a theory must have a high degree of internal consistency. To check for internal consistency, all of the *concepts* in each statement in the theory must be clearly defined, all of the *relationships* among the concepts in each statement must be clearly specified, and all of the *interrelationships* among the statements in the theory must be clearly delineated.

The complete articulation of the nature of the "systematically related" criterion requires an elaboration of the notion of "full formalization" in the philosophy of science. The essence of the full formalization of a theory is the complete, rigorous articulation of the entire syntactic and semantic structure of the theory. Bergmann (1957, p. 38) suggests, "One formalizes a scientific theory by replacing its descriptive words by 'marks on paper.' The logical words, which remain, are the only ones we 'understand.'" But full formalization implies much more than simply replacing descriptive words with "marks on paper." Figure 7.1 illustrates that *a fully formalized theory consists of a formal language system that has been axiomatized and appropriately interpreted.*[1] We must now turn to an examination of (1) formal language systems, (2) axiomatized formal systems, and (3) appropriately interpreted, axiomatized formal systems because to require theories to contain systematically related sets of statements implies that theories must, in principle, be amenable to formalization.

7.3.1 Formal Language Systems

Formal language systems must first be differentiated from natural language systems, such as English. Both formal language systems and natural language systems include (1) elements, (2) formation rules, and (3) definitions. The English language elements are the *words* of English, and the formation rules (the grammar or syntax) state the permissible ways in which words can be combined to form correct English sentences. For example, the statement "marketing advertising beneficial" is not a correct English sentence because it violates the *formation rule* that each English sentence must contain a verb.

In addition to elements and formation rules, both natural languages and formal language systems must have sets of definitions. The kinds of definitions that are required here are *nominal* definitions (Hempel 1970, p. 654) or *rules of replacement* (Rudner 1966, p. 15). These types of definitions should be carefully distinguished from definitions of the so-called *operational* variety. Roughly speaking, nominal definitions have to do with relationships among *terms alone* (syntactic considerations) and operational definitions have to do with relationships between terms and the *real world* (semantic considerations). We will treat operational definitions in the section probing the "empirically testable" criterion of theoretical constructions and will focus our present attention on nominal definitions.

A nominal definition states that one term, the *definiendum*, is equivalent to another term or groups of terms, the *definiens*. So, Alderson (1965) defines assortment:

$$\text{assortment} =_{df} \text{meaningful heterogeneous collection}$$

Figure 7.1 **The Full Formalization of a Theory**

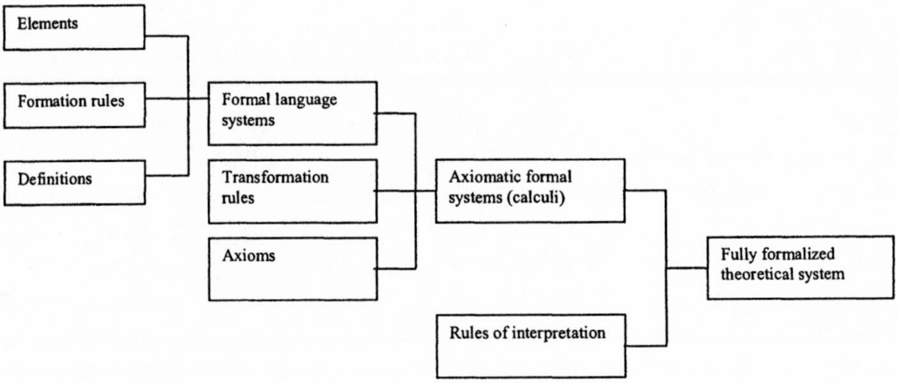

Source: Hunt (1991a). Reprinted by permission of the author.

In this instance, "assortment" is the definiendum and "meaningful heterogeneous collection" is the definiens. The significance of calling nominal definitions "rules of replacement" is that the truth value of any statement that includes the definiendum is maintained if the definiendum is replaced by the definiens (Rudner 1966, p. 16). That is, any statement that is true and contains the term *assortment* will likewise be true if "assortment" is replaced by "meaningful heterogeneous collection." Similarly, any false statement that contains the term *assortment* will remain false if "meaningful heterogeneous collection" is substituted for it.

But how does one define *meaningful heterogeneous collection*? We must either introduce other terms to define *meaningful heterogeneous collection,* or we must suffer circularity by defining:

$$\text{meaningful heterogeneous collection} =_{df} \text{assortment}$$

In either case, a little reflection reveals that in any language system there will be a set of *primitive* elements or terms. These primitive elements will be undefined within that system but will not necessarily be undefined within some other system. Also, all of the nonprimitive elements within the given language system can be defined by means of the primitives. Alderson (1965, p. 25) suggested that all of the subject matter in his conceptualization of marketing could be ultimately reduced by a series of definitions to three primitive terms: sets, behavior, and expectations. Although this conclusion may be open to question, Alderson clearly realized that all language systems contain primitive or undefined elements.

We require theories to contain systematically related sets of statements. The *systematically related* criterion implies a kind of systematization that is, at least in principle, amenable to formalization. A fully formalized theory implies, among other things, a formal language system. Insofar as both formal language systems and so-called natural languages include (1) elements, (2) formation rules, and (3) definitions, how do formal language systems differ from natural languages? Formal language systems differ from natural languages in that they identify all of the primitive elements, and they develop a complete "dictionary" that shows how all of the nonprimitive terms are derived from the primitive elements. Furthermore, rather than having the loose and continually evolving formation rules of natural languages, such as English, formal language systems rigorously and exhaustively specify the formation rules delineating the permissible ways of combining elements to form statements.

Summarizing, the full formalization of a theory requires the construction of a formal language system that includes a complete list of the primitive elements of the system, a "dictionary" showing how all of the system's nonprimitive terms are derived from the primitive elements, and a complete explication of the formation rules specifying how elements can be combined to form permissible statements (often called "wffs" or "well-formed formulations" in the philosophy of science literature). Nevertheless, the full formalization of a theory requires more than just a formal language system. The system must also undergo *axiomatization*, a subject to which we now turn.

7.3.2 Axiomatic Formal Systems

Figure 7.1 indicates that a fully formalized theory includes a formal language system that has been axiomatized. An axiomatized formal language system is referred to as a *calculus* in the philosophy of science. Axioms and their role in theory construction have already been discussed in section 6.2, which the reader might find helpful to review. The axiomatization of a formal language system requires (1) the adoption of rules of transformation and (2) the selection of appropriate fundamental statements or axioms. Recalling that formation rules detail the permissible ways in which elements can be combined to form statements, *transformation rules detail how statements can be combined to deduce other statements in the system.* A syllogistic example of a transformation rule from consumer demand theory should illustrate the kinds of rules that are required:

1. Bundle of goods *A* contains four oranges and two apples.
2. Bundle of goods *B* contains three oranges and three apples.

3. Bundle of goods *C* contains two oranges and four apples.
4. Consumer *X* indicates a preference for bundle *A* over bundle *B*.
5. Consumer X indicates a preference for bundle B over bundle C.
6. Therefore, consumer *X* will indicate a preference for bundle *A* over bundle *C*.

In consumer demand theory, statement 6 is deducible from statements 1–5 because demand theory assumes that consumer preferences follow the logical transformation rule known as *transitivity*. That is, if *A* is preferred to *B*, and *B* is preferred to *C*, then *A* is preferred to *C*. Therefore, to axiomatize a formal language system requires first that we adopt a series of transformation rules that dictate how some statements can be deduced from other statements.

After the permissible ways in which certain statements can be deduced from other statements have been delineated, the axiomatization of a formal language system requires the selection of appropriate fundamental statements or axioms to separate fundamental statements from derived or deduced statements. According to Popper (1959, p. 71), there are four criteria for selecting the *appropriate* fundamental statements for axiomatization. They must be: (1) free from contradiction, (2) independent, (3) sufficient, and (4) necessary. The first criterion requires that the fundamental statements be internally consistent to the extent that mutually exclusive outcomes or statements cannot be deduced from the fundamental statements. That is, if an appropriate set of transformations on the fundamental statements produces the statement that "*X* will occur," then there must *not* be some other permissible set of transformations that will produce the statement that "*X* will *not* occur." Thus, the first requirement is an internal consistency criterion. The second requirement, that the fundamental statements be *independent*, implies that no statement in the final set of fundamental statements can be deducible from the other statements. That is, the axioms must truly be *fundamental* in the system. The third requirement, that the fundamental statement be *sufficient*, implies that all of the statements that are part of the theory proper can be derived from the set of fundamental statements. Finally, to be *necessary* implies that all the statements in the fundamental set are *used* to derive other statements; that is, there are no superfluous statements.

Two points should be reemphasized here. First, as discussed in section 6.2, the fundamental statements or axioms of a theory are assumed to be true for *analytical* purposes only. That is, they are assumed to be true for the purpose of deriving other statements. The axioms are *not* assumed to be true for *empirical* purposes. Therefore, it is entirely appropriate and desirable to empirically test the axioms of a theory. Second, at least some of the fundamental or derived statements in the axiomatic formal system must have the characteristics of lawlike generalizations. Otherwise, the axiomatic formal system would not be a theoretical construction.

In summary, the axiomatization of a formal language system requires (1) the specification of the transformation rules that state the permissible ways in which statements can be combined in order to derive or deduce other statements, and (2) the delineation of a set of fundamental statements or axioms that are free from contradiction, independent, sufficient, and necessary. Every theory is, at least in principle, susceptible to axiomatization because every theory is composed of statements, and it should be possible to classify the statements in terms of whether they are (1) derived or (2) fundamental *within that theory*. For an excellent axiomatization of consumer demand theory, the reader is urged to consult the first fifty pages of Peter Newman's (1965) *The Theory of Exchange*. This writer knows of no strictly marketing theory that has been axiomatized. Whether marketing theorists should attempt to axiomatize and formalize their theories will be discussed later in this chapter.

7.3.3 Rules of Interpretation

Recapitulating, a fully formalized theoretical structure will include a formal language system that has been axiomatized. Recall, however, that the essence of the full formalization of a theoretical system is a complete, rigorous articulation of *both* the syntactic and semantic structure of the theory. The analysis, so far, has been purely syntactic; that is, only the requirements for the logical relationships among elements and combinations of elements (statements) have been articulated. We have developed the requirements for a formalized analytical-conceptual schema. Insofar as everything up to this point has dealt solely with Bergmann's "marks on paper," it is now time to bring in the meanings of the marks on paper. Alternatively stated, it is now time to bring in the real world by discussing the semantic rules of interpretation.

Referring again to Figure 7.1, an axiomatic formal language system becomes a fully formalized theoretical system when a complete set of appropriate semantic rules of interpretation for the elements or terms in the formal language system have been developed. Because theoretical systems are used to explain and predict phenomena, the elements in the theories must somehow be linked to observable entities and the properties of observable entities in the real world. The semantic rules of interpretation that accomplish this linkage are variously referred to as measures, indicants, operational definitions, coordinating definitions, correspondence rules, or epistemic correlations (Nagel 1961, p. 93).

Although a complete analysis of semantic rules of interpretation will be deferred to section 7.5 on the "empirically testable" criterion of theories, the *ideal goal* of these semantic rules should be stated here. The semantic rules of interpretation are optimal when for each possible interpretation of the axiomatized formal system by semantic rules that makes the fundamental statements (or axioms) true, all of the derived statements (or theorems) will likewise be true. Such a set of optimal semantic rules of interpretation would thus achieve a kind of *isomorphism* or "one-to-one correspondence" between the marks on paper of the theory and the real world.

Summarizing the preceding three sections, a theory is a systematically related set of statements, including some lawlike generalizations, that is empirically testable. To be *systematically related* is a desirable and consensus criterion of theory because science endeavors to increase scientific understanding by giving an organized account of the universe. A set of statements will fulfill the *systematically related* criterion when it exhibits a kind of systematization that is, at least in principle, amenable to full formalization. A fully formalized theoretical system consists of a formal language system that has been axiomatized and completely interpreted. Formal language systems contain (1) elements, (2) formation rules, and (3) a set of definitions (all three are rigorously specified). An axiomatic formal language system includes a set of transformation rules showing how some statements can be derived from other statements and a set of fundamental statements that are (1) free from contradiction, (2) independent, (3) sufficient, and (4) necessary. An axiomatized formal language system becomes a fully formalized theoretical system when a complete set of semantic rules of interpretation has been developed.

7.3.4 Issues in Formalization

Although theories are required to have a kind of systematization that is susceptible to formalization, four points must be made regarding formalization. First, the preceding discussion of *full formalization* in no way attempts to capture or describe the actual processes that theorists use to discover or create a theoretical structure. The formalization of a theory is *ex post*. That is, the process of formalization customarily begins in earnest only *after* the theory has been proposed. Second, some writers warn against the premature formalization of theories on the ground that formalization may actually inhibit scientific creativity. Thus, Kaplan suggests:

> The demand for exactness of meaning and for precise definition of terms can easily have a pernicious effect, as I believe it often has had in behavioral science. It results in what has been aptly named the *premature closure* of our ideas. That the progress of science is marked by successive closures can be stipulated; but it is just the function of inquiry to instruct us how and where closure can best be achieved. . . . There is a certain kind of behavioral scientist who, at the least threat of an exposed ambiguity, scurries for cover like a hermit crab into the nearest abandoned logical shell.

> But there is no ground for panic. That a cognitive situation is not as well structured as we would like does not imply that no inquiry made in that situation is really scientific. On the contrary, it is the dogmatisms outside science that proliferate closed systems of meaning; the scientist is in no hurry for closure. Tolerance of ambiguity is as important for creativity in science as it is anywhere else. (Kaplan 1964, p. 70)

Third, the complete formalization of any theory is an arduous task requiring great effort. Finally, it should be noted, few theories in any of the sciences have been fully formalized.

Many philosophers of science have questioned the role of formalization in theory development. Suppe (1977, pp. 110–15) has summarized their arguments. First, the systematic interconnections among the concepts of many theories are insufficiently specified to enable *fruitful* axiomatization. Suppe cites examples such as Darwin's theory of evolution, Hoyle's theory on the origin of the universe, Pike's theory of language structure, and Freud's psychology. Second, the formalization of a theory often leaves untouched many of the truly interesting philosophical problems. This is because formalization usually emphasizes syntactic rather than semantic considerations. Third, formalization is a static analysis revealing at best a "snapshot" of a theory at a point in time. Thus, formalization ignores the dynamics of theory development.

Suppe (1977) then replies to these criticisms by pointing out that the fact that some theories cannot be completely formalized ignores the possibility (and usefulness) of *partial* formalization. Furthermore, for studying the fine details of a structure, a "snapshot" is often much preferred to a "videotape." Suppe (1977, p. 62) concludes, "Rather surprisingly the various criticisms of the Received View have left this claim [that theories should be formalized] essentially unchallenged." Suppe's conclusion coincides with that of most writers. For example, MacKinnon suggests:

> Perhaps the most basic and obvious question to be asked concerning rational reconstructions of scientific theories is "Why bother?" Rational reconstructions have contributed little if anything either to the understanding of historically developing theories or to advancing their future development. The rather pragmatic point of view . . . is that in a rational reconstruction a scientific theory becomes an object of study, rather than a tool for studying some other domain. Reconstructing a theory is a help to understanding it, at least in the sense that we have some understanding of anything we can take apart and put back together. (MacKinnon 1979, p. 510)

The preceding analysis implies that the primary purpose of formalization lies in *evaluating* theoretical structures, not in discovering or creating them. Often, the attempt even to partially formalize a theory, by baring its essential structure or morphology, can sharpen the discussion of the theory and put it into a framework suitable for testing. *For many marketing theories, the partial formalization of the theory is an absolutely necessary precondition for meaningful analysis.* Two examples should illustrate this point. First, we shall consider the so-called general theory of marketing proposed by Robert Bartels (1968), and second, we shall explore the partial formalization of the Howard-Sheth "theory of buyer behavior" (1969) that was generated by Farley and Ring (1970).

7.3.5 The "General Theory of Marketing": A Partial Formalization

An article by Robert Bartels (1968) on marketing theory generated substantial debate concerning the nature of theoretical constructions in general and the components of a general theory of marketing in particular. Bartels proposed a general theory of marketing that included seven subtheories: (1) theory of social initiative; (2) theory of economic (market) separations; (3) theory of market roles, expectations, and interactions; (4) theory of flows and systems; (5) theory of behavior constraints; (6) theory of social change and marketing evolution; and (7) theory of social control of marketing. In order to analyze the basic nature of these seven "theories," the present writer found it necessary to partially formalize them. The reconstructions or partial formalizations of the seven theories were then used for evaluative purposes (Hunt 1971). A review of two of Bartels's theories will help to illustrate the process used for partial formalization. Bartels states his theory of flows and systems as follows:

> Flows are the movements of elements which resolve market separations. Marketing does not occur as a single movement, but rather as a number of movements, in series, parallel, reciprocal, or duplicatory. They occur in the complex relations among the individuals who have found an economic basis for their existence and for their participation in the marketing process. (Bartels 1968, p. 33)

Similarly, Bartels states his theory of behavior constraints in this way:

> Action in the marketing system is not determined wholly by any one individual or set of participants. It is governed by many determinants and occurs within constraints defined by society. Some of these constraints are economic in nature. Only that can be done which can be done within the bounds of economic feasibility. This may be determined through experience in the profitable combining of economic factors of production. However, much feasibility is predetermined and set forth in the form of marketing technology, know-how, or generalizations for behavior. This is reason for having thorough knowledge of marketing mechanics, or the relations of commodities-functions-institutions as set forth in conventional marketing theory.
>
> Constraints are also social, rather than economic or technical, in nature. These may be of an ethical nature, as that term is used broadly, indicating what is "right" to do under certain circumstances. Rightness may be determined by personal, legal, societal, and theistic standards, and each of these may differ from one society to another. As marketing is viewed more as a personal process rather than only a physical one, such constraints play a more prominent role in marketing theory. (Bartels 1968, p. 33)

The first steps in the formalization of any theory are to generate the basic statements of the theory in precise, succinct fashion and to array the statements in an orderly manner to facilitate theoretical analysis. One such reconstruction or (very) partial formalization of the first "theory" would be:

1. The elements in marketing can be classified into those that flow and those that do not flow.
2. The flowing elements of marketing can be further classified by type: series, parallel, reciprocal, and duplicatory.
3. a. The marketing flows are very important and should be studied by marketing students.
   b. The relationships among marketing flows are very complex.

Similarly, one possible reconstruction of the second "theory" would be:

1. Marketing behavior is constrained behavior.
2. a. Some of the constraints are designed by society.
   b. The societal constraints may be classified as economic, social, ethical, or technical.

As can easily be seen, these reconstructions, *even though they represent only the first modest steps toward formalizations*, are much more amenable to rigorous analysis than the original narrative discussions of the "theories." The present writer analyzed these reconstructions and concluded that none of the seven "theories" were theories at all. Rather, the seven "theories" were shown to be an assemblage of classificational schemata, some intriguing definitions, and exhortations to fellow marketing students to adopt a particular marketing perspective in attempting to generate marketing theory (Hunt 1971, p. 68). Pinson et al. (1972) then analyzed these same partial formalizations and came to different conclusions regarding their theoretical adequacy. The discussion of Pinson et al. prompted a rebuttal that concluded that Bartels's "theory" was "neither a theory of marketing nor a 'general' theory of marketing" (Hunt 1973, p. 70).

The point to be emphasized here is not whether Bartels's theory is or is not really a theoretical construction. Rather, the partially formalized reconstructions greatly facilitated theoretical analysis. In addition, a caveat is needed at this point: if the reconstructions do not accurately capture the basic structure, then, of course, any subsequent analysis will not do justice to the theory. In conclusion, in response to the question "Why formalize?" we respond, "In order to facilitate the analysis of theoretical and purportedly theoretical constructions." A second example of a partial formalization will reveal another benefit.

7.3.6 The Theory of Buyer Behavior: A Partial Formalization

Few theories in marketing have sparked more scholarly interest than the Howard-Sheth (1969) theory of buyer behavior. Figure 7.2 reproduces a summary of this theory. As can be observed, the theory consists of a large number of constructs, both exogenous and endogenous to the system. The constructs are interconnected by both direct causal linkages (the solid lines) and by feedback effects (the dashed lines).

Now, the fundamental question to be asked of any theoretical structure is: *how well does this theory represent the real world by explaining and predicting real-world phenomena*? To answer this question requires that the theory undergo empirical testing. Unfortunately, the theory as depicted in Figure 7.2 is not constructed in a form suitable for testing. Both the syntactic and semantic structure of the theory must first be reconstructed in at least partially formalized form to make the structure amenable to empirical testing. Farley and Ring (1970) addressed themselves to this task in their trailblazing study, "An Empirical Test of the Howard-Sheth Model of Buyer Behavior."

Farley and Ring's partial formalization of the Howard-Sheth (H-S) theory required the rigorous specification of the exact nature of the linkages among the constructs. They lament, "Indeed, in its [the model's] present form, the functional relationships among the variables are generally unspecified, although their directions are known" (Farley and Ring 1970, p. 427). The formalization of the theory culminated in a series of eleven simultaneous equations, each having the basic form:

$$Y_{(i)} = \sum_{\substack{j=l \\ (j \neq i)}}^{11} \beta_{i,j} Y_{(j)} + \sum_{k=l}^{K} Y_{i,j} X_{(k)} + Y_{i,o} + u_{(i)}; 1,\ldots,11.$$

Farley and Ring then obtained measures (the semantic rules of interpretation previously discussed) for each construct and conducted a test of the theory using both ordinary least squares and two-stage least squares regressions. Their results can be interpreted as weakly supporting the H-S theory.

Farley and Ring's efforts also sparked a critical appraisal of the basic structure of the H-S model by Hunt and Pappas (1972). This appraisal found that, because the actual variables used in the H-S model had been common knowledge in consumer behavior for some time, the major substantive contribution of the H-S theory was the postulation of certain *developmental linkages*. For example, Howard and Sheth propose the developmental linkage that attitude influences purchase only *through* intention to purchase. Any complete test of the H-S model must test for the existence or nonexistence of these developmental linkages. Because structural equation modeling programs were un-

Figure 7.2 **The Howard-Sheth Theory of Buyer Behavior**

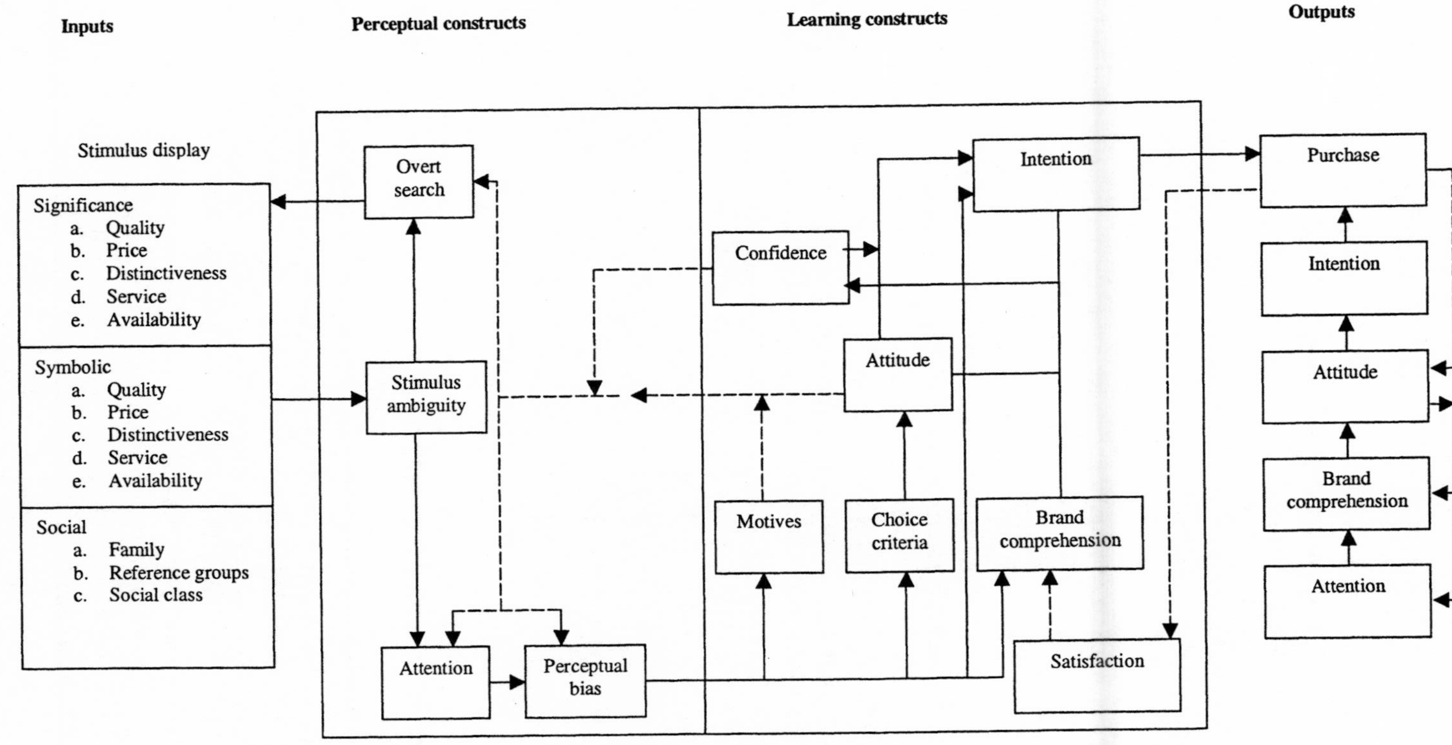

Source: Howard and Sheth (1969, p. 30). Reprinted by permission of John Wiley.

available at the time, a method using partial correlation coefficients was suggested as a possible procedure for testing the developmental linkages in the H-S model (Hunt and Pappas 1972, p. 347).

Subsequent empirical research by Lehmann, O'Brien, Farley, and Howard (1974) specifically tested for the developmental linkages postulated by the H-S model. Using the partial correlation coefficient procedure and cross-lagged correlation analysis, they concluded:

> Confidence levels for the Howard-Sheth model, as well as for the other two structures, were high enough to conclude that they are statistically significant, if yet very imperfect, representations of consumer information processing and decision making over time. In terms of finding strong support for the model, however, the results were disappointing. (Lehmann et al. 1974, p. 51)

Because of the weak support for the H-S version, Lehmann et al. constructed a revised model with different developmental linkages.

The pioneering efforts of Farley, Ring, Lehmann, O'Brien, and Howard conclusively demonstrate the desirability of formalization. Without their partial formalization of the Howard-Sheth theory, it would still be largely untested. Their partial formalization led to empirical testing (Farley and Ring 1970), then to theoretical appraisal and evaluation (Hunt and Pappas 1972), and then to retesting and redevelopment (Lehmann et al. 1974). In conclusion, the bogeyman of premature closure should deter no one from the formalization of theories, at least to the extent that formalization facilitates both theoretical analysis and empirical testing.

7.4 THE "LAWLIKE GENERALIZATIONS" CRITERION

The preceding sections have discussed the import of requiring the statements comprising a theory to be systematically related. Nevertheless, not all systematically related sets of statements are theoretical in nature. For example, definitional schemata, purely analytical schemata, and classificational schemata all contain systematically related statements, but they are not theories. For a systematically related set of statements to be a theory, at least some of the statements must be in the form of lawlike generalizations. A discussion of the nature of lawlike generalizations need not be repeated here, insofar as Chapter 5 has already explored this topic. It will suffice to recall that lawlike generalizations are statements having the basic form of generalized conditionals (statements of the "If *X* occurs, then *Y* will occur" variety) that (a) have empirical content, (b) exhibit nomic necessity, and (c) are systematically integrated into a body of scientific knowledge.

Why must theories contain at least some statements taking the form of lawlike generalizations? Because the purpose of theory is to increase scientific understanding through a systematized structure capable of both *explaining* and *predicting* phenomena. Being able to scientifically explain a phenomenon implies the ability to predict that phenomenon (see Chapter 4). Now, all of the models discussed in Chapter 3 that have explanatory power require lawlike generalizations to explain phenomena. That is, the deductive-nomological, deductive-statistical, and inductive-statistical models all rely on lawlike generalizations for their explanatory power. Models that do not include lawlike generalizations, for example, the pattern model, have been shown to yield inadequate scientific explanations of phenomena. *Therefore, all purportedly theoretical constructions must contain lawlike generalizations because a major purpose of theory is to explain phenomena, and all scientific explanations of phenomena contain lawlike generalizations.*

Once again, the *lawlike generalizations* criterion represents a consensus position in the philosophy of science. Thus, Kaplan (1964, p. 297) requires a "system of *laws*"; Bergmann (1957, p. 31) suggests a "group of *laws*"; Blalock (1969, p. 2) demands that theories contain "*lawlike* propositions"; and, finally, Bunge (1967a, p. 381) insists on "a system of hypotheses, among which *law* formulas are conspicuous." All of these authors are requiring theoretical constructions to contain what is referred to here as "lawlike generalizations."

Unfortunately, marketing theorists often seem to ignore the lawlike generalizations criterion in their efforts to develop marketing theory. Theorists create elaborate structures of systematically related statements composed exclusively of definitional and classificational schemata. As previously noted, a definition is a rule of replacement whereby an element (the definiendum) in a statement can be replaced by another element or elements (the definiens) without losing the truth value of the statement. A *definitional schema* is simply a systematically related set of definitions. All theories will contain definitional schemata, but a definitional schema is, by itself, not a theory.

Also frequently confused with theoretical schemata, a classificational schema is a kind of system that sets forth the conditions for the applicability of its categorial or classificatory terms. Classificational schemata always attempt to *partition* some universe of elements or statements into homogeneous groups.

7.5 THE "EMPIRICALLY TESTABLE" CRITERION

Having established that theories must contain systematically related statements, that at least some of these statements must be lawlike generalizations, and that classificational schemata should not be confused with theoretical schemata, there remains the task of exploring (1) what it means to require theories to be *empirically testable*, and (2) why they must be so required. First, why must theories be empirically testable? One powerful reason has been suggested by Popper (1959, p. 44). Scientific knowledge, in which theories are primal, must be *objective* in the sense that its truth content must be *intersubjectively certifiable*. Requiring a theory to be empirically testable ensures that it will be intersubjectively certifiable because different (but reasonably competent) investigators, with differing attitudes, opinions, and beliefs, will be able to make observations and conduct experiments to ascertain the truth content of the theory. Hempel (1970, p. 695) concurs, "Science strives for objectivity in the sense that its statements are to be capable of public tests with results that do not vary essentially with the tester." Scientific knowledge rests on the bedrock of empirical testability, which makes it intersubjectively certifiable. Most other kinds of knowledge (for example, theological knowledge, whose cornerstone is "faith") lack the capacity to be intersubjectively certifiable.

The second reason for requiring theories to be empirically testable springs from the purpose of theory itself. As previously discussed, the major purpose of theory is to increase scientific understanding through a systematized structure capable of both explaining and predicting phenomena. Any systematized structure that is *not* empirically testable will suffer from explanatory and predictive impotence: it will not be able to explain and predict phenomena. Hence, any structure that is not empirically testable will not be able to perform the tasks expected of genuine theoretical structures. Many purportedly theoretical constructions in marketing seem to lack explanatory and predictive power.

A final justification for requiring theories to be empirically testable lies in the desirability of distinguishing between theoretical schemata and what Rudner (1966, p. 28) refers to as *purely analytical schemata*. An analytical schema contains a systematically related set of statements, all of which are purely *analytic* rather than *synthetic*. "Products have life cycles" is a synthetic statement. "Either products have life cycles or products do not have life cycles" is purely analytic. Whether a synthetic statement is true or false can be ascertained only by examining the real-world facts. In contrast, whether a purely analytical statement is true or false can be determined solely by examining the order and nature of the logical terms (such as *either* and *or*) and the way in which certain descriptive terms (such as *products*) are defined. The real-world facts are completely irrelevant to the truth value of a purely analytical statement. Therefore, requiring theories to be empirically testable will screen out purely analytical schemata from being considered theories, which is desirable because we want the truth value of our theoretical construction to be relevant to the real world.

Summarizing, theories are required to be empirically testable in order that they be (a) intersubjectively certifiable, (b) capable of explaining and predicting phenomena, and (c) differentiated from purely analytical schemata. So far, we have been using the expression "empirically testable" as if it had perfect antecedent clarity. It is time to explore much more carefully exactly what it means to test a theory empirically.

7.5.1 The Nature of Empirical Testing

When confronted with any theory, ask the basic question, "Is the theory true?"[2] Less succinctly, ask the questions: "To what extent is the theory isomorphic with reality? Is the real world actually constructed as the theory suggests, or is it not? To what extent has the theory been empirically confirmed?" Numerous criteria have been proposed to evaluate the adequacy of theoretical constructions. Popper (1959, p. 32) has proposed the four criteria of internal consistency, logical form, comparison with other theories, and empirical testing. Dodd (1968, p. 31) reviewed the literature regarding criteria to evaluate theories and recorded seventy commonly used criteria, including accuracy, applicability, brevity, brilliance, and clarity. He then reduced the seventy to twenty-four criteria considered most relevant, including verifiability, predictivity, consistency, and reliability (Dodd 1968, p. 49). J.T. Clark (1969, p. 109) proposes the criteria of clarity, explanatory power, simplicity, and confirmation. Bunge (1967a, pp. 352–54) suggests twenty criteria to evaluate theories, grouped into (1) formal criteria, (2) semantic criteria, (3) epistemological criteria, (4) methodological criteria, and (5) metaphysical criteria. Zaltman et al. (1973, p. 104) used the Bunge groupings to develop their set of sixteen criteria, which they then employed to evaluate the Nicosia model of consumer decision processes, the Howard-Sheth theory of buyer behavior, and the Engel-Kollat-Blackwell model of consumer behavior.

What may be getting *lost* in all this generating of evaluative criteria is the realization that one criterion stands supreme over all others: *Is the theory true? To what extent has it been empirically confirmed?* Bunge (1967a, p. 347) clearly wanted his nonempirical criteria to be applied only for empirically equivalent theories: "Experience will be weighty, perhaps decisive at one point, in the evaluation of empirically *inequivalent* theories. But how does one proceed in the presence of one or more empirically equivalent theories?" Kaplan expresses the same belief:

> Norms of validation can be grouped according to the three major philosophical conceptions of truth: correspondence or semantical norms, coherence or syntactical norms, and pragmatic or functional norms. The first set is the basic one somehow; the others must be regarded as analyses or interpretations of correspondence. Sci-

> ence is governed fundamentally by the reality principle, its thought checked and controlled by the characteristics of the things it thinks about. (Kaplan 1964, p. 312)

The way to determine the truth content of any theory is to test it empirically. Figure 7.3 represents one (grossly compacted) conceptualization of the process of empirical testing. For a different and much more detailed conceptualization, see Bunge (1967b, p. 309).[3]

7.5.2 The Empirical Testing Process

Figure 7.3 shows that the first step in testing a theory empirically is to derive some bridge laws or guiding hypotheses from the theory proper. As discussed in section 6.2.1, a bridge law is a kind of derivative law whose function is to bridge the gap between a theory and the specific classes of phenomena under investigation. A researcher desirous of testing the role of *risk* in consumer behavior might develop bridge laws dealing specifically with the perceived risk involved in purchasing new homes. Similarly, the "fair price" theory is couched in terms of the prices of goods in general. To test the "fair price" theory one must develop bridge laws concerning *specific* stimuli, for example, the prices of gasoline used by Kamen and Toman (1970).

Neither theories nor bridge laws are directly testable; they are only *indirectly* testable. Because both theories and bridge laws are composed of statements in the form of generalized conditionals, neither can be tested by a direct confrontation with data. To illustrate, consider the bridge laws mentioned in section 6.2.1:

BL_1: Consumers will experience cognitive dissonance after the decision to purchase a major appliance.

BL_2: If retailers provide information to recent purchasers of major appliances, and if the information reassures the consumers that they made wise decisions, then the information will assist the consumers in their efforts to reduce cognitive dissonance.

As stated, these bridge laws are not susceptible to a direct comparison to data; they are not *directly* testable. In contrast, research hypotheses are directly testable. These are predictive-type statements that are (a) derived from the bridge laws and (b) amenable to direct confrontation with data. For example, a research hypothesis derived from the preceding bridge laws and actually tested was: "The subjects who received the post-transaction reassurances will have lower perceived dissonance scores (i.e., will be less dissonant) than the subjects in the control group" (Hunt 1970). The research hypothesis is directly testable because it refers to specific subjects in specific

Figure 7.3 **The Empirical Testing Process**

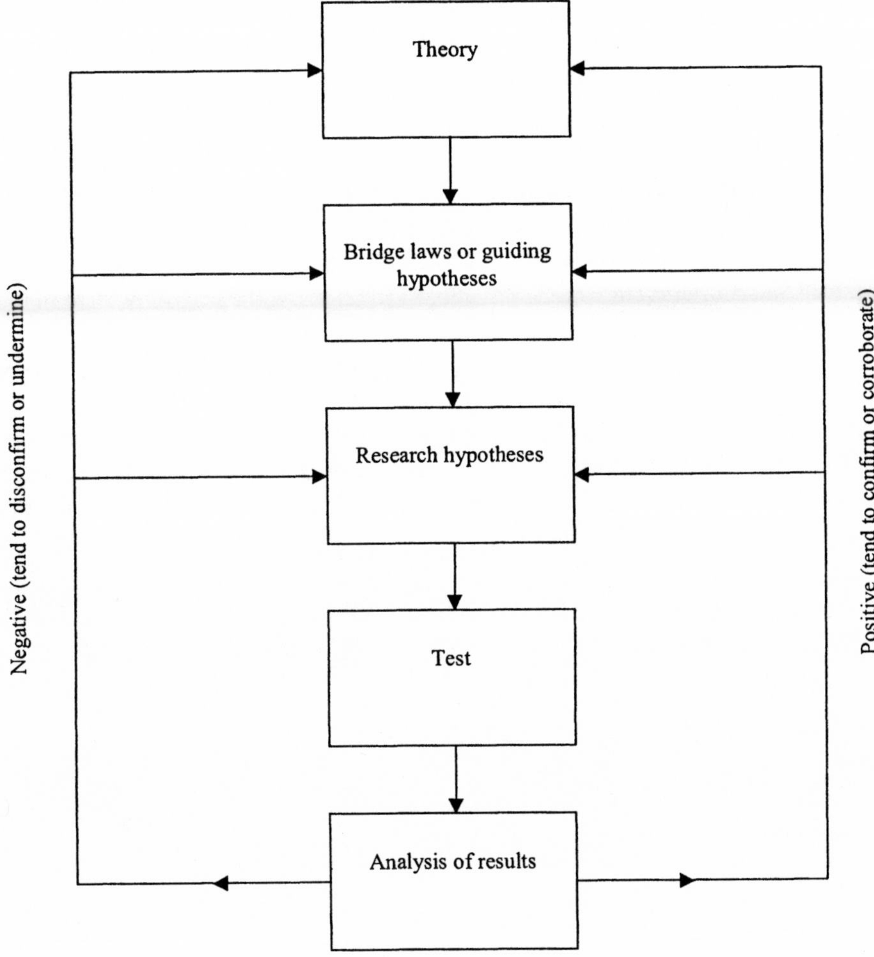

Source: Hunt (1991a). Reprinted by permission of the author.

groups (rather than consumers in general) and to specific scores on a measuring instrument (rather than dissonance in general).

The requirement that research hypotheses be predictive-type statements that are amenable to direct confrontation with data implies that all of the descriptive terms in the statements must have rules of interpretation containing empirical referents. These referents are sometimes referred to as reflective measures, operational definitions, formative indicators, or epistemic correlations. (See Diamantopoulos and Winklhofer [2001] for a good discussion of reflective versus formative indicators.) This does not mean that all of the terms in the theory proper must be "observables" or that every term in the theory must have an empirical referent. Rather, to require theories to be empirically testable implies that they must be capable of generating predictive-type statements (hypotheses) whose descriptive terms have empirical referents. The notion of empirical referents deserves some elaboration, especially insofar as it is closely intertwined with the school of thought commonly known as *operationalism.*

The position taken here should be carefully distinguished from the early forms of logical positivism or what Hempel (1970, p. 675) refers to as the *narrow thesis of empiricism.* According to the narrow thesis, "Any term in the vocabulary of empirical science is definable by means of observation terms; i.e,, it is possible to carry out a rational reconstruction of the language of science in such a way that all primitive terms are observation terms and all other terms are defined by means of them." This *radical empiricist* position was adopted by the school of thought known as *operationalism,* which was originated by P.W. Bridgman (1927). Three key propositions seem central to the doctrine of operationalism:

1. Only terms that have operational definitions are "meaningful." Terms without operational definitions are "meaningless," and, hence, have no value in scientific endeavor (Bridgman 1938).
2. Operational definitions always make reference ultimately to an instrumental operation (Bridgman 1951). That is, there must be some experiment or manipulation involved.
3. There must be only one operational definition for each scientific term (Bridgman 1927, p. 6).

The three propositions embodying the radical empiricism of the operationalists have been successfully challenged by Hempel (1970; Fetzer 1977) and others (Bergmann 1957, p. 58). Hempel (1970, p. 684) suggests that proposition 1 is untenable because (among other reasons) *theoretical constructs* play a vital role in science. These highly abstract concepts, for example, "channel of distribution," "self-image," "transvection," and "utility," often stoutly resist direct operational definitions. Such terms are not introduced piecemeal into a theory. "Rather, the constructs used in a theory are introduced jointly, as it were, by setting up a theoretical system formulated in terms of them and by giving this *system* an experiential interpretation, which in turn confers empirical meaning on the theoretical constructs" (Hempel 1970, p. 684). Thus, proposition 1 of the operationalists seems much too restrictive.

Hempel (1965b, p. 126) suggests that proposition 2 is also overly restrictive. Requiring direct experimenter manipulations is unnecessary to give experiential import to a term. Measures based on unobtrusive observations will often yield equally satisfactory results, maintaining intersubjective reliability. The important requirement is that different investigators be able to observe the phenomenon with reasonable agreement as to whether the requisite test conditions have been realized and the appropriate response obtained.

Concerning proposition 3, Bergmann (1957, p. 58) notes that some researchers refused "to 'generalize' from one instance of an experiment to the next if the apparatus had in the meantime been moved to another corner of the room or if the experimenter had, in the one case but not the other, blown his nose." The replication of an experiment would be logically impossible if proposition 3 were interpreted literally, because each instance would be a "different" operational definition. Furthermore, testing a theory under a variety of circumstances of application is extremely desirable in the process of confirmation. Yet, testing a theory under different circumstances may entail using different operational definitions for key constructs. The adoption of proposition 3 would imply that each time we change the circumstances in the testing of a theory we must consider ourselves to be testing a "new" theory. Science seems hardly to be advanced by the adoption of such a position. A much more viable position seems to be to acknowledge that alternative and equally valid operational definitions or measures may exist for the same concept, while maintaining constant vigilance to ensure that the alternative operational definitions or measures are, indeed, equally valid.

In conclusion, the preceding analysis suggests that the position of the radical empiricists is untenable. At the same time, metaphysical excesses are to be avoided. *Consequently, the requirement that theories be empirically testable shall be construed as being satisfied when a theory is capable (at least in principle) of generating predictive-type statements (hypotheses) whose descriptive terms have empirical referents, thus ensuring that the statements are amenable to a direct confrontation with real-world data.* This requirement is similar to the criterion of significance for theoretical terms suggested by Carnap (1956).

7.5.3 On Confirmation

Wartofsky has observed that

> No term in science suffers a greater ambiguity than does *hypothesis*. One could make up a list of contradictory statements about hypotheses and their status and use in scientific discussion which would make the scientific community look like something on the other side of Alice's looking glass. (Wartofsky 1968, p. 183)

Alas, the term *hypothesis* is commonly used as a general-purpose label synonymous with concepts such as law, lawlike generalization, derived law, theory, explanation, model, axiom, and theorem. The term *hypothesis* is overworked, overused, overbroad. Such abuse may result in little harm in ordinary conversation but may have serious, unintended consequences in research and scientific writing. Therefore, this writer suggests using the term *hypothesis* (or *research hypothesis*) to represent statements that are derived from laws or theories and are susceptible to direct testing by confrontation with real-world data. This usage is by no means a consensus position because there is no consensus concerning the term. However, the viewpoint expressed here is similar to Dubin's (1969, p. 212) position: "An hypothesis may be defined as the predictions about values of units of a theory in which empirical indicators are employed for the named units in each proposition."

The important consequence of reserving the label "hypothesis" for directly testable statements is that it highlights the notion of the empirical confirmation of theories. Because theories are not directly testable, they are not *strictly confirmable*. Theories cannot be shown to be conclusively true in an empirical sense. One can only say that certain research hypotheses have been derived from a theory and that these hypotheses have been directly tested. If the hypotheses are confirmed, then this provides empirical support that the theory is, indeed, empirically true; that is, the theory has been empirically corroborated by the confirmation of the research hypotheses. If the hypotheses are rejected by the data, then this provides empirical evidence that (a) the theory is false (reality just is not constructed as the theory suggests), (b) errors have been made in the empirical testing procedures, or (c) the rejected hypothesis was not properly derived from the theory.

The preceding discussion of the empirical testing procedure suggests that both *deduction* and *induction* play vital roles in the process of empirical confirmation. Because theories are not directly testable, one must *deduce* from them research hypotheses that are susceptible to direct confrontation with data. Once the tests of the research hypotheses have been conducted, the procedure of empirical confirmation is inherently *inductive*. To claim that empirically confirming a research hypothesis thus strictly confirms a theory is to fall prey to the logical fallacy of *affirming the consequent*. It would be claiming the following to be a valid syllogism:

> If theory X is true, then hypothesis h is true.
> Hypothesis h is empirically true.
>
> ---
>
> Therefore, theory X is true.

Obviously, hypothesis h could be true and yet theory X could be false. Therefore, when a theory has been tested many times and its hypotheses have been confirmed, we cannot say that the theory is empirically true; rather, we can say that the empirical tests have provided strong *inductive* support for the truth of the theory. In a sense, we are "weighing" the empirical evidence (Bunge 1967b, p. 319). The "heavier" the weight of the empirical evidence, the more likely it is that the theory accurately represents reality, and, thus, the more highly confirmed the theory is.

7.6 SUMMARY

This chapter has attempted to explicate the fundamental underpinnings of the nature and role of theory in scientific inquiry. The treatment here has proposed that the major role of theory is to *increase scientific understanding through a systematized structure capable of both explaining and predicting phenomena.* Consequently, theories become systematically related sets of statements, including some lawlike generalizations, that are empirically testable. Theories must contain a systematically related set of statements because science seeks to give an organized account of phenomena. Theories must contain lawlike generalizations because it is precisely these statements that give theories their explanatory and predictive power. Theories must be empirically testable in order that they may be (a) intersubjectively certifiable, (b) capable of explaining and predicting real-world phenomena, and (c) differentiated from purely analytical schemata. A theory is capable of being empirically testable when it is possible to derive from the theory certain predictive-type statements (hypotheses) that are amenable to direct confrontation with real-world data.

QUESTIONS FOR ANALYSIS AND DISCUSSION

1. Define and differentiate: theories, laws, hypotheses, models, generalizations, empirical regularities, propositions, and concepts. Show how these terms are related.
2. Do theories generate hypotheses, or do hypotheses lead to theories? How are theories generated?
3. Would marketing theory be useful to a marketing practitioner? To a government official? To a teacher of a basic marketing course?
4. "A theory is a systematically related set of statements, including some lawlike generalizations, that is empirically testable." We may therefore conclude that all theories can be shown to be either "true" or "false." Discuss.

5. Someone has said: "The problem with marketing research is the lack of an isomorphic relationship between concepts and their respective operational definitions." Evaluate.
6. Robert K. Merton makes a plea for "theories of the middle range" in sociology:

   > Throughout this book, the term *sociological theory* refers to logically interconnected sets of propositions from which empirical uniformities can be derived. Throughout we focus on what I have called theories of the middle range: theories that lie between minor but necessary working hypotheses that evolve in abundance during day-to-day research and the all-inclusive systematic efforts to develop a unified theory that will explain all the observed uniformities of social behavior, social organization, and social change. (Merton 1968, p. 39)

   Is Merton actually pleading for theories in sociology with greater extension? (See Chapter 6.) Evaluate the current work in marketing theory. How much of it appears to be in the middle range? Give examples of works that are in the middle range, more specific than the middle range, and more general than the middle range. Does Merton's plea also apply to marketing?
7. A major issue in marketing theory concerns the development of a general theory of marketing. Bartels (1968) suggests that "the broadest statement of marketing thought in any period is the 'general theory' of that day." Similarly, the subtitle of Alderson's (1965) last book was *A Functionalist Theory of Marketing*. Do you agree with Bartels's definition of a general theory of marketing? If yes, why? If no, suggest an alternative definition and show how it is superior to Bartels's definition. Will we ever have (i.e., is it possible to have) a general theory of marketing? What would be the role or purpose of a general theory of marketing if we did have one?
8. What is the relevance to the content of the chapter of the "garden in the jungle" epigraph at the beginning of the chapter?
9. Evaluate Bartels's perspective on the nature of theory:

   > Theory is a form in which knowledge is expressed, and the term is used with two meanings. First, it designates a tentative, speculative, or unproven generalization concerning a subject. In this sense, it is synonymous with "hypothesis" and presents an early stage in the logical process. Second, it means a summary or considered conclusion reached after analysis and synthesis of information, and, as such, it represents a mature stage in the development of thought. This second concept of theory is the sense in which the term is used hereafter. (Bartels 1970, p. 2)

10. Many theories or models in marketing consist primarily of a diagram

with little boxes, each having a single concept or construct and various arrows connecting the boxes. Is this a theory proper or a pictorial representation of a theory? To what extent is this procedure appropriate or inappropriate? Can it be abused?

11. Evaluate the following three characteristics of a good theory proposed by Baumol (1957):

    1. The model should be a sufficiently simple version of the facts to permit systematic manipulation and analysis.
    2. It must be a sufficiently close approximation to the relevant facts to be usable.
    3. Its conclusions should be relatively insensitive to changes in its assumptions.

12. In "Lawlike Generalizations and Marketing Theory" Hunt (1973) contends that "in order for generalizations to be considered lawlike, the *minimum* necessary conditions are that the generalizations specify a relationship in the form of a universal conditional (such as my example in the original note), which is capable of yielding predictive statements (hypotheses), which are composed of terms that have empirical referents and, thus, permit empirical testing." Are these the minimum necessary conditions?
13. El-Ansary (1979) in his "The General Theory of Marketing: Revisited" proposed that "a vertical marketing system, distribution channel, is a key integrative concept in marketing." Evaluate the contention that in a general theory of marketing the marketing channel would be the key integrative concept.
14. El-Ansary (1979) suggests that a major section of a general theory of marketing would be "a theory of micromarketing." Apparently, he believes that such a theory would include subtheories of product and brand management, pricing, promotion, physical distribution management, marketing research, financial aspects, and marketing program productivity. What would these subtheories attempt to explain and predict? Would such a collection of subtheories be appropriately referred to as a theory of micromarketing? Would a theory of micromarketing be positive or normative? Would it be possible to have a general theory of marketing that included both positive and normative components?
15. There is a famous paradox on how theories and laws are confirmed or corroborated by empirical testing. First proposed by Hempel (1945), the paradox is usually referred to as the "raven paradox" and can be roughly stated as:

a. The statement *P* "All ravens are black" is logically equivalent to the statement *P** "All nonblack things are nonravens."
b. One may empirically explore the validity of *P* by examining ravens and seeing whether they are black (tend to confirm) or nonblack (tend to disconfirm).
c. One may empirically examine *P** by looking at nonblack objects (e.g., roses) and determining whether they are nonravens (tend to confirm) or ravens (tend to disconfirm).
d. Any evidence that tends to confirm *P** must logically tend to confirm *P*.
e. Therefore, the fact that a rose may be red tends to confirm that ravens are black.
f. Statement *e* is intellectually disquieting.

Gardner discusses the paradoxical nature of ravens thus:

> We look around and see a yellow object. Is it a raven? No, it is a buttercup. The flower surely confirms (albeit weakly) that all nonblack objects are not ravens, but it is hard to see how it has any *relevance* at all to the statement "All ravens are black." If it does, it equally confirms that all ravens are white or any color except yellow. (Gardner 1976, p. 121)

Evaluate. (Remember that logic, like nature, is often surprising, sometimes fascinating, but never paradoxical.)

16. Do you agree that logic, like nature, is never paradoxical? If yes, why? If no, why not?
17. Alderson's law of exchange states: If *X* is an element in the assortment *A* and *Y* is an element in the assortment *B*, then *X* is exchangeable for *Y* if, and only if, the following three conditions hold:

    1. *X* is different from *Y*.
    2. The potency of the assortment *A* is increased by dropping *X* and adding *Y*.
    3. The potency of the assortment *B* is increased by adding *X* and dropping *Y*.

    Evaluate the law of exchange. To what extent does the law of exchange differ from conventional microeconomic demand theory? To what extent does the law of exchange have empirical content?
18. "In order for an economy to be characterized by many variations of the same basic product, it is necessary and sufficient that there be heterogeneity of demand." True? False? Why?

19. What is a transvection? Discuss the actual and potential usefulness of Alderson's transvection concept in marketing. Develop a hypothetical example of a transvection.
20. What is Alderson's (1965, p. 78) "discrepancy of assortments?" How does this concept attempt to explain the existence of intermediaries? Why is a wholesaler "most vulnerable when it purchases only a part of what the manufacturer supplies and sells to retailers only a small portion of what their customers demand?" Do you agree?
21. Bagozzi (1979) in "Toward a Formal Theory of Marketing Exchanges" proposes that "in their interactions with each other and with other social actors, the parties to an exchange are presumed to maximize"

$$U_d = U(Z_a, Z_c, Z_{mb})$$

where U_d is the utility for the dyad and Z_a = affect, Z_c = cognitions, and Z_{mb} = moral beliefs. To what extent does this equation differ from Alderson's Law of Exchange? Do you agree that the parties to an exchange maximize U_d?
22. Ferrell and Perrachione (1980, p. 159) contend that "one of Bagozzi's recurring goals or self-imposed criteria is to construct a theory that will go beyond description to explanation (and eventually prediction and control). Yet the models he has proposed, in spite of their frequent descriptive richness, are consistently insufficient when measured against the explanation criterion." Do you agree or disagree with this criticism?

NOTES

1. The succeeding discussion follows, in part, Rudner (1966, pp. 10–18) and Kyburg (1968).
2. See Hunt (1990) for a discussion and defense of the role of *truth* in marketing theory and research.
3. See Hunt (1992a, 1993, and 1994a) for more on empirical testing.

8 THEORY: ISSUES AND ASPECTS

A science is served in many ways: by intelligent discussion and fresh proposals, by the extension or completion of previously presented theories, by the fair-minded and unflinching evaluation of current proposals, by justly protesting, blowing the whistle, and pointing out that this kingly theory or that is not wearing a shred of evidence, by sometimes synthesizing and sometimes isolating, by daring to be explicit and—ironically—by daring to be suggestive. It is when scientists and philosophers of science cannot make up their minds as to which role they are playing or—what is worse—try to fill several roles at once, that matters go awry. Then the Ivory Tower and the Tower of Babel sound disturbingly alike.

—Paul Surgi Speck

The preceding chapter explored the nature of theoretical constructions. The purpose of this chapter is to examine several specific issues in marketing theory. Since classificational schemata are often confused with theoretical schemata, we shall begin by analyzing the nature of classifications in marketing. Next, we shall delineate the differences between positive theory, normative theory, deterministic theory, and stochastic theory. The chapter concludes with an examination of the nature of general theories.

8.1 CLASSIFICATIONAL SCHEMATA

Marketing is replete with classificational schemata. There are classificational schemata for different kinds of goods (convenience, shopping, etc.), stores (department stores, limited line stores, etc.), wholesalers (general merchandise, general line, etc.), pricing policies (cost-plus, demand-oriented, etc.), and numerous others. Classificational schemata play fundamental roles in the development of a discipline in that they are the primary means for *organizing* phenomena into classes or groups that are amenable to systematic investigation and theory development. Nevertheless, classificational schemata, no matter how elaborate or complex, are not by themselves theoretical, though most theoretical constructions will contain classificational schemata as components. As previously noted, an analysis of the seven subtheories of Bartels's general theory of marketing revealed them to be primarily classificational schemata that lacked the requisite lawlike generalizations to be considered as theories (Hunt 1971, p. 68).

Marketing has long-suffered from a lack of standardized classificational schemata. As Engel, Kollat, and Blackwell (1973, p. 659) pointed out, "The lack of standardized variable categories . . . makes it difficult to compare and integrate research findings." If having a variety of nonstandard classificational schemata for the same phenomenon is dysfunctional, how does one select the best classificational schema from the available alternatives? Because classificational schemata help to organize the elements of the universe, and because organizing phenomena often represents the first step in theory development, how can one differentiate the good classificational schema from the bad? This section will attempt to answer these questions, first by discussing the two basic approaches to generating classificational schemata and then by developing some criteria for evaluating any classificational schema.

Classificational systems always involve a partitioning of some universe of objects, events, or other phenomena into classes or sets that are homogeneous with respect to some categorical properties. There are two distinctly different procedures or methods for generating classificational schemata. Following the essence of Harvey's (1969, p. 334) terminology, one procedure is *logical partitioning* and the second is *grouping*. The procedure referred to here as logical partitioning is sometimes called "deductive classification," "*a priori* classification," or "classification from above." Grouping is probably a less satisfactory label for the second procedure (more accurately, second *set* of procedures). The grouping procedures are often called "inductive classification," "*ex post* classification," "classification from below," "numerical taxonomy," or "quantitative classification." The essential difference between the logical partitioning and grouping procedures is that with the former the classificational schema is always developed *before* the researcher analyzes any specific set of data (hence, "deductive," "*a priori*," and "from above"). In contrast, when using grouping procedures, researchers generate their schemata only *after* they analyze specific sets of data (hence, "inductive," "*ex post*," and "from below"). With logical partitioning, the researcher *imposes* a classificational system on the data; with grouping, the researcher lets the data suggest the system. Both kinds of procedures are used in marketing, and both have their strengths and weaknesses. After a (very) modest elaboration on the two procedures, we shall explore some criteria for evaluating any classification system.

8.1.1 Logical Partitioning

Logical partitioning starts with the careful specification of the marketing phenomena to be categorized—families, retailers, wholesalers, types of goods, brands of goods, and so forth. Next comes the delineation of the categorial terms. These are the properties or characteristics of the phenomena on which the classificational schema is to be based—for families this might be age, marital status, and number of children; for retailers it might be number of units and type of ownership. Finally, labels are given to the various categories that emerge from applying the categorial terms to the phenomena—thus, for families we have "newly married couples," the "full nest I," "empty nest," and so on, and for retailers we have independents, chain stores, and so on.

Several observations concerning logical partitioning are important to keep in mind. First, Sneath and Sokal (1973) point out that logical partitioning usually results in *monothetic* classifications. With monothetic classification systems, *all* members of a category possess *all* of the characteristics or properties used to identify the category. To illustrate this point, consider the commonly used stage in the family life cycle schema reproduced in Table 8.1. This schema is an example of logical partitioning with monothetic classifications. In order for a family to be classified as "full nest III," the family must satisfy *all* of the criteria; that is, the couple must be over forty-five years old, married, and the youngest child must be six years or older. If the couple satisfied the age and marital status criteria but had, by chance, a child under six years old, then it could not be classified as "full nest III." (In fact, it would not fit any category in the schema, a point to be discussed later.) Now, it may intuitively appear that all classificational schemata would be monothetic. But this is not the case, as will be shown when we discuss grouping procedures.

The second observation concerning logical partitioning is that the procedure can result in either single-level or multilevel schemata. Prominent among multilevel schemata are *hierarchical* classification systems that involve the ordering relation $\subset$ from set theory. Thus $A \subset B$ should be read, "The class of phenomena designated as *A* are contained in the class of phenomena designated as *B*." Hierarchies can be displayed by means of Euler-Venn diagrams from set theory or by *trees*. Figure 8.1 illustrates the common hierarchical classification of wholesalers by means of a tree. The ordering relation $\subset$ is both asymmetrical and transitive. Thus, $A \subset B$, being asymmetrical, implies that $B \not\subset A$ (brokers are a subset of the class known as agent wholesalers, but agent wholesalers are *not* a subset of the class called brokers). Similarly, $A \subset B$ and $B \subset C$ implies, by transitivity, $A \subset C$ (if a mail-order wholesaler is a kind of limited function wholesaler, and if a limited function wholesaler is a kind of merchant wholesaler, then a mail-order wholesaler is a kind of merchant wholesaler). Hierarchical classifications are preferable (other things

Table 8.1

The Stage in the Family Life Cycle Schema

	Age		Marital status		Children			
Category	Less than 45 years	45 years or older	Single	Married	No children	Youngest child under 6 years	Youngest child 6 years or over	No dependent children
1. The bachelor stage	X		X					
2. Newly married couples	X			X	X			
3. The full nest I	X			X		X		
4. The full nest II	X			X			X	
5. The full nest III		X		X			X	
6. The empty nest		X		X				X
7. The solitary survivors		X	X					X

Source: Adapted from a version originally proposed by the Survey Research Center, University of Michigan.

Figure 8.1 **Classification of Wholesalers**

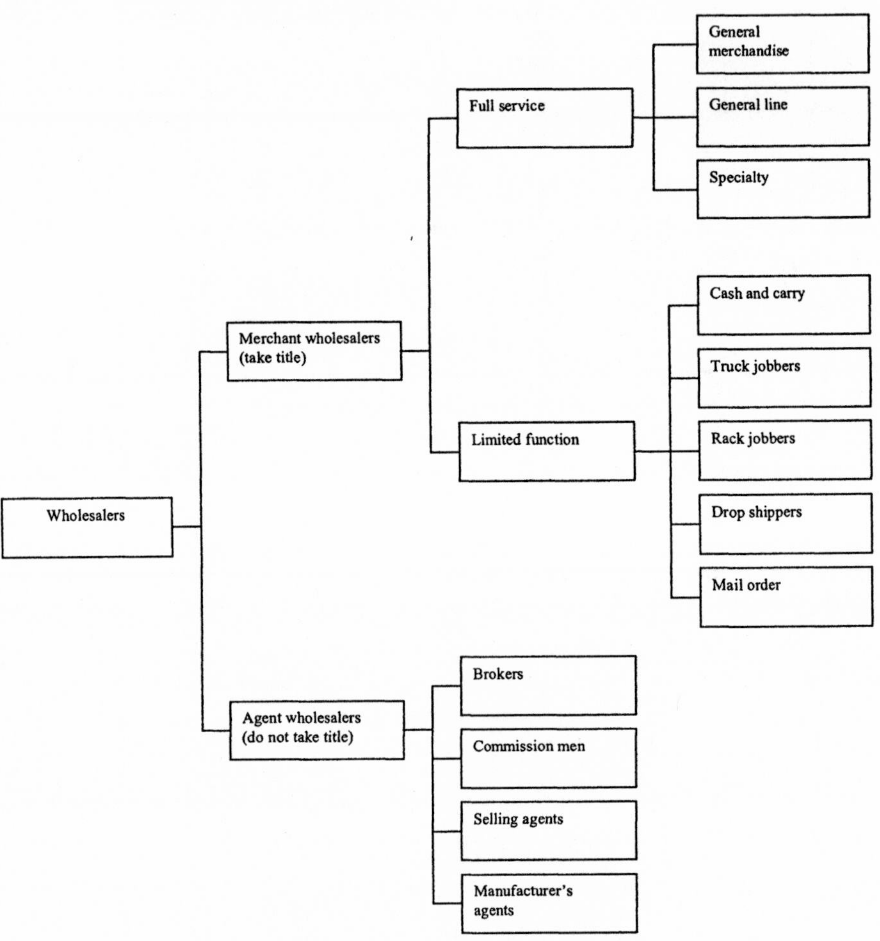

Source: Hunt (1991a). Reprinted by permission of the author.

equal) to single-level classifications because of their greater systemic power. That is, hierarchical classifications have greater power to systematically organize the phenomena under investigation.

The third observation about logical partitioning is that there may exist *empty classes*. That is, a proper application of the categorial terms may generate a class to which no phenomenon belongs. The importance of empty classes lies in the context of discovery; observing that empty classes exist may spur the researcher to inquire about the circumstances under which phenomena might be classified into the now empty set. For example, the existence of holes or empty classes in Mendeleev's periodic table of elements in chemistry suggested the existence of, and spurred the search for, previously unknown elements.

A final observation, suggested by Harvey (1969, p. 366), is that logical partitioning "presupposes a fairly sophisticated understanding of the phenomena being investigated, [or] else the classifications involved may be totally unrealistic, nothing better than an inspired guess." Any universe of phenomena can be classified in an infinite variety of ways. Which properties or characteristics are the important ones to use for classificatory purposes? Which classes would be most meaningful for research? Logical partitioning assumes substantial *a priori* knowledge about how to answer these questions. The procedures referred to previously as grouping procedures, which will be discussed next, require much less *a priori* knowledge about the phenomena to be classified.

8.1.2 Grouping Procedures

Like logical partitioning, all grouping procedures for classification start with the specification of the phenomena to be classified and the properties or characteristics on which the categorizing is to be done. However, grouping procedures are designed to conveniently accommodate larger numbers of properties than is the case with logical partitioning. As Frank and Green point out:

> Almost every major analytical problem requires the classification of objects by several characteristics—whether customers, products, cities, television programs, or magazines. Seldom are explicit classification systems with some combination of attributes, such as those used for measuring a customer's social class or stage in life cycle, found. Such classification systems typically represent self-imposed taxonomies; that is, taxonomies the researcher believes to be relevant because of a theory or prior experience. Although this approach [logical partitioning] can be useful, it has limitations. Regardless of the complexity of reality, it is difficult to classify objects by more than two or three characteristics at a time. If reality requires greater complexity, researchers are severely constrained by their conceptual limitations. (Frank and Green 1968, p. 84)

So, the first difference between logical partitioning and grouping is that the grouping procedures are better equipped to handle large numbers of categorial terms or properties. The second difference, and, perhaps, the most significant from a methodological perspective, is that *all grouping procedures share the common characteristic that they determine categories or classifications by an analysis of a specific set of data.* Consequently, they are referred to as "inductive," "*ex post*," or "classification from below" procedures.

Although all grouping procedures determine classifications by analyzing data, numerous basic models have been developed to accomplish the classificatory task, and many computer programs have been generated for each model. Among the most commonly used models are correspondence analysis, factor analysis, multiple discriminant analysis, multidimensional scaling, and cluster analysis. Thus, correspondence analysis has been used to classify soft drinks (Hoffman and Franke 1986), and factor analysis has been used to classify liquor preferences, job characteristics, and coffees (Stroetzel 1960; Hunt, Chonko, and Wood 1985; Mukherjee 1965). Multiple discriminant analysis has been used to classify types of patients (Dont, Lumpkin, and Bush 1990). Both pharmaceuticals and colors of automobiles (Neidell 1969; Doehlert 1968) have been classified by multidimensional scaling. Cluster analysis is the most frequently used technique (Hair et al. 1995). It has generated classifications of cities for test marketing and market survey respondents (Green, Frank, and Robinson 1967) and dissatisfaction response scores (Singh 1990). Finally, gasoline brands were classified by Kamen (1970) using "quick clustering" and by Aaker (1971) using "visual clustering." Although some of these models are often used for purposes other than classification, researchers are ever more frequently using them to organize phenomena for classification. The tremendous differences among the models notwithstanding, they share the common property of separating phenomena into groups that maximize both the degree of "likeness" *within* each group and the degree of differences *between* groups according to some objective function.

A detailed exposition of the specific models for grouping phenomena need not concern us here; interested readers are advised to consult the previously cited references for guidance as to which specific grouping model would be most appropriate for their needs. What shall concern us from a methodological perspective are certain fundamental characteristics of grouping procedures contrasted with logical partitioning. First, Sneath and Sokal (1973) observe that classificational schemata that are developed by grouping procedures usually have classes that are *polythetic*. Recalling that logical partitioning usually results in monothetic classes, with *polythetic* classes, the phenomena in any given class may share many characteristics in common; however, no individual phenomenon need possess *all* of the characteristics of the class. One simple example will illustrate this point. W.A.K. Frost (1969) used a clustering program to classify different television programs. One cluster contained the following programs: *World of Sport, Football, Sportsview, Horse Racing, Motor Racing, Boxing,* and *News*. All of the programs, save one, share (among other things) the common characteristic of being either sporting events (boxing, etc.) or solely concerned with sporting events (*Sportsview*). The *News* program must be perceived by viewers as being similar to the other members of its cluster *in toto*; yet, it does not share the *sports* characteristic common to its companions. It is in this respect that grouping procedures are polythetic.

Second, unlike logical partitioning, grouping procedures do not generate empty classes because classes can be formed only from existing observations. To the extent that empty classes serve the heuristic function of suggesting fruitful avenues for research, the inability to generate empty classes might be disadvantageous. In addition, at the risk of sounding tautologous, if researchers use a clustering program, they will get clusters. Aaker emphasizes this point when he advocates "visual clustering":

> [The results] indicate that the structure is not very well defined and that an unambiguous set of clusters does not exist. This observation, it should be noted, is not insignificant. Often an output which lists several clusters fails to convey this type of conclusion to those not intimate with the program. (Aaker 1971, p. 331)

Grouping procedures require substantially less *a priori* knowledge concerning which specific properties are likely to be powerful for classifying phenomena than is the case in logical partitioning. Furthermore, grouping procedures are uniquely equipped to accommodate large numbers of potentially useful categorial properties. These are powerful advantages for grouping procedures. Nevertheless, these procedures have not yet produced many *general* classificational schemata. Classifications developed through grouping procedures seldom are generalized beyond their original database. Rather than developing classification systems for marketing phenomena in general, the use of these procedures has been restricted to problems that are highly situation specific. Perhaps this is what Frank and Green are implying when they suggest that we refer to grouping procedures as "preclassification techniques":

> These taxonomic procedures may be called preclassification techniques since their purpose is to describe the natural groupings that occur in large masses of data. From these natural groupings (or clusters) the researcher can sometimes develop the requisite conceptual framework for classification. (Frank and Green 1968, p. 84)

Irrespective of the procedure used for classifying, either logical partitioning or grouping, the resultant classificational schema can be evaluated using the same criteria. The next section will attempt systematically to develop such criteria.

8.1.3 Criteria for Evaluating Classificational Schemata

Numerous criteria have been suggested for evaluating alternative classificational schemata. Although the following five criteria do not exhaust the possibilities, they would seem to make a useful starting point for any researcher who has a classification problem:

1. Does the schema adequately specify the phenomenon to be classified?
2. Does the schema adequately specify the properties or characteristics that will be doing the classifying?
3. Does the schema have categories that are mutually exclusive?
4. Does the schema have categories that are collectively exhaustive?
5. Is the schema useful?

Criterion 1 inquires whether the schema adequately specifies the phenomenon to be classified. That is, *exactly* what is being categorized? What is the universe? An analysis of the familiar classification of goods schema should help to explicate this criterion. Table 8.2 reproduces four versions of the classification of goods schema: the 1960 American Marketing Association (AMA) definition (which closely follows the original version by Copeland [1923]), the 1988 AMA definition (which is very similar to the 1960 version), the version suggested by Richard H. Holton (1958), and the version suggested by Louis P. Bucklin (1963) in his classic article "Retail Strategy and the Classification of Goods."

What is the universe that is being partitioned by the classification of goods schema? Is it products, brands of products, consumers' perceptions of products, or consumers' perceptions of brands of products? The answer is not altogether unambiguous. The two AMA definitions of convenience goods appears to be referring to *products*, yet both the Holton and Bucklin versions of convenience goods appear to be classifying consumers' *perceptions* of products. Holton (1958, p. 54) observed, "A given good may be a convenience good for some consumers and a shopping good for others." This would imply that the universe consists of perceptions of goods rather than goods *per se*. Thus, McCarthy (1971) suggests that the approach a marketing manager should take is to determine the proportion of consumers who perceive the product as a convenience good and compare this with the proportion who perceive it as either a shopping good or a specialty good. This approach implies that there will seldom, if ever, be anything that could be classified as a *convenience good*; rather, there are only a certain proportion of consumers who *perceive* a good to be a convenience good.

Similar ambiguity surrounds the specialty goods category, where people commonly cite specific *brands* as examples of specialty goods. Thus, for some consumers a particular *brand* of coffee would be a specialty good, and the universe being partitioned would be consumers' perceptions of brands of goods and not simply goods. Perhaps some of the debate that has centered on the classification of goods schema during the past decades can be explained by pointing out that this schema does not do well on criterion 1; it does not clearly specify the universe to be classified. Readers should ask themselves whether other classification schemata in marketing, such as the *product life cycle* schema, suffer from the same ambiguity. Does the product life cycle schema refer to an industry's product or to an individual company's product?[1]

Criterion 2 inquires whether the properties or characteristics that have been chosen to do the classifying have been adequately specified. Implicit in criterion 2 is the question: "Are these properties the *appropriate* properties for classificatory purposes?" One clue that the chosen properties may be inappropriate is when different properties are used throughout the schema, "changing horses in midstream," so to speak. Bunge (1967a, p. 75) addresses this issue: "One of the principles of correct classification is that the characteristics or properties chosen for performing the grouping should be stuck to throughout the work; for example, a shift from skeletal to physiological characteristics in the classification of vertebrates will produce not only different classes but also different systems of classes, i.e., alternative classification."

Referring once again to the classification of goods schema in Table 8.2, note that the two AMA schemata use three properties to identify convenience goods: purchased (a) frequently, (b) immediately or "often on impulse," and (c) with a minimum of effort. This would lead one to expect some other category to contain goods purchased (a) infrequently, (b) not immediately or not on impulse, and (c) with great effort. Yet, shopping goods are classified on the basic property of *comparison* or "gathering of information," and specialty goods are classified on the basis of *willingness to expend effort* or "multiple-store searching." The shifting from one set of properties for the classification of convenience goods to other properties for specialty goods and shopping goods is a strong sign that the schema is structurally unsound.

Consider now the revision suggested by Holton and detailed in the second column of Table 8.2. Holton uses the same two properties for classifying convenience goods and shopping goods: the consumer's perceptions of (a) the probable gain for making comparisons versus (b) the probable cost of such comparisons. Unfortunately, Holton then scraps these properties and uses the size of the market to classify specialty goods. Only the Bucklin version of the classification of goods schema consistently uses the same properties to do the job of classifying. These properties are (a) the existence of a preference map and (b) the nature of the preference map if one exists. To see that this is indeed the case, refer to Figure 8.2, which reformulates the essence of Bucklin's schema by means of a tree diagram. Bucklin's efforts are unique in terms of classifying goods because only his schema retains the conceptual richness of Copeland's original concepts, while at the same time rigorously and consistently explicating the properties used for classificatory purposes. Bucklin's version has much to recommend it.

Table 8.2

Classification of Goods' Schemata

Category	American Marketing Association (AMA)	Richard H. Holton[c]	Louis P. Bucklin[d]
Convenience goods	*AMA 1960.*[a] Those consumers' goods which the customer purchase frequently, immediately, and with a minimum of effort. *AMA 1988.*[b] Consumer goods and services . . . that are bought frequently, often on impulse, with little time and effort spent on the buying process. They usually are low-priced, and are widely available.	Those goods for which the consumer regards the probable gain from making price and quality comparisons as small compared to the cost of making such comparisons.	Those goods for which the consumer, before his need arises, possesses a preference map that indicates a willingness to purchase any of a number of known substitutes rather than to make the additional effort required to buy a particular item.
Shopping goods	*AMA 1960.*[a] Those consumers' goods which the customer in the process of selection and purchase characteristically compares on such bases as suitability, quality, price, and style. *AMA 1988.*[b] Products . . . for which the consumer is willing to spend considerable time and effort in gathering information on price, quality, and other attributes. Several retail outlets are customarily visited. Comparison of product attributes and complex decision processes are common.	Those goods for which the consumer regards the probable gain from making price and quality comparisons as large relative to the cost of making such comparisons.	Those goods for which the consumer has not developed a complete preference map before the need arises, requiring him to undertake a search to construct such a map before purchase.

Specialty goods	*AMA 1960.*[a] Those consumers' goods on which a significant group of buyers are habitually willing to make a special purchasing effort. *AMA 1988.*[b] Products that have unique attributes or other characteristics which make them singularly important to the buyer. Multiple-store searching, reliance on brand, and absence of extensive product comparisons are the rule.	Those convenience or shopping goods which have such a limited market as to require the consumer to make a special effort to purchase them.	Those goods for which the consumer, before his need arises, possesses a preference map that indicates a willingness to expand the additional effort required to purchase the most preferred item rather than to buy a more readily accessible substitute.

[a]American Marketing Association, *Marketing Definitions* (Chicago, 1960).
[b]Bennett (1988).
[c]Holton (1958).
[d]Bucklin (1963).

So one aspect of criterion 2 is whether the chosen properties are appropriate for classification. Second, one should ask whether the operational procedures for applying the classificatory properties are rigorous. *The procedures should be intersubjectively unambiguous*, a characteristic that is sometimes referred to as "high interjudge reliability." The procedures should be such that different people would classify the phenomena in the same categories. For example, the family life cycle schema in Table 8.1 has "marital status" as a categorial property with two categories, single and married. To be intersubjectively unambiguous, the schema must have rigorous procedures to enable different people reliably to classify widows, widowers, and divorcees.

Is the product life cycle schema intersubjectively unambiguous? Will different people categorize the same product in the same stage? A randomly selected group of a dozen products given to a group of students familiar with the product life cycle notion is hereby guaranteed to produce sobering results.

The third criterion for evaluating classificational schemata suggests that all the categories at the same level of classification should be *mutually exclusive*. That is, if an item fits one category or class, it will not fit any other class. No single item may fit two different categories at the same level. "At the same level" must be emphasized because, of course, in a hierarchical classificational schema the same item will fit different categories at different levels. Therefore, in Figure 8.1 a general line wholesaler is both a full-service wholesaler and a merchant wholesaler.

Many classifications in marketing do not meet the mutually exclusive criterion. The normal distinction between industrial goods and consumer goods typifies the problem. Common usage in marketing suggests, "Consumer goods are those goods and services destined for the ultimate consumer. These contrast with industrial goods, which are those goods and services destined for use in producing other goods and services" (McCarthy 1971, p. 300). Holloway and Hancock (1973, p. 683) have commented that this partitioning of goods does not result in mutually exclusive categories. "Relatively few goods are exclusively industrial goods. The same article may, under one set of circumstances, be an industrial good and under other conditions a consumer good." The lack of exclusivity is not a mortal blow to a useful classificational schema (consider, for example, the unquestionably useful male/female schema). However, exclusivity is an appropriate goal.

Criterion 4 suggests that classificational schemata should be *collectively exhaustive*. Every item that is to be classified should have a "home." Consider, once again, the family life cycle schema in Table 8.1. Into which category would a couple fall if they had the following characteristics: (a) over forty-five years old, (b) married, and (c) youngest child under six years old? Obviously, there is no home for this family. Now, all classification systems

Figure 8.2 **Bucklin's Classification of Goods Schema**

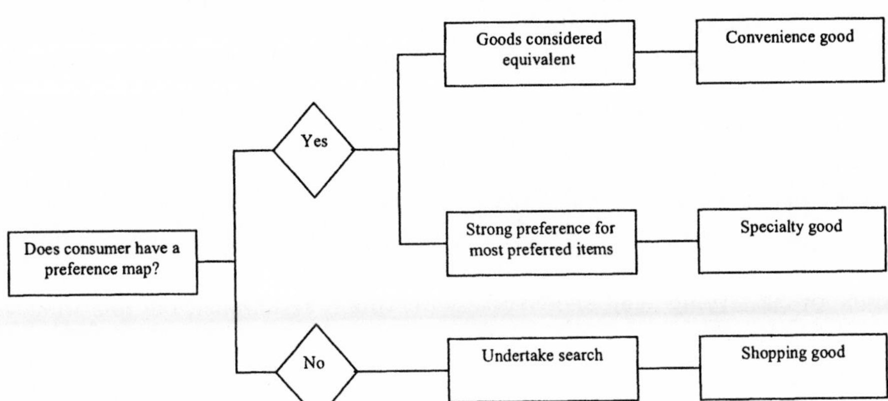

Source: Bucklin (1963). Reprinted by permission of the American Marketing Association.

can be made collectively exhaustive by the simple expedient of adding that ubiquitous category "other." However, the size of this category should be monitored carefully. If too many phenomena can find no home except other, then the system should be examined carefully for possible expansion by adding new categories.

Criterion 5 simply asks, "Is the schema useful?" Does it adequately serve its intended purposes? How well does it compare with alternative schemata? Of the five criteria, this one is "first among equals." Researchers do not create classificational schemata because they are possessed by some taxonomic devil. Rather, classifications are devised to attempt to solve some kind of problem. Harvey reminds us that we must keep in mind the purpose of the classificational system when evaluating it.

> Classification may be regarded as a means for searching reality for hypotheses or for structuring reality to test hypotheses. It may also be regarded as a beginning point or the culmination of scientific investigation. We possess, therefore, no means of assessing the adequacy or efficiency of a given classification independently of the job it is designed to do. (Harvey 1969, p. 326)

Therefore, the ultimate criterion is usefulness. How useful is the schema for helping marketing managers solve problems? In this regard, the product life cycle schema may pass muster if it simply reminds managers constantly to monitor their product line, because a company cannot afford to have all of its products in the "decline" stage. How *theoretically fruitful* is the schema? Have the concepts embodied in the schema been useful for developing lawlike generalizations? Many popular classificational schemata in marketing (e.g., the product life cycle) have exhibited extremely limited usefulness in generating lawlike statements. Much work remains to be done in this area.

In conclusion, classificational schemata are important in theory development because they are our primary means for organizing phenomena. Generating useful classificational systems frequently represents one of the first steps in theorizing. For this reason, we have spent considerable time analyzing classificational schemata. Nevertheless, classificational systems are a kind of nontheoretical construction because they lack the requisite lawlike generalizations that all theoretical constructions must contain. To develop useful systems for classifying is an endeavor worthy of any researcher, but this should not be confused with the construction of theory proper.

8.2 POSITIVE VERSUS NORMATIVE THEORY

Most of this book has focused on the nature of positive theories: systematically related sets of statements, including some lawlike generalizations, that are empirically testable and that increase scientific understanding through the explanation and prediction of phenomena. However, much of the theorizing in marketing is normative, not positive. How do normative theories differ from positive theories? As we shall see, these two kinds of theories differ as to (1) structure, (2) purpose, and (3) validation criteria. First, what is the nature of normative theories?

Normative theories are of at least two kinds. One embodies an *ethical* "ought"; the other, a *rational* "ought." There are normative theories that are essentially *ethical theories* that prescribe morally correct, desirable, or appropriate behavior. Such theories are found in the branch of philosophy generally known as "ethics," which has been a subject of philosophical inquiry since time immemorial. (See Hunt and Vitell [1986, 1992] for a theory of marketing ethics.)

However, when marketers discuss "normative theory," we are usually *not* referring to theories of ethical behavior. Rather, we are usually referring to some kind of model that assists a decision maker in rationally or systematically choosing from among a limited set of alternative actions or strategies, given certain (1) objectives, (2) consequences or payoffs, and (3) states of nature. As an example, consider the "high-assay model," reproduced in Figure 8.3, which was originally developed by the advertising agency of Young and Rubicam.

The high-assay model attempts to assist the advertising decision maker in scheduling media. The model incorporates the method of steepest ascent, which proposes that the user should purchase the insertion at each step that provides the greatest increase in effectiveness for the money expended. Statements 2

Figure 8.3 **High-Assay Model**

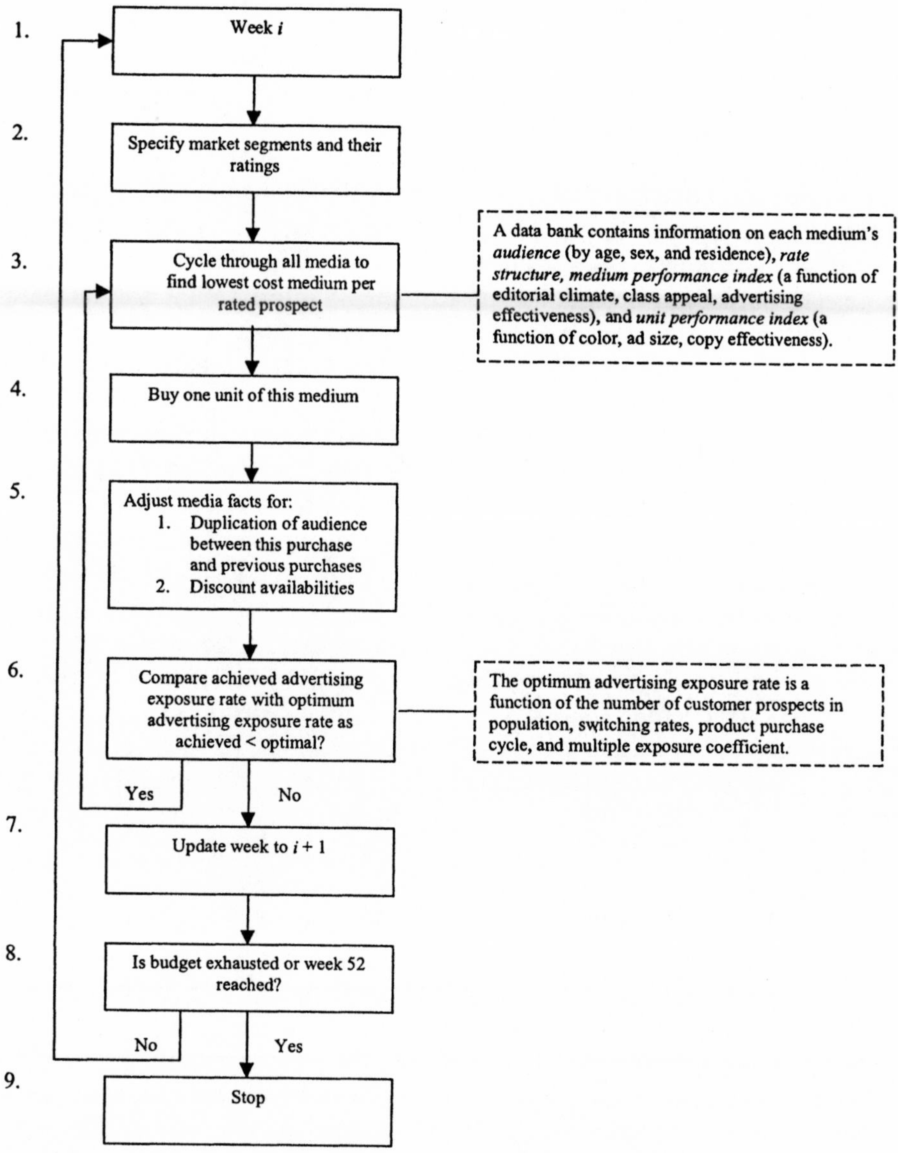

Source: Kotler (1971, p. 457). Reprinted by permission of the author.

and 3 are typical of the statements in normative decision theories: "Specify market segments and their ratings" and "Cycle through all media to find lowest cost medium per rated prospect." Note the *prescriptive* nature of these statements. The basic form of these statements is: "Under circumstances X_1,

X_2, X_3, . . . X_k, one should do Y in order to achieve G." All normative decision theories must contain such prescriptive statements.

On the other hand, all positive theories must contain not prescriptive statements, but lawlike generalizations. This is the fundamental *structural* difference between normative and positive theory. Because theories that are purely normative contain no lawlike generalizations, such structures cannot explain phenomena. Recall that it is precisely the lawlike generalizations in positive theories that carry the brunt of the load of explaining and predicting phenomena.

A second difference between normative and positive theory is one of purpose. The purpose or objective of positive theory in marketing is to increase our understanding of marketing phenomena by providing systematized structures capable of explaining and predicting phenomena. Because of their ability to explain and predict phenomena, positive theories are often extremely useful aids to decision making. Indeed, a stronger assertion is probably warranted: good normative theory is based on good positive theory. Understanding how the world *works* enables one to develop theories and models about how to make the world work *better*. Nevertheless, aiding decision making remains a favorable consequence of using theories. The *objective* of theory is to explain, predict, and understand.

In constrast, consider the purpose of the high-assay normative decision theory. Its objective is to help the advertising decision maker to better schedule media. Such is the situation with all normative decision theories. As another example, Massy and Weitz (1977) have developed a normative theory of market segmentation. The purpose of their theory is to provide specific guidelines for allocating marketing expenditures among various market segments. *Indeed, the entire purpose of creating normative decision models in marketing is to assist marketers in making better decisions.*

The final distinction between positive theory and normative decision theory lies in their differing validation criteria. How does one go about determining whether the theories are valid? The validity of a positive theory is determined by (1) checking the internal logic and mathematics of the theory and then (2) exposing it to empirical tests in the real world. Roughly speaking, we develop testable hypotheses of the following kind: "If theory X is valid, then every time we see circumstances C_1, C_2, C_3, . . . C_k in the real world, we would expect also to find phenomena P_1, P_2, P_3, . . . P_k." Note that it is the existence of lawlike generalizations in positive theory that enables us to derive testable hypotheses.

Consider the appropriate validation procedures for normative decision theories. The internal logic and mathematics of such a theory can be checked and verified. Further, the *usefulness* of the theory can be evaluated. That is, compared with other relevant theories, to what extent are the necessary data available, how expensive is the theory to use, how much time does it take to use the theory, and does the theory use the "best" objective function?

Although the usefulness and logic of normative decision theories can be validated, such theories cannot be empirically tested in the real world in the same sense as positive theories. Because normative decision theories do not contain lawlike generalizations, they cannot explain and predict phenomena, and, therefore, they cannot generate empirically testable hypotheses. As MacDonald has observed:

> Let it be admitted that all or most human beings are intelligent or rational. And that what is known by reason is certainly true. But, also, what can be known by unaided reason is what *must* be true, and perhaps what *ought* to be but never what *is* true of matter of fact. And statements which are logically certain are tautological or analytic and are neither verified nor falsified by what exists. *Statements about what ought to be are of a peculiar type which will be discussed later, but it is certain that they say nothing about what is.* (MacDonald 1968, p. 24; italics added)

It is precisely because normative decision theories are not empirically testable that many writers, including this one, prefer the label "normative decision *model*" instead of the label "normative decision theory."

8.3 DETERMINISTIC VERSUS STOCHASTIC THEORY

Unquestionably, much marketing theory uses tendency laws or tendency relationships. For example, "salespeople tend to be more satisfied with their jobs when they perceive that their immediate supervisor closely directs and monitors their activities" (Churchill, Ford, and Walker 1976, p. 331). It would seem that such relationships are inherently stochastic. Bass has been a proponent of the view that *all* marketing behavior may well be *fundamentally* stochastic:

> Despite growing evidence that individual consumer choice behavior is characterized by substantial randomness, the underlying premise or rationale which guides most of the current research in individual consumer behavior is that, in principle, behavior is caused and can therefore be explained. Thus, works such as those by Howard and Sheth and Engel, Kollat, and Blackwell, however valuable they may have been in providing structure and framework for empirical research, may have misdirected research by implicitly overemphasizing deterministic models of behavior. (Bass 1974, p. 1)

Nevertheless, many authors have expressed discomfort at and/or criticism of the use of stochastic instead of deterministic models as bases for marketing theory. For example, Morrison states:

> These models have been and can continue to be useful devices for describing and sometimes predicting consumer behavior, but there are many inherent factors which greatly limit the ability of [stochastic] brand switching models to help develop a theory of consumer behavior. (Morrison 1978, p. 5)

Is marketing theory *inherently* stochastic? To evaluate this issue requires a precise specification of the characteristics of deterministic theory.[2]

8.3.1 The Nature of Deterministic Theory

Intuitive conceptions of determinism connote some type of certainty—that is, if *A*, then *B*, *always*. The discussion here will attempt to make this notion more precise. Because the determinism of almost any current marketing theory might be open to dispute, we look to the physical sciences for an instructive example. We will begin, then, by considering Newtonian mechanics as the prototypical example of deterministic theory.

The theory of classical mechanics derives from the three laws promulgated by Newton, which are of strictly universal form. Under these laws, the mechanical state of a particle is completely specified by its position and momentum. Position and momentum are, therefore, the state variables of the theory. For a system of point masses, the mechanical state of the system is given by the mechanical states of all the particles in the system. With this information concerning a system at an arbitrary point in time, we need only specify the force function applying to the system in order to completely, uniquely specify the mechanical state of the system at any future time. As Nagel (1961, pp. 277–335), in his argument against the claimed indeterminacy of quantum mechanics points out, *this ability to predict a unique state over time is the essence of the determinism of classical mechanics.*

It is important to note that classical mechanics is deterministic only with respect to the mechanical state of the particle system, that is, its state variables. It says nothing, for example, about the chemical and electromagnetic states, nor does it deal with changes caused by these unspecified factors. *Thus, it is not necessary that a deterministic theory completely specify all aspects of a system.*

Moreover, in classical mechanics the positions and momenta of all particles are assumed to be known precisely at an instant in time. Obviously, in practice such perfect measurements can never be made. This imperfect knowledge of the initial state of the system causes mechanical equations to yield values for variables at a future time that are only approximate, that is, probabilistic. Again, uncertainty due to measurement does not damage the determinism of the theory.

In order to maintain that classical mechanics is a deterministic theory, it is necessary to treat it as an ideal state construct that is approximated in experiments. This is equivalent to stating that, *ignoring experimental error, classical mechanics is deterministic because of the logical relationships between statements of the theory*. Formally stated, "a theory is deterministic if, and only if, given the values of its state variables for some initial period, the theory logically determines a unique set of values for those variables for any other period" (Nagel 1961, p. 292).

This idea of determinism is quite inclusive. For example, there is no loss of uniqueness in allowing an infinite number of state variables. Furthermore, the state variables might be defined in terms of classes of individuals rather than individuals, for example, in terms of statistical parameters. If the state description of a theory is defined by the values of a set of statistical parameters, and if those parameters can be uniquely specified through the theoretical laws, given their values at some initial time, the theory would be deterministic.

8.3.2 Uncertainty in Explanation

As a prelude to analyzing the sources of uncertainty that lead to indeterminism in theory, we shall explore the sources of uncertainty in scientific explanations. The issues are the same in that scientific explanations contain exactly the same kinds of laws and lawlike generalizations as scientific theories. The analysis focuses on deductive-nomological (D-N), deductive-statistical (D-S), and inductive-statistical (I-S) explanations.

All three types of explanation suffer some kinds of uncertainty. However, this does not mean that all of the theories built on all three explanatory models are indeterministic. The definition of deterministic theory denotes uncertainty only in a specific sense. If the logical structure of the theory predicts two or more states of the system at a point in time based on the same initial conditions, this uncertainty with respect to prediction makes the theory indeterminate.

As noted earlier, one result of this restriction is that no form of measurement error affects the determinism of a theory. Such error does not affect the logic of the theory, only the ability of the scientist to test the predictions of the theory. The precision with which these predictions can be confirmed is a problem in determining the empirical adequacy of the theory, that is, its truth content. Whether a theory is empirically confirmed is a problem separate from that of logical analysis.

Because measurement error is the only form of uncertainty present in a deductive-nomological explanation, theories cast in this form must be deterministic. The explanandum is logically subsumed under the explanans, and the laws, universal in form, are assumed to be consistent. Therefore, the theory cannot predict two inconsistent versions of the explanandum.

In deductive-statistical explanations, the variables of the explanation are statistical parameters. The explanandum is logically subsumed and mathematically derived from the explanans. Given a fairly reasonable set of assumptions, a statistical parameter mathematically derived from another will be uniquely specified. Thus, with respect to statistical variables of state, any theory based on this type of explanatory model will be deterministic. Although the deductive form of the explanatory models in the deductive-nomological and deductive-statistical cases guarantees that any theory based on these models will be deterministic, the same reasoning does not apply to inductive-statistical explanations.

As noted earlier, inductive-statistical explanations confer some level of logical probability on the occurrence of the explanandum phenomenon. Conversely, they confer some likelihood of the nonoccurrence of the explanandum as well; that is, both the occurrence and the nonoccurrence of the explanandum are consistent with the truth of the explanans. In light of the definition given above, inductive-statistical explanations are not deterministic.

The preceding discussion is summarized in Table 8.3, which shows the three sources of uncertainty in the three kinds of explanations. The three sources of uncertainty result from (1) errors in measurement, (2) the logical relationships between statements in the explanans and the explanandum, and (3) the inability to predict the occurrence of individual phenomena. D-N explanations are deterministic because the only source of uncertainty arises from measurement error. D-S explanations have both measurement error and uncertainty resulting from their inability to predict the occurrence of individual phenomena. Yet, D-S explanations are deterministic because their explananda (a statistical parameter) are logically subsumed under the explanans. I-S explanations are indeterministic because they contain all three sources of uncertainty.

8.3.3 Determinism and Marketing Theory

The foregoing discussion of the nature of deterministic theory, the relationship of deterministic theory to explanatory models, and the uncertainty inherent in explanation can be used to assess the role of deterministic theory in marketing. Bass (1974) has argued that the presence of a stochastic element in consumer behavior makes it impossible to construct deterministic marketing theory. His argument centers on the claim that the stochastic element inherent in the individual actions of consumers makes it impossible to construct laws of universal form. Bass notes that even if this assumption were incorrect, the number of variables affecting consumer behavior might be so large that it would be pragmatically impossible to build deductive-nomological explanations of buyer behavior. Granting the assumption, it is true that it would

Table 8.3

Sources of Uncertainty in Scientific Explanation

Type of explanation	Measurement	Prediction	Logical relationship
Deductive-nomological	Yes	No	No
Deductive-statistical	Yes	Yes	No
Inductive-statistical	Yes	Yes	Yes

Source: Hunt (1991a). Reprinted by permission of the author.

be impossible to construct a deterministic theory predicting each consumer purchase, that is, deductive-nomological explanations of consumer behavior.

However, one could consider the long-run behavior of consumers toward a product or the behavior of a group of consumers toward a product and construct theories explaining brand loyalty, market share, or other statistical parameters or probabilities. Such theories, predicting particular values for the statistical variables of state, would be deterministic in that they would be based on a deductive-statistical model of explanation.

Thus, deterministic theory of some type is a legitimate goal of research in marketing. The critical question arising from this discussion is whether deterministic marketing theory is a desirable goal. And, if so, what implications does such a theoretical focus have for the conduct of theory construction and testing? In order to analyze this issue, it is necessary to return to the fundamental motivations for theory development in marketing.

Consider the buying behavior of a consumer. The "ideal" theory of consumer behavior would explain such behavior completely. Regarding a consumer facing a buying decision, the theory would allow one to predict the decision outcome with probability 1.0. Failing this, the theory might predict the outcome of the decision with some high likelihood—for example, "The consumer in this situation will buy with probability .9." This is an inductive-statistical explanation. As noted earlier, most marketing theory to date has been of this type.

Alternatively, by changing the focus of our considerations from one to many decisions, for example, the buying decision of an aggregate of consumers in a particular situation, the theory might predict market share. Depending on the precision of the estimate, the theory could be a deterministic one. Many so-called stochastic models of consumer choice provide exact predictions of parameters such as market share. To the extent that these models have a systematic basis, they represent deterministic theories. Again, the restriction of the determinism might be relaxed and a theory of inductive-statistical form developed to provide a range of estimates with varying probabilities.

The essential notion embodied in the above examples is that deterministic theory is an ideal toward which marketing theory is moving in a natural fashion. The implication is that, from a structural perspective, both the "deterministic" and "stochastic" schools of research in marketing are developing theory whose ultimate objective is deterministic.

8.4 THE NATURE OF GENERAL THEORIES

Starting from the perspective that theories are systematically related sets of statements, including some lawlike generalizations, that are empirically testable, how do general theories differ from the ordinary kind? In short, what is it that makes a general theory *general*?[3]

There are several ways that one theory can be more general than another. First, recalling that the purpose of theories is to increase scientific understanding through structures that can explain and predict phenomena, general theories can be more general by explaining and predicting *more* phenomena. (See sections 5.3 and 5.5.) That is, more general theories have a larger extension or domain than do less general theories. Dubin (1969, p. 41), for example, proposes that "the generality of a scientific model depends solely upon the size of the domain it represents." Zaltman, Pinson, and Angelmar (1973, p. 52) concur: "A second formal syntactical dimension of a [theoretical] proposition is its degree of generality. All propositions purport to refer to a particular segment of the world, their universe of discourse."

Second, theories can be more general by accommodating, integrating, or systematically relating a large number of concepts and lawlike generalizations from other theories. As Farber (1968, p. 173) suggests, in psychology "comprehensive theories, i.e., those serving to organize a considerable number of laws, depend on the state of knowledge in a given area." For example, perfect competition theory is more general than the theories of demand and supply because it integrates these more specific theories into a more general structure. Likewise, in neoclassical economics, general equilibrium theory takes the conditions for partial equilibrium (i.e., for equilibrium in each industry) and integrates them into a more general case.

A third and very important way that one theory can be more general than another is total theory *incorporation*. As used here, one theory may be said to incorporate another totally when the more general theory can satisfactorily explain the more limited theory's explanatory and predictive successes (Sellars 1963; Levy 1996). That is, it is not the case that the general theory adopts some or all of the concepts and assumptions of the less general theory. Rather, it is the case that the general theory explains why and under what circumstances the concepts and assumptions of the less-general theory explain and predict well.

The classic example of total incorporation, of course, is that Newtonian theory (which maintains that the acceleration of two masses increases as they approach each other) incorporates Galileo's law of descent (which assumes that acceleration is constant between two bodies) and thereby explains all the predictive successes of Galileo's law. Simply put, if *d* is the distance of a body from the surface of the earth and *D* is the radius of the earth, Galileo's law predicts well for most falling objects because the ratio *d*/*D* is–as the general principle is argued for in economics by Friedman (1953)—"close enough" to zero that assuming *g* to be constant in $S = 1/2\ gt^2$ is nonproblematic. Therefore, the foundations of Newtonian theory are such that they incorporate Galileo's law as a special case.

A fourth way that theories can be general is that their constructs may have a high level of abstraction. Blalock states:

> The general theory will be stated in highly abstract terms, with as few assumptions as possible as to the form of the equations, the values of the parameters, or (in the case of statistical theory) the specific distributions of the error terms. It will often be found that this very general theory cannot yield useful theorems, and so additional assumptions will be made in order to study important special cases . . . the principal value of a highly general theoretical formulation is that it enables one to place the various special cases in perspective and to prove general theorems appropriate to them all. (Blalock 1969, p. 141)

Howard and Sheth were cognizant of the relationship between "level of abstraction" and "level of generalization." Thus, they indicate "first, the theory is said to be at a moderate level of abstraction, because it deals only with buying behavior, but nevertheless to be abstract enough to encompass consumer buying, institutional buying, distributive buying, and industrial buying" (1969, p. 391).

Unfortunately, the phrase "high level of abstraction" does not have perfect antecedent clarity, and at least three different meanings seem possible. First, a high level of abstraction may indicate "more encompassing." This seems to be the usage suggested by Howard and Sheth when they propose that their theory of buyer behavior encompasses not only consumer buying but other forms of buying as well. This meaning of level of abstraction would make it consistent with the notion that a general theory encompasses and explains a large number of phenomena.

A second possible meaning of high level of abstraction might be that the terms in the theory are "far removed" from directly observable phenomena. Thus, empirical referents or operational definitions for the "highly abstract" constructs may be difficult, if not impossible, to develop. Given the requirement that all theories must be empirically testable, there appears to be a significant danger in developing theories that are too abstract, in the sense of being far removed from observable reality. To address this second meaning of "too abstract," the original logical positivist position required all terms or constructs in a scientific theory to have direct empirical referents, that is, be directly observable. Recognizing that this position was untenable, the positivists' successors, the logical empiricists, required all abstract or "theoretical" terms to be linked to directly observable terms via devices known as "correspondence rules."

Current analysis in the philosophy of science suggests that even the logical empiricist position is too stringent. Keat and Urry (1975) propose that attention be focused on the testability of *statements* rather than the observability of all terms *in* statements. Thus, they propose the following: "A statement is scientific only if it is possible to make observations that would count in some way for or against its truth or falsity" (p. 38). This principle suggests, as discussed in section 7.5.2, that the constructs in a theory cannot be allowed to become so abstract (so far removed from reality) that they render the theory incapable of generating hypotheses capable of being empirically tested, because such a theory would necessarily be explanatorily and predictively impotent.

In conclusion, one theory may be more general than another because it (1) explains and predicts more phenomena, (2) accommodates, integrates, or systematically relates a larger number of concepts and lawlike generalizations, (3) totally incorporates the less-general theory, and (4) has a higher level of abstraction. We will return to these characteristics of general theories in Chapter 9.

QUESTIONS FOR ANALYSIS AND DISCUSSION

1. Evaluate the classificational schema, discussed in Chapter 1, that used the three dichotomies of profit/nonprofit, micro/macro, and positive/normative to classify issues in marketing. Would the schema be a useful pedagogical tool? How well does it satisfy our criteria for classificational schemata?
2. Distinguish between normative and positive theory. Is price theory normative or positive? Is it appropriate for economists to use price theory to recommend that General Motors be broken up?
3. How would you classify (i.e., as a theory, law, definition, etc.) the statement "Effort in marketing takes two primary forms—either sorting or transformation" (Alderson 1965, p. 49)? Why?
4. Differentiate between *normative* theory and *positive* theory. Must the development of positive theory necessarily precede the development of normative theory? Do all normative theories rest upon an essentially positive base?

5. Someone has said, "We should always carefully distinguish between developing criteria for evaluating what constitutes a theory and developing criteria for evaluating what constitutes a good theory." Are these really two different notions? Could any single criterion be used for both purposes?
6. Find examples of two theories in marketing that are alike in that they address at least one phenomenon in common. Which theory is more general?
7. Would all theories that explain and predict more phenomena necessarily be better than theories that explain and predict fewer phenomena?
8. Wells (1993) is highly critical of certain kinds of consumer research. In particular, the "[s]earch for abstract, universal Theories has not increased our understanding of common behavior" (p. 500). He argues:

> So here we have four counts against Theory-oriented consumer research. Ego-involved Theorists persevere indefinitely in the face of Theory-disconfirming results. Theory "tests" are so imperfect that they can always be written off. When consumer behavior Theories are "tested," they do not get better or even change. And, Theory-oriented consumer researchers neither replicate their findings nor systematically investigate the range and limits of their work. In the absence of this essential segment of the research process, the "body of knowledge" cannot be expected to explain or predict real-world events. (Wells 1993, p. 497)

And he recommends:

> An alternative would be to start small and stay real—to forsake pursuit of high-level, abstract representations and seek ground-level generalizations that actually work. These generalizations might be called "theories" with a small *t* (Olson 1982); but they would always refer to real events. (pp. 497–98)

Evaluate (1) the problem that Wells identifies and (2) his proposed solution.

9. Is deterministic marketing theory a *desirable* goal? An undesirable goal? Why?

NOTES

1. Polli and Cook (1969) discuss this issue.
2. Parts of the following analysis are drawn from Nakamoto and Hunt (1980).
3. Parts of the following analysis are drawn from Hunt (1983a).

9 TOWARD A GENERAL THEORY OF MARKETING

Entrepreneur: "West Texas would be a good location for growing grapes and making wine."

Neoclassical economist: "Nonsense, if it were a good location, there would be wineries here."

—Anonymous

The title of this monograph, *Foundations of Marketing Theory*, is justified on the grounds that the explications of marketing, science, explanation, laws, and theories in the first eight chapters provide a foundation for developing and evaluating marketing theory. The subtitle of this work, *Toward a General Theory of Marketing*, is the subject of this chapter. Specifically, this chapter argues that a theory of competition developed by Robert M. Morgan and me, labeled resource-advantage theory, provides the foundations for, that is, it is *toward*, a general theory of marketing.[1]

This chapter argues on three different grounds that resource-advantage (R-A) theory provides the foundations for a general theory of marketing. First, because marketing takes place within the context of competition, a general theory of *marketing* should be consistent with the most general theory of *competition*. Accordingly, I argue that R-A theory is a general theory of competition, which makes it an appropriate foundation for working toward a general theory of marketing. Second, the closest thing to a general theory of marketing today is Alderson's (1957, 1965) functionalist theory of market behavior (Hunt 1983a). Therefore, I argue that R-A theory is toward a general theory of marketing because it accommodates key concepts and generalizations from Alderson's theory and integrates them into a broader theory. Third, R-A theory is a positive theory; yet much of marketing is normative. Furthermore, *is* does not imply *ought*. However, recall from section 8.2 that good positive theory can provide a foundation for good normative theory. Therefore, I argue that R-A is toward a general theory of marketing because it provides a foundation for the normative area of marketing strategy.

This chapter begins by overviewing R-A theory. It then argues that resource-advantage theory provides the foundations for a general theory of marketing by showing that it (1) is a general theory of competition, (2) accommodates and integrates key concepts and generalizations from Alderson's functionalist theory, and (3) provides a positive foundation for normative marketing strategy.

9.1 AN OVERVIEW OF R-A THEORY

Resource-advantage theory is a dynamic, process theory of competition that is interdisciplinary in the sense that it has been developed in the literatures of several different disciplines. These disciplines include marketing (Falkenberg 2000; Foss 2000; Hodgson 2000; Hunt 1997a, 1999, 2000b, 2000c, 2001a; Hunt and Arnett 2001; Hunt, Lambe, and Wittmann 2002; Hunt and Morgan 1995, 1996, 1997; Lusch 2000), management (Hunt 1995, 2000a; Hunt and Lambe 2000), economics (Hunt 1997b, 1997c, 1997d, 2000d, 2002) and general business (Hunt 1998; Hunt and Duhan, Forthcoming). R-A theory is also interdisciplinary in that it draws on and has affinities with numerous other theories and research traditions, including evolutionary economics, "Austrian" economics, the historical tradition, industrial-organization economics, the resource-based tradition, the competence-based tradition, institutional economics, transaction cost economics, and economic sociology.

At least in part because of its interdisciplinary nature, R-A theory has always been provocative (Hunt and Morgan 1996, 1997). Nonetheless, most commentators find aspects of R-A theory that they believe to be commendable. For example, Lusch (2000, p. 126) finds that, because of the theory's "unifying and integrative nature . . . it should be especially useful to educators, managers, and public policymakers." Likewise, Falkenberg (2000, p. 7) feels "confident that the text [i.e., Hunt (2000b)] will serve as a useful tool for understanding markets and competition, that it will inspire further research in the area, and that it will be required reading for students of marketing and strategy." Similarly, Hodgson (2000, p. 68) finds it to be "important and compelling" and Savitt (2000, p. 76) finds it "to be one of the most provocative treatises to come along in some time."

Resource-advantage theory is a general theory of competition that describes the *process* of competition. Figures 9.1 and 9.2 provide schematic depictions of R-A theory's key constructs and Table 9.1 provides its foundational premises. My overview will follow closely the theory's treatment in Hunt (2000b).

Figure 9.1 **A Schematic of the Resource-Advantage Theory of Competition**

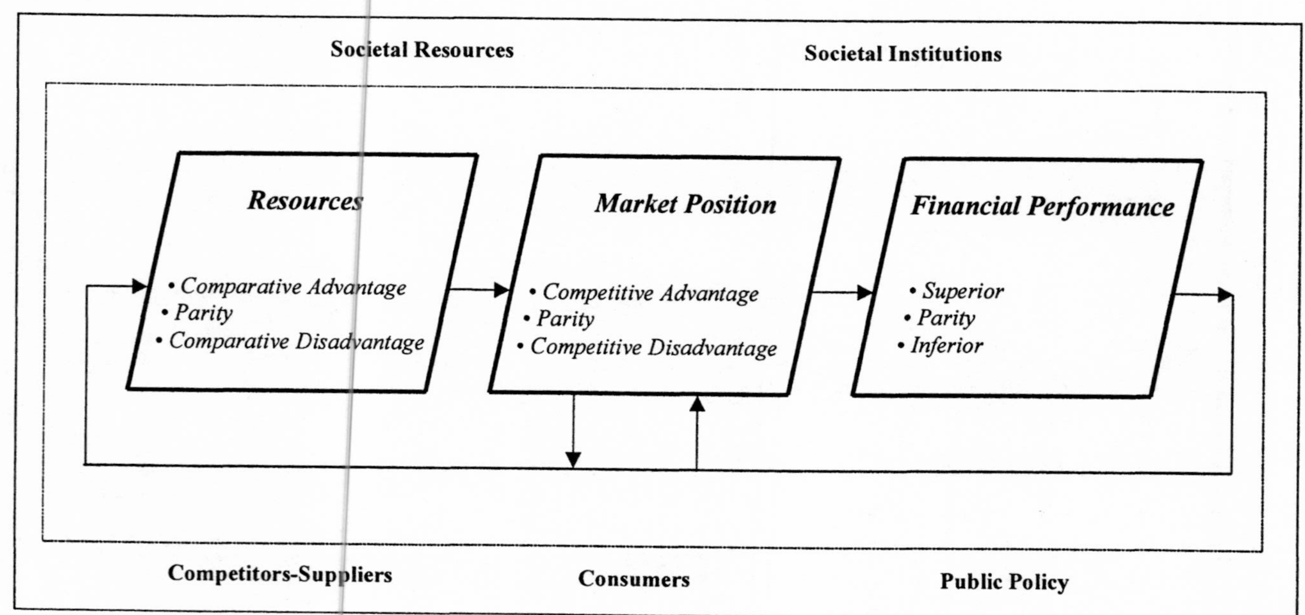

Read: Competition is the disequilibrating, ongoing process that consists of the constant struggle among firms for a comparative advantage in resources that will yield a marketplace position of competitive advantage, and, thereby, superior financial performance. Firms learn through competition as a result of feedback from relative financial performance "signaling" relative market position, which, in turn signals relative resources.

Source: Hunt and Morgan (1997). Reprinted by permission of the American Marketing Association.

Figure 9.2 **Competitive Position Matrix**[a]

Relative Resource-Produced Value

Relative Resource Costs	Lower	Parity	Superior
Lower	1 Indeterminate position	2 Competitive advantage	3 Competitive advantage
Parity	4 Competitive disadvantage	5 Parity position	6 Competitive advantage
Higher	7 Competitive disadvantage	8 Competitive disadvantage	9 Indeterminate position

Source: Adapted from Hunt and Morgan (1995). Reprinted by permission of the American Marketing Association.

[a]*Read:* The marketplace position of competitive advantage identified as cell 3 results from the firm, relative to its competitors, having a resource assortment that enables it to produce an offering for some market segment(s) that (a) is perceived to be of superior value and (b) is produced at lower costs.

9.1.1 The Structure and Foundations of R-A Theory

Using Hodgson's (1993) taxonomy, R-A theory is an evolutionary, disequilibrium-provoking, process theory of competition, in which innovation and organizational learning are endogenous, firms and consumers have imperfect information, and in which entrepreneurship, institutions, and public policy affect economic performance. Evolutionary theories of competition require units of selection that are (1) relatively durable, that is, can exist, at least potentially, through long periods of time, and (2) heritable, that is, can be transmitted to successors. For R-A theory, both firms and resources are proposed as the heritable, durable units of selection, with competition for comparative advantages in resources constituting the selection process.

Table 9.1

Foundational Premises of Resource-Advantage Theory

P_1: Demand is heterogeneous across industries, heterogeneous within industries, and dynamic.

P_2: Consumer information is imperfect and costly.

P_3: Human motivation is constrained self-interest seeking.

P_4: The firm's objective is superior financial performance.

P_5: The firm's information is imperfect and costly.

P_6: The firm's resources are financial, physical, legal, human, organizational, informational, and relational.

P_7: Resource characteristics are heterogeneous and imperfectly mobile.

P_8: The role of management is to recognize, understand, create, select, implement, and modify strategies.

P_9: Competitive dynamics are disequilibrium-provoking, with innovation endogenous.

Source: Adapted from Hunt and Morgan (1997). Reprinted by permission of the American Marketing Association.

At its core, R-A theory combines heterogeneous demand theory with the resource-based theory of the firm (see premises P_1, P_6, and P_7 in Table 9.1). Contrasted with perfect competition, heterogeneous demand theory views intra-industry demand as significantly heterogeneous with respect to consumers' tastes and preferences. Therefore, viewing products as bundles of attributes, different market offerings or "bundles" are required for different market segments within the same industry. Contrasted with the view that the firm is a production function that combines homogeneous, perfectly mobile "factors" of production, the resource-based view holds that the firm is a combiner of heterogeneous, imperfectly mobile entities that are labeled "resources." These heterogeneous, imperfectly mobile resources, when combined with heterogeneous demand, imply significant diversity as to the sizes, scopes, and levels of profitability of firms within the same industry. The resource-based theory of the firm, parallels, if not undergirds, what Foss (1993) calls the "competence perspective" in evolutionary economics and the "capabilities" approaches of Teece and Pisano (1994) and Langlois and Robertson (1995).

As diagrammed in Figures 9.1 and 9.2, R-A theory stresses the importance of (1) market segments, (2) heterogeneous firm resources, (3) comparative advantages/disadvantages in resources, and (4) marketplace positions of competitive advantage/disadvantage. In brief, market segments are defined as intra-industry groups of consumers whose tastes and preferences with regard to an industry's output are *relatively* homogeneous. Resources are defined as the tangible and intangible entities available to the firm that enable it to produce efficiently and/or effectively a market offering that has value for some marketing segment(s). Thus, resources are not just land, labor, and capital, as in neoclassical theory. Rather, resources can be categorized as financial (e.g., cash resources, access to financial markets), physical (e.g., plant, equipment), legal (e.g., trademarks, licenses), human (e.g., the skills and knowledge of individual employees), organizational (e.g., competences, controls, policies, culture), informational (e.g., knowledge from consumer and competitive intelligence), and relational (e.g., relationships with suppliers and customers). Each firm in the marketplace will have at least some resources that are unique to it (e.g., very knowledgeable employees, efficient production processes, etc.) that could constitute a comparative advantage in resources that could lead to positions of advantage (i.e., cells 2, 3, and 6 in Figure 9.2) in the marketplace. Some of these resources are not easily copied or acquired (i.e., they are relatively immobile). Therefore, such resources (e.g., culture and processes) may be a source of long-term competitive advantage in the marketplace.

Just as international trade theory recognizes that nations have heterogeneous, immobile resources, and it focuses on the importance of a comparative advantage in resources to explain the benefits of trade, R-A theory recognizes that many of the resources of firms within the same industry are significantly heterogeneous and relatively immobile. Therefore, analogous to nations, some firms will have a comparative advantage and others a comparative disadvantage in efficiently and/or effectively producing particular market offerings that have value for particular market segments.

Specifically, as shown in Figure 9.1 and further explicated in Figure 9.2, when firms have a comparative advantage in resources they will occupy marketplace positions of competitive advantage for some market segment(s). Marketplace positions of competitive advantage then result in *superior* financial performance. Similarly, when firms have a comparative disadvantage in resources they will occupy positions of competitive disadvantage, which will then produce *inferior* financial performance. Therefore, firms compete for comparative advantages in resources that will yield marketplace positions of competitive advantage for some market segment(s), and, thereby, superior financial performance. As Figure 9.1 shows, how well competitive processes work is significantly influenced by five environmental factors: the societal resources on which firms draw, the societal institutions that form the "rules of the game" (North 1990), the actions of competitors, the behavior of consumers and suppliers, and public policy decisions.

Consistent with its Schumpeterian heritage, R-A theory places great emphasis on innovation, both proactive and reactive. The former is innovation by firms that, although motivated by the expectation of superior financial performance, is not prompted by specific competitive pressures—it is genuinely entrepreneurial in the classic sense of *entrepreneur.* In contrast, the latter is innovation that is directly prompted by the learning process of firms' competing for the patronage of market segments. Both proactive and reactive innovation contribute to the dynamism of R-A competition.

Firms (attempt to) learn in many ways—by formal market research, seeking out competitive intelligence, dissecting competitor's products, benchmarking, and test marketing. What R-A theory adds to extant work is how the process of competition itself contributes to organizational learning. As the feedback loops in Figure 9.1 show, firms learn through competition as a result of the feedback from relative financial performance signaling relative market position, which in turn signals relative resources. When firms competing for a market segment learn from their inferior financial performance that they occupy positions of competitive disadvantage (see Figure 9.2), they attempt to neutralize and/or leapfrog the advantaged firm(s) by acquisition and/or innovation. That is, they attempt to acquire the same resource as the advantaged firm(s) and/or they attempt to innovate by imitating the resource, finding an equivalent resource, or finding (creating) a superior resource. Here, "superior" implies that the innovating firm's new resource enables it to surpass the previously advantaged competitor in terms of either relative costs (i.e., an *efficiency* advantage), or relative value (i.e., an *effectiveness* advantage), or both.

Firms occupying positions of competitive advantage can continue to do so if (1) they continue to reinvest in the resources that produced the competitive advantage, and (2) rivals' acquisition and innovation efforts fail. Rivals will fail (or take a long time to succeed) when an advantaged firm's resources are either protected by societal institutions such as patents or the advantage-producing resources are causally ambiguous, socially or technologically complex, tacit, or have time compression diseconomies.

Competition, then, is viewed as an evolutionary, disequilibrium-provoking process. It consists of the constant struggle among firms for comparative advantages in resources that will yield marketplace positions of competitive advantage, and, thereby, superior financial performance. Once a firm's comparative advantage in resources enables it to achieve superior performance through a position of competitive advantage in some market segment(s), competitors attempt to neutralize and/or leapfrog the advantaged firm through acquisition, imitation, substitution, or major innovation. R-A theory is, therefore, inherently dynamic. Disequilibrium, not equilibrium, is the norm. In the terminology of Hodgson's (1993) taxonomy of evolutionary economic theories, R-A theory is nonconsummatory: it has no end-stage, only a never-ending process of change. The implication is that, though market-based economies are *moving*, they are not moving toward some final state, such as a Pareto-optimal, general equilibrium.

9.2 R-A THEORY IS A GENERAL THEORY OF COMPETITION

Prior to the advent of resource-advantage theory, neoclassical perfect competition theory was the most general theory of competition. Other theories, for example, monopolistic competition (Chamberlin 1933/1962), were always discussed as (1) deviations from perfect competition and (2) societally *undesirable* deviations. Accordingly, this section compares R-A theory with perfect competition theory and argues that R-A theory is the more general theory because it (1) explains more phenomena and (2) (totally) incorporates perfect competition theory as a special case.

9.2.1 Explanatory Power

Even though R-A theory is relatively new, studies have shown that, when compared with perfect competition theory, it *better* explains and predicts numerous phenomena. Specifically, R-A theory (the following page numbers refer to Hunt [2000b]; see that source for additional references): contributes to explaining firm diversity (pp. 152–55), makes the correct prediction concerning financial performance diversity (pp. 153–55), contributes to explaining observed differences in quality, innovativeness, and productivity between market-based and command-based economies (pp. 169–70), shows why competition in market-based economies is dynamic (pp. 132–33), explains how competition is a process of knowledge discovery (pp. 29–30; 145–47), contributes to explaining why social relations constitute a resource only contingently (pp. 100–2), and explains how path dependence effects can occur (pp. 149–52).

Furthermore, R-A theory predicts correctly that technological progress dominates the K/L (i.e., capital/labor) ratio in economic growth (pp. 193–94), predicts correctly that increases in economic growth cause increases in investment (pp. 194–99), predicts correctly that most of the technological progress that drives economic growth stems from the actions of profit-driven firms (pp. 199–200), predicts correctly that R-A competition can prevent the economic stagnation that results from capital deepening (pp. 200–3), contributes to explaining the growth pattern of the (former) Soviet Union (pp. 201–3), explains why formal institutions promoting property rights and economic freedom also promote economic growth (pp. 215–28), and explains why informal institutions promoting social trust also promote economic growth (pp. 235–37).

Space limitations dictate that all the preceding instances of explanatory power cannot be reviewed here. Nonetheless, we can consider one example: the issue of financial performance diversity.

Financial Performance Diversity. Why are some firms more profitable than others? If, as in perfect competition theory, (1) firms are viewed as combiners of homogeneous, perfectly mobile resources by means of a standard production function and (2) intra-industry demand is viewed as homogeneous, then the variance in financial performance across firms and their business-units must result from industry factors such as collusion. This, of course, is the standard view of the structure→ conduct→ performance model in industrial organizational economics (Bain 1956). As Schmalensee (1985, p. 342) observes, a "central hypothesis in virtually all [neo]classical work was that increases in seller concentration tend to raise industrywide profits by facilitating collusion." Empirically, therefore, neoclassical theory predicts that "industry effects" should explain most of the variance in firms' performance and "firm effects" should explain little, if any. In contrast, if firms are viewed as combiners of heterogeneous, imperfectly mobile resources and intra-industry demand is viewed as heterogeneous, as in R-A theory, then "firm effects" should dominate "industry effects."

Schmalensee's (1985) study investigated the issue of industry effects versus firm effects using variance components analysis. Using the Federal Trade Commission's (FTC) line of business data and 1975 business-unit return on assets as the measure of financial performance, Schmalensee (1985, p. 349) finds industry effects to account for 19.5 percent of the variance of business-unit return on assets and corporate effects to be not significant. He concludes: "[This] supports the classical focus on industry level analysis as against the revisionist tendency to downplay industry differences."[2] However, Rumelt (1991) pointed out that Schmalensee's use of only one year's data not only confounded stable industry effects with transient annual fluctuations but also made it impossible to separate the effects of the overall corporation from those of the individual business-unit. When Rumelt (1991) supplemented Schmalensee's 1975 data with the FTC data for 1974, 1976, and 1977, he found that, whereas industry effects explained only 8 percent of the variance, corporate and business-units effects explained 2 percent and 44 percent, respectively. Therefore, he finds "total firm" effects of 46 percent (2 percent + 44 percent) to be almost six times those of industry effects.

Supporting Rumelt's findings, Roquebert, Phillips, and Westfall (1996) find industry, corporate, and business-unit effects to be 10 percent, 18 percent, and 37 percent, respectively (resulting in "total firm" effects of 18 percent + 37 percent = 55 percent). Notably, their database was much larger (over 6,800 manufacturing corporations), from a more recent time period (1985–91), used a longer time period (seven years versus four), had a broader base (over 940 SIC, 4–digit categories), and it (unlike FTC data) included both small and large corporations. Similarly, McGahan and Porter (1997) find industry, corporate, and business-unit effects for their sample of 7,003 corporations (for the time period 1982–88) to be 19 percent, 4 percent, and 32 percent, respectively (resulting in "total firm" effects of 4 percent + 32 percent = 36 percent).[3] Likewise, Mauri and Michaels (1998) use a sample of 264 single-business companies from 69 4–digit SIC code industries, for the time period 1988–92, and find industry and firm effects to be 5 percent and 30 percent, respectively. Similarly, for the time period 1978–92, Mauri and Michaels find the comparable figures to be 4 percent and 19 percent.

In summary, depending on the database used, it appears that industry effects account for 4–19 percent of the variance in performance, as measured by return on assets, and firm effects account for 19–55 percent. That is, "firm effects" account for 2–6 times the variance accounted for by "industry effects." In short, industry is the "tail" of competition; the firm is the "dog."

The empirical studies on the diversity of financial performance indicate that R-A theory makes the correct prediction on the issue of financial performance diversity. Competition simply does not produce the requisite "as if" conditions and/or the competitive circumstances in the United States economy are not "close enough" to the assumptions of perfect competition to enable neoclassical theory to make the correct prediction. In contrast, because R-A theory proposes that firms are *best* construed as combiners of heterogeneous, imperfectly mobile resources and intra-industry demand is *best* construed as substantially heterogeneous, then the fact that "firm effects" dominate "industry effects" is precisely what one expects. That is, the descriptively more accurate premises of R-A theory enable it to make the correct prediction.

Although R-A theory better explains and predicts numerous phenomena, there are, of course, times when perfect competition does explain and/or predict well. Why this is the case is addressed next.

9.2.2 Perfect Competition Theory and R-A Theory

The finding discussed in section 9.2.1 that firm effects (the focus of R-A theory) dominate industry effects (the focus of neoclassical theory) supports viewing the *process* identified by R-A theory in Figures 9.1 and 9.2 as the general case of the *process* of competition. Therefore, because a theory is derived from its assumptions, the evidence supports viewing each of R-A theory's foundational premises in Table 9.1 to be either descriptively realistic, or, at least, "close enough" (Friedman 1953). Hunt (2000b) argues that the foundational premises of perfect competition are, indeed, special cases of R-A theory, and, consequently, R-A theory incorporates perfect competition. A key part of the argument is the following issue: how should the foundational premises of R-A theory in Table 9.1 be interpreted?

Note that each assumption in Table 9.1 could be viewed as an idealized state that anchors an end-point on a continuum. That is, demand (P_1) could be conceptualized as a continuum with perfect homogeneity and perfect heterogeneity as idealized anchor-points. Similar continua could be conceptualized for information and its cost (P_2 and P_5) and for the homogeneity-heterogeneity and mobility-immobility of resources (P_7). However, whereas perfect competition is customarily interpreted in the idealized, anchor-point manner, in no case is R-A theory to be interpreted as the anchor-point *opposite* perfect competition. Rather, each foundational premise of R-A theory is proposed as the descriptively realistic general case. Therefore, intra-industry demand (P_1) is to be interpreted for R-A theory as *substantially* heterogeneous. Similarly, information for both firms (P_5) and consumers (P_2) is substantially imperfect and costly. Likewise, many, but not all, resources (P_6) are substantially heterogeneous and immobile. Space limitations prevent a full discussion of all of R-A theory's premises, as is done in Hunt (2000b). Instead, this section illustrates the argument by focusing only on P_1 and P_9.

Consider intra-industry demand (P_1) and the case of footwear. R-A theory views consumers' tastes and preferences for footwear, which is classified by the U.S. Census as "SIC #314," to be substantially heterogeneous and constantly changing. Furthermore, consumers have substantially imperfect information concerning footwear products that might match their tastes and preferences, and obtaining such information is often costly in terms of both time and money. The implication of heterogeneity is that few—if any—*industry* markets exists: there are only market segments *within* industries. There is no "market for shoes," (SIC #314) or even separate markets for women's shoes (#3144) and men's shoes (#3143). Even though all consumers require footwear and one can readily identify a group of firms that manufacture shoes, there is no shoe-industry *market*. That is, the firms that constitute the shoe industry do not collectively face a *single*, downward sloping demand curve—for such an industry demand curve would imply homogeneous tastes and preferences.

For R-A theory, to the extent that demand curves exist at all, they exist at a level of (dis)aggregation that is too fine to be an "industry." For example, even if there were a men's walking shoe market, one certainly would not speak of the men's walking shoe *industry*. The fact that intra-industry demand is substantially heterogeneous in *most* industries (even at the 4–digit SIC level) contributes to R-A theory's ability (and neoclassical theory's inability) to make the correct prediction as to the diversity in business-unit financial performance. Likewise, the fact that intra-industry demand is relatively homogeneous ("close enough") in at least *some* commodity-type industries, for example, gold ores (SIC #1041), contributes to explaining those special cases where perfect competition predicts well. Therefore, R-A theory's premise P_1 is the general case; perfect competition's premise concerning intra-industry demand is the special case.

Premise P_9, the issue of competitive dynamics, raises the following question: under what set of circumstances will the process of R-A competition (which is disequilibrium-provoking, with innovation endogenous) result in perfect competition (which is equilibrium-seeking, with innovation exogenous)? Consider the following scenario. First, assume that a set of firms producing an offering for a particular market segment within an industry has been competing according to R-A theory. Therefore, because of resource heterogeneity (say, different levels of a key competence), the firms are distributed throughout the nine marketplace positions in Figure 9.2. Some firms, because of their comparative advantage in resources, are enjoying superior returns; others, because of their comparative disadvantage in resources, have inferior returns; and still others, because of their parity resources, have parity returns (see Figure 9.1).

Next, assume that, over time, both disadvantaged and parity firms (1) gradually learn how the advantaged firms are producing their offerings more efficiently and/or effectively and (2) successfully imitate the advantaged firms by acquiring or developing the requisite resources. For example, assume that they gradually develop competences equivalent to the advantaged firms. Then assume that, even though all firms seek *superior* financial performance, no firm finds it possible to acquire, develop, or create new resources (e.g., developing a new competence) that will enable it to produce a market offering more efficiently or effectively than any other firm. That is, for some reason or set of reasons, all competition-induced innovation stops, both proactive and reactive. Consequently, all competition-induced technological change stops. Under these economic conditions, then, the resources of all firms serving this market segment become relatively homogeneous and there will be parity resources producing parity offerings.

Next, assume that the tastes and preferences of consumers in all other market segments served by the firms in this industry shift toward the original segment. Industry consumer demand will then become relatively homogeneous. Suppose further that consumers' tastes and preferences remain stable throughout a significant period of time and that consumers become very knowledgeable about the relative homogeneity of firms' offerings. There will then be parity resources producing parity offerings, which results in all firms having parity marketplace positions (cell 5 in Figure 9.2).

Next, assume that firms have accurate information about competitive conditions and there are no institutional restraints preventing them from producing their market offerings in the profit-maximizing quantity. Under these economic circumstances, the industry experiences no endogenous technological change, firms become price-takers, and a static equilibrium theory of competition, such as perfect competition, applies. That is, there will be parity resources producing parity offerings, which results in parity marketplace positions and parity performance (see Figure 9.1). The industry has now become a candidate for "industry effects" to dominate "firm effects" in empirical studies, for collusion and barriers to entry to become viable explanations for any industrywide, superior financial performance, and, in general, for industry-level theoretical analyses to be appropriate.

Next, assume that the preceding process occurs in every industry in an entire economy. Then, if this set of economic circumstances persists over time, all competition-induced technological change ceases, all endogenous technological progress stops, all endogenous growth ceases, and a long-run, general equilibrium theory applies (such as Walrasian general equilibrium). In such an economy, growth comes only from exogenous sources, including those sources (e.g., government R&D or a state planning board) that might develop innovations that result in exogenous technological progress, as in neoclassical growth theory (see Hunt 2000b, pp. 179–83).

Note that the preceding analysis began with the process of R-A competition for a market segment and sketches the special economic circumstances that must prevail for the competitive process to result in a static-equilibrium situation in an industry. Among other conditions, it showed that a very important circumstance is that all endogenous innovation must stop (or be stopped). Such a stoppage might come as a result of collusion, complacency, institutional restrictions, governmental fiat, or lack of entrepreneurial competence. The analysis then sketched the special circumstances for a long-run general equilibrium to develop, and, again, it showed that all endogenous technological progress in all industries—hence, all endogenous economic growth—in an economy must cease. Therefore, the statics of perfect competition, both partial equilibrium and general equilibrium, may be viewed as a special case of the dynamics of R-A theory. R-A theory relates to perfect competition in the same way that Newtonian mechanics relates to Galileo's law: the former incorporates the latter. In this manner, R-A theory explains the predictive successes (when such successes occur) of neoclassical perfect competition theory.

9.3 THE THEORY OF MARKET PROCESSES

Alderson (1957; 1965), in developing his functionalist theory of market processes, drew heavily on several sources. Most notably, he was influenced by Clark's (1954; 1961) theory of effective competition. Therefore, before discussing Alderson's work, I first review Clark's.

9.3.1 Effective Competition

In the 1930s and 1940s, Clark (1940) developed the concept of workable competition. In the 1950s and 1960s, Clark (1954, 1961) abandoned the label *workable* competition and replaced it with *effective* competition for reasons he states clearly:

> I am shifting the emphasis from "workable" to "effective competition" because "workable" stresses mere feasibility and is consistent with the verdict that feasible forms of competition, while tolerable, are still inferior substitutes for that "pure and perfect" competition which has been so widely accepted as a normative ideal. And I have become increasingly impressed that the kind of competition we have, with all its defects—and these are serious—is better than the "pure and perfect" norm, because it makes for progress. Some departures from "pure and perfect" competition are not only inseparable from progress, but necessary to it. The theory of effective competition is dynamic theory. (Clark 1961, p. ix)

Because a dynamic theory of competition would have different standards of appraisal, Clark inquires as to the objectives society would want competition to accomplish. He suggests that competition should provide or promote an adequate variety of products (including low-priced products, high-quality products, and new products), economic opportunity, social mobility, a productive economy, rewards to innovators, low search costs, a diffusion of the gains of progress, high and stable employment, business freedom, the elimination of process inefficiencies, and an appropriate balance of desirable and undesirable effects on individuals (Clark 1954, pp. 323–24; 1961, pp. 63, 74, 77, 78, 81, 82, 86).

Taken collectively, the desirable outputs of competition would seem to be a tall order. Yet, Clark maintains that effective, dynamic competition could come tolerably close to achieving all his suggested goals. But effective, dynamic competition does not imply that firms would be price-takers, or that they would seek to maximize profits, or that competition is a struggle with only one winner (1961, p. 18). What, then, does effective competition imply?

Acknowledging his "kinship" with Schumpeter's "creative destruction," competition is:[4]

> [A] form of independent action by business units in pursuit of increased profits . . . by offering others inducements to deal with them, the others being free to accept the alternative inducements offered by rival business units. Active competition consists of a combination of (1) initiatory actions by a business unit, and (2) a complex of responses by those with whom it deals, and by rivals. (Clark 1954, p. 326)

Clark's definition of dynamic competition is remarkably compact. Indeed, his entire 1961 book is devoted to "unpacking" it. A good starting point for us is his view that firms pursue increased profits rather than maximum profits.

Clark (1961, p. 9) specifically alerts readers that his "profit-minded" firms are not profit maximizers. He argues that firms do not maximize profit because all firms at all times face such conditions of uncertainty as to consumers' and rivals' actions that they lack the necessary information to maximize (pp. 93, 471). He further argues that some firms at some times (1) sacrifice profits for growth (p. 96), (2) sacrifice profits in favor of community responsibilities (p. 91), and (3) sacrifice profits because of following the "morals of trade" (p. 479). By substituting "increased profits in the face of uncertainty" for the neoclassical "maximum profits in the face of perfect information," Clark makes competition dynamic. That is, the continuing pursuit of increased profits, *more* profits, prompts changes in the "inducements to deal."

When firms are successful in effecting changes in inducements targeted at specific customers, for example, by providing market offerings of higher quality or lower prices, such firms have a "differential advantage" over rivals (1954, p. 327). It is the pursuit of differential advantages over rivals that prompts the innovations that constitute "aggressive competition" (1961, p. 14). For Clark, the sum of innovations that result in differential advantages over rivals constitutes the technological progress required for a "dynamically progressive system," that is, for economic growth (1961, p. 70). Therefore, mandating the homogeneity of demand and supply—as argued for by many defenders of perfect competition theory—would necessitate the "stoppage of growth and progress, a price we should be unwilling to pay" (1961, p. 70). Indeed, "perfect competition . . . define[s] a model from which competitive progress would be ruled out; progress could come only by government fiat" (1954, p. 329).

For Clark, the innovations resulting from aggressive competition can come from small firms, as stressed by Marshall (1890/1949), or from large firms, as stressed by Schumpeter (1950). Contrasted with Schumpeter (1950), however, the innovations by firms large and small can be such that they only modestly improve quality or lower costs. Cumulatively, however, Clark points out that small innovations are important to the firm and economy. Whether an innovation is brought about by small firms or large ones, whether it is industry-shaking or only a modest improvement, "the life history of a successful innovation is a cycle. It is developed, profitably utilized, and ultimately loses its value as a source of special profit" (Clark 1961, p. 189).

An innovation loses its value to produce superior profits when it is either superseded by something better (i.e., Schumpeter's "creative destruction") or when it is diffused among rivals and becomes standard practice by "defensive competition." Thus, when an innovation is diffused among rivals, it becomes—rather than a differential advantage for the originator—much like the "ante" in a poker game. Both aggressive and defensive competition are required for *effective* competition: "without initiatory moves, competition does not begin, without defensive responses, it does not spread" (Clark 1961, p. 429). Aggressive competition creates innovations and differential advantages; defensive competition diffuses innovations and neutralizes such advantages. As to the speed of neutralization:

> If a potential innovator expects neutralization to be complete before he has recovered the costs of innovation, his incentive vanishes. . . . On the other hand, if neutralizing action were permanently blocked, the initiator would have a limited monopoly, in the sense of a permanent differential advantage. . . . The desirable case lies somewhere between too prompt and too slow neutralization. I will not call it an "optimum," because that term suggests a precision which no actual system could attain. (Clark 1954, pp. 327–28)

Clark's hope was that his dynamic theory of effective competition would provide a framework for understanding actual forms of competition and for fostering the ones most conducive to a dynamic welfare ideal. He knew, however, that "the threat of failure looms large, in that readers whose conception of theory is identified with models of determinate equilibrium are likely to decide that no theory has been produced" (1961, p. x). He was prescient, to say the least. His 500–page 1961 book—having not a single differential equation or geometrical representation—was not incorporated into mainstream economics. However, it did have a significant impact on Alderson's (1957, 1965) functionalist theory of market processes.

9.3.2 Alderson's Functionalist Theory

Alderson (1957, 1965) was strongly influenced by Chamberlin's (1933) heterogeneous demand theory and by Clark's (1954, 1961) theory of effective, dynamic competition. He was also impressed by Merton's (1949) functionalist, systems approach to theory development. Furthermore, his background in marketing, with its historical interest in groups of manufacturers, wholesalers, and retailers that form channels of distribution, pointed him toward developing a theory of marketing systems. Accordingly, his functionalist theory of market processes may be viewed as a functionalist, systems approach to integrating theories of heterogeneous demand, differential advantage, and channels of distribution.[5]

Alderson (1957, p. 16) views functionalism as "that approach to science which begins by identifying a system of action, and then tries to determine how and why it works as it does." He identifies (1) firms as the subsystems that produce goods and (2) households as the subsystems that constitute the basic consuming units. He (1965, p. 39) notes that firms evolve in a society when specialization of labor results in removing the production function for some goods from the household. Extending Chamberlin's (1933) view that intra-industry demand is substantially heterogeneous, he notes that the particular assortment of goods that is viewed as meaningful or desirable by any one household is likely to differ greatly from that of others. Thus, the macrosystems that he seeks to understand and explain are those that involve firms taking tangible resources in their natural state and transforming them into a variety of marketplace goods that ultimately winds up as meaningful assortments of goods in the hands of particular households.

Although firms pursue profit, Alderson (1957, p. 54) maintains that they do so *as if* they had a primary goal of survival. The survival goal results from firm owners and employees believing that they can obtain more in terms of financial and nonfinancial rewards by working toward the survival of their existing firms than by acting individually or by become members of other firms. Firm growth, therefore, is sought because of the conviction that growth is necessary for survival (1957, pp. 103–8). In a market-based economy, however, survival depends crucially on a firm's ability to compete with other firms in seeking the patronage of specific (1) intermediate buyers and/or (2) ultimate households.

A firm can be assured of the patronage of intermediate buyers and/or groups of households only when buyers have reasons to prefer its output over that of competing firms. Therefore, each competing firm will seek some advantage over other firms to assure the patronage of some group of either intermediate buyers or ultimate households. Citing the work of Clark (1954), Alderson labels the process "competition for differential advantage" (1957, p. 101). Indeed, "no one enters business except in the expectation of some degree of differential advantage in serving his customers, and . . . competition consists of the constant struggle to develop, maintain, or increase such advantages" (1957, p. 106). Therefore:

> The functionalist or ecological approach to competition begins with the assumption that every firm must seek and find a function in order to maintain itself in the market

> place. Every business firm occupies a position, which is in some respects unique. Its location, the product it sells, its operating methods, or the customers it serves tend to set it off in some degree from every other firm. Each firm competes by making the most of its individuality and its special character. It is constantly seeking to establish some competitive advantage . . . [because] an advanced method of operation is not enough if all competitors live up to the same high standards. What is important in competition is differential advantage, which can give a firm an edge over what others in the field are offering. (Alderson 1957, pp. 101–2)

Alderson (1957, pp. 184–97) identifies six bases of differential advantage for a manufacturing firm: market segmentation, selection of appeals, transvection, product improvement, process improvement, and product innovation. By market segmentation having the potential for a differential advantage, Alderson means that firms may have an advantage over competitors when they (1) identify segments of demand that competitors are not servicing (or rivals are servicing poorly) and (2) they subsequently develop market offerings that will appeal strongly to those particular segments. On the other hand, by "selection of appeals" he means that some firms can achieve advantage by the images that are conveyed to consumers through advertising and other promotional means. Similarly, by "transvection" he means an advantage in reaching a market segment through a unique channel of distribution.

The existence of a differential advantage gives the firm a position in the marketplace known as an "ecological niche" (1957, p. 56). The "core" and "fringe" of a firm's ecological niche consists of the market segments for which the firm's differential advantage is (1) ideally suited and (2) satisfactorily suited, respectively. A firm can survive attacks by competitors on its "fringe" as long as its "core" remains intact; it can survive attacks on its "core" as long as it has the will and ability to find another differential advantage and another core (1957, pp. 56–57). Therefore, given heterogeneity of demand and competition for differential advantage, heterogeneity of supply is a natural phenomenon. That is, manufacturers will respond to heterogeneity of demand by producing a variety of different goods and many variations of the same generic kind of good (1957, p. 103).

To reach households, however, manufacturing firms require market intermediaries, that is, channels of distribution. Market processes involving intermediaries are essentially "matching" processes, that is, matching segments of demand with segments of supply. In a *perfectly* heterogeneous market, each small segment of demand, that is, each household, could be satisfied by just one unique segment of supply, that is, one firm (1965, p. 29). In most markets, however, there are partial homogeneities. That is, there are groups or segments of households *desiring* substantially similar products and there are groups of firms *supplying* substantially similar products.

The major job of marketing intermediaries is to effect exchange by matching segments of demand with segments of supply. The matching process comes about as a result of a sequence of sorts and transformations (1965, p. 26). A sort is the assignment of goods, materials, or components to the appropriate facilities. A transformation is the change in the physical form of a good or its location in time or space.

With the preceding as a backdrop, Alderson (1965, p. 26) can provide an answer to the question that prompted his functionalist theory. Given heterogeneity of demand, heterogeneity of supply, competition for differential advantage, and the requisite institutions (intermediaries) to effect the sorts and transformations necessary to match segments of demand with segments of supply, market processes will take resources in the natural state and bring about meaningful assortments of goods in the hands of households.

9.3.3 Market Processes and R-A Theory

With respect to the nature of competition, both Alderson's functionalist theory and Clark's effective competition rely on the concept of competition for differential advantage. Therefore, I use the label *differential advantage theory* ("D-A theory") to refer to the combination of their respective views. This section argues that R-A theory accommodates and integrates key concepts and generalizations of D-A theory into its general theory of competition.

First, both differential advantage theory and R-A theory maintain that competition is dynamic. Indeed, they share a similar propulsion mechanism. For D-A theory, the mechanism is increased profits; for R-A theory, it is the more general concept (and more completely explicated concept) of superior financial performance. That is, R-A theory proposes that the firm's primary objective of superior financial performance (P_4 in Table 9.1) is pursued under conditions of imperfect (and often costly to obtain) information about extant and potential market segments, competitors, suppliers, shareholders, and production technologies (P_5 in Table 9.1). Superior financial performance is indicated by measures such as profits, earnings per share, return on investment, and capital appreciation. Here, "superior" equates with both "more than" and "better than." It implies that firms seek a level of financial performance exceeding that of some referent. For example, the referent can be the firm's own performance in a previous time period, the performance of rival firms, an industry average, or a stock-market average, among others. Affecting the process of competition, both the specific measure and specific referent will vary somewhat from time to time, firm to firm, industry to industry, and culture to culture.

Firms are posited to pursue superior financial performance because superior rewards—both financial and nonfinancial—will then flow to owners, managers, and employees. However, superior financial performance does not equate with the neoclassical concepts of "abnormal profits" or "rents" (i.e., profits differing from the average firm in a purely competitive industry in long-run equilibrium) because R-A theory views industry long-run equilibrium as such a rare phenomenon that "normal" profits cannot be an empirical referent for comparison purposes. Furthermore, the actions of firms that collectively constitute competition do not force groups of rivals to "tend toward" equilibrium. Instead, the pursuit of *superior* performance implies that actions of competing firms are disequilibrating, not equilibrating. That is, R-A competition is necessarily dynamic because all firms cannot be superior *simultaneously*.

As a second point of similarity, neither D-A theory nor R-A theory is defended on the ground that its theory of competition represents "second best" or "workable" approximations of perfect competition. Instead, both theories deny that the equations of general equilibrium, relying as they do on perfect competition, represent the appropriate welfare ideal. For both D-A and R-A theory, the appropriate welfare ideal must accommodate, at the minimum, competition-induced technological progress. The more general R-A theory, contrasted with D-A theory, explicates in detail how R-A competition produces increases in productivity and economic growth (Hunt 2000b).

Third, both D-A and R-A theory share the view that competition involves both initiatory and defensive actions. The "aggressive competition" and "defensive competition" of D-A theory parallel the "proactive innovation" and "reactive innovation" of R-A theory. Thus, competition-induced innovations, whether large or small, by huge corporations or solitary entrepreneurs, play a major role in both theories.

Fourth, both D-A and R-A theory share the view that competition involves the struggle among rivals for *advantages*. For D-A theory, the concept of the kinds of advantages that firms pursue are of an unspecified (or only limitedly specified) nature. For R-A theory, firms pursue two kinds of advantages: advantages in resources and advantages in marketplace position. Specifically, they pursue comparative advantages in resources that will yield marketplace positions of competitive advantage, and, thereby, superior financial performance (see Figures 9.1 and 9.2). Furthermore, R-A theory explicates the nature of resources that will make effective neutralization by rivals less likely or at least more time consuming: when resources are imperfectly mobile, inimitable, and imperfectly substitutable, they are more likely to thwart effective neutralization. That is, when resources are tacit, causally ambiguous, socially or technologically complex, interconnected, or when they exhibit mass efficiencies or time-compression diseconomies, they are *less* likely to be quickly and effectively neutralized and *more* likely to produce a sustainable competitive advantage.

Finally, both D-A theory and R-A theory are developed in a natural language, that is, English. They are not developed in the language of mathematical equations. But R-A theory's preference for natural-language exposition should not be interpreted as being anti-equation. Rather, unlike D-A theory, the more general R-A theory is argued to be a theory of competition that incorporates perfect competition theory as a special case, and, thereby, explains when the equations in the neoclassical tradition will predict accurately.

9.4 A POSITIVE FOUNDATION FOR STRATEGY

Good positive theory, as discussed in section 8.2, can provide a firm foundation for good normative theory. R-A theory is a positive theory of competition. That is, it purports to describe, explain, and predict—and thus it contributes to *understanding*—how competition *works*. In contrast, marketing strategy is inherently normative. That is, marketing strategy prescribes how strategic decisions within the firm *should* be made. However, because good normative strategies always presume a set of assumptions as to how the world of competition actually does *work*, the thesis of this section is that R-A theory (a positive theory) provides a foundation for marketing strategy (a set of normative theories). Because marketing strategy is inexorably intertwined with business strategy, this section (1) begins with a brief overview of business strategy, before (2) discussing three major concepts in marketing strategy. Section 9.5 shows how R-A theory provides a positive foundation for both business and marketing strategy.

9.4.1 Business Strategy

Modern business strategy traces to the works on administrative policy of Kenneth Andrews and his colleagues at Harvard (Andrews 1971, 1980, 1987; Christianson et al. 1982; Learned et al. 1965). Viewing business strategy as the match a business makes between its internal resources and skills and the opportunities and risks created by its external environment, they developed the SWOT framework: *S*trengths, *W*eaknesses, *O*pportunities, *T*hreats. In this framework, the main task of corporate-level strategy is identifying businesses in which the firm will compete (Andrews 1971). Alternative strategies for the firm are developed through an appraisal of the opportunities and threats it faces in various markets, that is, *external* factors, and an evaluation of its strengths and weaknesses, that is, *internal* factors. Good strategies are those that are explicit (for effective implementation) and effect a good match or "fit." Such strategies avoid environmental threats, circumvent internal weaknesses, and exploit opportunities through the strengths or distinctive competences of the firm. Since the work of Andrews and his colleagues, research on strategy has centered on three approaches: industry-based strategy, resource-based strategy, and competence-based strategy.

Industry-based Strategy. An "external factors" approach, the industry-based theory of strategy, as exemplified by Porter (1980; 1985), turns industrial-organization economics "upside down" (Barney and Ouchi 1986, p. 374). That is, what was considered anticompetitive and socially undesirable under neoclassical, industrial-organization economics, forms the basis for normative competitive strategy. In this view, choosing the industries in which to compete and/or altering the structure of chosen industries to increase monopoly power should be the focus of strategy because:

> Present research [i.e., Schmalensee (1985)] continues to affirm the important role industry conditions play in the performance of individual firms. Seeking to explain performance differences across firms, recent studies have repeatedly shown that average industry profitability is, by far, the most significant predictor of firm performance. . . . In short, it is now uncontestable that industry analysis should play a vital role in strategy formation. (Montgomery and Porter 1991, pp. xiv–xv)

Porter's (1980) "five forces" framework maintains that the profitability of a firm in an industry is determined by (1) the threat of new entrants to the industry, (2) the threat of substitute products or services, (3) the bargaining power of its suppliers, (4) the bargaining power of its customers, and (5) the intensity of rivalry among its existing competitors. Therefore, because "a firm is not a prisoner of its industry's structure" (Porter 1985, p. 7), strategy should aim at choosing the best industries (usually those that are highly concentrated) and/or altering industry structure by raising barriers to entry and increasing one's bargaining power over suppliers and customers.

After choosing industries and/or altering their structure, Porter (1980) advocates choosing one of three "generic" strategies: (1) cost leadership, (2) differentiation, or (3) focus. That is, superior performance can result from a competitive advantage brought about by a firm, relative to others in its industry, having a lower cost position, having its offering being perceived industrywide as being unique, or having a focus on one particular market segment and developing a market offering specifically tailored to it. Although it is possible to pursue successfully more than one strategy at a time (and the rewards are great for doing so), "usually a firm must make a choice among them, or it will become stuck in the middle" (Porter 1985).

After choosing one of the three generic strategies, internal factors come into play. Specifically, Porter (1985) argues that the firm should implement its strategy by managing well the activities in its "value chain," because "[t]he basic unit of competitive advantage . . . is the discrete activity" (1991, p. 102). If value is defined as "what buyers are willing to pay," then "superior value stems from offering lower prices than competitors for equivalent benefits or providing unique benefits that more than offset a higher price" (1985, p. 4).

For Porter (1985), activities in the firm's value chain are categorized as either primary or support. Primary activities include inbound logistics, operations, outbound logistics, marketing and sales, and service. Support activities include procurement, technology development (improvement of product and process), human resource management, and firm infrastructure (e.g., general management, planning, finance). Doing these activities well improves gross margin, promotes competitive advantage, and thereby produces superior financial performance. Therefore, the fundamental strategic thesis of industry-based strategy is that, to achieve competitive advantage, and, thereby, superior financial performance, firms should (1) choose industries and/or modify their structure, (2) select one of three generic strategies, and (3) manage well the activities in its value chain.

Resource-based Strategy. Because (1) empirical studies show that highly concentrated industries are no more profitable than their less concentrated counterparts (Buzzell et al, 1975; Gale and Branch 1982; Ravenscraft 1983), and (2) similar studies show that the industry market share-profitability relationship is spurious (Jacobson and Aaker 1985; Jacobson 1988), many business strategy theorists have questioned the focus on external factors of industry-based theory. In particular, those labeled "resource-based" theorists argue for the primacy of heterogeneous and imperfectly mobile resources.

Resource-based theory in business strategy traces to the long-neglected work of Edith Penrose (1959). Avoiding the term "factor of production" because of its ambiguity, she viewed the firm as a "collection of productive resources" and pointed out that "it is never *resources* themselves that are the 'inputs' to the production process, but only the *services* that the resources can render" (pp. 24–25; italics in original). Viewing resources as bundles of possible services that an entity can provide, "It is the heterogeneity . . . of the productive services available or potentially available from its resources that gives each firm its unique character" (pp. 75, 77). Therefore, contrasted with the neoclassical notion of an *optimum* size of firm, "the expansion of firms is largely based on opportunities to use their existing productive resources more efficiently than they are being used" (p. 88).

Works drawing on Penrose (1959) to explicate resource-based theory in business strategy include the seminal articles of Lippman and Rumelt (1982), Rumelt (1984), and Wernerfelt (1984) in the early 1980s, followed by the efforts of Dierickx and Cool (1989), Barney (1991, 1992), and Conner (1991) in the late 1980s and early 1990s. The resource-based theory of strategy maintains that resources (to varying degrees) are both significantly heterogeneous across firms and imperfectly mobile. "Resource heterogeneity" means that each and every firm has an assortment of resources that is at least in some ways unique. "Imperfectly mobile" implies that firm resources, to varying degrees, are not commonly, easily, or readily bought and sold in the marketplace (the neoclassical factor markets). Because of resource heterogeneity, some firms are more profitable than others. Because of resource immobility, resource heterogeneity can persist over time despite attempts by firms to acquire the same resources of particularly successful competitors. Therefore, the fundamental strategic thesis of the resource-based view is that, to achieve competitive advantage, and, thereby, superior financial performance, firms should seek resources that are valuable, rare, imperfectly mobile, inimitable, and nonsubstitutable.

Competence-based Strategy. A second "internal factors" theory of business strategy is competence-based theory. The term "distinctive competence" traces to Selznick (1957) and was used by Andrews (1971) and his colleagues in the SWOT model to refer to what an organization could do particularly well, relative to its competitors. Stimulating the development of competence-based theory in the early 1990s were the works of Chandler (1990), Hamel and Prahalad (1989, 1994a, 1994b), Prahalad and Hamel (1990, 1993), Reed and DeFillippi (1990), Lado, Boyd, and Wright (1992), and Teece and Pisano (1994). Numerous other theoretical and empirical articles have been developing competence-based theory (Aaker 1995; Bharadwaj, Varadarajan, and Fahy 1993; Day and Nedungadi 1994; Hamel and Heene 1994; Heene and Sanchez 1997; Sanchez, Heene, and Thomas 1996; and Sanchez and Heene 1997, 2000).

Prahalad and Hamel (1990, p. 81) argue that "the firm" should be viewed as both a collection of products or strategic business units and a collection of competences because "in the long run, competitiveness derives from an ability to build, at lower cost and more speedily than competitors, the core competencies that spawn unanticipated products." For Hamel and Prahalad (1994a), business strategy should focus on industry foresight and competence leveraging. *Foresight* involves anticipating the future by asking what new types of benefits firms should provide their customers in the next five to fifteen years and what new competences should be acquired or built to offer such benefits. *Resource leveraging* focuses on the numerator in the productivity equation. Specifically, they argue that too much attention in analyses of firm productivity has been devoted to resource efficiency—the denominator—and too little on resource effectiveness—the numerator.

For competence-based theorists, productivity gains and competitive advantage come through the resource leveraging that results from "more effectively concentrating resources on key strategic goals . . . more efficiently accumulating resources . . . complementing resources of one type with those of another to create higher-order value . . . conserving resources whenever possible, and . . . rapidly recovering resources by minimizing the time between expenditure and payback" (Hamel and Prahalad 1994a, p. 160). Therefore, the fundamental strategic thesis of the competence-based view of strategy is that, to achieve competitive advantage, and, thereby, superior financial performance, firms should identify, seek, develop, reinforce, maintain, and leverage distinctive competences.

9.4.2 Marketing Strategy

Marketing strategy, of course, overlaps significantly with business strategy. That is, strategic decisions in the areas of product, promotion, distribution, pricing, and the sales force, though significantly developed in marketing, are frequent topics in business strategy. Therefore, this section will focus on three topics that are, to a significant extent, distinctively *marketing* in character: market segmentation, market orientation, and relationship marketing.

Market Segmentation Strategy. The view that market segmentation is a key dimension of marketing strategy traces to Chamberlin's (1933) argument that intra-industry heterogeneity of demand is natural and to Smith's (1956) seminal marketing article that argued: "market segmentation may be regarded as a force in the market that will not be denied" (6). Since Smith's article, research on segmentation analysis has focused on the "basis variables" for segmenting markets and on data analysis techniques for generating market segments empirically. Common basis variables include demographics, psychographics, social class, stage in the family life cycle, personality, consumption patterns, and benefits sought. Common data analysis techniques include factor analysis, cluster analysis, latent class modeling, the automatic interaction detector, and multidimensional scaling (Myers 1996). The fundamental strategic thesis of market segmentation is that, to achieve competitive advantage, and, thereby, superior financial performance, firms should (1) identify segments of demand, (2) target specific segments, and (3) develop specific marketing "mixes" for each targeted market segment.

Market Orientation Strategy. The idea of market orientation traces to the marketing concept, which has been considered a marketing cornerstone since its articulation and development in the 1950s and 1960s. The marketing concept maintains that (a) all areas of the firm should be customer-oriented, (b) all marketing activities should be integrated, and (c) profits, not just sales, should be the objective. As conventionally interpreted, the concept's customer-orientation component, that is, knowing one's customers and developing products to satisfy their needs, wants, and desires, has been considered paramount. Historically contrasted with the production and sales orientations, the marketing concept is considered to be a philosophy of doing business that should be a major part of a successful firm's culture (Baker, Black, and Hart 1994; Wong and Saunders 1993). For Houston (1986, p. 82), it is the "optimal marketing management philosophy." For Deshpandé and Webster (1989, p. 3), "the marketing concept defines a distinct organizational culture . . . that put[s] the customer in the center of the firm's thinking about strategy and operations."

In the 1990s, the marketing concept morphed into market orientation. In this view, for Webster (1994, pp. 9, 10), "The customer must be put on a pedestal, standing above all others in the organization, including the owners and the managers." Nonetheless, he maintains, "having a customer orientation, although still a primary goal is not enough. Market-driven companies also are fully aware of competitors' product offerings and capabilities and how those are viewed by customers." At the same time, Narver and Slater (1990) and Slater and Narver (1994) were characterizing a market orientation as having the three components of customer orientation, competitor orientation, and interfunctional coordination. And Kohli and Jaworski (1990, p. 6) defined a market orientation as "the organizationwide *generation* of market intelligence pertaining to current and future customer needs, *dissemination* of the intelligence across departments, and organizationwide *responsiveness* to it" (italics in original). Therefore, the fundamental thesis of market orientation strategy is that, to achieve competitive advantage, and, thereby, superior financial performance, firms should systematically (1) gather information on present and potential customers and competitors and (2) use such information in a coordinated way across departments to guide strategy recognition, understanding, creation, selection, implementation, and modification (Hunt and Morgan 1995).

Relationship Marketing Strategy. The strategic area of relationship marketing was first defined by Berry (1983, p. 25) as "attracting, maintaining, and—in multi-service organizations—enhancing customer relationships." Since then, numerous other definitions have been offered. For example, Berry and Parasuraman (1991) propose that "relationship marketing concerns attracting, developing, and retaining customer relationships." Gummesson (1999, p. 1) proposes that "relationship marketing (RM) is marketing seen as relationships, networks, and interaction." Gronroos (1996, p. 11) states that "relationship marketing is to identify and establish, maintain, and enhance relationships with customers and other stakeholders, at a profit, so that the objectives of all parties involved are met; and that this is done by a mutual exchange and fulfillment of promises." Also for him, relationship marketing is "marketing . . . seen as the management of customer relationships (and of relationships with suppliers, distributors, and other network partners as well as financial institutions and other parties)" (Gronroos 2000, pp. 40–41). Sheth (1994) defines relationship marketing as "the understanding, explanation, and management of the ongoing collaborative business relationship between suppliers and customers." Sheth and Parvatiyar (1995) view relationship marketing as "attempts to involve and integrate customers, suppliers, and other infrastructural partners into a firm's developmental and marketing activities." Morgan and Hunt (1994) propose that "relationship marketing refers to all marketing activities directed towards establishing, developing, and maintaining successful relational exchanges."

Although the various perspectives on relationship marketing differ, one common element is that all view relationship marketing as implying that, increasingly, firms are competing through developing relatively long-term relationships with stakeholders such as customers, suppliers, employees, and competitors. Consistent with the Nordic School (Gronroos and Gummesson 1985; Gronroos 2000) and the IMP Group (Hakansson 1982; Ford 1990; Axelsson and Easton 1992), the emerging thesis seems to be: to be an effective *competitor* (in the global economy) requires one to be an effective *cooperator* (in some network) (Hunt and Morgan 1994). Indeed, for Sheth and Parvatiyar (1995), the "purpose of relationship marketing is, therefore, to enhance marketing productivity by achieving efficiency and effectiveness."

It is important to point out that none of the previously cited authors naively maintains that a firm's efficiency and effectiveness are always enhanced by establishing relationships with all potential stakeholders. Clearly, advocates of relationship marketing recognize that firms should at times avoid developing certain relationships. As Gummesson (1995, p. 15) observes, "Not all relationships are important to all companies all the time . . . some marketing is best handled as transaction marketing." Indeed, he counsels firms: "Establish which relationship portfolio is essential to your specific business and make sure it is handled skillfully" (p. 15). Therefore, the fundamental thesis of relationship marketing strategy is that, to achieve competitive advantage, and, thereby, superior financial performance, firms should identify, develop, and nurture a relationship portfolio.

9.5 STRATEGY AND R-A THEORY

This section argues that resource-advantage theory is toward a general theory of marketing because it provides a positive theory that forms a foundation for the normative area of strategy. Each of the six theories of strategy overviewed in sections 9.4.1 and 9.4.2 will be discussed, but in slightly different order. Indeed, the best place to begin is with market segmentation.

9.5.1 Market Segmentation Strategy and R-A Theory

As discussed, the fundamental strategic thesis of market segmentation is that, to achieve competitive advantage and superior financial performance, firms should (1) identify segments of industry demand, (2) target specific segments of demand, and (3) develop specific marketing "mixes" for each targeted market segment. A positive theory of competition that could ground normative market segmentation theory (1) must permit a segmentation strategy to be successful and (2) contribute to explaining why and/or when (i.e., under what circumstances) such a strategy may be successful.

First, consider foundational premise P_1 in Table 9.1. It states that demand is heterogeneous across industries, heterogeneous within industries, and dynamic. "Heterogeneous within industries" implies that demand in the overwhelming majority of industries is *substantially* heterogeneous. Hence, it makes no sense to draw demand curves for most industries. There are far more industries like motor vehicles (SIC #3711), women's footwear (#3144), and book publishing (#2731) than there are industries like corn (SIC #0115), gold ores (#1041), and industrial sand (#1446).

Now consider the nature of competition. For R-A theory, as shown in Figures 9.1 and 9.2, competition consists of the constant struggle among firms for comparative advantages in resources that will yield marketplace positions of competitive advantage for some market segment(s,) and, thereby, superior financial performance. Therefore, R-A theory views market segments as the basic unit of competition. Firms compete against each other on a segment-by-segment basis, not on an industrywide basis.

Now consider the nature of *product* or what R-A theory refers to as *market offering*. For R-A theory, a market offering is a distinct entity that is (1) comprised of a bundle of attributes, which (2) may be tangible or intangible, objective or subjective, and that (3) may be viewed by some potential buyer(s) as a want satisfier. Most market offerings have blends of tangible (e.g., an automobile's engine, tires, and transmission) and intangible attributes (e.g., an automobile's warranty, reliability, and prestige). If tangible attributes predominate, market offerings are referred to as goods; if intangibles predominate, they are services. Attributes are relatively more objective or subjective depending on the degree of uniformity across buyers as to (1) the importance weights given to different attributes, (2) the extent to which different market offerings have or do not have different attributes, and (3) the extent to which different offerings have different levels of attributes. In all cases, consumer perceptions—subjective factors—are dispositive. Market offerings perceived by consumers to be closer to their ideal constellation of attributes and their ideal level of each attribute are more valuable.

Now consider Figure 9.2 and cells 8 and 9. In cell 8, the firm's market offering is viewed by members of the segment as being of parity value. However, the value produced by the firm is achieved at higher resource costs than competitors. This position leads to inferior financial performance. In cell 9, the market offering is viewed as being of superior value, but because the value is achieved at higher resource costs, financial performance (depending on the relative value/relative costs ratio) may be inferior, parity, or superior, when compared with rivals.

Therefore, the preceding analysis shows why R-A theory *permits* the success of segmentation strategy and provides guidance as to when it will be successful. R-A theory permits the success of segmentation strategy because (1) intra-industry demand is presumed to be heterogeneous, (2) competition is considered to be segment by segment, (3) market offerings tailored closely to a segment's ideal constellation of attributes will be perceived by the segment as more valuable, which can lead (4) to marketplace positions of competitive advantage, and, thereby, (5) to the firm's objective of superior financial performance.

The preceding also provides guidance as to when a market segmentation strategy will be successful. The strategy will be more successful (or more likely to be successful) when (1) intra-industry demand is *more* heterogeneous, (2) the target segment of demand is relatively large, (3) the market offering is well tailored to the segment's tastes and preferences, (4) competitors' offerings are not well tailored to each segment, and (5) the firm's resource costs, relative to competitors, of catering to each segment does not push the firm into cells 8 or 9 in Figure 9.2.

With regard to point (5) in the preceding conditions, for example, consider firms *A* and *B* in industry *X* competing for segments X_1, X_2, and X_3. *A* produces a single "general purpose" market offering, whereas *B* produces three offerings, each one closely tailored to a different segment. If *B* is able to maintain parity resource costs, it will occupy cell 6, and, relative to *A* (who will occupy cell 4), have a position of competitive advantage for X_1, X_2, and X_3. Now assume that *A*'s resource costs are substantially lower than *B*'s (because, for example, of the production efficiencies in producing only one standard offering) and *A*'s offering is viewed by X_1 and X_2 as "good enough" and by X_3 as "not nearly good enough." Under these circumstances, *A* will occupy cell 2 for X_1 and X_2 and cell 1 for X_3. Conversely, *B* will occupy cell 8 for X_1 and X_2 and cell 9 for X_3. That is, *A* will have a competitive advantage for X_1 and X_2, but (by virtue of its low value produced/resource cost ratio) be at a competitive disadvantage for X_3. *B* will have a competitive advantage for X_3 (because of its high value produced/resource cost ratio), but be at a competitive disadvantage for X_1 and X_2.

In conclusion, R-A theory, a positive theory of competition, provides a foundation for the normative theory of market segmentation. R-A theory permits a segmentation strategy to work and gives guidance as to when it will be successful.

9.5.2 Resource-based Strategy and R-A Theory

As discussed, the fundamental thesis of resource-based strategy is that, to achieve competitive advantage, and, thereby, superior financial performance, firms should seek resources that are valuable, rare, imperfectly mobile, inimitable, and nonsubstitutable. A positive theory of competition that could ground normative, resource-based strategy (1) must permit such a strategy to be successful and (2) contribute to explaining why and when (i.e., under what circumstances) such a strategy may be successful.

First, R-A theory permits resource-based strategy to be successful because it specifically adopts a resource-based view of the firm. As P_7 in Table 9.1 notes, firms are viewed as combiners of heterogeneous and imperfectly mobile resources—which is the fundamental tenet of the "resource-based view" (Conner 1991). Indeed, competition for R-A theory consists of the constant struggle among firms for comparative advantages in such resources.

Note, however, that R-A theory adopts "a" resource-based view of the firm, not "the" view. As extensively discussed by Schulze (1994), many resource-based theorists view competition as an equilibrium-seeking process. Indeed, firms are often described as seeking "abnormal profits" or "economic rents," which in the neoclassical tradition imply "profits different from that of a firm in an industry characterized by perfect competition" and "profits in excess of the minimum necessary to keep a firm in business in long-run competitive equilibrium." Thus, because perfect is posited as ideal, that is, it is *perfect*, viewing competition as equilibrium-seeking and the goal of the firm as *abnormal* profits or *rents* implies that the achievement of sustained, superior financial performance by firms is detrimental to social welfare.

In contrast, R-A theory denies that competition is equilibrium-seeking and that perfect competition is the ideal competitive form. The achievement of superior financial performance—both temporary and sustained—is pro-competitive when it is consistent with and furthers the disequilibrating, ongoing process that consists of the constant struggle among firms for comparative advantage in resources that will yield marketplace positions of competitive advantage, and, thereby, superior financial performance. It is anti-competitive when it is inconsistent with and thwarts this process. Therefore, R-A theory maintains that when superior financial performance results from pro-competitive ("pro" in the sense of R-A theory) factors, it contributes to social welfare because the dynamic process of R-A competition furthers productivity and economic growth through both the efficient allocation of scarce tangible resources, and, more important, the creation of new tangible and intangible resources.

Specifically, the ongoing quest for superior financial performance, coupled with the fact that all firms cannot be simultaneously superior, implies that the process of R-A competition will not only allocate resources in an efficient manner, but also that there will be both proactive and reactive innovations developed that will contribute to further increases in efficiency and effectiveness. Indeed, it is the process of R-A competition that provides an important mechanism for firms to learn how efficient-effective, inefficient-ineffective, they are. (See the learning, feedback loops in Figure 9.1.) Similarly, it is the quest for superior performance by firms that results in the proactive and reactive innovations that, in turn, promote the very increases in firm productivity that constitute the technological progress that results in economic growth.

As to why and when a strategy of seeking resources that are "valuable, rare, imperfectly mobile, inimitable, and nonsubstitutable" will be successful, consider the "valuable" criterion. An entity may be valuable in many ways. For example, a firm's assets may include a section of land, or a building, or a painting that has value in the marketplace (and appears in the firm's balance sheet). But what R-A theory highlights is that *marketplace value* is not the key for understanding the nature of competition. Rather, a resource is "valuable" when it contributes to a firm's ability to efficiently and/or effectively produce a marketplace offering that *has value* for some market segment or segments. And, as discussed in section 9.5.1, consumer perceptions of value are dispositive.

Now consider the recommendation that valuable resources should be *rare*. Entities may be "rare" in many ways. What R-A theory highlights and emphasizes is that a valuable, "rare" resource is one that enables a firm, when competing for a market segment's patronage, to move upward and/or to the right in the marketplace position matrix (Figure 9.2). That is, valuable, *rare* resources enable firms to compete by being, relative to competitors, more efficient and/or more effective.

Now, in light of R-A theory's emphasis on proactive and reactive innovation, consider the recommendation that resources should be "inimitable and nonsubstitutable." To the list, R-A theory adds "nonsurpassable" (Hunt 1999). Firms occupying positions of competitive disadvantage (cells 4, 7, and 8 in Figure 9.2) will be motivated to engage in three forms of reactive innovation: (1) imitating the resource of an advantaged competitor, (2) finding (creating) an equivalent resource, or (3) finding (creating) a superior resource. Many authors have tended to focus on the equilibrating behavior of resource imitation and substitution. Although imitation and substitution are important forms of competitive actions, R-A theory highlights the fact that reactive innovation can also prompt disequilibrium-provoking behaviors. That is, reactive innovation in the form of finding (creating) a superior resource results in the innovating firm's new resource assortment enabling it to *surpass* the previously advantaged competitor in terms of either relative efficiency, or relative value, or both. By leapfrogging competitors, firms realize their objective of *superior* returns, make competition dynamic, shape their environments, and renew society. In so doing, the process of reactive innovation stimulates the kinds of major innovations described as creative destruction by Schumpeter (1950). Imitation brings parity returns; parity returns are never enough.

9.5.3 Competence-based Strategy and R-A Theory

The fundamental thesis of competence-based strategy is that, to achieve competitive advantage, and, thereby, superior financial performance, firms should identify, seek, develop, reinforce, maintain, and leverage distinctive competences. Organizational competences, all strategy theorists agree, have components that are significantly intangible (e.g., knowledge and skills) and are not *owned* by the firm (i.e., not capable of being *sold* by the firm). Recall that R-A theory acknowledges that both tangible and intangible entities can be resources. Recall also that entities need not be owned by firms to be resources. Rather they need only be *available* to firms.

Premise P_6 in Table 9.1 classifies firm resources as financial, physical, legal, human, organizational, informational, and relational. For R-A theory, therefore, a firm competence is a kind of *organizational* resource. Specifically, competences are "higher order" resources that are defined as socially and/or technologically complex, interconnected, combinations of tangible basic resources (e.g., basic machinery) and intangible basic resources (e.g., specific organizational policies and procedures and the skills and knowledge of specific employees) that fit coherently together in a synergistic manner. Competences are distinct resources because they exist as distinct packages of basic resources. Because competences are causally ambiguous, tacit, complex, and highly interconnected, they are likely to be significantly heterogeneous and asymmetrically distributed across firms in the same industry. Therefore, R-A theory permits competence-based strategy to be successful.

Differences in specific competences explain why some firms are simply better than others at *doing* things (Langlois and Robertson 1995; Hamel and Heene 1994; Sanchez, Heene, and Thomas 1996; Heene and Sanchez 1997; Sanchez and Heene 1997). For example, firms can have superior entrepreneurial competences (Foss 1993), research and development competences

(Roehl 1996), production competences (Prahalad and Hamel 1990), marketing competences (Conant, Mokwa, and Varadarajan 1990; Day 1992), and competitive agility competences (Nayyan and Bantel 1994).

Highlighted by R-A theory is the role of *renewal* competences, such as those described by Teece and Pisano (1994) and Teece, Pisano, and Shuen (1997) as "dynamic capabilities," by Dickson (1996) as "learning how to learn," and by Hamel and Prahalad (1994a, 1994b) as "industry foresight." Specifically, renewal competences prompt proactive innovation by enabling firms to (1) anticipate potential market segments (unmet, changing, and/or new needs, wants, and desires), (2) envision market offerings that might be attractive to such segments, and (3) foresee the need to acquire, develop, or create the required resources, including competences, to produce the envisioned market offerings. Therefore, because firms are not viewed by R-A theory as just passively responding to changing environment or looking for the best "fit" between existing resources and market "niches," it contributes to explaining why and when a firm developing a renewal competence will be successful. A strategy of developing a renewal competence will be successful when (1) the marketplace is turbulent, (2) competitors are "sleepy," and/or (3) the proactive innovations spawned by a renewal competence promotes turbulence.

9.5.4 Industry-based Strategy and R-A Theory

The fundamental thesis of industry-based strategy is that, to achieve competitive advantage, and, therefore, superior financial performance, firms should (1) choose industries and/or modify their structure, (2) select one of three generic strategies, and (3) manage well the activities in its value chain. Of course, as discussed in section 9.2.1, R-A theory rejects the notion that "choosing industry" is the key factor for strategy success. Indeed, empirical works on financial performance show clearly that "firm effects" dominate "industry effects" and competition is market segment by market segment. However, R-A theory does contribute to understanding when a strategy of expanding the firm's offerings to new segments in (1) the same industry or (2) a new industry will be successful. Such a strategy is more likely to be successful when the resources that the firm has (or can reasonably acquire or develop) are believed to be such that they enable it to produce a market offering that will occupy cells 2, 3, or 6 in Figure 9.2. That is, R-A theory highlights the role of resources in implementing a segment-based variant of industry-based strategy.

R-A theory also addresses the issue of the propriety of the recommendation that firm strategy should be directed at *altering* industry structure. As Fried and Oviatt (1989) point out, the "alter structure" recommendation is often (if not *most* often) interpreted as taking actions that will (1) drive competitors out of the marketplace in order to (2) increase industry concentration, and, thereby, (3) achieve superior financial performance. Therefore, the "alter structure" recommendation is customarily interpreted as advocating predatory practices—in potential violation of antitrust law.

As shown in Figure 9.1, R-A theory views competition as "embedded" (Granovetter 1985) within, for example, societal institutions and public policy. It is true that firms are often harmed by the actions of competitors. For example, if a firm introduces at competitive prices a new product that performs better than its rivals, then rival firms' sales and profits will likely be affected. However, R-A theory maintains that the harm to competitors is, or ought to be, a by-product of the process of competition, not the focus of competitors' actions. The goal of R-A competition is superior financial performance, not the harming of competitors. Because the goal can be achieved through competing for comparative advantages in resources, success neither implies nor depends on violating norms of public policy.

Finally, consider the recommendation of industry-based strategy that firms should perform well those activities in their value chains. Unfortunately, the value *chain* metaphor has limited applicability beyond manufacturing firms. Service firms and knowledge-based firms are poorly represented by linear, input-output chains of activities. However, though R-A theory minimizes the role of value chains, it highlights the importance of value creation as a key component of strategy. Indeed, value creation is central to Figure 9.2, the marketplace position matrix. Furthermore, R-A theory provides an explanation for the claim that some firms are superior to others in performing value creation activities: superior-performing firms in terms of value creation have a comparative advantage in resources, for example, specific competences related to specific value-producing activities.

9.5.5 Market Orientation Strategy and R-A Theory

The fundamental thesis of market orientation (MO) strategy is that, to achieve competitive advantage and superior financial performance, firms should systematically (1) gather information on present and potential customers and competitors and (2) use such information in a coordinated way to guide strategy recognition, understanding, creation, selection, implementation, and modification. R-A theory permits MO strategy to succeed because premise P_5 in Table 9.1 assumes that the firm's information is imperfect and premise P_6 indicates that information can be a resource.[6] That is, the (1) systematic acquisition of information about present and potential customers and competitors and the (2) coordinated use of such information to guide strategy may contribute to the firm's ability to efficiently and/or effectively produce market offerings that have value for some market segments.

If a firm is market oriented and its competitors are not, then an MO strategy may be a resource that moves the firm's marketplace position upward and to the right in Figure 9.2. Note, however, that premise P_5 in Table 9.1 also points out that information acquisition is costly. The implication is that if implementing an MO strategy is *too* costly, then the firm's position in Figure 9.2 will shift downward toward positions of competitive disadvantage. Therefore, whether an MO strategy provides a resource that leads to a position of competitive advantage in Figure 9.2 depends on the relative value/relative cost ratio of MO implementation.

Because it consists of a synergistic combination of more basic resources (Hunt and Lambe 2000), the effective implementation of a market orientation may be viewed as an organizational competence. To implement an MO strategy, firms deploy tangible resources, such as information systems to store, analyze, and disseminate information about competitors and customers. In addition, firms use intangible resources to implement MO. That is, organizational policies must be in place to encourage MO action, and managers must have the knowledge and experience required to utilize customer and competitor information effectively.

Specifically, a market orientation may be viewed as a kind of renewal competence discussed in section 9.5.3. That is, a competence in MO will prompt proactive innovation by enabling firms to anticipate potential market segments, envision market offerings that might be attractive to such segments, and prompt the need to acquire, develop, or create the required resources to produce the offerings. Furthermore, a competence in MO will assist efforts at reactive innovation because it provides valuable information about existing competitors and customers.

9.5.6 Relationship Marketing Strategy and R-A Theory

The fundamental thesis of relationship marketing strategy is that, to achieve competitive advantage, and, thereby, superior financial performance, firms should identify, develop, and nurture a relationship portfolio. Consider what is required for a theory of competition to permit a relationship marketing strategy to succeed. First, because relationships are intangible, the theory must permit intangibles to be resources. Second, because relationships are not owned (and, therefore, firms cannot buy and sell relationships in the "factor" markets), firm ownership must not be a criterion for an entity to be a firm resource. Third, because each relationship has unique characteristics (and, therefore, one cannot take the first derivative of any equation in which a relationship appears), unique entities must be allowed. Fourth, because (at least some) relationships involve cooperation among firms in order for them to compete, the theory must permit some relationships to be pro-competitive (and not presumptively assume all instances of cooperation to be anti-competitive *collusion*).

Now consider R-A theory with regard to its view of resources. A firm resource is any tangible or *intangible* entity *available* to the firm that enables it to produce efficiently and/or effectively a market offering that has value for some market segment(s). Therefore R-A theory satisfies criteria (1) and (2). Now recall that R-A theory views firm resources as significantly heterogeneous (premise P_7 in Table 9.1). Therefore, it satisfies criterion (3). Finally, because R-A theory assumes that (at least some) firm resources are imperfectly mobile (premise P_7), yet such resources can nonetheless enable firms to produce offerings efficiently and/or effectively, the theory satisfies criterion (4). That is, at least some cooperative relationships are *relational* resources (premise P_6), making them pro-competitive.

As discussed in Hunt (1997a), R-A theory implies that firms should periodically conduct a strategic resource audit as a standard part of its corporate planning. The strategic resource audit should pay close attention to the competences of the organization and the role that relationships with suppliers, customers, employees, and competitors can play in enhancing the total "mix" of strategic competences. From the perspective of relationship marketing, therefore, firms should develop a relationship portfolio or "mix" that complements existing competences (as discussed in section 9.5.3) and enables it to occupy positions of competitive advantage, as identified in Figure 9.2. However, it is important to recognize that relationship portfolios are *developed* not *selected.*

Because it conjures the image of being like a portfolio of stocks, Gummesson's (1999) concept of a relationship portfolio has the same systemic ambiguity as the marketing mix. The standard, textbook versions of the marketing mix concept often imply that some marketing manager sits down at a specific point in time and *selects* both a target market and a particular combination of price, product, place, and promotion that is believed to be optimal. Although this may occur on rare occasions, much more commonly these decisions are made sequentially, that is, over time. Therefore, it could well be the case that the first decision actually made was the nature of the product. Then a market segment is targeted for the product. Following that, the price, channels of distribution, and promotional programs are developed. The point is that, in contrast with standard textbook treatments, marketing mixes are most often developed over time, not selected at a point in time.

A similar ambiguity emerges in the concept of a relationship portfolio. Even more so than the marketing mix, relationship portfolios are not selected at a point in time, but developed over time. Indeed, good relationships take time to develop (Lambe, Spekman, and Hunt 2002). Therefore, though it is important to develop a relationship portfolio that complements existing organizational competences in an optimal manner and it is important to strategically plan for such relationships, the relationships that comprise the relationship portfolio can be developed only over time. Though both are *portfolios*, the relationship portfolio differs dramatically from a portfolio of stocks, for it is at least possible to select a portfolio of stocks at a single point in time. Consequently, a relationship marketing strategy will be more successful when it is a long-term strategy.

9.6 A FINAL NOTE

This work takes a philosophy of science approach to marketing theory. Unfortunately, much of the theory in marketing falls substantially short of fulfilling the requirements detailed in this monograph. Substantial evidence exists suggesting that the shortcomings of marketing theory can be attributed in large measure to misperceptions by marketing theorists as to the fundamental nature of theoretical constructions. It is the hope of this writer that the preceding analysis can play a constructive role in assisting theorists in their efforts to develop theory in marketing. The task of theory development is arduous, but the rewards are commensurate with the challenge.

The philosophy of science tool kit that has been developed here provides the theoretical analyst with a set of powerful instruments for analyzing theoretical and purportedly theoretical constructions in marketing. The evaluative criteria that have been developed are stringent. Therefore, a caveat for the would-be theoretical analyst: it is much easier to criticize someone else's theory than it is to develop one's own. Be constructive, not destructive, in your analysis. Furthermore, a caveat to existing and would-be marketing theorists: obtuse armchair philosophy does not constitute theory. Keep in mind that your theory must contain a systematically related set of statements, including some lawlike generalizations, that are empirically testable. Also keep in mind that the purpose of developing your theory is to increase scientific understanding through a systematized structure capable of explaining and predicting marketing phenomena.

This final chapter has argued that resource-advantage theory is a step toward developing a general theory of marketing because R-A theory (1) is a general theory of competition, (2) accommodates and integrates key concepts and generalizations from Alderson's functionalist theory, and (3) provides a positive foundation for normative marketing strategy. Why "toward" a general theory of marketing? Because much work needs to be done to further (1) test the micro-positive and macro-positive dimensions of the theory, (2) develop the theory's micro-normative and macro-normative implications, and (3) use the theory to explain the four fundamental explananda detailed in section 4.5. Like the process of R-A competition, the process of marketing research is nonconsummatory. Just as there is always a higher level of performance for competitors to seek, there is always more about marketing for researchers to learn.

QUESTIONS FOR ANALYSIS AND DISCUSSION

1. The purpose of scientific theories is to explain and predict phenomena, thereby contributing to understanding phenomena. What should a theory of competition explain and predict? Why?
2. Resource-advantage theory is claimed to be an interdisciplinary theory. In particular, it "draws on" and "has affinities with" numerous other theories and research traditions. What is the difference between *draws on* and *has affinities with*? Is this distinction important? If so, why? If not, why not?
3. "Although patents are not legal resources, a trademark and a license to produce a product granted by the patent holder are." Evaluate this position.
4. What is the difference between an *efficiency* advantage and an *effectiveness* advantage? *Ceteris paribus*, which kind of advantage is likely to last longer? Upon which kind of advantage has marketing historically focused? Why? Upon which kind of advantage has neoclassical economics focused? Why?
5. What does it mean to claim that innovation is endogenous to resource-advantage competition, but exogenous to perfect competition? Why is it important to have a theory of competition in which innovation is endogenous? Why is it the case that neoclassical economics cannot adopt the simple expedient of allowing perfect competition to have innovation be endogenous?
6. Clark maintains that competition should result in "a diffusion of the gains of progress." What does he mean by the "gains of progress?" To *whom* should the gains be diffused? Does R-A theory diffuse the gains of progress? If so, how? If not, should the theory be modified to accommodate the diffusion of gains?
7. Alderson (1965, p. 186) writes: "To state the essence of market segmentation more succinctly, it is the policy of selecting a group of

customers with relatively homogeneous demands out of an area of consumer use which is heterogeneous in the aggregate and so deriving production economies from that selection." Evaluate.

8. Neoclassical economics has historically viewed "product differentiation" as being contrary to the best interests of consumers because it establishes "monopoly." On the other hand, Alderson (1965, p. 185) states: "Chamberlin began with product differentiation and only in his later years came to realize that heterogeneity is inherent on the demand side of the market and is not necessarily created by the supplier." Why is it important to distinguish between "inherent" heterogeneity and "created" heterogeneity? Is "created heterogeneity" antisocial? Why or why not?
9. What is the difference between " profit-maximization" and "superior financial performance?" Why is this difference important?
10. As Barney and Ouchi (1986, p. 374) point out, when strategy is guided by industrial-organization economics, I-O theory is "turned upside down." That is, what was considered anticompetitive and socially undesirable under neoclassical, industrial-organization economics becomes the basis for normative competitive strategy. Discuss the implications for firms and societies of adopting industry-based strategies.
11. There is a *Journal of Market Segmentation*, but there is no *Journal of Product Differentiation*. Why?
12. How does the marketing concept differ from a firm being market oriented?
13. Is it important to have a theory of competition that provides a theoretical grounding for marketing strategy? If so, why? If not, why not?
14. Is it important to distinguish between adopting "a" resource-based view of the firm and not "the" resource-based theory of the firm? If so, why? If not, why not?
15. Find a type of marketing strategy other than market segmentation, market orientation, and relationship marketing. Would resource-advantage theory provide a positive foundation for the strategy you identify? If so, why? If not, why not?
16. What is the difference, if any, between viewing a market orientation as an aspect of a firm's *culture* and viewing it as a kind of firm *strategy*? Discuss the pros and cons of viewing market orientation as culture versus strategy. Could it be *both* culture and strategy?

NOTES

1. Sheth (2001) argues that Hunt (2000b) should have been titled *A General Theory of Marketing* instead of *A General Theory of Competition*. In contrast, the view here is that R-A theory *is* a general theory of competition, but it is only *toward* a general theory of marketing.

2. By the time of McGahan and Porter (1997), the entire nature of the debate over firm performance had changed dramatically. Originally, advocates of industry-based strategy (e.g., Montgomery and Porter 1991) were citing Schmalensee (1985) to justify their focusing on "choosing industry" as the key strategic decision. After Rumelt's (1991) replication and extension of Schmalensee found firm factors to account for almost six times the variance of industry factors (46 percent vs. 8 percent), the debate shifted toward whether industry choice matters *at all*. Thus, McGahan and Porter's (1997) study, which finds that firm effects dominate industry effects by *only* 36 percent to 19 percent, is interpreted by its authors as confronting the challenge from Rumelt and others that industry, far from being *key*, doesn't seem to matter at all. The point to be emphasized here is that no one now claims empirical support for the neoclassical position. That is, after Rumelt's (1991) and other studies, no one argues seriously the neoclassical position that either industry is everything or industry effects dominate firm effects. Stated differently, despite the fact that Schmalensee (1985) is still cited frequently, no one arguing the neoclassical position on firm performance can now be taken seriously.

3. The discussion here and in the next section follows closely the review in Hunt (2000b).

4. Throughout his 1961 book, Clark (pp. 9, 13, 18, 213) gives definitions of "competition." Although each is consistent with his 1954 work, cited here, none appears to be as complete, yet still succinct.

5. Surveys of marketing scholars identify Alderson as the scholar who has most contributed to the development of marketing theory (Chonko and Dunne 1982). See Hunt, Muncy, and Ray (1981) for a detailed explication of Alderson's functionalist theory of market processes.

6. The discussion here follows the analysis in Hunt and Morgan (1995) and Hunt and Lambe (2000).

REFERENCES

Aaker, David A. 1971. "Visual Clustering Using Principal Components Analysis." In *Multivariate Analysis in Marketing*, ed. David A. Aaker, 321–24. Belmont, CA: Wadsworth.

———. 1995. *Strategic Market Management*. New York: Wiley.

Abel, T. 1948. "The Operation Called *Verstehen*." *American Journal of Sociology* 54, no. 2: 211–18.

Adler, Lee. 1967. "Systems Approach to Marketing." *Harvard Business Review* 45 (May–June): 104–11.

Alderson, Wroe. 1957. *Marketing Behaviòr and Executive Action*. Homewood, IL: Irwin.

———. 1965. *Dynamic Marketing Behavior*. Homewood, IL: Irwin.

Anderson, Don S. 1936. "The Consumer and the A.A.A." *Journal of Marketing* 1 (July): 3–8.

Anderson, Paul F. 1983. "Marketing, Scientific Progress and Scientific Method." *Journal of Marketing* 47 (Fall): 18–31.

———. 1986. "On Method in Consumer Research: A Critical Relativist Perspective." *Journal of Consumer Research* 13 (September): 155–73.

Andrews, Kenneth R. 1971/1980/1987. *The Concept of Corporate Strategy*. Homewood, IL: Irwin.

Angeles, Peter A. 1981. *Dictionary of Philosophy*. New York: Barnes and Noble.

Arndt, Johan. 1981a. "The Conceptual Domain of Marketing: An Evaluation of Shelby Hunt's Three Dichotomies Model." *European Journal of Marketing* (Fall)): 27–36.

———. 1981b. "The Political Economy of Marketing Systems: Reviving the Institutional Approach." *Journal of Macromarketing* 1 (Fall): 36–47.

———. 1985. "The Tyranny of Paradigms: The Case for Paradigmatic Pluralism in Marketing." In *Changing the Course of Marketing: Alternative Paradigms for Widening Marketing Theory*, ed. N. Dholakia and S. Arndt, 3–26. Greenwich, CT: JAI Press.

Axelsson, B., and G. Easton. 1992. *Industrial Networks: A New View of Reality*. London: Gower.

Bagozzi, Richard P. 1974. "Marketing as an Organized Behavioral System of Exchange." *Journal of Marketing* 38 (October): 77–81.

———. 1979. "Toward a Formal Theory of Marketing Exchanges." In *Conceptual and Theoretical Developments in Marketing*, ed. O.C. Ferrell, Stephen Brown, and Charles Lamb, 431–47. Chicago: American Marketing Association.

———. 1980. *Causal Models in Marketing*. New York: Wiley.

Bain, Joe S. 1956. *Barriers to New Competition*. Cambridge, MA: Harvard University Press.

Baker, Michael J.; C.D. Black; and S.J. Hart. 1994. "Competitive Success in Sunrise and Sunset Industries." In *The Marketing Initiative*, ed. J. Saunders, 58–71. London: Prentice Hall.

Barger, Harold. 1955. *Distribution's Place in the Economy Since 1869*. Princeton: Princeton University Press.

Barney, Jay. 1991. "Firm Resources and Sustained Competitive Advantage." *Journal of Management* 17, no. 1: 99–120.

———. 1992. "Integrating Organizational Behavior and Strategy Formulation Research: A Resource-based Analysis." In *Advances in Strategic Management*, ed. P. Shriviastava, A.S. Hugg, and J.E. Dutton, 39–61. Greenwich, CT: JAI Press.

Barney, Jay, and William G. Ouchi. 1986. *Organizational Economics*. San Francisco: Jossey-Bass.

Bartels, Robert. 1951. "Can Marketing Be a Science?" *Journal of Marketing* 15, no. 3: 319–28.

———. 1962. *The Development of Marketing Thought*. Homewood, IL: Irwin.

———. 1968. "The General Theory of Marketing." *Journal of Marketing* 32 (January): 29–33.

———. 1970. *Marketing Theory and Metatheory*. Homewood, IL: Irwin.

Barwise, Patrick. 1995. "Good Empirical Generalizations." *Marketing Science* 14, no. 3: G29–35.

Bass, Frank N. 1969. "A New Product Growth Model for Consumer Durables." *Management Science* (January): 215–27.

———. 1974. "The Theory of Stochastic Brand Preference and Brand Switching." *Journal of Marketing Research* 11 (February): 1–20.

———. 1995. "Empirical Generalizations and Marketing Science: A Personal View." *Marketing Science* 14, no. 3: G6–19.

Bass, Frank N., and Thomas L. Pilon. 1980. "A Stochastic Brand Choice Framework for Econometric Modeling of Time Series Market Share Behavior." *Journal of Marketing Research* 17 (November): 486–97

Bass, Frank N., and Jerry Wind. 1995. "Introduction to the Special Issue: Empirical Generalizations in Marketing." *Marketing Science* 14, no. 3: G1–5.

Bauer, Raymond. 1960. "Consumer Behavior and Risk Taking." In Proceedings of the Forty-third Conference of the American Marketing Association, 389–98.

———. [1965] 1973. "A Revised Model of Source Effect." Presidential Address to the American Psychological Association Annual Meeting. Reprinted in *Buyer Behavior*, ed. John A. Howard and Lyman E. Ostland, 124–38. New York: Knopf.

———. 1967a. "Games People and Audiences Play." Paper presented at Seminar on Communication in Contemporary Society, University of Texas.

———. 1967b. "Risk Taking in Drug Addiction: The Role of Company Preference." In *Risk Taking and Information Handling in Consumer Behavior*, ed. Donald Cox. Boston: Harvard Business School.

Baumol, W.J. 1957. "On the Role of Marketing Theory." *Journal of Marketing* 21 (April): 18–22.

Belk, R.W.; M. Wallendorf; and J.F. Sherry. 1989. "The Sacred and the Profane in Consumer Behavior—Theodicy on the Odyssey." *Journal of Consumer Research* 16, no. 1: 1–38.

Bennett, Peter D. 1988. *Dictionary of Marketing Terms*. Chicago: American Marketing Association.

Bentler, P.M. 1990. "Comparative Fit Indices in Structural Models." *Psychological Bulletin* 107, no. 3: 238–46.

Berelson, Bernard, and Gary Steiner. 1964. *Human Behavior: An Inventory of Scientific Findings*. New York: Harcourt Brace Jovanovich.

Bergmann, Gustav. 1957. *Philosophy of Science*. Madison: University of Wisconsin Press.

———. 1968. "Imperfect Knowledge." In *Readings in the Philosophy of the Social Sciences*, ed. May Brodbeck, 415–35. Toronto: Collier Macmillan.

Berry, L.L. 1983. "Relationship Marketing." In *Emerging Perspectives on Services Marketing*, ed. L. Berry, G.L. Shostock, and G.D. Upah, 25–28. Chicago: American Marketing Association.

Berry, L.L., and A. Parasuraman. 1991. *Marketing Services*. New York: Free Press.

Bettman, James R., and J. Morgan Jones. 1972. "Formal Models of Consumer Behavior: A Conceptual Overview." *Journal of Business* (October): 544–62.

Bharadwaj, Sundar; P. Rajan Varadarajan; and John Fahy. 1993. "Sustainable Competitive Advantage in Service Industries: A Conceptual Model and Research Propositions." *Journal of Marketing* 57, no. 4: 83–99.

Blalock, Hubert M. 1969. *Theory Construction*. Englewood Cliffs, NJ: Prentice Hall.

Blanchard, C.H.; C.R. Burnett; R.G. Stoner; and R.L. Weber. 1972. *Introduction to Modern Physics*. Englewood Cliffs, NJ: Prentice Hall.

Blattberg, Robert C.; Richard Briesch; and Edward J. Fox. 1995. "How Promotions Work." *Marketing Science* 14, no. 3: G122–32.

Blaug, Mark. 1980. *The Methodology of Economics*. Cambridge, UK: Cambridge University Press.

Bloom, Alan. 1987. *The Closing of the American Mind*. New York: Simon and Schuster.

———.1990. *Giants and Dwarfs: Essays 1960–1990*. New York: Simon and Schuster.

Bock, R.D., and R.E. Borgman. 1966. "Analysis of Covariance Structures." *Psychometrics* 31: 507–34.

Bogart, Leo. 1962. "How Do People Read Newspapers?" *Media/Scope* 6 (January).

Bollen, K.A. 1989. *Structural Equations with Latent Variables*. New York: Wiley.

Borden, Neil. 1942. *The Economic Effects of Advertising*. Homewood, IL: Irwin.

Braithwaite, Richard B. 1968. *Scientific Explanation*. Cambridge, UK: Cambridge University Press.

Bridgman, P.W. 1927. *The Logic of Modern Physics*. New York: Macmillan.

———. 1938. "Operational Analysis." *Philosophy of Science* 5, no. 2: 114–31.

———. 1951. "The Nature of Some of Our Physical Concepts—I." *British Journal for the Philosophy of Science* 1, no. 3: 257–72.

Brodbeck, May. 1962. "Explanation, Prediction, and 'Imperfect' Knowledge." In *Scientific Explanation, Space, and Time*, ed. Herbert Feigl and Grover Maxwell, 231–72. Minneapolis: University of Minnesota.

———, ed. 1968. *Readings in the Philosophy of the Social Sciences*. New York: Macmillan.

———. 1982. "Recent Developments in the Philosophy of Science." In *Marketing Theory: Philosophy of Science Perspectives*, ed. Ronald F. Bush and Shelby D. Hunt, 1–7. Chicago: American Marketing Association.

Brody, B.A. 1972. "Toward an Aristotelian Theory of Scientific Explanation." *Philosophy of Science* 39, no. 1: 20–31.

Brody, Robert, and Scott Cunningham. 1968. "Personality Variables and the Consumer Decision Process." *Journal of Marketing Research* 5 (February): 50–57.

Bromberger, S. 1966. "Why Questions." In *Mind and Cosmos: Explorations in the Philosophy of Science*, ed. R. Colodny, 86–111. Pittsburgh: University of Pittsburgh Press.

Brubacher, John S., and Willis Rudy. 1976. *Higher Education in Transition: A History of American Colleges and Universities. 1636–1776*. New York: Harper and Row.

Bucklin, Louis P. 1963. "Retail Strategy and the Classification of Goods." *Journal of Marketing* 27 (January): 50–55.

———. 1972. *Competition and Evolution in the Distributive Trades*. Englewood Cliffs, NJ: Prentice Hall.

———. 1978. *Productivity in Marketing*. Chicago: American Marketing Association.

Bunge, Mario. 1961. "Kinds and Criteria of Scientific Laws." *Philosophy of Science* 28, no. 3: 260–81.

———. 1967a. *Scientific Research. Vol. 1: The Search for a System*. New York: Springer-Verlag.

———. 1967b. *Scientific Research. Vol. 2: The Search for Truth*. New York: Springer-Verlag.

Buzzell, Robert D. 1963. "Is Marketing a Science?" *Harvard Business Review* 41 (January–February): 32–40, 166–70.

Buzzell, Robert D.; Bradley T. Gale; and Ralph G.M. Sutton. 1975. "Market Share: A Key to Profitability." *Harvard Business Review* 53 (January–February): 97–106.

Campbell, N.R. 1952. *What Is Science?* New York: Dover.

Canton, Irving D. 1973. "A Functional Definition of Marketing." *Marketing News* (July 15): 2.

Carmen, James M. 1973. "On the Universality of Marketing." *Journal of Contemporary Business* 2 (Autumn): 1–16.

Carnap, Rudolf. 1950. *Logical Foundations of Probability*. Chicago: University of Chicago Press.

———. 1956. "The Methodological Character of Theoretical Concepts." In *The Foundations of Science and the Concepts of Psychology and Psychoanalysis*, Minnesota Studies in the Philosophy of Science, ed. Herbert Feigl and Michael Scriven, vol. 1, 38–76. Minneapolis: University of Minnesota Press.

———. 1962. "The Aim of Inductive Logic." In *Logic Methodology and Philosophy of Science*, ed. E. Nagel, P. Suppes, and A. Tarski, 303–18. Stanford, CA: Stanford University Press.

Chamberlin, Edward. 1933/1962. *The Theory of Monopolistic Competition*. Cambridge, MA: Harvard University Press.

Chandler, Alfred D. 1990. *Scale and Scope: The Dynamics of Industrial Capitalism*. Cambridge, MA: Harvard University Press.

Chonko, Lawrence B., and Patrick M. Dunne. 1982. "Marketing Theory: A Status Report." In *Marketing Theory: Philosophy of Science Perspectives*, ed. R.F. Bush and S.D. Hunt, 43–46. Chicago: American Marketing Association.

Christianson, C.R.; K.R. Andrews; J.L. Bower; G. Hamermesh; and M.E. Porter. 1982. *Business Policy: Text and Cases*. Homewood, IL: Irwin.

Churchill, Gilbert A., Jr.; Neil M. Ford; and Orville C. Walker. 1976. "Organizational Climate and Job Satisfaction in the Salesforce." *Journal of Marketing Research* 13 (November): 323–32.

Clark, Desmond M. 1979. "Discussion: Teleology and Mechanism: M. Grene's Absurdity Argument." *Philosophy of Science* 46, no. 3: 321–25.

Clark, John M. 1940. "Toward a Concept of Workable Competition." *American Economic Review* 30 (June): 241–56.

———. 1954. "Competition and the Objectives of Government Policy." In *Monopoly and Competition and Their Regulation*, ed. E. Chamberlin, 317–37. London: Macmillan.

———. 1961. *Competition as a Dynamic Process*. Washington, DC: Brookings Institution.

Clark, Joseph T. 1969. "The Philosophy of Science and the History of Science." In *Critical Problems in the History of Science*, ed. Marshall Clagett, 103–40. Madison: University of Wisconsin Press.

Cohen, Morris R., and Ernest Nagel. 1934. *Logic and the Scientific Method*. New York: Harcourt Brace Jovanovich.

Conant, Jeffrey S.; Michael P. Mokwa; and P. Rajan Varadarajan. 1990. "Strategic Types, Distinctive Marketing Competencies, and Organizational Performance." *Strategic Marketing Journal* 11 (September): 365–83.

Conner, Kathleen. 1991. "A Historical Comparison of Resource-Based Theory and Five Schools of Thought Within Industrial-Organization Economics: Do We Have a New Theory of the Firm?" *Journal of Management* 17 (March): 121–54.

Converse, Paul D. 1945. "The Development of a Science of Marketing." *Journal of Marketing* 10 (July): 14–23.

———. 1949. "New Laws of Retail Gravitation." *Journal of Marketing* 14 (October): 379–84.

Cooke, Roger M. 1981. "Discussion: A Paradox in Hempel's Criterion of Maximal Specificity." *Philosophy of Science* 48 (June): 327–28.

Copeland, Melvin T. 1923. "Relation of Consumers' Buying Habits to Marketing Methods." *Harvard Business Review* 1 (April): 282–89.

Cowan, Donald R.G. 1960. "A Pioneer in Marketing: Louis H.D. Weld." *Journal of Marketing* 24 (October): 63–66.

Cox, Donald F., and Raymond Bauer. 1964. "Self-Confidence and Persuasibility in Women." *Public Opinion Quarterly* 27 (Fall): 453–66.

Cox, Reavis. 1965. *Distribution in a High Level Economy*. Englewood Cliffs, NJ: Prentice Hall.

Coyne, J.C. 1982. "A Brief Introduction to Epistobabble." *Family Therapy Networker* 6: 27–28.

Dawson, Leslie. 1971. "Marketing Science in the Age of Aquarius." *Journal of Marketing* 35 (July): 66–72.

Day, George S. 1992. "Marketing's Contribution to the Strategy Dialogue." *Journal of the Academy of Marketing Science* 20 (Fall): 323–30.

Day, George S., and Prakesh Nedungadi. 1994. "Managerial Representations of Competitive Advantage." *Journal of Marketing* 58 (April): 31–44.

Day, George S., and R. Wensley. 1983. "Marketing Theory with a Strategic Orientation." *Journal of Marketing* 47 (Fall): 43–55.

Deshpandé, Rohit, and Frederick E. Webster, Jr. 1989. "Organizational Culture and Marketing: Defining the Research Agenda." *Journal of Marketing* 53 (January): 3–15.

Dewey, John. 1938. *Logic: The Theory of Inquiry*. New York: Holt, Rinehart and Winston.

Diamantopoulos, Adamantios, and Heidi M. Winklhofer. 2001. "Index Construction with Formative Indicators: An Alternative to Scale Development." *Journal of Marketing Research* 38 (May): 269–77.

Dickson, Peter R. 1996. "The Static and Dynamic Mechanics of Competitive Theory." *Journal of Marketing* 60 (October): 102–6.

Dieks, D. 1980. "Discussion: On the Empirical Content of Determinism." *Philosophy of Science* 47, no. 1: 124–30.

Dierickx, Ingemar, and Karel Cool. 1989. "Asset Stock Accumulation and Sustainability of Competitive Advantage." *Management Science* 35 (December): 1504–11.

Dodd, S.C. 1968. "Systemmetrics for Evaluating Symbolic Systems." *Systemmatics* 6, no. 1: 27–49.

Doehlert, David H. 1968. "Similarity and Preference Mapping: A Color Example." *Marketing and the New Science of Planning*, ed. Robert L. King, 250–58. Chicago: American Marketing Association.

Donagan, Alan. 1966. "The Popper-Hempel Theory Reconsidered." In *Philosophical Analysis and History*, ed. W. Dray, 127–59. New York: Harper and Row.

Dont, Rajiv P.; James R. Lumpkin; and Robert P. Bush. 1990. "Private Physicians or Walk-In Clinics: Do the Patients Differ?" *Journal of Health Care Marketing* 10, no. 2: 25–35.

Dubin, Robert. 1969. *Theory Building*. New York: Free Press.

Duncan, Greg J. 1984. *Years of Poverty, Years of Plenty: The Changing Economic Fortunes of American Workers and Families*. Ann Arbor: University of Michigan Institute for Social Research.

Edwards, Paul. 1951. "Bertrand Russell's Doubts about Induction." In *Logic and Language*, ed. A.G.N. Flew, 55–79. Oxford: Basil Blackwell.

———. 1972. *The Encyclopedia of Philosophy*, vol. 3. New York: Macmillan and Free Press.

Ehrenberg, A.S.C. 1971. "Laws in Marketing: A Tailpiece." In *New Essays in Marketing Theory*, ed. G. Fisk, 28–39. Boston: Allyn and Bacon.

———. 1994. "Theory or Well-Based Results: Which Comes First?" In *Research Traditions in Marketing*, ed. Gilles Laurent, Gary L. Lilien, and Bernard Pras, 79–108. Boston: Kluwer.

———. 1995. "Empirical Generalizations, Theory, and Method." *Marketing Science* 14, no. 3: G20–28.

Einstein, Albert. 1923. *Sidelights on Relativity*. New York: Dutton.

El-Ansary, Adel. 1979. "The General Theory of Marketing: Revisited." In *Conceptual and Theoretical Developments in Marketing*, ed. O.C. Ferrell, Stephen W. Brown, and Charles Lamb Jr., 399–407. Chicago: American Marketing Association.

Engel, James E.; David B. Kollat; and Roger Blackwell. 1973. *Consumer Behavior*, 2d ed. New York: Holt, Rinehart and Winston.

Enis, Ben M. 1986. "Comments on Marketing Education in the 1980s and Beyond: The Rigor/Relevance Rift." In *Marketing Education: Knowledge Development, Dissemination, and Utilization*, ed. Joseph Giltinan and Dale Achabal, 1–4. Chicago: American Marketing Association.

Etgar, Michael. 1977. "Comment on the Nature and Scope of Marketing." *Journal of Marketing* 41 (October): 14, 16, 146.

Falkenberg, A.W. 2000. "Competition and Markets." *Journal of Macromarketing* 20 (June): 8–9.

Farber, I.E. 1968. "Personality and Behavioral Science." In *Readings in the Philosophy of Social Sciences*, ed. May Brodbeck, 145–79. New York: Macmillan.

Farley, John U., and Harold J. Leavitt. 1971. "Marketing and Population Problems." *Journal of Marketing* 35 (July): 28–33.

Farley, John U., and L. Winston Ring. 1970. "An Empirical Test of the Howard-Sheth Model of Buyer Behavior." *Journal of Marketing Research* 7 (November): 427–38.

Fenner, Frank, and David White. 1976. *Medical Virology*. New York: Academic Press.

Ferber, Robert. 1970. "The Expanding Role of Marketing in the 1970's." *Journal of Marketing* 34 (January): 20–30.

Ferrell, O.C.; Stephen W. Brown; and Charles W. Lamb, Jr., ed. 1979. *Conceptual and Theoretical Developments in Marketing*. Chicago: American Marketing Association.

Ferrell, O.C., and J.R. Perrachione. 1980. "An Inquiry into Bagozzi's Formal Theory of Marketing Exchanges." In *Theoretical Developments in Marketing*, ed. C. Lamb and P. Dunne, 158–61. Chicago: American Marketing Association.

Festinger, Leon. 1957. *A Theory of Cognitive Dissonance*. Evanston, WY: Harper and Row.

Fetzer, James H. 1977. "Book Review of Robert J. Ackerman. *The Philosophy of Karl Popper*." *Philosophy of Science* 44, no. 4: 491–93.

Feyerabend, Paul K. 1970. "Against Method." In *Analysis of Theories and Methods of Physics and Psychology*, ed. Michael Radan and Stephen Winokur, 17–130. Minneapolis: University of Minnesota Press.

Fishbein, Martin, and Icek Ajzen. 1972. "Attitudes and Opinions." *Annual Review of Psychology* 23: 487–543.

Fisk, George. 1967. *Marketing Systems: An Introductory Analysis*. New York: Harper and Row.

———. 1971. *New Essays in Marketing Theory*. Boston: Allyn and Bacon.

———. 1982. "Editor's Working Definition of Macromarketing." *Journal of Macromarketing* 2 (Spring): 3–4.

Ford, D. 1990. *Understanding Business Markets: Interaction, Relationships, and Networks*. London: Academic Press.

Fornell, Claes. 1983. "Issues in the Application of Covariance Structure Analysis: A Comment." *Journal of Consumer Research* 9: 443–48.

Foss, Nicolai. 1993. "Theories of the Firm: Contractual and Competence Perspectives." *Journal of Evolutionary Economics* 3: 127–44.

———. 2000. "The Dangers and Attractions of Theoretical Eclecticism." *Journal of Macromarketing* 20 (June): 65–67.

Frank, Ronald E., and Paul Green. 1968. "Numerical Taxonomy in Marketing Analysis: A Review Article." *Journal of Marketing Research* (February): 83–94.

Fried, Vance, and Benjamin Oviatt. 1989. "Michael Porter's Missing Chapter: The Risk of Anti-Trust Allegations." *Academy of Management Executive* 3, no. 1: 49–56.

Friedman, Milton. 1953. "The Methodology of Positive Economics." In *Essays in Positive Economics*, ed. M. Friedman, 3–43. Chicago: University of Chicago Press.

———. 1970. "The Social Responsibility of Business Is to Increase Its Profits." *New York Times Magazine*, September 13: 658–69.

Frost, W.A.K. 1969. "The Development of a Technique for TV Programming Assessment." *Journal of Marketing Research Society* 9 (January): 25–44.

Fullerton, Ronald. 1987. "The Poverty of Ahistorical Analysis: Present Weakness and Future Cure in U.S. Marketing Thought." In *Philosophical and Radical Thought in Marketing*, ed. A.F. Firat et al., 89–103. Lexington, MA: Lexington.

Gabor, Andre; Clive Granger; and Anthony Sowter. 1971. "Comments on Psychophysics of Prices." *Journal of Marketing Research* 8 (May): 251–52.

Gale, Bradley T., and Ben S. Branch. 1982. "Concentration Versus Market Share: Which Determines Performance and Why Does It Matter?" *Antitrust Bulletin* 27 (Spring): 83–103.

Garb, Gerald. 1965. "Professor Samuelson on Theory and Realism: Comment." *American Economic Review* (December): 1151–53.

Gardenfors, Peter. 1980. "A Pragmatic Approach to Explanations." *Philosophy of Science* 47, no. 4: 404–23.

Gardner, M. 1976. "On the Fabric of Inductive Logic." *Scientific American* 234, no. 2: 119–26.

Gaski, John F. 1985. "Nomic Necessity in Marketing: The Issue of Counterfactual Conditionals." *Journal of the Academy of Marketing Science* 13, no. 3: 320–21.

Gieryn, Thomas F. 1983. "Boundary-Work and the Demarcation of Science from Non-Science." *American Sociological Review* 48 (December): 370–86.

Gist, Ronald R. 1971. *Marketing and Society*. New York: Holt, Rinehart and Winston.

Goble, Ross L., and Roy Shaw. 1975. *Controversy and Dialogue in Marketing*. Englewood Cliffs, NJ: Prentice Hall.

Goodman, Nelson. 1965. *Fact, Fiction, and Forecast*. Indianapolis: Bobbs-Merrill.

Gordon, Robert A., and James E. Howell. 1959. *Higher Education for Business*. New York: Columbia University Press.

Granbois, Ronald H. 1971. "Decision Processes for Major Durable Goods." In *New Essays in Marketing Theory*, ed. G. Fisk, 172–205. Boston: Allyn and Bacon.

Granger, C.W.J. 1969. "Investigating Causal Relationships by Econometric Methods." *Econometrics* 37 (July): 424–38.

Granovetter, Mark. 1985. "Economic Action and Social Structure: The Problem of Embeddedness." *American Journal of Sociology* 91, no. 3: 481–510.

Gray, Elisha. 1968. "Changing Values in the Business Society." *Business Horizons* 11 (August): 26.

Green, Paul E.; Roland Frank; and Patrick Robinson. 1967. "Cluster Analysis in Test Market Selection." *Management Science* 13 (April): 387–400.

Green, Paul E., Donald S. Tull, and Gerald Albaum. 1988. *Research For Marketing Decisions*. Englewood Cliffs, NJ: Prentice Hall.

Greeno, James G. 1966. "Explanation and Information." In *The Foundations of Scientific Inference*, ed. W. Salmon, 89–104. Pittsburgh: University of Pittsburgh Press.

Grene, Marjorie. 1976. "To Have a Mind . . ." *Journal of Medicine and Philosophy* 1, no. 2: 177–99.

Gronroos, C. 1996. "Relationship Marketing: Strategic and Tactical Implications." *Management Decision* 34, no. 3: 5–14.

———. 2000. *Service Management and Marketing: A Customer Relationship Management Approach*. New York: Wiley.

Gronroos, C., and E. Gummesson, eds. 1985. *Service Marketing-Nordic School Perspectives* [Research Report R], Department of Business Administration, University of Stockholm, Stockholm.

Gummesson, Evert. 1995. "Focus Shifts in Marketing: A New Agenda for the Third Millennium." Presentation at the Twentieth Anniversary Program of the Marketing Technology Center, Stockholm, Sweden.

———. 1999. *Total Relationship Marketing*; *Rethinking Marketing Management: From 4Ps to 30Rs*. Woburn, MA: Butterworth-Heinemann.

Hair, Joseph F., Jr.; Rolph E. Anderson; Ronald L. Tatham; and William C. Black. 1995. *Multivariate Data Analysis*. Englewood Cliffs, NJ: Prentice Hall.

Hakansson, H., ed. 1982. *International Marketing and Purchasing of Industrial Goods: An Interaction Approach*. Chichester, UK: Wiley.

Halbert, M. 1965. *The Meaning and Sources of Marketing Theory*. New York: McGraw-Hill.

Hamel, Gary, and Aime Heene. 1994. *Competence-Based Competition*. New York: Wiley.

Hamel, Gary, and C.K. Prahalad. 1989. "Strategic Intent." *Harvard Business Review* (May–June): 63–76.

———. 1994a. *Competing for the Future*. Cambridge, MA: Harvard Business School Press.

———. 1994b. "Competing for the Future." *Harvard Business Review* (July–August): 122–28.

Hanson, Norwood R. 1958. *Patterns of Discovery*. Cambridge: Cambridge University Press.

———. 1963. *The Concept of Positivism: A Philosophical Analysis*. Cambridge: Cambridge University Press.

Harré, Rom. 1986. *Varieties of Realism*. Oxford, UK: Basil Blackwell.

Harré, Rom, and E.H. Madden. 1975. *Causal Powers*. Totawa, NJ: Rowman and Littlefield.

Harvey, David. 1969. *Explanation in Geography*. New York: St. Martin's Press.

Headen, Robert S.; Jay Klompmaker; and Roland Rust. 1979. "The Duplication of Viewing Law and Television Media Schedule Evaluation." *Journal of Marketing Research* 16 (August): 333–40.

Heene, Aimé, and Ron Sanchez. 1997. *Competence-Based Strategic Management*. New York: Wiley.

Hempel, Carl G. 1945. "Studies in the Logic of Confirmation." *Mind* 54, no. 1: 1–26, 97–121.

———. 1959. "The Logic of Functional Analysis." In *Symposium on Sociological Theory*, ed. Llewellyn Gross, 271–307. New York: Harper and Row.

———. 1965a. "Aspects of Scientific Explanation." In *Aspects of Scientific Explanation and Other Essays in the Philosophy of Science*, ed. Hempel, 331–496. New York: Free Press.

———, ed. 1965b. *Aspects of Scientific Explanation and Other Essays in the Philosophy of Science*. New York: Free Press.

———. 1965c. "Studies in the Logic of Explanation." In *Aspects of Scientific Explanation*, ed. Hempel, 245–90. New York: Free Press.

———. 1965d. "The Theoretician's Dilemma." In *Aspects of Scientific Explanation*, ed. Hempel, 173–228. New York: Free Press.

———. 1966. *Philosophy of Natural Science*. Englewood Cliffs, NJ: Prentice Hall.

———. 1968. "Maximal Specificity and Lawlikeness in Probabilistic Explanation." *Philosophy of Science* 35, no. 1: 116–33.

———. 1969. "Logical Positivism and the Social Sciences." In *The Legacy of Logical Positivism*, ed. Peter Achinstein and Stephen F. Borker, 163–94. Baltimore: Johns Hopkins University Press.

———. 1970. "Fundamentals of Concept Formation in Empirical Science." In *Foundations of the Unity of Science*, vol. 2, ed. Otto Neurath, Rudolf Carnap, and Charles Morris, 651–745. Chicago: University of Chicago Press.

Hill, Martha, et al. 1985. *Research Report: Motivation and Economic Mobility*. Ann Arbor: University of Michigan Survey Research Center.

Hintikka, Jaakko. 1988. "On the Incommensurability of Theories." *Philosophy of Science* 55, no. 1: 25–38.

Hirschman, Elizabeth C. 1986. "Humanistic Inquiry in Marketing Research: Philosophy, Method, and Criteria." *Journal of Marketing Research* 23 (August): 237–49.

———. 1987. "Marketing Research: To Serve What Purposes?" In *Marketing Theory: 1987 AMA Winter Educator's Conference*, 204–8. Chicago: American Marketing Association.

———. 1989. "After Word." In *Interpretive Consumer Research*, ed. Elizabeth C. Hirschman, 209. Provo, UT: Association for Consumer Research.

Hodgson, Geoffrey M. 1993. *Economics and Evolution*. Ann Arbor: University of Michigan Press.

———. 2000. "The Marketing of Wisdom: Resource-Advantage Theory." *Journal of Macromarketing* 20 (June): 68–72.

Hoffman, Donna L., and George R. Franke. 1986. "Correspondence Analysis: Graphical Representation of Categorical Data in Marketing Research." *Journal of Marketing Research* 23 (August): 213–27.

Holbrook, Morris B. 1986. "The Place of Marketing Research on the Business-Research Continuum." In *Marketing Education: Knowledge, Development, Dissemination, and Utilization*, ed. Joseph Guiltinan and Dale Achabal, 11–15. Chicago: American Marketing Association.

———. 1987. "What Is Consumer Research?" *Journal of Consumer Research* 14 (June): 128–32.

Holbrook, Morris B., and Mark W. Grayson. 1986. "The Semiology of Cinematic Consumption: Symbolic Consumer Behavior in 'Out of Africa.'" *Journal of Consumer Research* 13 (December): 374–81.

Hollander, Stanley. [1960] 1969. "The Wheel of Retailing." *Journal of Marketing* (July): 37–42). Reprinted in *Marketing Classics*, ed. Ben M. Erin and Keith Cox, 331–39. Boston: Allyn and Bacon.

Holloway, Robert J., and Robert S. Hancock. 1964. *The Environment of Marketing Behavior*. New York: Wiley.

———. 1968. *Marketing in a Changing Environment*. New York: Wiley.

Holton, Richard H. 1958. "The Distinction Between Convenience Goods, Shopping Goods, and Specialty Goods." *Journal of Marketing* 23 (July): 53–56.

Hopkins, Donald R. 1983. *Princes and Peasants: Smallpox in History*. Chicago: University of Chicago Press.

Hostiuck, K., and David L. Kurtz. 1973. "Alderson's Functionalism and the Development of Marketing Theory." *Journal of Business Research* 1 (Fall): 141–56.

Houston, Franklin. 1986. "The Marketing Concept: What It Is and What It Is Not." *Journal of Marketing* 50 (April): 81–87.

Howard, John A. 1965. *Marketing Theory*. Boston: Allyn and Bacon.

Howard, John A., and Jagdish N. Sheth. 1969. *The Theory of Buyer Behavior*. New York: Wiley.

Hugstad, Paul S. 1983. *The Business School in the 1980s: Liberalism Versus Vocationalism*. New York: Praeger.

Hume, David. 1911. *A Treatise of Human Nature*. New York: Dutton.

Hunt, Shelby D. 1970. "Post Transaction Communications and Dissonance Reduction." *Journal of Marketing* 34 (July): 46–51.

———. 1971. "The Morphology of Theory and the General Theory of Marketing." *Journal of Marketing* 35 (April): 65–68.

———. 1973. "Lawlike Generalizations and Marketing Theory." *Journal of Marketing* 37 (July): 69–70.

———. 1976a. *Marketing Theory: Conceptual Foundations of Research in Marketing*. Columbus, OH: Grid.

———. 1976b. "The Nature and Scope of Marketing." *Journal of Marketing* 40 (July): 17–28.

———. 1976c "The Three Dichotomies Model of Marketing: An Evaluation of Issues." In *Proceedings of Macro-Marketing Conference*, ed. Charles C. Slater, 52–56. Boulder: University of Colorado.

———. 1978. "A General Paradigm of Marketing: In Support of the Three Dichotomies Model." *Journal of Marketing* 42 (April): 107–10.

———. 1983a. "General Theories and the Fundamental Explananda of Marketing." *Journal of Marketing* 47 (Fall): 9–17.

———. 1983b. *Marketing Theory: The Philosophy of Marketing Science*. Homewood, IL: Irwin.

———. 1984. "Should Marketing Adopt Relativism?" In *Scientific Method of Marketing*, ed. Paul F. Anderson and Michael J. Ryan, 30–34. Chicago: American Marketing Association.

———. 1987. "Marketing Research: Proximate Purpose and Ultimate Value." In *Proceedings of the 1987 Winter Marketing Educators' Conference*, ed. Belk et al., 209–13. Chicago: American Marketing Association.

———. 1989a. "Naturalistic, Humanistic, and Interpretive Inquiry: Challenges and Ultimate Potential." In *Interpretive Consumer Research*, ed. Elizabeth Hirschman, 185–98. Provo, UT: Association for Consumer Research.

———. 1989b. "Reification and Realism in Marketing." *Journal of Macromarketing* 9 (Fall): 4–10.

———. 1990. "Truth in Marketing Theory and Research." *Journal of Marketing* 54 (July): 1–15.

———. 1991a. *Modern Marketing Theory: Critical Issues in the Philosophy of Marketing Science*. Cincinnati: South-Western.

———. 1991b. "Positivism and Paradigm Dominance in Consumer Research: Toward Critical Pluralism and Rapprochement." *Journal of Consumer Research* 18 (June): 32–44.

———. 1991c. "The Three Dichotomies Model of Marketing Revisited: Is the Total Content of Marketing Thought Normative?" In *Proceedings of the 1991 AMA Winter Educators' Conference*, ed. Terry L. Childers et al., 425–30. Chicago: American Marketing Association.

———. 1992a. "For Reason and Realism in Marketing." *Journal of Marketing* 56 (April): 89–102.

———. 1992b. "Marketing Is . . ." *Journal of the Academy of Marketing Science* 20 (Fall): 301–11.

———. 1993. "Objectivity in Marketing Theory and Research." *Journal of Marketing* 57 (April): 76–91.

———. 1994a. "A Realist Theory of Empirical Testing: Resolving the Theory Ladenness/Objectivity Debate." *Philosophy of the Social Sciences* 24, no. 2: 133–58.

———. 1994b. "On Rethinking Marketing: Our Discipline, Our Practice, Our Methods." *European Journal of Marketing* 28, no. 3: 13–25.

———. 1994c. "On the Rhetoric of Qualitative Inquiry: Toward Historically Informed Argumentation in Management Inquiry." *Journal of Management Inquiry* 3 (September): 221–34.

———. 1995. "The Resource-Advantage Theory of Competition: Toward Explaining Productivity and Economic Growth." *Journal of Management Inquiry* 4 (December): 317–32.

———. 1997a. "Competing Through Relationships: Grounding Relationship Marketing in Resource Advantage Theory." *Journal of Marketing Management* 13: 431–45.

———. 1997b. "Evolutionary Economics, Endogenous Growth Models, and Resource-Advantage Theory." *Eastern Economic Journal* 23, no. 4: 425–39.

———. 1997c. "Resource-Advantage Theory: An Evolutionary Theory of Competitive Firm Behavior?" *The Journal of Economic Issues* 31 (March): 59–77.

———. 1997d. "Resource-Advantage Theory and the Wealth of Nations." *The Journal of Socio-Economics* 26, no. 4: 335–57.

———. 1998. "Productivity, Economic Growth, and Competition: Resource Allocation or Resource Creation?" *Business and the Contemporary World* 10, no. 3: 367–94.

———. 1999. "The Strategic Imperative and Sustainable Competitive Advantage: Public Policy and Resource Advantage Theory." *Journal of Academy of Marketing Science* 27, no. 2: 144–59.

———. 2000a. "The Competence-Based, Resource-Advantage, and Neoclassical Theories of Competition: Toward a Synthesis." In *Competence-Based Strategic Management: Theory and Research*, ed. R. Sanchez and A. Heene, 177–208. Greenwich, CT: JAI Press.

———. 2000b. *A General Theory of Competition: Resources, Competences, Productivity, Economic Growth.* Thousand Oaks, CA: Sage.

———. 2000c. "A General Theory of Competition: Too Eclectic or Not Eclectic Enough? Too Incremental or Not Incremental Enough? Too Neoclassical or Not Neoclassical Enough?" *Journal of Macromarketing* 20, no. 1: 77–81.

———. 2000d. "Synthesizing Resource-Based, Evolutionary and Neoclassical Thought: Resource-Advantage Theory as a General Theory of Competition." In *Resources, Technology, and Strategy*, ed. N.J. Foss and P. Robertson, 53–79. London: Routledge.

———. 2001a. "A General Theory of Competition: Issues, Answers, and an Invitation." *European Journal of Marketing* 35, no. 5/6: 524–48.

———. 2001b. "The Influence of Philosophy, Philosophies, and Philosophers on a Marketer's Scholarship." *Journal of Marketing* 64 (October): 117–24.

———. 2003. *Controversy in Marketing Theory: For Reason, Realism, Truth, and Objectivity.* Armonk, NY: M.E. Sharpe.

———. 2002. "Resource-Advantage Theory and Austrian Economics." In *Entrepreneurship and the Firm: Austrian Perspectives on Economic Organization*, ed. N.J. Foss and P. Klein. Cheltenham, UK: Edward Elgar.

Hunt, Shelby D., and Dennis Arnett. 2001. "Competition as an Evolutionary Process and Antitrust Policy." *Journal of Public Policy and Marketing* 20, no. 1: 15–25.

Hunt, Shelby D.; Lawrence B. Chonko; and Van R. Wood. 1985. "Organizational Commitment and Marketing." *Journal of Marketing* 49 (Winter): 112–24.

Hunt, Shelby D., and Dale F. Duhan. Forthcoming. "Competition in the Third Millennium: Efficiency or Effectiveness?" *Journal of Business Research.*

Hunt, Shelby D., and C. Jay Lambe. 2000. "Marketing's Contribution to Business Strategy: Market Orientation, Relationship Marketing, and Resource-Advantage Theory." *International Journal of Management Reviews* 2, no. 1: 17–44.

Hunt, Shelby D.; C. Jay Lambe; and C.M. Wittman. 2002. "A Theory and Model of Business Alliance Success." *Journal of Relationship Marketing* 1, no. 1: 17–36.

Hunt, Shelby D., and Robert M. Morgan. 1994. "Relationship Marketing in the Era of Network Competition." *Marketing Management* 3, no. 1: 19–28.

———. 1995. "The Comparative Advantage Theory of Competition." *Journal of Marketing* 59 (April): 1–15.

———. 1996. "The Resource-Advantage Theory of Competition: Dynamics, Path Dependencies, and Evolutionary Dimensions." *Journal of Marketing* 60 (October): 107–14.

———. 1997. "Resource-Advantage Theory: A Snake Swallowing Its Tail or a General Theory of Competition?" *Journal of Marketing* 61 (October): 74–82.

Hunt, Shelby D., and Scott M. Vitell. 1986. "A General Theory of Marketing Ethics." *Journal of Macromarketing* 6 (Spring): 5–15.

———. 1993. "The General Theory of Marketing Ethics: A Retrospective and Revision." In *Ethics in Marketing*, ed. N.C. Smith and J.A. Quelch, 775–84. Homewood, IL: Irwin.

Hunt, Shelby D.; James A. Muncy; and Nina M. Ray. 1981. "Alderson's General Theory of Marketing: A Formalization." In *Review of Marketing*, ed. Ben M. Enis and Kenneth J. Roering, 267–82. Chicago: American Marketing Association.

Hunt, Shelby D., and James L. Pappas. 1972. "A Crucial Test for the Howard-Sheth Model of Buyer Behavior." *Journal of Marketing Research* 9 (August): 346–48.

Hutchinson, Kenneth D. 1952. "Marketing as a Science: An Appraisal." *Journal of Marketing* 16 (January): 286–93.

Hyman, Michael R.; Robert Skipper; and Richard Tansey. 1991. "Two Challenges for the Three Dichotomies Model." In *Proceedings of the 1991 AMA Winter Educators' Conference*, ed. Terry L. Childers et al., 417–22. Chicago: American Marketing Association.

Jacobson, Robert. 1988. "Distinguishing Among Competing Theories of the Market Share Effect." *Journal of Marketing* 52 (October): 68–80.

Jacobson, Robert, and Franco M. Nicosia. 1981. "Advertising and Public Policy: The Macroeconomic Effects of Advertising." *Journal of Marketing Research* 18 (February): 29–38.

Jacobson, Robert, and David A. Aaker. 1985. "Is Market Share All That It's Cracked Up to Be?" *Journal of Marketing* 49 (Fall): 11–22.

Jastram, Roy W. 1955. "A Treatment of Distributed Lags in the Theory of Advertising Expenditure." *Journal of Marketing* 20 (July): 36–46.

Jeffrey, Richard C. 1966. "Statistical Explanation vs. Statistical Inference." In *The Foundations of Scientific Inference*, ed. W. Salmon, 89–104. Pittsburgh: University of Pittsburgh Press.

Jevons, William Stanley. 1968. "Philosophy of Inductive Reference." In *Philosophy of Science*, ed. Joseph J. Kockelmans, 137–46. New York: Free Press.

Jobe, Evan K. 1976. "Discussion: A Puzzle Concerning D-N Explanation." *Philosophy of Science* 43, no. 4: 542–49.

Joreskog, K.G. 1968. "A General Method for Analysis of Covariance Structure." In Proceedings of the Psychometric Society, 120–38. Chapel Hill: University of North Carolina Press.

———. 1973. "A General Method for Estimating a Linear Structural Equation System." In *Structural Equation Models in the Social Sciences*, ed. A.S. Goldberger, 85–112. New York: Seminar Press.

Kaiser, Mattias. 1993. "Discussion: Philosophers Adrift? Comments on the Alleged Disunity of Method." *Philosophy of Science* 60, no. 3: 500–12.

Kalyanaram, Gurumurthy; William T. Robinson; and Glen L. Urban. 1995. "Order of Market Entry: Established Empirical Generalizations, Emerging Empirical Generalizations, and Future Research." *Marketing Science* 14, no. 3: G212–221.

Kalyanaram, Gurumurthy, and Russell S. Winer. 1995. "Empirical Generalizations from Reference Price Research." *Marketing Science* 14, no. 3: G161–69.

Kamen, Joseph M. 1970. "Quick Clustering." *Journal of Marketing Research* 7 (May): 199–204.

Kamen, Joseph M., and Robert Toman. 1970. "Psychophysics of Prices." *Journal of Marketing Research* 7 (February): 27–35.

———. 1971. "Psychophysics of Prices: A Reaffirmation." *Journal of Marketing Research* 8 (May): 252–57.

Kangun, Norman. 1972. *Society and Marketing*. New York: Harper and Row.

Kant, Immanuel. [1783] 1968. "Prolegomena and Metaphysical Foundations of Natural Science." In *Philosophy of Science*, ed. Joseph J. Kockelmans, 17–27. New York: Free Press.

Kaplan, Abraham. 1964. *The Conduct of Inquiry*. Scranton, PA: Chandler.

Kassarjian, Harold H. 1989. "Book Review." *Journal of Marketing* 53 (January): 123–26.
Katoma, George. 1960. *The Powerful Consumer*. New York: McGraw-Hill.
Keat, Russell, and John Urry. 1975. *Social Theory as Science*. London: Routledge and Kegan Paul.
Kerin, Roger A., and Raj Sethuraman. 1999. "'Revisiting Marketing's Lawlike Generalizations': A Comment." *Journal of the Academy of Marketing Science* 27, no. 1: 101–4.
Keynes, John Neville. 1891. *The Scope and Method of Political Economy*. London: Macmillan.
Kincaid, Harold. 1990. "Defending Laws in the Social Sciences." *Philosophy of the Social Sciences* 20, no. 1: 56–83.
Kohli, Ajay K., and Bernard Jaworski. 1990. "Market Orientation: The Construct, Research Propositions, and Managerial Implications." *Journal of Marketing* 54 (April): 1–18.
Kotler, Philip. 1971. *Marketing Decision Making*. New York: Holt, Rinehart and Winston.
———. 1972a. "Defining the Limits of Marketing." In *Marketing Education and the Real World* (1972 Fall Conference Proceedings), ed. Boris W. Becker and Helmut Becker, 48–56. Chicago: American Marketing Association.
———. 1972b. "A Generic Concept of Marketing." *Journal of Marketing* 36 (April): 46–54.
———. 1972c. *Marketing Management*, 2d ed. Englewood Cliffs, NJ: Prentice Hall.
Kotler, Philip, and Sidney Levy. 1969a. "Broadening the Concept of Marketing." *Journal of Marketing* 33 (January): 10–15.
———. 1969b. "A New Form of Marketing Myopia: Rejoinder to Professor Luck." *Journal of Marketing* 33 (July): 55–57.
Kotler, Philip, and Gerald Zaltman. 1971. "Social Marketing: An Approach to Planned Social Change." *Journal of Marketing* 35 (July): 3–12.
Kruger, Lorenz. 1976. "Are Statistical Explanations Possible?" *Philosophy of Science* 43, no. 1: 129–46.
Kuhn, Thomas S. 1962. *The Structure of Scientific Revolutions*. Chicago: University of Chicago Press.
Kyburg, Henry E. Jr. 1968. *Philosophy of Science*. New York: Macmillan.
Lado, Augustine; Nancy Boyd; and P. Wright. 1992. "A Competency-Based Model of Sustainable Competitive Advantage." *Journal of Management* 18, no. 1: 77–91.
Lakatos, Imre. 1978. *The Methodology of Scientific Research Programmes*, vol. 1. Cambridge, UK: Cambridge University Press.
Lambe, C. J.; Robert N. Spekman; and Shelby D. Hunt. 2002. "Alliance Competence, Resources, and Alliance Success: Conceptualization, Measurement, and Initial Test." *Journal of the Academy of Marketing Science* 30, no. 2: 141–58.
Lambert, Karel, and Gordon G. Brittan, Jr. 1970. *An Introduction to the Philosophy of Science*. Englewood Cliffs, NJ: Prentice Hall.
Lange, Marc. 1999. "Laws, Counterfactuals, Stability, and Degrees of Lawhood." *Philosophy of Science* 66, no. 2: 243–67.
Langlois, Richard N., and P.L. Robertson. 1995. *Firms, Markets and Economic Change: A Dynamic Theory of Business Institutions*. London: Routledge.
Laudan, Larry. 1977. *Progress and Its Problems: Towards a Theory of Scientific Growth*. Berkeley: University of California Press.
Lavidge, Robert J. 1970. "The Growing Responsibilities of Marketing." *Journal of Marketing* 34 (January): 25–28.
Lavidge, Robert J., and Gary A. Steiner. 1961. "A Model for Predictive Measurements of Advertising Effectiveness." *Journal of Marketing* 25 (October): 59–62.
Lavin, Marilyn, and Thomas J. Archdeacon. 1989. "The Relevance of Historical Method for Marketing Research." In *Interpretive Consumer Research*, ed. Elizabeth C. Hirschman, 60–68. Provo, UT: Association for Consumer Research.
Lazer, William. 1962. "The Role of Models in Marketing." *Journal of Marketing* 26 (April): 9–14.
———. 1969. "Marketing's Changing Social Relationships." *Journal of Marketing* 33 (January): 3–9.
Lazer, William, and Eugene Kelly. 1962. "Systems Perspective of Marketing Activity." In

Managerial Marketing Perspectives and Viewpoints, rev. ed., ed. William Lazer and Eugene Kelly, 191–98. Homewood, IL: Irwin.

———. 1973. *Social Marketing*. Homewood, IL: Irwin.

Learned, E.P.; C.R. Christiansen; K.R. Andrews; and W.D. Guth. 1965. *Business Policy: Text and Cases*. Homewood, IL: Irwin.

Leftwich, Richard H. 1966. *The Price System and Resource Allocation*. New York: Holt, Rinehart and Winston.

Lehmann, Donald R.; Terrence V. O'Brien; John Farley; and John Howard. 1974. "Some Empirical Contributions to Buyer Behavior Theory." *Journal of Consumer Research* 1 (December): 43–55.

Leone, Robert P., and Randall L. Schultz. 1980. "A Study of Marketing Generalizations." *Journal of Marketing* 44 (Winter): 10–18.

Leplin, Jarrett. 1984. *Scientific Realism*. Berkeley: University of California Press.

Lerner, Abba P. 1965. "Professor Samuelson on Theory and Realism: Comment." *American Economic Review* (December): 1153–55.

Levin, Michael E. 1991. "The Reification-Realism-Positivism Controversy in Macromarketing: A Philosopher's View." *Journal of Macromarketing* 11 (Spring): 57–65.

Levitt, Theodore. 1958. "The Dangers of Social Responsibility." *Harvard Business Review* 36 (September–October): 41–50.

———. 1960. "Marketing Myopia." *Harvard Business Review* 38 (July–August): 24–27.

Levey, G.B. 1996. "Theory Choice and the Comparison of Rival Theoretical Perspectives in Political Sociology." *Journal of Philosophy of the Social Sciences* 26 (March): 26–60.

Levy, Sid. 1976. "Marcology 101 or the Domain of Marketing." In *Marketing: 1776–1976 and Beyond*, ed. Kenneth L. Bernhardt, 577–81. Chicago: American Marketing Association.

Lincoln, Yvonna S., and Egon G. Guba. 1985. *Naturalistic Inquiry*. Beverly Hills, CA: Sage.

Lippman, S.A., and R.P. Rumelt. 1982. "Uncertain Imitability." *Bell Journal of Economics* 13: 418–38.

Little, John D.C. 1970. "Models and Managers: The Concept of a Decision Calculus." *Management Science* (April): 466–85.

Lockley, Lawrence C. 1964. "An Approach to Marketing Theory." In *Theory in Marketing*, ed. Reavis Cox, Wroe Alderson, and Stanley Shapiro, 37–50. Homewood, IL: Irwin.

Longman, Kenneth A. 1971. "The Management Challenge to Marketing Theory." In *New Essays in Marketing Theory*, ed. George Fisk, 9–19. Boston: Allyn and Bacon.

Louch, A.R. 1979. "Human Conduct Requires Ad Hoc Explanations." In *Philosophy and Science*, ed. Frederick Mosedale, 281–85. Englewood Cliffs, NJ: Prentice Hall.

Luck, David J. 1969. "Broadening the Concept of Marketing—Too Far." *Journal of Marketing* 33 (July): 53–55.

Luck, David J.; Hugh G. Wales; and Donald A. Taylor. 1970. *Marketing Research*. Englewood Cliffs, NJ: Prentice Hall.

Lusch, R.F. 2000. "Review: A General Theory of Competition: Resources, Competences, Productivity, Economic Growth." *Journal of Marketing* 64 (April): 126–27.

Lutz, Richard J. 1979. "Opening Statement." In *Conceptual and Theoretical Developments in Marketing*, ed. O.C. Ferrell, S.W. Brown, and C.W. Lamb, 3–6. Chicago: American Marketing Association.

Lynn, Kenneth S. 1965. *The Professions in America*. Boston: Houghton-Mifflin.

MacDonald, Margaret. 1968. "The Natural Laws and Natural Rights." In *Readings in the Philosophy of the Social Sciences*, ed. May Brodbeck, 719–36. New York: Macmillan.

Machlup, Fritz. 1964. "Professor Samuelson on Theory and Realism." *American Economic Review* (September): 733–36.

MacKenzie, Scott B. 2001. "Opportunities for Improving Consumer Research Through Latent Variable Structural Equation Modeling." *Journal of Consumer Research* 28, no. 1: 159–66.

Mackie, J.L. 1965. "Causes and Conditions." *American Philosophical Quarterly* 2, no. 2: 245–64.

MacKinnon, Edward. 1979. "Scientific Realism: The New Debates." *Philosophy of Science* 46, no. 4: 501–32.

Mahner, Martin, and Mario Bunge. 2001. "Function and Functionalism: A Synthetic Perspective." *Philosophy of Science* 68 (October): 75–94.

Malinowski, Bronislaw. 1936. "Anthropology." In *Encyclopedia Britannica*. suppl., vol. 1, Chicago: Encyclopaedia Britannica Educational Corporation.

———. 1944. "The Functional Theory." In *A Scientific Theory of Culture*, ed. B. Malinowski, 145–76. Chapel Hill: University of North Carolina Press.

———. 1954. *Magic, Science, and Religion*. New York: Doubleday.

Manicas, Peter T. 1987. *A History and Philosophy of the Social Sciences*. New York: Basil Blackwell.

Marketing Staff of the Ohio State University. 1965. "Statement of Marketing Philosophy." *Journal of Marketing* 29 (January): 43–44.

Marshall, Alfred. [1890] 1949. *Principles of Economics*. London: Macmillan.

Martilla, J.A. 1971. "Word of Mouth Communication in the Industrial Adoption Process." *Journal of Marketing Research* 8 (May): 173–78.

Masey, Gerald J. 1965. "Professor Samuelson on Theory and Realism: Comment." *American Economic Review* (December): 1153–63.

Masland, T.; R. Norland; M. Liu; and J. Contreras. 1992. "Slavery." *Newsweek* 4 (May): 30–39.

Massy, William, and Barton Weitz. 1977. "A Normative Theory of Market Segmentation." In *Behavioral Models for Marketing Action*, ed. M. Nicosia and Y. Wind, 121–44. Hinsdale, IL: Dryden Press.

Mauri, Alfredo, and Max P. Michaels. 1998. "Firm and Industry Effects Within Strategic Management." *Strategic Management Journal* 19, no. 3: 211–21.

McCarthy, E.J. [1960] 1971. *Basic Marketing*, 4th ed. Homewood, IL: Irwin.

McGahan, A.M., and M. Porter. 1997. "How Much Does Industry Matter, Really?" *Strategic Management Journal* 19 (Summer Special Issue): 15–30.

McGarry, Edmund D. 1936. "The Importance of Scientific Method in Advertising." *Journal of Marketing* 1 (October): 82–86.

McMullin, Ernan. 1984. "A Case for Scientific Realism." In *Scientific Realism*, ed. J. Leplin, 8–40. Berkeley: University of California Press.

McNair, Malcolm P. 1958. "Competitive Trends and Developments to the Postwar Period." In *Competitive Distribution in a Free, High Level Economy and Its Implications for the University*, ed. A.B. Smith. Pittsburgh: University of Pittsburgh Press.

Meehl, Paul E. 1986. "What Social Scientists Don't Understand." In *Metatheory in Social Science*, ed. Fiske and Shweder, 315–38. Chicago: University of Chicago Press.

———. 1990. *Psychological Reports: Why Summaries of Research on Psychological Theories Are Often Uninterpretable*. Minneapolis: University of Minnesota.

Meixner, John. 1979. "Homogeneity and Explanatory Depth." *Philosophy of Science* 46, no. 3: 366–81.

Merton, Robert K. 1938. "Science, Technology and Society in Seventeenth Century England." *Osiris* 4, no. 3: 360–62.

———. [1949] 1968. *Social Theory and Social Structure*. New York: Free Press.

Meyer, Robert, and Eric J. Johnson. 1995. "Empirical Generalizations in the Modeling of Consumer Choice." *Marketing Science* 14, no. 3: G180–89.

Meyers, James H., and William Reynolds. 1967. *Consumer Behavior and Marketing Management*. New York: Houghton Mifflin.

Mick, David Glen. 1986. "Consumer Research and Semiotics: Exploring the Morphology of Signs, Symbols, and Significance." *Journal of Consumer Research* 13 (September): 196–213.

Mindak, William A., and H. Malcolm Bybee. 1971. "Marketing's Application to Fund Raising." *Journal of Marketing* 35 (July): 13–18.

Monroe, Kent B. 1971. "Psychophysics of Prices: A Reappraisal." *Journal of Marketing Research* 8 (May): 248–50.

Monroe, Kent B., et al. 1988. "Developing, Disseminating, and Utilizing Marketing Knowledge." *Journal of Marketing* 52 (October): 1–25.

Monroe, Kent B.; William C. Wilkie; Linda J. McAleer; and Albert R. Wildt. 1986. "Report of the AMA Task Force on the Development of Marketing Thought." In *Marketing Education: Knowledge, Development, Dissemination, and Utilization*, ed. Joseph Guiltinan and Dale Achabal, 8–9. Chicago: American Marketing Association.

Montgomery, Cynthia, and Michael E. Porter. 1991. *Strategy: Seeking and Securing Competitive Advantage*. Boston: Harvard Business School.

Moore, Wilbert E. 1970. *The Professions: Roles and Rules*. New York: Russell Sage Foundation.

Morell, Ben. 1956. *The Role of American Business in Social Progress*. Indianapolis: Clarendon Press.

Morgan, Robert M., and Shelby D. Hunt. 1994. "The Commitment-Trust Theory of Relationship Marketing." *Journal of Marketing* 58 (July): 20–38.

Morris, Charles W. 1955. "Scientific Empiricism." In *Foundations of the Unity of Science*, vol. 1, ed. Otto Neurath, Rudolf Carnap, and Charles Morris, 63–75. Chicago: University of Chicago Press.

Morrison, Donald G. 1978. "The Use and Limitations of Brand Switching Models." In *Behavioral and Management Science in Marketing*, ed. Harry L. Davis and Alvin J. Silk, 5–11. New York: Wiley.

Moyer, Reed. 1972. *Macro-Marketing*. New York: Wiley.

Mukherjee, Bishwa Nath. 1965. "A Factor Analysis of Some Qualitative Attributes of Coffee." *Journal of Advertising Research* 5 (March): 35–38.

Myers, James H. 1996. *Segmentation and Positioning Strategies for Marketing Decisions*. Chicago: American Marketing Association.

Myers, John G. 1979. "What Is Appropriate Orientation for the Marketing Academician?" (In panel discussion edited by William H. Peters.) In *Conceptual and Theoretical Developments in Marketing*, ed. O.C. Ferrell et al., 49–75. Chicago: American Marketing Association.

Myers, John G.; Stephen A. Greyser; and William F. Massy. 1979. "The Effectiveness of Marketing's 'R&D' for Marketing Management: An Assessment." *Journal of Marketing* 43 (January): 17–29.

Myers, John G.; William F. Massy; and Stephen A. Greyser. 1980. *Marketing Research and Knowledge Development: An Assessment for Marketing Management*. Englewood Cliffs, NJ: Prentice Hall.

Nagel, Ernest. 1961. *The Structure of Science*. New York: Harcourt Brace Jovanovich.

———. 1963. "Assumptions in Economic Theory." *American Economic Review* 53 (May): 211–19.

Nakamoto, Kent, and Shelby D. Hunt. 1980. "Deterministic Theory and Marketing." In *Theoretical Developments in Marketing*, ed. Charles W. Lamb, Jr. and Patrick M. Dunne, 244–47. Chicago: American Marketing Association.

Narver, John C., and Stanley F. Slater. 1990. "The Effect of Market Orientation on Business Profitability." *Journal of Marketing* 54 (October): 20–35.

Nayyan, Praveen, and Karen Bantel. 1994. "Competitive Agility = A Source of Competitive Advantage Based on Speed and Variety." *Advances in Strategic Management* 10A: 193–222.

Neidell, Lester A. 1969. Physician Perception and Evaluation of Selected Ethical Drugs: An Application of Nonmetric Multidimensional Scaling to Pharmaceutical Marketing, Ph.D. dissertation, University of Pennsylvania.

Newman, Joseph W., and Richard A. Werbel. 1973. "Multivariate Analysis of Brand Loyalty for Major Household Appliances." *Journal of Marketing Research* (November): 404–9.

Newman, Peter. 1965. *The Theory of Exchange*. Englewood Cliffs, NJ: Prentice Hall.

Neurath, Otto; Rudolf Carnap; and Charles Morris, ed. 1955. *Foundations of the Unity of Science*. vol. 1. Chicago: University of Chicago Press.

Nickels, William G. 1974. "Conceptual Conflicts in Marketing." *Journal of Economics and Business* 26 (Winter): 140–43.

Nicosia, Francesco W. 1966. *Consumer Decision Processes*. Englewood Cliffs, NJ: Prentice Hall.

Niiniluoto, Ilkka. 1978. "Discussion: Dretske on Laws of Nature." *Philosophy of Science* 45, no. 4: 431–39.

———. 1999. *Critical Scientific Realism.* Oxford, UK: Oxford University Press.

North, Douglass C. 1990. *Institutions, Institutional Change, and Economic Performance.* Cambridge, UK: University of Cambridge.

O'Brien, Terrence. 1971. "Stages of Consumer Decision Making." *Journal of Marketing Research* (August): 283–89.

Osigweh, Chimezie A.B. 1986. "Management and Professionalism." *Mid Atlantic Journal of Business* 24 (Summer): 1–20.

Parasuraman, A. 1982. "Is a 'Scientist' Versus 'Technologist' Research Orientation Conducive to Marketing Theory Development?" In *Marketing Theories: Philosophy of Science Perspectives*, ed. Ronald A. Bush and Shelby D. Hunt, 78–79. Chicago: American Marketing Association.

Palda, Kristian S. 1966. "The Hypothesis of a Hierarchy of Effects: A Partial Evaluation." *Journal of Marketing Research* (February): 13–24.

Parsons, Talcott. 1949. *Essays in Sociological Theory.* New York: Free Press.

Pauling, Linus. 1956. *College Chemistry.* San Francisco: W.H. Freeman.

Pechmann, Cornelia. 1990. "Response to President's Column, September 1989." *ACR Newsletter* (June): 5–7.

Penrose, Edith T. 1959. *The Theory of the Growth of the Firm.* London: Basil Blackwell and Mott.

Peter, J. Paul, and Jerry C. Olson. 1983. "Is Science Marketing?" *Journal of Marketing* 47 (Fall): 111–25.

Peters, William H. 1980. "The Marketing Professor-Practitioner Gap: A Possible Solution." *Journal of Marketing Education* (Fall): 4–11.

Peterson's Annual Guide to Four-Year Colleges. 2000. Princeton, NJ: Peterson's Guides.

Pierce, David A., and Larry D. Haugh. 1977. "Causality in Temporal Systems." *Journal of Econometrics* 5 (May): 265–93.

Pierson, Frank C. 1959. *The Education of American Businessmen.* New York: McGraw-Hill.

Pinson, Christian R.A.; Reinhard Angelmar; and Eduardo L. Roberto. 1972. "An Evaluation of the General Theory of Marketing." *Journal of Marketing* 36 (July): 66–69.

Phillips, D.C. 1987. *Philosophy, Science, and Social Inquiry.* Oxford: Pergamon Press.

Plato. 1942. *Republic: Book II, in Five Great Dialogues*, ed. Louise R. Loomis. Roslyn, NY: Walter J. Block.

Polli, Rolando, and Victor Cook. 1969. "Validity of the Product Life Cycle." *Journal of Business* (October): 395–400.

Pondy, Louis R. 1967. "Organizational Conflict: Concepts and Models." *Administrative Science Quarterly* 12 (September): 296–320.

Popper, Karl R. 1959. *The Logic of Scientific Discovery.* New York: Harper and Row.

———. 1960. *The Poverty of Historicism*, 2d ed. London: Routledge and Kegan Paul.

Porter, Michael E. 1980. *Competitive Advantage.* New York: Free Press.

———. 1985. *Competitive Strategy.* New York: Free Press.

———. 1991. "Towards a Dynamic Theory of Strategy." *Strategic Management Journal* 12, no. 2: 95–117.

Prahalad, C.K., and Gary Hamel. 1990. "The Core Competence of the Corporation." *Harvard Business Review* (May–June): 79–91.

———. 1993. "Strategy as Stretch and Leverage." *Harvard Business Review* (March/April): 73–76.

Radcliffe-Brown, A.R. 1952. *Structure and Function in Primitive Society.* London: Cohen and West.

Ravenscraft, David J. 1983. "Structure-Profit Relationships at the Line of Business and Industry Level." *Review of Economics and Statistics* 65 (February): 22–31.
Ray, Michael. 1973. "Marketing Communication and the Hierarchy of Effects." In *New Models for Mass Communications Research*, vol. 2, ed. Peter Clark, 147–76. Beverly Hills, CA: Sage.
Reed, Richard, and Robert J. DeFillippi. 1990. "Causal Ambiguity, Barriers to Imitation, and Sustainable Competitive Advantage." *Academy of Management Review* 15 (January): 88–117.
Reed, Virgil. 1930. *Planned Marketing*. New York: Ronald Press.
Rescher, Nicholas. 1970a. *Scientific Explanation*. New York: Free Press.
———, ed. 1970b. *Essays in Honor of Carl G. Hempel*. Dordrecht, Holland: D. Reidel.
Rigby, Paul. 1965. *Conceptual Foundations of Business Research*. New York: Wiley.
Rigdon, E.E. 1995. "A Necessary and Sufficient Identification Rule for Structural Models Estimated in Practice." *Multivariate Behavioral Research* 30, no. 3: 359–84.
Rigdon, E.E., and C.E. Ferguson, Jr. 1991. "The Performance of the Polychoric Correlation Coefficient and Selected Fitting Functions in Confirmatory Factor Analysis with Ordinal Data." *Journal of Marketing Research* 28, no. 4: 491–97.
Robin, Donald P. 1974. "Success in Social Marketing." *Journal of Business Research* 3 (July): 303–10.
———. 1977. "Comment on the Nature and Scope of Marketing." *Journal of Marketing* 41 (January): 136–38.
———. 1978. "Comment on the Nature and Scope of Marketing." *Journal of Marketing* 42 (July): 6–42.
Roehl, Tom. 1996. "The Role of International R&D in the Competence-Building Strategies of Japanese Pharmaceutical Firms." In *Dynamics of Competence-Based Competition*, ed. R. Sanchez, A. Heene, and H. Thomas, 377–96. New York: Elsevier Science.
Roquebert, Jaime A.; Robert L. Phillips; and Peter A. Westfall. 1996. "Markets Versus Management: What 'Drives' Profitability?" *Strategic Management Journal* 17, no. 8: 653–54.
Rossiter, John R. 1994. "Commentary." In *Research Traditions in Marketing*, ed. Gilles Laurent, Gary L. Lilien, and Bernard Pras, 116–22. Boston: Kluwer Academic.
Rudner, Richard. 1966. *Philosophy of Social Science*. Englewood Cliffs, NJ: Prentice Hall.
Rumelt, Richard P. 1984. "Toward a Strategic Theory of the Firm." In *Competitive Strategic Management*, ed. R. Lamb, 556–70. Englewood Cliffs, NJ: Prentice Hall.
———. 1991. "How Much Does Industry Matter?" *Strategic Management Journal* 12, no. 2: 167–85.
Ryle, G. 1949. *The Concept of the Mind.* London: Hutchinson.
Salmon, Wesley C. 1963. *Logic*. Englewood Cliffs, NJ: Prentice Hall.
———. 1971. *Statistical Explanation and Statistical Relevance*. Pittsburgh: University of Pittsburgh Press.
———. 1984. *Scientific Explanation and the Causal Structure of the World.* Princeton: Princeton University Press.
Samuelson, Paul A. 1963. "Problems of Methodology—Discussion." *American Economic Review* (May): 231–36.
———. 1964. "Theory and Relativism: A Reply." *American Economic Review* (September): 736–39.
———. 1965. "Professor Samuelson on Theory and Realism: A Reply." *American Economic Review* (December): 1164–72.
Sanchez, Ron, and Aimé Heene. 1997. *Strategic Learning and Knowledge Management*. New York: Wiley.
———, eds. 2000. *Theory Development for Competence-Based Management*. Vol. 6(A) of the *Advances in Applied Business Strategy Series*. Greenwich, CT: JAI Press.
Sanchez, Ron; Aimé Heene; and Howard Thomas. 1996. *Dynamics of Competence-Based Competition*. New York: Wiley.
Savitt, R. 2000. "A Philosophical Essay About a General Theory of Competition: Resources, Competences, Productivity, Economic Growth." *Journal of Macromarketing* 20 (June): 73–76.

Schiffman, Leon G., and Vincent Gaccione. 1974. "Opinion Leaders in Institutional Markets." *Journal of Marketing* 38 (April): 49–53.

Schlaifer, Robert. 1959. *Probability and Statistics for Business Decisions*. New York: McGraw-Hill.

Schmalensee, Robert. 1985. "Do Markets Differ Much?" *American Economic Review* 75, no. 3: 341–50.

Schmidt, Stuart M., and Thomas A. Kochon. 1972. "Conflict: Toward Conceptual Clarity." *Administrative Science Quarterly* 17 (September): 359–70.

Schulze, William S. 1994. "The Two Schools of Thought in Resource-Based Theory." In *Advances in Strategic Management*. Vol. 10A, ed. P. Shrivastaba, A.S. Huff, and J.E. Dutton, 127–51. Greenwich, CT: JAI Press.

Schumpeter, Joseph A. 1950. *Capitalism, Socialism, and Democracy*. New York: Harper and Row.

Schwartz, George. 1963. *Development of Marketing Theory*. Cincinnati: South-Western.

———. 1965. "Nature and Goals of Marketing Science." In *Science in Marketing*, ed. George Schwartz, 1–19. New York: Wiley.

Scott, Richard A., and Norton E. Marks. 1968. *Marketing and Its Environment*. Belmont, CA: Wadsworth.

Sellars, Wilfrid. 1963. *Science, Perception and Reality*. New York: Humanities Press.

Selznick, P. 1957. *Leadership in Administration*. New York: Harper and Row.

Shapiro, Benson P. 1973. "Price Reliance: Existence and Sources." *Journal of Marketing Research* 10 (August): 286–93.

Sherry, John F., Jr. 1983. "Gift Giving in Anthropological Perspective." *Journal of Consumer Research* 10 (September): 157–68.

Sheth, Jagdesh N. 1994. "The Domain of Relationship Marketing." Handout at the Second Research Conference on Relationship Marketing, Center for Relationship Marketing, Emory University, Atlanta, Georgia, June 9–11.

———. 2001. "The Future of Marketing." Unpublished presentation at the Academy of Marketing Science Tenth Biennial World Marketing Congress, Cardiff, Wales, UK.

Sheth, Jagdesh N., and A. Parvatiyar. 1995. "The Evolution of Relationship Marketing." *International Business Review* 4, no. 1: 397–418.

Sheth, Jagdesh N., and Rajendra S. Sisodia. 1999. "Revisiting Marketing's Lawlike Generalizations." *Journal of the Academy of Marketing Science* 27 (Winter): 71–87.

Shrader, Douglas W. 1977. "Discussion: Causation, Explanation, and Statistical Relevance." *Philosophy of Science* 44, no. 1: 136–45.

Siegel, Harvey. 1985. "What Is the Question Concerning the Rationality of Science?" *Philosophy of Science* 55, no. 4: 517–37.

———. 1987. *Relativism Refuted*. Dordrecht: D. Reidel.

Simon, Hermann. 1994. "Marketing Science's Pilgrimage to the Ivory Tower." In *Research Traditions in Marketing*, ed. Gilles Laurent, Gary L. Lilien, and Bernard Pras, 27–43. Norwell, MA: Kluwer.

Simon, Julian. 1969. *Basic Research Methods in Social Science*. New York: Random House.

Sims, C.A. 1972. "Money, Income, and Causality." *American Economic Review* 6 (September): 540–52.

Singh, Jagdip. 1990. "A Typology of Consumer Dissatisfaction Response Styles." *Journal of Retailing* 66, no. 1: 57–99.

Slater, Charles C. 1977. *Macromarketing: Distributive Processes from a Societal Perspective*. Boulder: Business Research Division, Graduate School of Business, University of Colorado.

Slater, Stanley, and John C. Narver. 1994. "Does Competitive Environment Moderate the Market Orientation Performance Relationship?" *Journal of Marketing* 58 (January): 46–55.

Smith, Wendell. 1956. "Product Differentiation and Market Segmentation as Alternative Marketing Strategies." *Journal of Marketing* 21 (July): 3–8.

Sneath, R.H.A., and R.R. Sokal. 1973. *Numerical Taxonomy*. San Francisco: Freeman Press.

Snyder, Paul. 1978. *Toward One Science*. New York: St. Martin's Press.

Sosa, Ernest, ed. 1975. *Causation and Conditionals*. London: Oxford University Press.

Stallo, J.B. 1960. *The Concepts and Theories of Modern Physics* (1882), ed. Percy W. Bridgeman. Cambridge, MA: Harvard University Press.

Stern, Barbara B. 1989a. "Literary Explication: A Methodology for Consumer Research." In *Interpretive Consumer Research*, ed. Elizabeth C. Hirschman, 48–59. Provo, UT: Association for Consumer Research.

———. 1989b. "Literary Criticism and Consumer Research: Overview and Illustrative Analysis." *Journal of Consumer Research* 16 (December): 322–34.

Stewart, Paul F.; James F. Dewhurst; and Larry Field. 1939. *Does Distribution Cost Too Much?* New York: Twentieth Century Fund.

Stinchcombe, Arthur L. 1968. *Constructing Social Theories*. New York: Harcourt, Brace, and World.

Strevens, Michael. 2000. "Do Large Probabilities Explain Better?" *Philosophy of Science* 67, no. 3: 366–90.

Stroetzel, Jean. 1960. "A Factor Analysis of Liquor Preferences of French Consumers." *Journal of Advertising Research* 1 (December): 7–11.

Suppe, Frederick. 1977. *The Structure of Scientific Theories*, 2d ed. Chicago: University of Illinois Press.

Taylor, C. 1967. "Teleological Explanation—A Reply to Dennis Noble." *Analysis* 27, no. 1: 141–43.

Taylor, Weldon J. 1965. "Is Marketing a Science? Revisited." *Journal of Marketing* 29 (July): 49–53.

Teece, David, and Gary Pisano. 1994. "The Dynamic Capabilities of Firms: An Introduction." *Industrial and Corporate Change* 3, no. 3: 537–56.

Teece, David; Gary Pisano; and Amy Shuen. 1997. "Dynamic Capabilities and Strategic Management." *Strategic Management Journal* 18, no. 7: 509–33.

Tellis, Gerald J., and C. Merle Crawford. 1981. "An Evolutionary Approach to Product Growth Theory." *Journal of Marketing* 45 (Fall): 125–32.

Thompson, Craig J.; William B. Locander; and Howard R. Pollio. 1989. "Putting Consumer Experience Back into Consumer Research: The Philosophy and Method of Existential-Phenomenology." *Journal of Consumer Research* 16 (September): 133–46.

Tucker, W.T. 1964. "The Development of Brand Loyalty." *Journal of Marketing Research* 1 (August): 32–35.

———. 1967. *Foundations for a Theory of Consumer Behavior*. New York: Holt, Rinehart and Winston.

Utz, Stephen. 1977. "Discussion: On Teleology and Organisms." *Philosophy of Science* 44, no. 2: 313–20.

Van Fraassen, Bas C. 1980. *The Scientific Image*. Oxford: Clarendon Press.

Vollmer, Howard M., and Donald L. Mills. 1966. *Professionalism*. Englewood Cliffs, NJ: Prentice Hall.

Walker, Orville C., Jr., and Richard F. Santer. 1974. "Consumer Preferences for Alternative Retail Credit Terms." *Journal of Marketing Research* (February): 70–78.

Wartofsky, Marx W. 1968. *Conceptual Foundations of Scientific Thought*. New York: Macmillan.

Watkins, John. 1984. *Science and Skepticism*. Princeton: Princeton University Press.

Webster, Frederick E., Jr. 1974. *Social Aspects of Marketing*. Englewood Cliffs, NJ: Prentice Hall.

———. 1994. "Executing the Marketing Concept." *Marketing Management* 3, no. 1: 9–16.

Weitz, Barton. 1981. "Effectiveness in Sales Interaction: A Contingency Framework." *Journal of Marketing* 45 (Winter): 360–70.

Weld, L.D.H. 1920. *The Marketing of Farm Products*. New York: Macmillan.

Wells, William D. 1993. "Discovery-Oriented Consumer Research." *Journal of Consumer Research* 19, no. 4: 489–504.

Wernerfelt, Birger. 1984. "A Resource-Based View of the Firm." *Strategic Management Journal* 5, no. 2: 171–80.

Westing, J. Howard. 1977. "Marketing Educators Must Switch to Helping Real World Meet Real Problems." *Marketing News* 29 (July): 2.

———. 1979. Comments in "What Is the Appropriate Orientation for the Marketing Academician? A Panel Discussion." Originally appearing in *Conceptual and Theoretical Developments in Marketing*, ed. O.C. Farrell, Stephen W. Brown, and Charles W. Lamb, Jr., 49–75. Chicago: American Marketing Association.

Whewell, William. [1840] 1968. "The Philosophy of the Inductive Sciences." Reprinted in *Philosophy of Science*, ed. Joseph J. Kockelmans, 51–79. New York: Free Press.

White, P., and W.S. Hayward. 1924. *Marketing Practice*. New York: Doubleday Page.

Wish, John R., and Stephen H. Gamble. 1971. *Marketing and Social Issues*. New York: Wiley.

Wong, V., and J. Saunders. 1993. "Business Organization and Corporate Success." *Journal of Strategic Marketing* 1 (March): 20–40.

Wood, Van R.; Lawrence B. Chonko; and Shelby D. Hunt. 1986. "Social Responsibility and Personal Success: Are They Compatible?" *Journal of Business Research* 14, no. 2: 193–212.

Wright, Larry. 1977. "Discussion: Rejoinder to Utz." *Philosophy of Science* 44, no. 3: 321–25.

Zaltman, Gerald; Christian R.A. Pinson; and Reinhard Angelmar. 1973. *Metatheory and Consumer Research*. New York: Holt, Rinehart and Winston.

Zaltman, Gerald, and Ilan Vertinsky. 1971. "Health Service Marketing: A Suggested Model." *Journal of Marketing* 35, no. 3: 19–27.

Zikmund, William G., and William J. Stanton. 1971. "Recycling Solid Wastes: A Channels of Distribution Problem." *Journal of Marketing* 35 (July): 34–39.

INDEX

SHELBY D. HUNT is the Jerry S. Rawls and P.W. Horn Professor of Marketing at Texas Tech University, Lubbock, Texas. A past editor of the *Journal of Marketing* (1985–87), he is the author of *Modern Marketing Theory: Critical Issues in the Philosophy of Marketing Science* (South-Western, 1991) and *A General Theory of Competition: Resources, Competences, Productivity, Economic Growth* (Sage Publications, 2000). He has written numerous articles on competitive theory, macromarketing, ethics, channels of distribution, philosophy of science, and marketing theory. Three of his *Journal of Marketing* articles, "The Nature and Scope of Marketing" (1976), "General Theories and Fundamental Explananda of Marketing" (1983), and "The Comparative Advantage Theory of Competition" (1995) (with Robert M. Morgan) won the Harold H. Maynard Award for the "best article on marketing theory." His 1985 *Journal of Business Research* article with Lawrence B. Chonko, "Ethics and Marketing Management," received the 2000 Elsevier Science Exceptional Quality and High Scholarly Impact award. His 1989 article, "Reification and Realism in Marketing: in Defense of Reason," won the *Journal of Macromarketing* Charles C. Slater Award. For his contributions to theory and science in marketing, he received the 1986 Paul D. Converse Award from the American Marketing Association, the 1987 Outstanding Marketing Educator Award from the Academy of Marketing Science, and the 1992 American Marketing Association/Richard D. Irwin Distinguished Marketing Educator Award.